Discovering Cork

DISCOVERING
CORK

Daphne D.C. Pochin Mould

BRANDON

First published in 1991 by
Brandon Book Publishers Ltd
Dingle, Co. Kerry, Ireland

Text and photographs © Daphne D. C. Pochin Mould 1991

Drawings © Jack Roberts 1991

British Library Cataloguing in Publication Data

Mould, Daphne Desiree Charlotte Pochin
  Discovering Cork
  I. Title
  914. 19504824

   ISBN 0 86322 129 7

The publishers wish to thank the Ordnance Survey
for permission to reproduce the map of County Cork
used in this book.

Cover design: Jean McCord
Internal design: Brandon
Typesetting: Koinonia Ltd, Manchester
Printed by the Bath Press, England

CONTENTS

I

Discovering Cork

A CIRCLE OF WHITE and glittering peaks around a sunlit plain; this can be one impression of Ireland's largest county, Cork. Most of these mountains do not belong to Cork, but they come close enough to set a term to the distant view, whether from the air or from the ground. If the winter has been a cold one, these circling heights can be as brightly white as the high Alps. From the air you see it all: a county that is a semi-circle backing on the sea, the eye ranging from east to west, from the hard outline of the Comeragh plateau (County Waterford) to the pyramidal shapes

Lough Ine

Knockmealdowns, the elegant grace of the Galtees (County Tipperary) and then the lumpy, snowy uplands of north Cork, around to the drama of the Kerry hills (big Mangerton and sharp Crohane, the sparkling line of the MacGillycuddy Reeks, Ireland's highest hills) and finally back into the county itself, the great rocky mount that is Hungry Hill and the high moorland mass of Beara. Now and again, but rarely, the snow sweeps down from the hills and you fly over a county entirely white, from mountain-top to high tide mark. The snow etches every ridge and fold of the land in high relief, and the little towns, usually so gay, are drained of all colour and the world is rendered entirely in black and white. At sunrise and sunset the colour may return and the white peaks of the Galtees turn gold and pink as they catch the reflections of bright winter dawn or evening.

The coastline

There are other days, too, when the county, seen from the air, takes on another character. The hills retreat into the cloud and the horizon out to sea merges into a grey torment of water and sky. There are days when the coastline assumes a character of sheer and utter savagery, a snarling ocean that has wrecked ships on almost every rock of Cork's shores. The headlands seem to be thrusting out into the heaving sea, which throws itself high on the rock faces and hangs a mist of spume and spray over the long neck of the Old Head of Kinsale. There is a feeling, and a true one, of struggle, of the grey-blue sea locked in conflict with the long rocky fingers of the land which thrusts like a claw into the thundering waves.

More often, waves pattern lines of delicate, lacy foam along the sunny length of the Long Strand and the sun gleams on ranks of parked cars at popular beaches. Small sailing boats with white or coloured sails compete in races in the wide expanse of Cork Harbour or off Kinsale; further out, sea anglers' boats heave gently on long Atlantic swells.

Seasons

It is a constantly changing pattern of colour, from winter to spring, and spring to summer, and summer to autumn. In spring the wide farmlands of east and central Cork are ploughed, and paler lines show where the walls of smaller, older field divisions have been knocked, show, too, the circles and outlines of destroyed ring forts. The ploughs move fast these days, and suddenly the whole of the land is brown, chequered with the green of pasture. The newly turned ground is sown and changes again to pale, then dark green and by August to gold. The combines move in to harvest the grain, leaving surrealist patterns of cast straw, till the balers follow and scoop it up. The forests change, too, the conifers a steady green but the larches palest green in spring and yellow gold in autumn; sap running purple in the birches of spring; the flush of new leafage, a green mist that darkens and thickens and ends in autumn golds. Spring sees the hedges and wastelands of Cork ablaze with golden furze (gorse); in autumn the dwarf furze gilds the cliff edges like burnished bronze. Hawthorn blossom turns hedges into lines of whipped cream and the pilot looks down on the riotous colours of rhododendron and azalea in the gardens of the great houses.

It is, in fact, from the air that the varied face of the county is most vividly appreciated. To the north, the heathy uplands, now widely afforested, the Nagles and Boggeragh Mountains and high cold uplands around them; to the south and east is rolling farmland, breathing an aura of quiet prosperity. Fly west and the country roughens under your wings, fat pastures and wide cornfields changing to small mountainy crofts, the rocky bones of the land breaking through the thin skin of soil. Ultimately you see the rocky divide where Cork marches with Kerry.

To the east, the coast has a certain plainness, a directness of line that is entirely lost in the west. Here the rias, drowned valleys, finger deep inland in long narrow bays, and the sea is set with islands like gems, green and magical in shimmering ocean: Carbery's Hundred Isles; the Fastnet Rock like a black swan sailing on a magic sea. There are days here of sun and sudden showers which spill rainbows and hailstones and set the land between the downpours all aglitter with light and colour. And calm evenings, when the pilot sees the shadows of stone circles longer than the gallauns (standing stones) themselves, and the low sun picks up the faintest traces of bank and fosse, the archaeology that is part and parcel of looking at Cork from the air.

All this land is marked with traces of the past, as well as evidence of the present. There are ring forts on land that was fertile, alone or in village-like clusters. There are deep trenches and walls of fortified headlands and sharp star patterns of 17th-century James and Charles Forts. Little valleys have old mills cunningly tucked into them with carefully planned take-offs for the water to turn their wheels. Deep quarries scar the land: slate at Ben Duff and Drinagh, limestone at Castlemore and Ballybeg and many more places. New factories cluster around Cork Harbour or are buildings set in countryside. Most of Cork's towns are by the sea or astride rivers. It is a maritime county and some of the big rivers were once highways for small ships. Old castle, Big House, modern housing estate, the county's life, past and present

The land

Buildings

Carbery's Hundred Isles

Mizen peninsula

– all these show most clearly from the air. So do the traces of now closed railway lines, old and present roads, airport and airstrip. Old and new jostle as the brightly painted helicopters scuttle off to the platforms of the offshore gasfield, flying over the grass-grown railway lines and furze-gilt circles of the ring forts.

The county is indeed enormous and a microcosm, both in geography and history, of all Ireland. For the record, its area is 1,849,686 acres, 748,567 hectares. In some countries, even so big an area could be all of a piece, a uniformity; but not in Ireland, not in Cork. The kind of land and its shape are rich in variety, and the dominant colours change as you move about the county. West Cork would seem to be the most brilliantly coloured part of all Ireland. At any time of the year it can take on so luminous a brilliance, such a subtle rainbow of colours and perfection of form, as to be almost overwhelming. 'Mid-September in West Carbery can yield such days as heaven's climate is made of,' wrote Edith Somerville. She was not far wrong, and it has colour and shape to match. Cork's air is still clear and unpolluted except when an established anticyclone in spring, with easterly winds, brings British and Continental smog west over Ireland. The air is normally damp, if not actually moisture-laden, and this, as in the West Highlands of Scotland, gives a jewel-like brilliance when the sun is shining.

Colour and shape

Many things go into the making of the colour of a district: rock and soil, mountain and plain, the relation of land to sea, crops and natural vegetation. A land divided into large and undulating fields like much of east Cork, will appear smiling and prosperous, if perhaps a trifle dull. In late summer it is a checker of green and gold – green pasture and root crop; golden grain – and there is a smell of ripening barley in the air. North Cork has rounded, neither very big nor very dramatic mountains, the Nagles and Boggeraghs, which left to themselves have the brown of heather in winter and its purple in summer, with small, abandoned green fields high on their slopes. Fortunately they have not been left entirely to themselves and beautiful forestry plantations, with some splendid walks, have transformed much of the bleaker uplands and scented all the minor roads with hot pine on a summer day.

Loch na Madra

High mountains introduce another element, a skyline shattered, dramatic. They control for half the year the amount of light that can come directly into their deeper valleys. For this reason, Bantry Bay divides the brilliant colours and miniature hills of West Cork from the more subdued tints of the mountains of Beara, where Kerry meets with Cork at 2,000 feet along the heights – high, rocky, with creamy white waterfalls after rain; grassy rather than heathery, good sheep country. Glengarriff itself is subtropical and forested, green with flames of exotic blossoms; Beara is mountain, reddish rock and green sward rising steeply from the bright sea.

Around Cork city and its harbour, the colours are bright – blue sea, green fields and woods – but the shape of the land, its level fertility, reduces their impact. It seems that it is the broken character of West Cork, its multitude of inlets and islands, its little fields like the facets of a jewel, that give it its special sparkle. At the Old Head of Kinsale and to the west the cliffs rise dark, almost black, in savage fangs; for some peculiar reason, those to the east of the harbour, where red beds appear, seem more benign, though they have wrecked just as many ships.

Cork city, in its deep trench, is liable to a temperature inversion which traps the town's smoke in the valley and may send a long, smoggy trail downwind, beyond Cobh and on toward Midleton. In wintertime, when the lights begin to flick on and people light their fires, the trails of smoke lie over the city and snake up its side valleys, recalling the traditional picture of Auld Reekie herself. These smoke trails do not normally rise into the sky but lie close upon the city roofs. Fog, on the larger scale, can lie in bands along the county's river valleys whilst the ridges above are in sunshine. Some of the more interesting Cork fogs are those from the sea: very damp air is blown gently inland and, as it rises over each little headland of the coast, condenses into little puffs of cloud, capping each small rise.

East Cork, with its wide fields, is a region of great views and open skies and

Seals at Glengarriff

Deer in Farran Wood

cloudscapes. North Cork is a land of fertile farmland as well as of hills, with the long green valley of the Blackwater set with great house and ruined castle. In Muskerry – the terrain between Cork and Macroom and beyond to the county bounds – it is rougher and rockier but without the intense brilliance of the similar terrain of coastal West Cork. 'Beyond the Leap, beyond the Law,' the saying once went, and it is this area, from Rosscarbery and Leap to Bantry Bay, that holds the most vibrant colour. In autumn, there is a Turkish carpet of heather and dwarf furze on the hillsides, hedges that drip cascades of the red bells of fuchsia, a tangle of vivid yellowness of tide-bared rocks, salt water broken up by inlet and island, and open sky with a view to mountains yet not overshadowed by them. Here is the most splendidly coloured part of the county and, it could be claimed, of all Ireland.

In outline then, this is the shape and colour of County Cork, and the world which this book sets out to explore.

Near Galley Head

II

Cork Rock

THE WORLD OVER, rocks determine the shape and the potential of the land. In County Cork there is a direct link between the geology and the visible countryside which has been shaped both by the nature and the structure of the underlying rocks and by the passage of the Ice Age glaciers.

Roughly speaking, the rocks are Old Red Sandstone/Devonian and Carboniferous in age; folded together along east/west axes – a result of the Hercynian mountain-building movements after the end of the Carboniferous period. From just east of the Kerry border, right across the county, you can see the land thrown into these regular east/west ridges and valleys. No pilot in fine weather, knowing these ridges, could be lost in Cork, for they are like a compass reading drawn on the living world, and you can pick up a ridge at Inchigeelagh and follow it due east to Cork airport (sited on top of this particular line) and beyond, if you wish, into the long ridge of Great Island and Cobh. The Carboniferous outcrops in the valley floors, while the Old Red Sandstone is bared along the ridge crests. Vegetation changes as you climb the slope. Rhododendron, heather and blueberries flourish on the Old Red Sandstone on the heights but avoid the lime-rich land of the valleys.

In most of the county the bedrock is very largely concealed by the drift, the Ice Age deposits of boulder clay and sands and gravels sorted from it by melt-waters. But in the west, as the country roughens and the mountains lift, there are more and more outcrops of rock, until the exposure in the Sugar

Ridges and valleys

Hungry Hill

Sugar Loaf
Hungry Hill

Loaf and Hungry Hill is almost continuous. Here it is mostly a red or red-dish sandstone, in which you can trace dune bedding and sometimes sun-cracks, for its origin was in shallow water where currents criss-crossed and dunes could be formed and sand dry out long enough for the sun to crack its surface into hexagons. In fact, a great many Cork flagstones are shallow-water deposits, and ripple prints are a frequent sight in quarry and roadside exposure. Millions of years separate these ancient ripples and their modern twins on the present Cork beaches.

Cliffs

There is continuous exposure of rocks along the cliffs of the county, and here even the uninitiated in geology can get an impression of the complexi-ty and variety of the Cork rocks and the violent folding which they have undergone. Detailed studies of these rocks have been and are being made. Almost every little bay has given a name to a formation or sub-division, and a story has emerged of how each was formed. In outline, in Old Red

Akinkeen, County Bounds

Sandstone/Devonian times, there was a depression in the earth's crust, which geologists call the Munster Basin. To the east, the north and the south-west were mountains and from them rivers flowed, carrying the material they had eroded from the heights. The rivers ran over wide plains to the south and on to the sea. Sometimes they flooded the plains and left a spread of mud. Later on, a marine delta developed between Kenmare and Cork, and sand was deposited on it (the Coomhola Formation). With the beginning of the Carboniferous period, the sea began to encroach on the land and the water deepened. It was warm, and the Carboniferous limestone, which outcrops today north of a line from Kenmare to Cork, was formed in a coral sea. Its corals and other shell-bearing creatures, the extinct sea lilies (crinoids) and a variety of molluscs, appear as numerous fossils in the rocks today – often showing up well on the polished surfaces of cut-limestone buildings in Cork city. This sea continued to deepen, and dark mudstones and sandstones (mud and sand in origin) were deposited. In north-west Cork, there are the later Coal Measures, which represent forest growth on swampy deltas and wetlands. Cork coal is not of high quality and is difficult to work, as the later intense folding has squeezed it into lenses in the crook of the folds, but it was mined in the 18th and 19th centuries.

Coomhola

All the rocks of subsequent geological ages deposited on top of the Carboniferous have, on the mainland, been completely eroded away. They do, however, survive out to sea, under water on the Continental Shelf, where oil and gas explorations take place in them. It is probable that the little nodules of flint, used by the early people in Cork to make tools, came from these undersea deposits.

In the intense folding under pressure and heat which the Cork rocks underwent, there was much mineralisation. Everywhere you will see the rocks veined with white quartz (SiO_2) which came in, fluid, to crystallise along cracks and lines of weakness during this stage. It is often associated

Lough Brackderg, County Bounds

Lough Gortavehy under Caherbarnagh

Sheep's Head
Crookhaven

Ice Age

Macroom

Dunmanus

Bantry

Nagles
Caherbarnagh

with other minerals; Cork's rocks are quite highly mineralised and copper, lead and manganese have been mined on a commercial scale. Gold and silver also occur, the gold only in traces in the old copper mines at Kilcrohane in the Sheep's Head peninsula and at Carrigacat, Crookhaven. Barytes occur in some quantity in West Cork and have been extensively mined there – indeed it is claimed that Cork had the world's first barytes mine.

The final shaping of the land came as a result of the Ice Age, which was, of course, very long, involving a whole series of advances and retreats of the ice-sheets. Ice moving over the land picked up stones and grit and carried them along, acting as a gigantic rasp on the underlying bedrocks, and ultimately dropping all the debris to form boulder clay when it melted.

Where the ice-sheets grated over solid rock, they shaped it into long ridges, like the backs of whales or sheep, so that they go by the French name of *roches moutonnées,* sheep rocks. In West Cork these little ridges are everywhere, smooth and steep. Carrigaphooca Castle near Macroom is perched on top of one, utilising the rock shape for defence. Another castle on such a ridge is Dunmanus in the Mizen peninsula. Another sort of ridge formed under the ice is the drumlin (Irish, little ridge, one of the names Ireland has given to science). Drumlins are little green elongated hills usually to be found in swarms; they are made of sand and gravel, not of solid rock. Both the ice movement above and water flowing under the ice seems to have influenced their shaping. There are very fine examples around Bantry in the west of the county.

The ice never covered all of Cork. There were some hills which rose above it, for example the Nagles and Caherbarnagh on the county bounds with Kerry. Climb up these heights and you will come on deeply weathered sandstone, rock which took all the hammering of Ice Age cold without the protection of deep ice cover. Then, too, there were local glaciers in the hollows of the hills, hollows filled with ice accumulating, alternately melting and

Glacial spillway: Pass of Keimaneigh

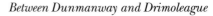
Between Dunmanway and Drimoleague

freezing against the rock, so that it slowly dug deeper and deeper into the hill. The result, when the ice melted, was a corrie, often with a lake where the ice had lain, and below it a moraine, where the foot of the glacier had melted and dumped the gravel and sand it had worn off the mountain above. Barley Lake near Glengarriff is one such corrie; there are a number of others in Beara including the two rock-cut ones halfway up the stony face of Hungry Hill.

When the ice finally melted vast quantities of water were released with enormous erosive power. In the west the ice-shed, the great mass of ice, lay in Bantry Bay and the Kenmare River. As it began to break up, water was dammed between the ice and the land, and from this great temporary lake made its escape through the Pass of Keimaneigh. This rocky gut was cut by the melt-water; today only a trickle flows down it. The same applies to many deep, sometimes wooded glens in east Cork (what Scots would call *cleughs*) where melt-water cut deep into the older glacial deposits and bedrock. These wind-gaps and almost dry valleys include a very fine example at Mountain Barrack, north of Kilworth. In Cork city, Gouldings Glen is interesting. Ice lay in the Blackpool valley and, as it melted, it formed a lake in which a delta developed, coarse material coming down in summer when the melt was going on at a fast rate, the finer material in winter. The gravel quarries in the glen show these alternating layers; the water finally escaped from the district by cutting a V gap, the present Gouldings Glen.

The sorting of the glacial boulder clay into sand and gravel by melting ice water is, in County Cork, of great economic importance. The gravels are extensively quarried, and the clays have been utilised for brick-making and pottery.

The great ice-sheets travelled far and could transport rocks, some very large, in or on them, from one part of the country to another. Thus boulders of one sort of rock are found resting on bedrock of quite another period and type. The Golden Rock (so called because treasure was supposed to be buried under it) at Ringaskiddy, Cork Harbour, is limestone, one of many such blocks resting on flagstones. The movement of the ice-sheets can be traced by some of the farther travelled erratics: one ice-sheet came down to Cork from Connemara and brought with it boulders of the Galway granite with its big, deep pink feldspar crystals. Examples of Galway granite have been found near Midleton, and at Desert, an old church site south of Castlelyons, a block of Galway granite was utilised to form a millstone for a nearby horizontal mill.

In the mountains of West Cork erratics of the local sandstone are perched all over the hillsides, adding much to the scene in their peculiar shapes and positions. There are also – for instance back from Glengarriff – areas of vast jumbled boulder fields, which must represent massive but local erosion by ice.

It is not only the erratics which show the way the ice was moving. Very

Glengarriff

Hungry Hill

Bantry Bay

Keimaneigh

Kilworth
Cork city

Ringaskiddy

Midleton
Castlelyons

Mount Gabriel

frequently in the rocky parts of the county you will see ice-smoothed surfaces on *roches moutonnées* or in places like the rocky gut followed by the road over Mount Gabriel, which are deeply scratched. These scratches are produced by stones in the ice rasping along the rocks, and by taking a compass bearing on them, you can work out the way the local ice was going.

Drowned valleys

In all of south-west Ireland, you are looking at a partly submerged landscape. The deep sea inlets are not fiords but rias, drowned valleys; Roaring Water Bay, Dunmanus, Bantry Bay. The islands are the heights of a country lost to the ocean. The full story of the changes of sea level relative to the land in Ireland has still to be teased out, but the evidence of past changes are very obvious in Cork. All along the coast, rapid erosion can be seen going on along the cliffs and islands.

There is a very marked preglacial or inter-glacial raised beach, marking a time when the sea stood higher then it does today. You can follow this raised beach very well along the cliffs at Howes Strand and Coolmain, and again at Man o' War cove near Rocky Bay. On the old beach shelf, you can still see the old beach deposit with its white quartz pebbles, and on top of that the glacial boulder clay and 'head' (broken soil and rock debris). As well, there is a 200 foot peneplain in east Cork which may represent preglacial marine erosion – it is very well seen between Midleton and Youghal with Youghal itself sited on the old raised beach feature with the ancient cliff line behind it.

Youghal

Rivers

The great rivers of Cork – Blackwater, Lee, Bandon – with their long west-to-east courses and sudden right-angled turns south to the sea, are a puzzle. The older theory was that north-to-south rivers were formed on a now-eroded land surface, and that in the course of ages, as the rocks were worn away and the rivers came to flow on the underlying strata, their west/east tributaries became dominant. But this theory really flies in the face of the shape of the land. Nobody who has spent much time flying over the county and looking down on the rivers can doubt that the wide west-to-east trenches, huge and mature (in the case of the Blackwater extending on to Dungarvan;

Inishannon and Bandon River

of the Lee to Midleton and beyond; of the Bandon down the Owenaboy to Crosshaven) are the original valleys. One has the impression of great rivers, rising perhaps originally in much more extensive and higher mountains to the west, flowing straight as arrows down the long valleys to the east and the sea. What swung them, near their mouths, so sharply south into deep-cut, immature trenches? Changes in the land and sea relationship; water dammed back by the ice? Furthermore, where they enter the sea, the valleys continue under the water. The Lee is actually flowing in alluvium, river mud and sand, over its original rock-cut course as it comes to Cork; its original bed is 40 feet down in the soil at Carrigrohane, 90 feet at Cork. It is possible that some of these deep-cut and undersea channels are preglacial; certainly we are dealing with a landscape which has undergone, indeed is undergoing, massive changes in relative sea levels.

When the naval dockyard at Haulbowline in Cork Harbour was being constructed in the last century, tree stumps were found in the slob. This is not the only place to have fossil forests, and often deposits of peat, below present tide levels. More tree trunks have been exposed at Garrylucas strand, just west of the Old Head of Kinsale. There is a stone *fulacht fiadh*, an ancient cooking place, embedded in a peat layer temporarily exposed on the strand – sand normally covers all this – where, in the past, local people found enough peat to make it worth while collecting it. At Rostellan, a megalithic tomb stands half submerged at high tide. The sea cliffs are everywhere being very rapidly eaten into. Rock arches and caves abound, and the Old Head of Kinsale is on the road to becoming an island. Caves run right through its neck and a small boat can make its way through, from one side of the head to the other. Duneendermotmore headland fort on Toe Head,

Haulbowline

Garrylucas

Rostellan

Old Head of
Kinsale
Toe Head

*Low water on Lee reservoir
reveals old tree roots*

Tree roots in bog

occupied as late as the 17th century, has almost all fallen into the sea – it is certainly no longer habitable. Neither is another promontory fort, Dunoure, on the Galley Head. Castle Downeen, a 16th-century tower-house, was set on a rocky cliff near Rosscarbery; it is now totally isolated, or rather insulated, by the collapse of the land that linked it to the mainland. The old church on the Skeames Islands is in grave danger from the sea and the islands themselves, now being rapidly eroded, were obviously originally a single island. Low Island, beside High Island off Glandore, is now the mere bones of an island, yet not so long ago people went to cut hay on it. The few grassy relics show the lines of old lazy beds and it is said to have had a graveyard.

The flora and fauna of County Cork includes those Lusitanean species which occur along the west coast, and particularly today in Kerry; but the further extent of their distribution is south, in the Iberian peninsula, not east across Ireland or to Britain. They include the arbutus (the strawberry tree) and the Kerry bog violet, the splendid purple-flowering butterwort (*Pinguicula grandiflora*). The Kerry violet is widespread on the Cork hills, as is the spotted Kerry slug. It seems likely that the Lusitanean flora may be a survival from preglacial times of plants and some animals that existed on land, some of which is now submerged, that remained unglaciated. Certainly in Greenland a rich flora, good grass, dwarf scrubby forest and many alpines grow happily right up to the ice margins in the few green valleys of that ice-covered land.

We know in some detail the changes in climate and vegetation since the end of the Ice Age. Pollen grains are distinctive of the plant and tree from which they come, and they are preserved in peat and in the silts of lakes. From their study, a picture of the past may be built up of an Ireland first very cold, with tundra-like expanses and little hillocks – which the Eskimos call pingos – formed by unmelted lenses of ice just under the soil surface. When the ice finally melted the hillock collapsed and left a more or less circular ring of earth to mark its site. Such pingo sites can be found in some

Downeen near Rosscarbery

quantity in Ireland, and they occur in Cork – for instance near Glanworth. Juniper scrub, then pines and the deciduous trees moved in as the climate warmed up. The pine died out, to be reintroduced in plantings on the big estates from the 17th century on, but its timbers and roots (bog deal) are frequent in the peat bogs, as well as bog oak. In deep cuttings, the peat shows these old forest layers, often high on the mountainsides, right up on the 2,000-foot contour on the boundary with Kerry, and reminds us that these hills were once forested.

But much of the peat growth is surprisingly recent. The copper mines of West Cork, on Mount Gabriel, are of Bronze Age date and were entirely hidden by later peat growth – at nearby Derrycarhoon, 15 feet of peat covered the old workings. Early people came to an Ireland which possessed far less extensive peat bogs than were known later. At the present time the peat on the hilltops is being eroded again into peat hags.

Mount Gabriel

The skeletons and antlers of that most splendid of deer, the Irish 'elk', have turned up in Cork both in bogs and in caves. The limestone districts of

Kilcolman bog

the county contain numerous caves, cut by water seeping through the soluble rock: the big Ovens (Coleman's) Cave in Muskerry, many around Midleton and Cloyne and yet others along the Blackwater (by Castletownroche, in the Awbeg cliffs and up the Blackwater toward Mallow). There are more caves in the Doneraile area. The Blackwater caves have yielded bones of long extinct animals which once roamed Ireland before man arrived: mammoth, Irish 'elk' , reindeer, bear, hyena and the Norwegian lemming. Mammoth and deer bones found in these caves had been gnawed by the hyenas. The Irish 'elk' is not an elk at all but is big brother to the elegant fallow deer we know today. Properly it is known as the Giant Irish Deer, *Megaloceros giganteus,* and the male's antlers could have a span of 9.5 feet across. The animal was widely distributed, ranging from Russia to Ireland and south to Greece, but the Irish specimens are the biggest. Climatic change with resultant changes in vegetation and habitat seem to have resulted in the extinction of this most magnificent animal, which is thought to have died out in Ireland about 10,500 years ago – before the arrival of man. Reindeer survived a little longer, to about 10,000 years ago.

Caves

Just over the county border, east from Mitchelstown, in County Tipperary, the Mitchelstown caves are to be found; they are very extensive, very magnificent and now very accessible. However, to the speleologists, the County Cork caves provide a great deal of sport and adventure. Most of the limestone outcrop in Cork is hidden under drift and soil, but around Midleton it rises into little rocky hillocks with a real feel of limestone terrain – white dusty paths, Burren-like outcrops and lime-loving wild flowers.

III

The Megaliths

T HE IRELAND INTO which early people made their way was very different from the Ireland of today. It was heavily forested. Bogs had not been drained, but much of the peat cover was yet to form. Wolves and red deer prowled the woods; eagle and osprey soared in the skies, and the seas and rivers teemed with fish. People may have come to Cork as much as 6,000 years ago. As yet we have no definite early dates, but along the coast and at various inland sites worked flints are to be found. The source of the flint, which is not in any of the local rock, was from the boulder clay and offshore chalk, and the nodules worked are mostly small. There is then the possibility that people of the Mesolithic Middle Stone Age were in County Cork.

Around Cork Harbour are the remains of shell middens, accumulations of oyster shells for the most part. The harbour was famous for its oysters and, while it is possible that some of these are prehistoric accumulations, others are certainly later – one mound at Carrigtwohill produced pottery fragments dated to 1250-1400 AD. Some of the mounds are very large, for instance in the inner harbour at Brick Island and Brown Island. The Brick Island deposit was once over 1,000 feet long but was cut into to provide material for brick-making and road work. Today, Cork's modern oyster farm is in the same part of the harbour.

Shell middens

Knockakilla

Stone circle and alignment, Baurgorm

Arderawinny
Ahaglaslin

Glanworth
Boggeragh
West Cork

It is with the Megalithic (Greek, 'big stone') people that we really begin to make contact with the early inhabitants of the county. Two portal tombs in which a great capstone is perched on three uprights, are found at Arderawinny west of Schull, and at Ahaglaslin near Rosscarbery. These are of Neolithic age but most of the monuments seem to be of Bronze Age date and many are associated with the copper-bearing areas of West Cork. Stone circles, wedge-tombs, boulder burials, stone alignments and standing stones are what they built. Some wedge-tombs and stone circles are found by Glanworth and in central and east Cork, but the main concentration is in the Boggeragh Mountains and in West Cork. There is a suggestion that the stone circle and wedge-tomb builders may have been different groups: in Beara and Mizen, the tombs are numerous but the circles rare. While the West Cork monuments are in the copper-bearing areas near the Bronze Age copper mines of Mount Gabriel, those of the Boggeraghs are far from any mineral source and suggest something quite other, a kind of holy ground around the mountain Mushera with its summit holy well.

There are several things to remember about this remote period, at least 4,000 years ago. First, the sea was never a barrier but a highway, and over it people could sail to settle in or trade with other countries. Cork's long coast-line was always open to people and ideas. It has been suggested that these bronze-working, wedge-tomb-building people were cattle farmers.

The sheer size of the stones they set up – even the small ones are quite difficult to shift – indicates a good knowledge of the logistics of the job and the availability of enough workers to carry it out. Plenty of suitable stones

Gallauns, Ballingeary

Gallauns, Ceancullig

were available. On rocky outcrops the flagstones were naturally weathered into the right shape for stone circle gallauns. Erratic blocks provided another source. But Ireland was wooded, and in England a Woodhenge has been found, as well as a Stonehenge. If the circles were both temple and observatory, and their builders living in areas without suitable stone, they could have constructed the same structures in timber, of which, naturally, no trace now remains.

The stones used were what was locally available so that there is a considerable difference in the shape and size of standing stones around the county. In parts of West Cork it was possible to come by very long slender pillars of sandstone – an ogham-inscribed one near Eyeries is 17.5 feet high, and an ordinary pillar stone, lately fallen and broken, near Ballingeary was claimed to be the tallest in Ireland at about 20 feet. But around Midleton and Castlelyons, limestone was used for some of the standing stones, and because of the way it breaks and weathers, the gallauns tend to be much more clumpy and pocked with typical limestone weathering hollows.

Midleton

Castlelyons

Quartz

Quartz boulders are often associated with the stone circles. However, quartz does not normally weather into a pillar-like shape and so could not usually be used for the circle itself. It is possible, if not probable, that because quartz was associated with the much desired copper – the ore occurs in the quartz veins – it may have had a lucky significance. Certainly today people on a beach will pick up the white quartz pebble first of all; they

Gallaun with ogham inscriptions,
Eyeries

Gallaun of quartz, Larravolta
near Newcestown

are in themselves very attractive. They were used sometimes as counters at holy wells and can be found in numbers at some early Christian sites. At the well on Church Island in Valentia Harbour in Kerry, 6,800 quartz pebbles were counted. Around Crookstown and Kilmurry large round boulders of quartz were, most unusually, obtainable and were seized upon for the main, big stone of boulder burials. Toward Newcestown in Larravolta townland there is a tall, fat quartz standing stone; two small quartz uprights form the outliers of a five-stone circle at Knockraheen in the Boggeragh mountains.

Crookstown Kilmurry

The stone circles, the alignments of standing stones, even the alignment of the long axis of a single standing stone, raise the questions of astro-archaeology and these structures' orientation. Early people seem to have explored the heavens before the earth, and to have gained a good working knowledge of the movements of sun, moon and stars. Once people were settled farmers, they needed to have some sort of a calendar for reckoning the seasons. It was not necessary for it to be of a high degree of accuracy, and in the Irish climate cloudy skies could prevent observations for many days. At Newgrange the sun shines directly into the inmost chamber for some two weeks around the shortest day of the year.

Admiral Somerville, brother of author Edith Somerville of Castletownsend, was a pioneer in investigating the orientations of Cork circles and alignments. Edith described how, one midsummer, they went to the Three Fingers, close to their home. 'Our archaeological hearts beat, and then, precisely at the sunrise hour in the gap, the first gleaming spark of the sun's rim appeared. The Fingers had been truly aligned.' Near Castlelyons, I have seen the winter evening's sun go down through a gap in the uplands, in line with the main axis of one of the chunky limestone gallauns of the area.

Stone circles

Cork stone circles come in two kinds: those of more than five stones, and those of five only. The basic orientation of the multiple-stone circles is a line drawn between the two tallest portal stones, across the circle to an opposite recumbent, elongate stone. The orientations of these circles have a 107 degree splay, with the portal stones on the sunrise side of the ring and the recumbent on the sun. The stone alignments end to a similar

Three Fingers   *Drombeg*

north-east/south-west alignment. It needs to be noted that having laid down a permanent baseline of standing stones, any other angle and orientation could very easily be got from it, with temporary posts and strings.

According to Professor Alexander Thom, the forest of standing stones at Carnac in Brittany can be used to find the rising and setting sun throughout the year: 'no comparable accuracy was possible until the invention of the telescope'. In the New World the Indians set up 'medicine wheels' which appear, from work done by astronomer John Eddy in 1972, to be observatories lining up with the rising and setting sun, with the moon's movements and with the three brightest stars of the period when the wheel was in use, thought to be 1400-1700 AD.

Although astro-archaeology is a young science and may be sometimes inclined to claim too much for itself, the Cork circles and alignments have been measured and seem to tie in with some heavenly event far too often for it to be mere chance. John Barber (1972) noted that the circles have a bilateral symmetry – opposite stones match each other across the main axis – and he went on to claim that they were laid out to an accuracy of about 6 inches (15 centimetres). He, too, went on to try to use stellar events to put a date on the time of the circles' building. An orientation on the maximum southern declination of Venus would suggest the period 3000-2000 BC; the circles with stellar alignments suggest 1700 to 500 BC, with a concentration around 1100 BC. At the moment, such work is speculative and open to a lot of criticism, but the basic idea of a definite orientation, from Stonehenge and Newgrange on, seems sound enough.

It is probable also that the circles were centres of a religious cult – religion and early science may have gone hand in hand – and one can speculate whether the right-handed *deiseal* or sunwise round of pilgrims at Irish holy wells and 'stations' does not go back to the customs of stone circles. Certainly the early Church found it easy to transfer people's allegiance from the sun to the 'son of justice' who knows no setting, the new Helios, Christ.

Stone circle, Kealkill

Stone circle, Maulatanvally and Carrigfadda

Burials are associated with some circles, but one may question the speculation that there was a dedicatory killing and interment at, for instance, Drombeg. We do not know. We do know that many have been buried in churches and cathedrals, not as dedicatory sacrifices but because it was holy ground and an honour to rest there.

Mushera

The concentration around Mushera in the Boggeragh Mountains is very striking. Mushera rises to 2,118 feet, has a well on the summit and is a landmark for many miles around. North of it is the Blackwater, south the Lee and its various tributaries. The climate was rather better and the present peat cover not developed when all this area was almost built over with stone circles, wedge-tombs, stone alignments, stone pairs and solitary standing stones. Later settlement is marked by numerous ring forts. Of stone circles alone, 17 of Cork's total of 89 (extant or now destroyed) are in the Boggeragh area.

Wells

Wells on mountain-tops are rare in Ireland. On Mount Brandon in Kerry there is one at St Brendan's hermitage site on the summit. Mushera's is dedicated to St John the Baptist, the Christian saint who took over the great midsummer festival of June 24th, the celebration of which must be at least as old as the coming of settled farming communities. Mushera has two holy wells: one at the summit for sick animals and one on its northern slopes for humans, at which Mass is celebrated at midsummer. Just west of Mushera, in County Kerry, are the twin Paps of Dana with their massive, perhaps Neolithic summit cairns, and on their northern slopes the still visited 'City' – a stone ring fort at which rounds are made on May Eve and Mayday and from whose spring water is taken for sick animals. In the old days, the sick animals were brought on pilgrimage to the 'City', and were, I think, driven between May bonfires. Bonfires are still lit in County Cork for midsummer eve, curiously now a custom much more honoured in the city than in the country.

Cairns

The summit cairns continue east from the Paps: one on the hill-fort of

Carriganimmy

Bohonagh

Claragh above Millstreet, others on Mount Hilary, the Nagles and Corrin Hill at Fermoy, all overlooking the Blackwater valley. One is drawn inescapably to speculate that here is not only evidence of much early settlement, but of holy ground, a great cult centre, which still, 4,000 years later, draws its pilgrims and a crush of parked cars at the Mushera Mass.

Three of the multiple stone circles of Cork have been excavated: Drombeg, Reanascreena South and Bohonagh. Bohonagh is just east of Rosscarbery, on a cultivated upland ridge with a good outlook. There is a fine boulder burial alongside. Here the excavator, Dr Fahy, experimented with methods of re-erecting some of the fallen stones, using ropes and pegstones, and found it relatively simple to shift them. Drombeg, like Bohonagh, is near the sea, on a sunny plat close to Glandore. It has a well preserved *fulacht fiadh* (ancient cooking place) and hut circles alongside. Drifts of bluebells decorate this site in spring. Reanascreena is a very fine circle but much harder to locate, being set in the middle of fields on upland with no road immediately adjacent. I located it first from the air and afterwards found it at ground level only by asking the way.

Reanascreena is unusual in having an external fosse or ditch surrounding the ring of stones, and thus getting itself into the 'henge' category of monuments and ritual sites. There is another smaller and even harder to find circle of this type in Cork, on the west flanks of Mushera, Glantane East. Like a number of the circles, this Glantane East site had two big gallauns (for sighting purposes?) outside of its ring; one is deeply buried and fallen but one can feel its extent and it is thought it would have stood some five metres high. Over in Kerry, at Killarney, the Lissyviggeen circle has similarly two enormous outlying gallauns, side by side, while the stones of the circle itself are tiny. Tucked away in a hollow of glaciated rocks, just west of Coppeen, is a curious little circle of small stones, Gortroe, with an internal ditch just inside the ring of stones, unless this has been tramped out by animals ambling round, which is perhaps unlikely.

There is a considerable difference in the size of the stones used in building the circles. This obviously would depend on the size of stone locally

Bohonagh

Reanascreena

Glantane

Gortroe

Reenascreena

Gallaunagarra
Gortanimill

Ardgroom
Outward

Castletownbere

Dunbeacon

Drombeg

Templebryan
Gowlane North

Lissacresig

Knockraheen

available, and perhaps on the number and enthusiasm of the builders. East of Mushera is Gallaunagarra, a little circle of very small stones with two little outliers in boggy land high on a hill-slope. Gortanimill, between Bally-vourney and Reananerree, is also of small stones, though not so small as Gallaunagarra's; again it is high on the moors, in a slight hollow. But many circles are of big stones. The very fine one at Ardgroom Outward in Beara stands on level upland ground below the main rise of the mountains, with a wide outlook over the Kenmare River, and the fine circle just west of Castle-townbere is in the same area. Over the Kerry border, at the head of the valley that runs up from Lauragh into the heart of a horseshoe of mountains – which give a lovely ridge walk along the county bounds – is another fine stone circle, which the visitor to Ardgroom Outward would do well to seek out.

The circles, then, can be high on the hillside, like Dunbeacon with its twin outliers (knocked down and now re-erected) in the Mizen peninsula; in sunny nooks like Drombeg; or on lowland like Carrigagulla's fine 17-stone ring under Mushera. There may be a stone set up inside the circle – there is one at Carrigagulla – and sometimes this is of quartz, for instance in Gortanimill and at Templebryan (near Clonakilty and just outside an old church site). Gowlane North, to the east of Mushera near Bweeng, is unusual in having a kind of porch to its entry, two additional stones set outside the portal ones.

There are 49 known five-stone circles in County Cork, 40 multiple-stone ones. Five stones hardly make a proper ring and the 'circles' tend to be D-shaped. Again, they vary very much in the size of stone. Enormous blocks were used at Lissacresig (just north of the Half Way House on the Macroom/Ballyvourney road). They mingle with the multiple-stone circles: there is a five-stone one quite close to Carrigagulla's 17-stone circle; indeed, there is a whole ring of them around Mushera. Knockraheen to the west of the mountain has, as already noted, two quartz outliers, and there is another

Carrigagulla

Dunbeacon

charming little circle above Carriganimmy on a westerly spur of Mushera-beg. Just off the road along the north flanks of the Mushera group is Knocknakilla, with two (one fallen) outlier gallauns to dwarf its moderately sized circle stones. There is the ruin of a cairn close by. These are all high level sites with fine outlooks over the surrounding country, except for Carrigagulla, which is set low down under the hills. So, too, near Glengarriff, is Mill Little, on a plat beside a stream below the Priest's Leap, and with two of its stones set to form a kind of entry to the ring of the other three. Adjacent, on a line running north/south, are three boulder burials and two small gallauns and some fallen stones to the south of the group. This is the only reported association of boulder burials with five-stone circles, though they occur on a number of occasions with the multiple-stone ones.

Mill Little

Only one five-stone circle has been excavated in Cork, that at Kealkill on the road between Gougane Barra and Ballylickey. Although evidence of a single burial with cremated bones was found at both Reanascreena and Bohonagh, and evidence of two, one in an urn, was found at Drombeg, nothing of this sort was discovered at Kealkill. What was found was a cruciform trench which the excavator suggested might have contained wooden beams to support some sort of upright structure, perhaps for sighting on sun or star. It reminds us that we have only the stones left to us, and that there may have been extensive wooden structures going with them.

Kealkill

At Kealkill, as at other sites, there is a cairn alongside; Knockraheen has several cairns in its vicinity which are thought to be associated with the circle. Kealkill is a splendid hillside site with extensive views over West Cork and down Bantry Bay. The circle of five medium-sized stones has two very tall outliers. One cannot but be impressed by the care the builders seem to have taken in picking nicely marked stones; the circle stones and some of the outliers have beautiful fossil ripple prints on them. So, too, do some of the stones at Breeny More, about 400 metres (something over a quarter of a mile) south-west of the Kealkill monument. Breeny More is a ruined

Breeny More

Stone circle, Derreenataggart West

Mill Little

multiple-stone circle enclosing four fine boulder burials. The view from Breeny More of Bantry Bay and the circling mountains is even more magnificent than Kealkill's. Not very much further away is yet another multiple-stone circle, on the side of the hill near its crest and above Cappanaboul Lough with its white water-lilies.

Standing stones

From the circles turn to the other standing stones: alignments, pairs and solitary gallauns. The solitary stones are, even now when many have been knocked as a result of their impeding machinery in enlarged fields, very numerous in the county. They may have been erected for a variety of purposes: to mark where some great event took place, or perhaps where some great person was buried; to mark a route; or simply for the convenience of cows to scratch themselves. Sometimes standing stones occur in a line, say three in three adjacent fields. Where a standing stone is rearing itself up on the crest of a ridge, one cannot but suspect a marker on an old cross-country track. There is a line of stones up along the upper Lee valley to Macroom and over toward Millstreet, which could be markers along a route.

The pilgrim route along the Ross of Mull to Iona is still marked by big standing stones, and 'path marked by cairns' has been a common feature of many lands. In Iceland, you can travel the modern road and see the old trail, for ponies, alongside with its regular cairn markers. It needs to be remembered that the made highway belongs to regular wheeled transport. The ancient routes for walkers and horses and droves of animals can have many vague patches, and nobody who has been crossing a strange mountain pass in mist and sees the next cairn looming up in the right place can have any doubt that some of the Irish gallauns served the same purpose. Markers

Stone alignment excavation, Kealkill

Kealkill

on the crests of ridges and tops of passes are particularly useful in bad weather: there is a gallaun in the Cousane Gap in Cork; others on the pass west from the Black Valley, under Carrantuohill, in Kerry; another on the crest of the Monavullaghs in County Waterford, to give three obvious examples.

Pairs of very large megaliths occur around the Mushera district and elsewhere in the county, and are separate from the outlier pairs attached to the stone circles. Theories of male and female stones seem more imaginative than capable of proof; it is possible that the two big surviving stones relate to adjacent structures built in timber and now vanished. There are fine pairs at Monkey's Bridge, near Bweeng; south of Mushera, at Ballynagree; and another at about 800 metres west of Cooper's Rock. Where the Cousane Gap road leaves the Kilmichael/Dunmanway road, a fine pair stands on a sandy ridge to the south of it. Again, one often comes on one tall gallaun and then its companion lying beside it or half-buried in peat growth and heather. One such couple is high on a spur of Musherabeg, west of the Cusloura river headwaters, and at over 1,000 feet with most commanding views. Another is set equally high on a spur of Shehy Mountain.

The alignments, consisting of anything from three stones upwards, appear from recent research in the county to be astronomically aligned, as the Somervilles realised so many years ago. There are still a good number of them in County Cork, varying from those with very massive stones to those with quite small ones. Sometimes they grade in height from one end of the line to the other. At Reananeree, to the south of Ballyvourney, is a five-stone circle of smallish stones and close by, running through a field fence and line of trees, a little alignment of six stones carefully graded from 50 centimetres at one end to 150 centimetres at the other. Particularly fine alignments are those of Castlenalacht, just north of Bandon; An Seisear ('The Six'), 800 metres from Beenalaght bridge on the Bweeng road, and one in Piercetown townland, on the south slope of Doolieve between Carrigaline and Bally-martle. The Somervilles' 'Three Fingers' at Castletownsend was originally

Cousane Gap

Monkey's Bridge
Ballynagree

Musherabeg

Shehy

Alignments

Reananeree

Castlenalacht
Piercetown
Castletownsend

'An Seisear'

Stone circle, Breeny More

Stone circle, Pookeen

Stone circle, Cappanaboul

Stone alignment, Lettergorman

Stone alignment, Leitry

Stone alignment, Murrahin

Stone alignment, Cullenagh

five, but one of the Townshend ladies appropriated one for a rockery; another has fallen. There are other reports of big standing stones being broken up to make tombstones.

Nobody looking down on a standing stone or stone circle can fail to see, at times, a resemblance to people seen at a distance. Martin Martin in his *Description of the Western Islands of Scotland* (*c.* 1695) writes of North Uist: 'There are three stones erect about five feet high, at a distance of a quarter of a mile from one another, on eminences about a mile from Loch Maddy, to amuse invaders; for which reason they are still called false sentinels.' *Na Fir Bhréige* – 'the False Men' – the Scots Gaelic called them; and stones on Cape Clear Island have exactly the same name and the same tradition – that they were to 'amuse' (frighten off) invaders, in this case the French.

Cape Clear

Wedge-tombs, contemporary with the stone circles, are widely spread over the county. In plan, they are roughly wedge-shaped stone boxes in which the broader end usually faces south-west or thereabouts and narrows in the opposite direction. The tomb is divided into an inner and outer portion by a cross-set slab or slabs, and its outer wall is normally double. The whole would, originally, have been covered with a mound of earth and stones. Today, it is the centre box, with its great capping stones and slab sides, that is normally all that remains. Cork has a number in good condition and many more in various stages of ruin; the county also has the biggest of the type in Ireland, Labbacallee near Glanworth.

Wedge-tombs

Labbacallee, the old woman's grave – and female bones were found in it – is on an upland site with a far-ranging view all around it. The tomb is built of the local limestone, with a lot of fossils in some of the blocks, and the

Labbacallee

Wedge-tomb, Rostellan

Wedge-tomb, Keamcorravooly

Wedge-tomb, Altar

Wedge-tomb, Inchincurka

Wedge-tomb, Arderawinny

Wedge-tomb, Lahardane More

Wedge-tomb, Mourne Abbey

Wedge-tomb, Ballynahown

biggest of the three capstones is estimated to weigh 100 tonnes. Island, near Burnfort (east of the Mallow/Cork main road) was excavated not too long ago and gives a good idea of the plan of a big wedge-tomb and enclosing cairn, but the wedge is partially ruined. So, too, to a far greater extent, is another wedge-tomb of Labbacallee proportions, which the Ordnance Survey maps mark as 'St Laser's church', in Killaseragh townland, south-west of Ballynoe in east Cork. There was a big standing stone across the field to the west of the ruined tomb but it was bulldozed into the ditch recently (*c.* 1982/3). A scatter of the tombs continues across the county from the east to the west where, with more abundant stone and less intensive agriculture, they are more numerous. At Cloyne there is a large ruined one of limestone in the grounds of Castlemary, and at Rostellan a portal tomb rather than a wedge, up which the tide rises half way. The Rostellan dolmen, to use the old name for these structures, has been argued over and some have claimed it is a comparatively modern construction, of the time when people built such romantic follies. But this could hardly be the case with Rostellan, for though the now destroyed Big House had, along the shore, a folly tower and an ornamental column, both are set firmly and sensibly on dry land. It is true that the capstone had fallen and was replaced, but the location must rule out any idea of garden ornament. There seems to have been a local memory, too, that there was a stone circle near it, or at least other stones, and that these have all disappeared in the water and mud of the little estuary within the last 100 years or so. Rostellan seems rather a case showing the relative rise of sea level since the tomb was built, and it can be matched in West Cork with a boulder dolmen at Dunmanus, in salt marsh with the sea fingering around it.

Leaba Diarmaida, on the Old Head of Kinsale, was probably another wedge-tomb, but is now destroyed; it was on the east side of the lighthouse road soon after it leaves the old lighthouse site for the present one.

Well preserved wedge-tombs around Mushera include the Bealick in Lackaduv (with a second tomb hidden in a field fence lower down the hillside); a very fine specimen near the Glantane East stone circle and, across the valley and up on the hills west of Carriganimmy, a magnificent tomb in Carrigonirtane. Stone alignments occur in the same area. Keamcorravooly is another good example, just east of the county bounds between Ballyvourney and Inchigeelagh, in the district where the old mountain track of Lackabaun leads into Kerry. There are, in fact, a number of wedge-tombs in the area around Shehy and Douce near Gougane Barra. Another county bounds' site, of which only a few of the side stones remain in the moor, lies near the Cork summit of the old Esk road from the head of Bantry Bay to Kenmare.

There are still more fine examples of wedge-tombs in the Mizen and Beara peninsulas. In the Mizen peninsula two of the best are the one at Altar and, near by, Arderawinny, which is claimed as a portal tomb. In Beara, near the old church site of Kilmackowen, is a small wedge up on the hillside with a

Island

Killaseragh

Cloyne
Rostellan

Mushera

Shehy
Douce

Altar
Arderawinny
Kilmackowen

Rock art

standing stone near it; inside the tomb is a slab with well cut cup-marks.

Rock art – circles, lines and cup-marks – occurs all over West Cork and is to be seen on smooth glaciated rock surfaces as well as on boulders, standing stones and tombs. Examples are often difficult to locate when they are on natural surfaces on the hillside; easy to find when they are on known monuments. Whether the designs are merely ornamental or have some symbolic significance seems impossible to determine. One should be careful about identifying cup-marks because very similar natural hollows can be weathered out in the Cork rocks.

Boulder burials

Boulder burial – a burial over which a single more or less round stone is set, perched firmly on several smaller ones – is confined to West Cork and Kerry and is very much simpler then the wedge-tomb. As already remarked, a group of people on the ridge between Crookstown and Kilmurry had access to large boulders of quartz and were able to use some of them as the main stone. At other sites, a quartz boulder may be used for one of the smaller supporting stones. There is a fine example of a boulder burial about 400 metres north of the Castlenalacht alignment, the one in the salt marsh at Dunmanus in the Mizen peninsula, and a great concentration in the Beara peninsula, especially at the Castletownbere/Allihies section of it. Again, however, a note of caution: glacial erratics can equally be perched on a cluster of smaller stones, and in some cases could ape the boulder burial.

Barrows

Another type of burial found in the east and north of the county is an earthen tumulus or barrow; most of them have been, it seems, largely destroyed by agriculture. Large pottery food vessels have turned up from some of the burials – sometimes in sand and gravel workings; sometimes in farm bulldozing operations. Ring barrows, most of which seem to be Bronze Age, are the most easily destroyed of monuments, little mounds enclosed in a small circular earthwork. Some survive in County Cork and recently I

*Cup-marked stone,
Castlemehigan*

*Inscribed stone,
Knockdrum fort*

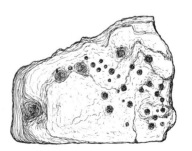

discovered from the air a very perfect example in Dromlough townland, on the banks of the Caha River between Coppeen and the Cousane Gap.

Undoubtedly the most magnificently sited are the mountain-top stone burial cairns, which date from Neolithic times. Two urns came from the great cairn of Corrin Hill at Fermoy long ago. Most of the cairns are now ruinous but some certainly, like the much damaged Corrin one, were chambered. The sites are all worth visiting for the hill walks and views they provide, and the county list is long. It properly begins in Kerry with the two Paps of Dana, the great cairns forming the actual nipples of the breasts. These cairns are at 2,273 and 2,284 feet. Moving east, in Cork, there is a huge, much ruined cairn on the lower peak of Caherbarnagh at 2,001 feet. Claragh, overlooking Millstreet (1,486 feet) has the remains of a cairn inside its hill-fort enclosure. There is another on the east end of Mount Hilary (1,200 feet). There is a group of them on the Nagles Mountains; a very large one on *Súideacháin na Mná Finne* (the resting place of the Fingalian women) at 1,340 feet. Across a col, or pass, there is another, lesser cairn on the higher summit at 1,406 feet, and yet another large one to the west of Seefin (Fionn's resting place) at 1,392 feet. Corrin (only about 600 feet) ends the Nagles ridge to the east, and is an outstanding landmark for many miles around. There was another cairn, now buried in forest, on Cahergall (772 feet) north of Dungourney; possibly one on Caher Hill (771 feet) further east, but again in impenetrable forest at present. Toward Lisgoold is an upland ridge called Slieve Corrin with the remains of a cairn on it. The cairn on the crest of Currabinny Hill, opposite Crosshaven, has been excavated, and is now very ruined. One on Ram's Hill opposite was destroyed in the building of Camden Fort. There is another massive ruined cairn on Doolieve (606 feet) on the ridge immediately south of Cork airport, which it overlooks.

Cairns
Corrin Hill

Caherbarnagh
Claragh
Mount Hilary
Nagles

Seefin
Corrin

Currabinny Hill

Doolieve

Boulder burial, Castlenalacht

Boulder burial, Rathruane More

Cape Clear

Cape Clear Island has Cnoc Charn Tonn on its heights, much ruined and traditionally said to be the burial place of a chieftain, Tonn. Explored in 1984, it appears to be a passage tomb and the decorated stone, now in Cork Public Museum, came from it.

Skeagh

Mount Corrin

Knocknacorrin

Moving into mainland West Cork, there is an immense but very ruined cairn at a place called Skeagh (499 feet) north-west of Skibbereen, presently in forest but accessible. Here there is a tradition of a midwinter, Christmas festival which drew people from miles around, but it has long died out. There is another big cairn on the Corrin Hill (Mount Corrin, 946 feet) in the Mizen peninsula, overlooking Durrus, with a more recent tall cairnlet built atop the ancient ruin. Finally there is Knocknacorrin (596 feet) between Glengarriff and Adrigole, with a great view down Bantry Bay. It is unlikely that this list is exhaustive and there could well be more Cork hilltop cairns of ancient date. There are, of course, plenty of the ordinary modern ones that people build on hilltops, which are not burial sites. People are always building cairns on hills; in the past, as landmarks, today often just for amusement!

Merely listing the sites, detailing structures, dates and possible uses, does not convey the glamour that these great stone monuments of County Cork have for anyone who goes in search of them. One gains a special sense of awe when touching the rough rock that people set up so long ago in such splendid places. The act of seeking them out mingles history with hill walking, the scents of furze and heather, the wind off the sea. Great cairns of deeply weathered pink sandstone command vast views to all the mountain

Gallaun with rock art near Rosscarbery

Burial cairn, Caherbarnagh, at 2,000 feet. The original cairn exists only in its foundations

chains of Kerry and Cork, Tipperary, Waterford and away into Limerick. It is possible as well to check the orientations of circle and alignment and come at dawn or sunset and see the sun rise or set over the ancient stones on the appointed date.

Ring barrow, Dromlough, east of Cousane Gap

Ballybane carved rock

IV

Dún, Cashel and Rath

ORK WAS WELL populated from early times. Even today, after centuries of destruction, the county is spotted with the circles of the ring forts, the homesteads of farmers and landowners of Early Christian times. T. J. Westropp counted the ring forts marked on the first edition (1840) of the six inches to the mile Ordnance Survey maps and made a grand total of ring forts for all Ireland of about 30,000. Many more could be added from aerial survey and local knowledge, not to mention those totally destroyed in the more remote past. Cork alone could well have had 4,000 ring forts. In addition, there are the hill-forts and the fortified headlands along the coast.

When the Romans went into southern Britain, the inhabitants were occupying numerous hilltop forts. Many of these remain, massive banks and ditches surrounding and defending a hilltop. There are far fewer such structures in Ireland – 200 or so. Cork has one of the finest Irish examples in Cashel Hill, four miles north-east of Bandon. Here a vast oval enclosure is defended by double banks and ditches; although only 598 feet high, the hill is a mighty swelling in the land and commands enormous prospects. So does Carn Tigheragh, Corrin Hill, by Fermoy, where the recent afforestation has partly

Hilltop forts

Cashel Hill

Corrin Hill

Cashel hill-fort

obliterated the banks of the old hill-fort. Corrin, as already noted, encloses a huge burial cairn, as does little round Claragh above Millstreet, whose hill-fort's banks can still be traced fairly readily. Corrin is 700 feet high; Claragh is 1,486 feet, and its steep flanks make it a favourite launching place for hang-gliders.

Claragh

Caherdrinny, west of Kilworth Camp on the Fermoy-Mitchelstown road, is 695 feet, a long swelling ridge dominating the surrounding country. Topped by the ruin of a medieval castle, it seems originally to have been a hill-fort with concentric banks defending its summit. Other less dramatic but possible hill-forts in the east of County Cork are Glenaphuca (506 feet), immediately east of Dungourney, and another large enclosure, presently on the edge of a state forest, south of the Leamlara River valley and about one and a half miles west of the site of Ballyedmond House. In both these two examples, these are very large enclosures, bigger and more irregular than the typical ring fort.

Caherdrinny

Glenaphuca

Perhaps the most unusual of Cork's hilltop forts is Kilmacoo in north Cork, east-north-east of Newmarket and just west of Bawn Cross, at about 600 feet. Here is a very large circular enclosure with deeply entrenched bank and ditch defences which seems to have been a hill-fort later taken over by the Church. A small graveyard inside the great circle of the fort is all that is left of what may have once been a Celtic establishment spread over the whole area.

Kilmacoo

Promontory forts are numerous in Cork for the simple reason that the coast is well supplied with suitable headlands. It was easy to put a bank and ditch across the neck and make a defensible position. Today, the sea has encroached very seriously on a great many, if not all, of these sites, so we do not see them as their builders knew and used them. Cork does not appear to have any inland promontory forts like the famous Caherconree in Kerry. At Caherconree, a large, cliff-ringed spur of the Slieve Mish mountains at a height of about 2,000 feet is defended by a massive stone wall with a ditch in front of it. Legend has been busy with traditions about this fortress, if fortress it is – certainly there is no supply of water within the walls to allow

Promontory forts

Ardahill

Knockdrum

the survival of a prolonged siege.

In happier times in Lebanon, Ralph and Molly Izzard made a delightful journey through that country (*Smelling the Breezes*, London 1959), and one evening saw a shepherd corral his flock on just such a Caherconree spur, blocking off the neck with temporary brushwood. Everywhere in Ireland cattle used to go up to the mountain pastures for the summer, and it could be that Caherconree was where their owners lived and where they could pen the animals at night or when a neighbour might be expected to come raiding. After all, the stones for the wall's building are there for the picking up and Caherconree would probably represent a lot less of an outlay than a modern farmer's milking parlour. It was while thinking these heretical thoughts about Caherconree and some of our defended headlands that I came on a remark of Charles Smith in his *Ancient and Present State of the County and City of Cork* (1750). Speaking of Dunworly at the Seven Heads between Courtmacsherry and Inchydoney, he wrote that there were 'the ruins of an old castle defended by square bastions to prevent people from landing ... This was a place where the Irish formerly secured their cattle at night: there are many such on the coast, particularly one in the west, defended by a wall, a castle and two turrets.' (This last must be Three Castles on the Mizen.)

The biggest defended headland on the Cork coast is the Old Head of Kinsale. The name is of interest in that it is Norse. The Norsemen knew this great jutting-out headland and called it *Olde Nes: nes*, a headland, and *oddi*, a long tongue-shaped bit of land. A defensive ditch was thrown across the narrow root of the tongue, and later the de Courcys built a wall with towers to defend the approaches to the headland. On this site were the remains of hut circles and small ring forts, all now swept away by land reclamation, as well as the already mentioned megalithic tomb, Leaba Diarmaida. The Old Head would represent a whole settlement of houses and fields which could halt entry by defending a very narrow pass that linked it to the mainland. The Galley Head was somewhat on the same lines: a big headland, though not on the scale of the Old Head, with a defensive structure across its neck. Like the Old Head, the Galley Head had a later medieval defence built across it, of which some part remains mingling with the present farm

Marginal notes:
Dunworly

Old Head of Kinsale

Galley Head

Galley Head

buildings there. A third, enormous, promontory fort was only first recorded in 1990 as a result of local people informing the County Cork Archaeological Survey. It is Crow Head at the tip of the Beara peninsula, and its neck is defended by a massive series of banks and ditches.

More typical of headland forts is Dunoure, on the west flank of the Galley Head. It is now nearly destroyed. All that remains are a fragment of wall and foundations of buildings, on a rapidly diminishing little headland linked to the mainland by a thin catwalk kneck that must soon be eroded away. The ruins are medieval, but could be on an earlier site. Duneendermotmore (Big Dermot's Little Fort) on the west side of the Toe Head is in similar plight. It was rapidly disintegrating when M. J. O'Kelly excavated it in the 1940s, and more has gone since. It is a very splendid place, on the cliffs of Toe Head looking out to sea to the Stags Rocks which, though they still appear massive, are also much-eroded remnants.

O'Kelly found that Duneendermotmore had been first fortified by putting a deep ditch across the neck of the headland, but he found virtually nothing connected with this first structure. What he did find was all to do with the medieval occupation: the wall around the perimeter of the headland, the house, and massive building on the neck to make a causeway, defensive walls and a drawbridge. For the excavators, O'Kelly writes, after they had cleaned up this structure, 'our only means of entry to the fort ... was by means of a plank laid down in the position which the drawbridge would have occupied and this enabled us to form a realistic impression of the whole structure as it must have been when first completed by its medieval builder. Few of the visitors who came to the dig at this time were prepared to "walk the plank", especially if the day were windy and the tide full, for the waves crashed against the sides of the isthmus, making the crossing look more dangerous than it actually was.'

Crow Head

Dunoure

Duneendermot-
more

Promontory fort, Dunoure Castle, Galley Head

*Promontory fort, Duneendermotmore,
and Stags Rocks*

The finds from the medieval house were extensive, and included much pottery imported from places as far away, the excavators believed, as Cologne, Holland and England. It included colourful majolica ware and plates with multicoloured hand-painted patterns. There was a very contemporary looking pickaxe, a piece of pewter, broken quern stones and flint fragments that may have come from making the flints needed to fire old-fashioned muskets. A number of musket-balls were found and appear to date as late as the 17th century. The end of the house came when it burned down. According to tradition, Dermotmore was a local freebooter, but the exact dates of his existence are uncertain. What is certain is that whoever lived out on the little headland was quite well-to-do, and that the sea has made enormous inroads on the cliffs since that time.

Portadoona
Carrigillihy

O'Kelly excavated two other headland forts in West Cork: Portadoona on the east side of Toe Head and Carrigillihy on the west side of Glandore Harbour. Both had very strong defending walls, but they yielded virtually nothing in the way of finds: traces of two hearths at Portadoona, nothing in

Dunoure

Carrigillihy. But a little way off from the Carrigillihy headland, on the lands of a nearby farm close to an old church site, was an oval mound with indications of a house inside it. O'Kelly thought it might be where the promontory fort builders had lived, and excavated it, revealing a house inside an enclosing and massive wall. The little house had had stone walls and a thatched roof and O'Kelly spent some time reconstructing the roof and rafters to see exactly how it was done; there is a model of the reconstruction in Cork City Museum. Finds, which included fragments of pottery and a bronze awl, dated the site to the early Bronze Age, and O'Kelly claimed it as an early ring fort. But Carrigillihy is a very far cry from the carefully marked out circle of a ring fort; the ring fort is a very sophisticated bit of construction, whereas Carrigillihy appears much more as a house with a wall round it.

The ring forts, which are typically Irish with some small overspill into the Isle of Man are, so far as present knowledge goes, mostly of Early Christian date, but some were in use as late as the 17th century and others go back to pre-Christian times. They are traditionally called 'fairy forts', and, if they were in use so late, that must be a comparatively recent tradition. Nor are they forts in the normal use of the word; their security arrangements, which appear quite impressive, are perhaps no more than the equivalent of present day locks and grills, to keep out the casual marauder rather than take the brunt of sustained attack.

Ring forts

Archaeology calls them 'ring forts', but the Irish word *rath* is better and less misleading. When the walls are of drystone, they are a *caiseal*, anglicised cashel. *Cathair*, anglicised caher and common in placenames like Caher Hill, would imply a big rath or a hill-fort; it is sometimes translated 'city', and the big stone rath under the Paps of Dana in Kerry at which the Mayday rounds are made is known in English as the 'City'. *Lios an Uisge* (Lisanisky), means water liss and suggests that the ditch could be or was filled with water. One near Crossbarry has a very deep ditch with water in it; it is a large oval close to a couple of holy wells and suggests, in fact, a church site rather than a

Cahervaglier near Coppeen

Remains of stone-built rath near Carriganimmy

typical rath. *Dún* indicates a large and important rath.

The typical rath is a near perfect circle, usually a single bank and ditch but sometimes, in the big examples, with two or three massive enclosing banks which even today may still rise to a considerable height. Raths vary in size; the big ones can be 40 or 50 metres across, and they vary very much in their look as one sees them from the air, which is really the best way to appreciate them fully. The pilot has the impression that raths have different architectural styles. Some big raths may have low banks; some small ones very massive banks.

From the air, the raths seem to cluster in almost village-like groups or are strung out along the good farmland. Their distribution is very much that of their successors, the present day, fairly large Irish farm. They do not go down into the boggy valleys, which were then undrained, and they do not climb too high into the hills; one or two reach the 1,000-foot contour (e.g. under Caherbarnagh near Rathmore) but not many. Most have earthen banks but where stone is available, as one moves into the hills of West Cork, for instance, the walls are drystone. Stone and earth may be mixed, as at Caher-

Cahervaglier

vaglier with its massive stone-built entry. Cahervaglier, near Coppeen, on the road to the Cousane Gap from Crookstown, is on the edge of the real mountainy, rocky land and an area, too, with very numerous ring forts, in which you can trace the increasing use of stone as you move west. But stone was

Garryduff

used in some of the raths of east Cork also, as at Garryduff, and a much overgrown rath between Garryduff and Clonmult, where the double banks are of cyclopean masonry, to use the old phrase for construction in gigantic stones.

While the raths are situated on well-drained, often south-facing slopes with wide outlooks, they are not normally on actual hilltops. But some of them are. Several raths in the Bantry area are sited on the very top of drumlin ridges. At Terelton, three miles north of Coppeen, a large rath with an

Terelton

underground passage is placed on the very summit of a conical 825-foot hill. No less than two large forts (with underground passage and a standing stone) crowned the height of Caherdesert, above the old church site of

Caherdesert

Desert, one and a half miles south-west of Britway. At 500 feet, Caherdesert commands an enormous view to all the distant mountain ranges – Ballyhouras, Galtees, Knockmealdowns – and must have been one of the most interesting ring fort sites in the county. One ring fort, the gallaun and the underground passage were bulldozed completely in the last few years; the second ring fort, of the same size and close to the first, has only been revealed by aerial photography. Garryduff I is sited on a long whale-back of a hill, at 531 feet, two miles south of Ballynoe; the hill is being rapidly reduced by quarrying but the fort, on its very crest, is a landmark for many miles around. Most dramatic of all is the enormous, largely stone-built Rath,

Rath

on the border of Cork with Waterford, which stands on the summit of a round hill about 500 feet high and commanding all the countryside. Rath is two miles east of Mount Uniacke and about five miles north-west of Youghal.

The Ireland in which the occupants of the ring forts lived and farmed looked very different from the Ireland of today. It was still heavily forested with mixed timber. Bogs were undrained. There were no field fences on the scale of today, though some plots may have been enclosed. Animals needed a herdsperson when grazing. In summer the cattle might go up to the mountains pastures, as they still do in Switzerland, and so leave the plots of grain on the farm free from molestation. There seem to have been good trails. In tradition Tara was the centre of main roads radiating out, much as the present ones from Dublin, to the different parts of the country. Annals and lives of the saints suggest it was quite easy to move about Ireland. The sea and the great rivers, as well as the land, were important highways, and overseas trade was a part of life.

The farmers who lived in the raths were primarily cattlemen, but they also had sheep, pigs, horses and dogs. Each rath was a self-contained unit: grain was ground on the hand quern or at a local horizontal mill (see chapter XII), wool was spun and woven into cloth, and iron was smelted for tools. Iron slag is a common find in the raths. If a group of small huts inside a rath seems to have offered a very primitive way of life, the people who lived in them were anything but primitive. Poetry and literature flourished. The glitter of Celtic ornament came out of ring-fort factories and the great illuminated manuscripts from equally simple hutments in the monasteries.

The huts were normally of timber and wattle with thatched roofs, but in the stonier areas would be of drystone with thatch or of stone corbelled in a beehive shape. Most raths have underground passages as well, called 'earth houses', or 'weems' in Scotland, 'fogous' in Cornwall, though archaeology has opted for the French 'souterrain'. These passages probably provided additional storage space but their utility as hiding places seems limited by the fact that people must have known a rath would have one or more. A very large number are known from County Cork – frequently being discovered by a tractor wheel going through the roof. Not all are in ring forts or rath sites; some are associated with moated sites, with other houses, or with no known structure above ground.

Souterrains

There were two ways of making a souterrain. One was by tunnelling into the rock or clay, when the clay was solid enough not to cave in. Pits were dug to gain access to the tunnel and these were filled in when the job was done. The souterrain at Templebryan (near Clonakilty) is of this type. Or one could have a souterrain entirely stone lined, and here the trench was dug out open to the sky, the stones set in it and then covered over. Souterrains can be complex with several chambers, with ventilation shafts and creep-holes between, and even have hearths and chimneys in them. A complex rock-cut one, under the old church site and the Beamish Tower at Dunisky, is thought not to belong to the main series of earth houses but to be a much later construction. It has some seven chambers and has been compared to French medieval souterrains with the suggestion that the De Cogans, who

Templebryan

Dunisky

owned the adjacent (now destroyed) castle, could have been its builders. Anglo-Saxon coins, of the time of Aethelstan and Eadmund, turned up in an earth house at Castlefreke. The strangest Cork souterrain story comes from Peake, just north of Coachford, where in 1755 one alleged to have had 15 chambers was found. In them was an enormous number of human skeletons, perhaps of people trapped and killed in the souterrain.

Evidence that they could be used as hiding places comes from the life of St Ruadhan, who hid a man on the run in an underground room under a chapel. Not wanting to tell a lie, and closely questioned about the man's whereabouts, Ruadhan said: 'I don't know where he is, unless he's under my feet.'

From the Icelandic *Book of the Settlements* (*Landnámabók*) comes another story about Leif, the foster-brother of Ingolfur Arnarson (first permanent settler of Iceland in 784 AD). Before they set off for Iceland, Leif went on a Viking trip to Ireland and came to a big earth house (*iard hús* in Icelandic). It was very dark but Leif went down into it and eventually came on a man with a sword from which light shone. He killed the Irishman and bore off the sword and other treasure, and was known ever afterwards as Sword Leif.

Very many ogham stones have been recovered from souterrains. In fact, the biggest find ever of ogham-inscribed stones was made at a souterrain in Cork at a place called Ballyknock, first explored in 1889. No less than 15 stones were found, most of which are on exhibition in the 'Stone Corridor' of University College, Cork, together with oghams from other districts. Oghams were cut on tall slender pillar-stones and slabs, and these proved just the right shape for roofing a stone-built earth house. Ballyknock's

Kilcascan ogham stone

Toberatemple

souterrain was in a large ring fort with three banks; practically nothing survives of this rath now, and nothing at all of the Anglo-Norman castle later built on it. Ballyknock is about two miles south of Ballynoe in north-east Cork.

Ogham, named from the god Oigmiú who in Irish mythology invented writing, may have originated *c.* 300 AD, but continued in use for a very long time. Cutting oghams on stones may have ended in the 7th century, but the code was known long after that: there is a treatise on it in the *Book of Bally-mote* and it was even occasionally used by Irish people in 18th- and early 19th-century manuscripts. Ogham is a straightforward code, very much like the Morse code though a little easier to learn. Like Morse, it is based on the Latin alphabet. There are up to five strokes in each letter code and these can be above, below or across a baseline. On a wooden post or a standing stone, the edge made a convenient baseline; and the inscription is read from bottom up, and then down the other side if it continues. The inscriptions mean very little to us, as they simply say 'so-and-so, son of so-and-so'. They must have meant as little to the souterrain builders who took them so readily for roofing slabs.

Ogham is an Irish thing, and a southern Irish thing at that, for the most part. It appears in Wales and Cornwall, areas settled and visited by Irish people. Cork has the tallest ogham-inscribed pillar, 17.5 feet, at Ballycrovane between Eyeries and Ardgroom in Beara. It reads MAQI DECCEDDAS AVI TURI-ANIAS (of the son of Deich, descendant of Torainn) and still stands in its original site, facing out to sea on a rocky outcrop. The source of the long slender pillar is a short way inland, up the hillside. Around Cork county, other ogham stones remain in their original positions, apart from those taken for earth houses.

Eyeries

R. A. S. MacAlister believed ogham could be a secret means of communication between people knowing the code, using their five fingers and different hand positions to spell it out – which would be quite easy to do. Ogham should be clearly distinguished from Runic, which is a Scandinavian alphabet in its own right, not a code based on an alphabet.

Apart from standing stones with oghams cut on them, there is a curious association in County Cork of a single standing stone set beside a rath. Did the rath builders set up the stone, or choose the site because of some ancient association indicated by the gallaun?

Today it is difficult to realise how self-contained small communities were, and, even recently, how many trades were carried on in the ordinary small town. The rath communities were very largely self-sufficient, but they also imported items from overseas and made use of the services of specialists. According to a story in one of the Irish saints' lives, there were contractors who travelled the country constructing raths, and their fee was the fill of the fort with cattle – a considerable amount. There were travelling craftsmen of various trades who moved around the country – St Ciaran of Clonmacnois came of one such family – and they would survive for centuries as tinkers. But some trades needed a fixed base from which to operate (a factory in modern terms) and as far back as the Bronze Age there was a bronze-making industry settled in the hill-fort of Rathgall in County Wicklow. In County Cork the excavation of Garranes rath revealed that the place had been a metal-workers' site, producing all the brilliant items of Celtic ornament and design.

Garranes

Garranes is one of the very large, three-ring (trivallate) raths of Cork. It stands on the great anticlinal ridge between the rivers Bride and Bandon, the ridge on which Cork airport is sited, and just off the road from Clough-duv to Templemartin, and is about 525 feet above sea level. It is known as Lisnacaheragh, but its ancient name was Rath Raithleann, supposed stronghold of the Uí Eachach, forebears of the O'Mahonys. This identification was made by way of an Irish poem which lists all the other raths one could see from Rath Raithleann: it is the middle of a great complex of raths, of which a number are now ploughed out. The rath is very large, 220 feet across inside the in-most ring, and it had four or five gates at its entrance, very strongly constructed against attack. But finds of military use were nil: the excavators found instead a multitude of little crucibles, clay and stone moulds and iron fragments that may have been smiths' tools – pincers, awls, shears. There were the multi-stranded coloured glass rods (millefiori) used in Celtic ornament, fragments of bronze and an unfinished penannular brooch in that metal, a couple of lumps of tin (imported one supposes from Cornwall) and glass beads. A great deal of pottery was found, of which the most striking specimens were large, comb-surfaced jars – amphorae. They must have been imported from the continent of Europe and may have contained wine or oil.

Ballycatteen

The central date for the occupation of Garranes would seem to be 500 AD; the second enormous trivallate ring fort that was excavated in Cork, Bally-catteen, is a little later, 600 AD. Ballycatteen sits on top of a long ridge that runs down to Ballinspittle village, just back from the coast at Garretstown. Again, the whole district is crowded with raths. The interior of the rath at

Bronze pot found when ploughing near Ballyandreen

Ballycatteen is 200 feet across and the whole structure covers an area of three acres. It had elaborate defences, featuring palisades as well as banks and a complex entrance; but again, as at Garranes, the evidence did not point to either military or much domestic use. There were three souterrains in the area excavated, which was only a quarter of the whole interior. Finds included a kiln, pottery (but not the amphorae of Garranes), bronze items (which included a penannular brooch and a piece of horse trapping), glass beads and one of amber and a broken jet bracelet. There were some crucibles – but only nine, as against the 39 complete ones and 2,500 fragments from Garranes – iron slag, quern fragments and a spindle whorl. The excavators thought the rath had been used by craft-workers, working in metal, and that the place could have served as a stronghold for the neighbourhood in the case of an attack on the local tribe. They believed the souterrains had been constructed during a later phase of occupation. The

Ballycatteen

pottery, very similar to that at Garranes, was made on the wheel and most likely had been imported from Gaul. One fragment, of a yellow jug, could have come from the factories of the Lower Rhine. Today it is perhaps hard to visualise, on the grassy banks of the raths, how their owners imported their crockery from continental Europe, running it into the little harbours of Cork in small sailing ships.

Garryduff

Garryduff I was a domestic site which had boasted a wealthy owner, and excavation turned up a great many finds. The most exciting item, adopted as the logo of the Cork Archaeological and Historical Society, was the Garryduff bird. This is a tiny little bird, intended as a brooch ornament (you can buy and wear a replica today), worked in beaded gold wire on a golden disc – probably the sort of thing Garranes could produce. Its technique looks back, on the one hand, to a gold granulation type from Eastern Mediterranean countries, and forward to its further development, the beaded gold wire used in the Tara brooch.

Garryduff I is Lios Árd, High Fort, and is set on its hill; on the slope of the fields below is Lios Íseal, the low-lying rath. M. J. O'Kelly, after so rich a haul in the little stone fort on the heights, went down to excavate the much larger Lios Íseal, and found exactly nothing! He suggested that this second rath could have been simply a cattle fold. There are two other raths in the immediate vicinity and the same townland – just west from Garryduff I across a little valley and atop the steeply rising hillside. One has been ploughed out; the other is an enormous structure with banks still rising some 12 feet high from the deep ditch. It is far larger than Lios Íseal, and it would be very interesting to excavate it.

Woodstock

A striking feature of the raths is that normally they have no internal water supply, nor even one within immediate reach. Carrying buckets of water must have been part of the daily round. Lios Aimhreidh, in Woodstock townland on the ridge immediately north of Carrigtwohill, has what appears to be a stone-cut well in its deep inner ditch. This Woodstock rath is another very fine example, double ringed and with, unusually, a split-level interior, there being a sharp change in level across the diameter of the structure.

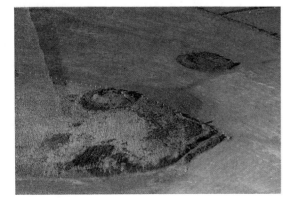

*The two raths
of Garryduff*

Like Ballycatteen, it covers some three acres of land.

A few of the Cork raths use a natural cliff for one side of the structure, thus saving considerably in construction costs. There is nothing on the scale of Dún Aengus in the Aran Islands, but there are a few little semi-circular raths here or there, for instance, using a bank of the Dripsey River high up in the hills.

The souterrains normally tend today to be closed up, so that animals do not fall into them. At a number of Cork raths you will be told that there is an underground passage that was used during the 'Troubles' as a secret hiding place for arms. In fact, one or two modern souterrains were constructed then for just that purpose. The big, mostly rock-cut souterrain at the stone fort of Knockdrum, near Castletownsend, is open and can be seen, but was badly vandalised in the past.

Knockdrum

In 1987 the excavation of Lisnagun (the hound's fort) on the lands of Darrara college near Clonakilty was begun. It is one of a whole complex of ring forts in the area. Remains of cattle, sheep, pig and red deer bones were found and of wheat, rye, barley, flax, radish and hazel nuts, together with iron slag, quern stones and a blue glass bead. The excavation was followed by the reconstruction of the rath. The banks were raised and steepened, and topped again by a palisade; posts went back into the post-holes found in the 'dig' and a round house and animal sheds rose again in wattle and daub. Thatching was complete by the end of 1990. One of the souterrains was made safe for the public to crawl through. This is the first time a ring fort has been restored in this fashion in Ireland.

Lisnagun

From the air, the forts still dot the countryside, or show up as pale outlines in new plough – a ring of stones, thinner soil where their banks have been thrown down or, later in the season, a "crop mark" – a change in the colour of the crop over the different, stonier soil. Destruction has been particularly extensive around Cork Harbour which was originally, it seems, well settled by the rath farmers. But the very dry summer of 1989 really revealed how much has gone. Aerial survey then found crop marks of destroyed ring forts,

Ploughed-out ring fort near Cork Airport

ring barrows and old field fences in nearly every field carrying an arable crop. These new crop marks were particularly numerous, running into hundreds in north Cork, from the Kanturk area across toward Fermoy and the border with Waterford. The banks of the surviving raths are often grown with furze and hawthorn, so that through spring they stand out like gold collars on the green with the bright furze blossom, and later, like rings of whipped cream, with that of the whitethorn. They are particularly beloved, too, of the wild hyacinth, the bluebell, and in late spring are circles of vivid blue. The badger may make his sett in the high banks of the old rath and the explorer come on the winter's bedding turned out by that housekeeperly animal. Often one may wonder why or how the tradition linking these old farmsteads to the fairies came into being.

V

Boiled Venison

URING THE SUMMER months, the Fianna went hunting. They used 'to dig two pits in the yellow clay of the moorland, and put some of the meat on spits to roast before the fire; and to bind another portion of it in dry bundles and set it to boil in the larger of the two pits and keep plying them with stones that were in the fire, making them seethe often until they were cooked. And these fires were so large that their sites are today burned to blackness, and these are now called *Fulacht Fian* by the peasantry.' So wrote Keating in his *Forus Feasa*. They are also known as *Fulacht fiadh* (deer roast), but the *Book of Lismore* calls them *Fulacht na Morrigna*.

Fulacht fiadh

There are many thousands of *fulachta fiadh* in County Cork, the most inconspicuous but most numerous ancient monuments, if you can so call them, of all. At best they show as a low overground mound, often horseshoe shaped, built of black soil and fire reddened stones. Many have been ploughed out and show as a spread of dark soil and burned stones. They were ignored by the Ordnance Surveyors until the third edition of the six-inch map was prepared, *c.* 1930, at which time the *fulachta* had been pointed out to them, and they marked a great number of the more obvious examples on the maps. But the careful examination of *fulacht* ground is turning up very many more. They are normally near a stream or spring, in boggy ground, so that the trough could be easily supplied with water.

Some of the mounds are very big. One at Passage West is reported to be 80 feet in diameter and six feet high. But they occur in clusters, maybe six or so quite close together in a field, and no one can say whether they were all in action together or used and abandoned in turn.

Passage West

When M. J. O'Kelly completed his excavation at the St Gobnet site at Ballyvourney, he turned to a *fulacht fiadh* in a field close to the bridge over the Sullane, on the way up to the shrine. Here he found a wooden trough for the boiling and a stone-lined oven for the roasting of meat, and the post-holes of a hut. Putting poles into these ancient holes, he reconstructed the little hut which he thought had been used to store the meat. He went further. He lit a fire and heated stones in it and got the old tank going again. In half an hour, the 100 gallons it held was boiling. Ten pounds of meat wrapped in straw was put in, more hot stones were added to keep the water boiling and, using modern cookbook times for boiling (3hrs 40mins),

Ballyvourney

it came out perfectly cooked. He was equally successful with the stone oven, which could be heated by piling a fire around it and heating the interior with faggots, the ashes of which were swept out before the meat was put in.

Professor O'Kelly not only got a *fulacht fiadh* working again after centuries, but set a fashion for so doing. The Ballyvourney *fulacht*, like most, was a wooden trough; at Drombeg, beside the stone circle there, is a fine stone one and E. M. Fahy excavated this, as well as the circle, and successfully cooked in it. It was working again for an RTE television feature on ancient Ireland.

Modern people find a *fulacht fiadh* quite hard work. You must gather enough sticks and enough stones (sandstone that will not break up too readily in the water) to get the water boiling and to keep it boiling till the meat is cooked. On the other hand, the method is far more efficient and far easier than spit-roasting a large quantity of meat: outdoors, it is difficult to avoid part being burned and part being half raw, the whole being smoked, and the fats and juices lost to the fire. *Fulacht fiadh* boiling, on the other hand, seals in the whole goodness of the meat and gives a perfectly even cooking.

But their enormous numbers are mysterious and we do not really know by whom or for what they were used. Were they a feature of hunting parties as tradition claims, or of great ceremonial gatherings, or were they just local communal cooking places? We know from excavation and finds that some are prehistoric, but it seems likely that the method continued to be used until much later. Certainly Keating, for instance, knew in the 17th century how it worked.

At Drombeg near Glandore students from UCC get a fulacht fiadh *working again for an RTE television programme*

Leg of lamb cooked in the Drombeg fulacht fiadh

In 1935 the priests of Millstreet parish and Timothy Broker, who drove them to the Station Masses, compiled a list of their findings gathered at the Masses. For this one parish of north-west Cork they came up with a total of 196 raths and 177 *fulachta*: there were 905 houses in the parish at that time. In the townland of Cúil an Áirne were two of particular interest. One was under seven feet and the other under 13 feet of peat, which would date them to a period prior to the formation of this peat. The one with the 13 feet of peat over it had a space about 14 feet square planked with hatchet-dressed timber that looked like bog deal. This was destroyed in about 1897. It sounds somewhat like a horizontal mill's base. In 1892 a trough about nine inches deep, scooped from a tree trunk, was found at a lesser depth. But most of the *fulacht* mounds are just on the surface of the ground, grassed over or grown with bushes. As the writers of the Millstreet booklet note: 'Looking at them today, one would not be surprised to hear that they had been dumped out of a cart into their present position, say some ten years ago to allow for the growth of grass on them.'

Millstreet

Fulacht fiadh, *Trinity Well, Newmarket*

There seems a definite suggestion that some were used to cater for crowds at religious assemblies. There is the very fine stone trough at the Drombeg stone circle. There are *fulacht* mounds at St John the Baptist's well near Templeboden in east Cork, and at St Brigid's well in Ballyrobert townland near Castlelyons. Brigid's well was, in the past, the centre of a very big and boisterous pilgrimage whose 'round' included a now-destroyed standing stone. Brigid's Day, 1 February, marks the beginning of spring; John the Baptist's, 24 June, midsummer – both very ancient festivals Christianised. Near Newmarket in north-west Cork, an area very rich in *fulachta*, one has been actually converted into a holy well, of the Trinity, the water coming from the old trough site in the middle of the mount.

Because *fulachta fiadh* are so easy to overlook, it is probable that their full distribution in Ireland has yet to be worked out. That they are recorded as being so numerous in Cork and Waterford is likely to be a matter of their having been spotted there; counties without present records of them may actually have many. They are also reported from sites in England and Wales. Cooking by dropping red hot stones into a pot or trough is still carried on by some primitive peoples, but no one knows how long people went on using the method in Ireland.

Templeboden
Castlelyons

Newmarket

VI

The Cross on the Stone

OVER ALL THE county are reminders of the first centuries of Christianity: church sites, holy wells, saints' names of whom, today, little more is known. It is vital to try to visualize the country in which this dramatic flowering of the new creed came about. There were no towns – the Vikings had yet to come and build the first of them. People lived in scattered farms or clustered settlements, cultivated the land and raised cattle and sheep, but there were vast forests. Trails marked by cairns and standing stones led from one place to another, but the sea was perhaps the easier highway. It was quite simple to sail across from Cork to continental Europe; trade and people and ideas had been moving in and out that way from very early in men's coming to Ireland. Patrick's mission would come later and be to the north and the midlands of Ireland. The first news of Christianity could be expected to come in along the south coast, and the strong tradition of the 'pre-Patrician' saints shows that it did. If we accept this tradition – and it fits neatly into the geography and the sea routes – Ireland's first Christian and first missionary was a Corkman, Ciaran, 'first born of the saints of Ireland,' as the old accounts style him.

St Ciaran

Cape Clear

Ciaran was born on Cape Clear, crossed over on one of the many small ships making the run to continental Europe, and learned about Christianity there. He came back to begin preaching it in Ireland; first, it would seem, in the Cape; then moving inland to found a great monastery at Saighir, on the western foothills of the Slieve Bloom mountains. Ciaran's father is said to have come from that part of Ireland, but to have fallen in love with a Cork girl called Líadin when making a journey through the south. Ciaran is said to have been born near the White Strand on Cape Clear, and to have been brought up there – legend has it that he worked a miracle even as a youngster, rescuing a fledgling from a hawk! (Perhaps Ciaran should be the patron of the present, internationally famous bird observatory on Cape Clear.)

This was the way the new faith spread: people like Ciaran who had been abroad returned with the new gospel, and it spread slowly over the land. Patrick did not come to Cork, but Cork would eventually become part of the whole national Irish Church which Patrick's mission probably helped to consolidate.

The Christianity which Ciaran and the Irish saints who would follow him brought to Ireland was not the stuffy, overly organised, irrelevant thing that was later to be made of it. It came with a flash of lightning, a roll of thunder, a new vision of reality, of God and God's relation to man. It came with the blinding light of the Transfiguration and of the Resurrection: 'Christ is risen from the dead, by his death conquering death and giving life to those in the tombs' (Easter troparion, Orthodox rite).

It was new, exciting, transforming. Celtic Christianity was a part of the Western Patriarchate, centred on Rome, and its liturgy was in Latin, but the whole organisation was freer and looser than it would later become, and was more on the lines of the present Orthodox Church. The monastic life was also something new; hermits had gone out into the desert to find God and to fight with devils, and God and the devils were real, and there in the desert the first monastic communities had been set up. Each founder of a settlement, there or in Ireland, was a pioneer, picking up the basic ideas of how to be a monk or a nun and applying them to local people and local circumstances.

Only if we understand the excitement of the new faith and the violent enthusiasm it aroused, can we begin to understand why Cork county is full of old church sites that were once monasteries and hermitages, and why Cork people still pray to long-dead saints, of whom now only the name, and the person-to-person contact in prayer, remain.

On Cape Clear is St Ciaran's well and stone and the ruin of a little medieval church on his church site. Islanders point it out as 'the oldest church in Ireland'; the present structure above ground is not, of course, but the site very probably is. The stone is a massive gallaun, smoothed and shaped like a phallus, and cut on it, small and neat, is a Latin cross. The new religion had taken over the old.

We know next to nothing of what that old religion was, except that in Ireland Christianity scored a bloodless and martyrless victory over it. What is intriguing is this link between the standing stones, stone tombs and stone circles and the new faith: it suggests that they had retained some aura of holiness, were the centre of some religious cult, for well over 2,000 years at the very least. The legend of St Patrick relates how he overthrew Crom Cruach, a massive standing stone beside a stone circle. The fact is that early church sites in Ireland, Scotland and elsewhere may be associated with megalithic monuments. At Carnac in Brittany, with its ranked standing stones, St Michael's Church is built on a megalithic tumulus. In the Mourne Mountains, St Donard is said to have used a megalithic hilltop cairn as a hermitage on the summit of Slieve Donard. The official Church, in Councils of the 5th, 6th and 7th centuries, condemned the worship of stones and wells and trees; equally it had to live with people's ingrained habits, and St Gregory would advise St Augustine on his English mission to Christianise the ancient customs and gatherings. This was the most sensible policy and the one which was carried out, so that the Church's liturgical year replaced the old seasonal festivals with new Christian ones: the light of Christ coming in the dark of midwinter at Christmas; Easter, the Resurrection of Christ and the resurrection of plant and animal life with spring. St John the Baptist took the midsummer slot; All Saints and All Souls, the beginning of real winter, in November. The cross was cut small and neat by Ciaran on the standing stone, but it would soon spread itself over the whole rock and end with the full splendour of the Irish High Cross, the Christian version of the ancient gallaun.

The list of megalithic remains associated with early church sites in Cork is quite impressive. The standing stone on Cape Clear is associated with Ciaran. A very large wedge-tomb, which the Ordnance map calls 'St Laser's Church', is linked with the monastic enclosure of Killaseragh near Ballynoe. A group of four gallauns stands beside Labbamolagga near Mitchelstown. A stone circle is beside Templebryan near Clonakilty. A small, ruined megalithic tomb, 'St Brigid's Chair', lies beside Britway church, just south of Castlelyons. St Abban's grave, a cairn with ogham stones set around it, is close to St Gobnet's in Ballyvourney. Down in the Beara peninsula, the impressive ancient site of Kilmackowen is quite close to a wedge-tomb and standing stone on the opposite hillside. There are likely to be others in addition to these examples.

Killaseragh
Labbamolagga
Templebryan
Britway

Ballyvourney
Kilmackowen

In continental Europe and in Britain, the Church was town-based (*pagan* means a countryman), and the bishop had his seat in the town's big church or cathedral. The bishop's diocese, his area of jurisdiction, spread out from the town over the surrounding countryside. It was neat and orderly, based no doubt on Roman civil administration. But Ireland was Celtic and devoid

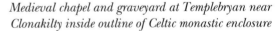

Tullylease

Medieval chapel and graveyard at Templebryan near Clonakilty inside outline of Celtic monastic enclosure

of towns, and the Church had to find itself a different way of life. It became predominantly monastic. One reason for this was that the total dedication of the monastic calling had an enormous appeal to enthusiastic Irish Christians, another that the monastery was the most viable unit in the circumstances. The big landowners and farmers lived in their self-contained raths; the Church simply took over the self-contained rath idea and turned it into a monastery. Here the monks could live, farm the surrounding land and serve the local people with liturgy and sacrament. It meant downgrading the bishop to his purely sacramental and religious functions and giving much greater power to the abbot or abbess. By and large the system worked very well, and from it were mounted the great evangelising missions of Irish saints to Scotland and to mainland Europe.

Because Irish monasteries tended to attract large numbers of monks and students, the monastic rath was, in general, bigger than the secular model accommodating one farmer and his family. It tended to be more irregular, less perfectly circular, than the rath. Preserved in faint earthworks, some-

Church site inside hill-fort at Kilmacoo

times only visible from the air, or in field fences still following the ancient circuit, County Cork has a long list of these large and ancient monastic enclosures. After the coming of the Anglo-Normans and of the continental religious Orders, the old monasteries faded away and today, occupying a mere spot in the great acreage of the original enclosure, you often find a small, ruined, medieval church and a rectangular graveyard around it.

At Templebryan the ancient enclosure is preserved in the stone field fences, as also is the enclosure at Bawnatemple in the Lee valley near Carrig-adrohid, a site which recently turned up a boulder with a Maltese cross cut on it. Labbamolagga and Killeenemer (near Glanworth), both with very ancient churches, have extensive circular earthworks around them, clearly visible from the air and to some extent on the ground. Ballymodan, just south of Bandon, only really shows its enclosure from the air, and only from the air is the faint outline of the monastic enclosure of Kilnaruane visible at Bantry, the site of the famous Bantry pillar stone. Kilmackowen retains much of its original massive cashel stone wall. Fanlobbus, by Dunmanway, is marked out again by the field walls. Killaseragh had part of its original oval retained in the present field walls, which were recently knocked; it is still traceable from the air and on the ground. Aglish, between Bawnatemple and Farran, had a very large oval enclosure, again really only visible now from the air as a soil mark and faint earthwork. Olan's Aghabulloge still shows part of its oval enclosure in field fences. Kilmacoo in north Cork is on its own, because here the Church seems to have moved into a massive and ancient hill-fort site. In the same part of the county, Kilcorcoran to the south-east of Newmarket has a more modern graveyard attached outside of the original big circular enclosure.

Killeagh rath, north-north-east of Carrignavar, was a compact, massive ring fort, inside of which was a church, according to the first edition of the Ordnance map, and it must have been one of the more unusual church sites in the county. All is now swept away except for a bullaun stone in the ditch. Doon Peter, with a holy well and graveyard inside what seems a rather large, irregular rath near Glenville, could also have been a rath taken over by the Church.

Cork has numerous *cill* or *cillín*, sites, though a number have been now ploughed out. The *cillín* (killeen) or little church represents the small hermitage or the little church serving the area round about. The great spread of ancient church sites in Ireland reminds one of places like Patmos in Greece, where there is one or more great central monastic citadels, but over the whole countryside a spread of chapels, from cliff edge to hilltop. Today, some may only have a liturgy once a year on their saint's feast day, but they give an idea of why a heavily Christianised country like Ireland had so many church sites, and the gay interior of these Orthodox churches can remind us, too, that the early Irish churches, of which only bare walls now survive here and there, were once as brightly and profusely decorated.

Templebryan
Bawnatemple
Labbamolagga
Killeenemer

Ballymodan

Kilnaruane
Kilmackowen
Fanlobbus
Killaseragh

Aglish

Aghabulloge
Kilmacoo

Kilcorcoran

Killeagh

Doon Peter

The *cill* was, in many cases, abandoned from medieval times on, but people still felt it had some aura of holiness, some memory of a saint, and so they buried there unbaptised children, who had no claim to the consecrated ground around the church in current use. Boulders, uncut and unmarked, indicate in their thick-set abundance how high infant mortality was, how many were stillborn or died within hours or days of their birth. 'Children's graveyard' is often marked on the Ordnance Survey maps at the old *cill* sites.

The *cillín*, like the big monastic site, is circular; indeed, this is a characteristic of all the early monastic sites, and is even preserved in part of the enclosing wall round St Multose's church in Kinsale town. But in many places the outline of the original enclosure has been obliterated.

Kinsale

The monasteries and churches are normally set in pleasant places, each with an adjacent spring-water supply, now a holy well. Many of them are on the fertile farmlands like the ring forts, but a certain number seem to have chosen fertile hilltop or hillside locations ('a city set on a hill cannot be hid'). Kilmacoo is situated in a hill-fort; Kilnaruane stands on a height at Bantry; Templebreedy perches on the cliffs near Crosshaven where the church spire would later be a landmark for ships entering Cork Harbour; the old church on Myross island in West Cork stands on a ridge. Kilourfin, just north of Carrigtwohill, is another high site, with Caheragh to the west of it. Kilcounty further east is on a high slope with wide views to the south. Kilpatrick near Tracton, Donoughmore and Castle Ventry near Leap are yet other high locations of ancient monasteries.

Kilmacoo
Kilnaruane
Templebreedy
Myross
Kilourfin
Kilcounty
Kilpatrick
Donoughmore
Castle Ventry

There are ancient church sites on islands, too, and we need to remember that the islands then were bigger than they are today, and the climate was

Cross at cillín, *Ballymacrown, near Baltimore*

warmer and drier. The Celtic saints were amphibious animals, very used to travel and the handling of small boats. But they were also lovers of inland solitude, seeking out hermitages in the forests with only the wild animals for company, and these places still bear the name of desert. There are a number of them in County Cork: Desert, south of Castlelyons, which was later to be a parish church, and where from the air you can see the faint arc of a large enclosure; Desert More, a little hillock in the river Bride valley between Kilumney and Kilcrea in West Cork; Desertserges on the river Bandon at Enniskean. Desertserges, too, became a parish in which no less than seven *cill* sites have been recorded. The saint's hermitage would soon attract disciples and visitors and in the end, as with St Kevin's Glendalough, grow into a large monastery.

Of the actual buildings on the monastic sites of the Celtic Church, very little is left. A *cillín* at Croagh Bay near Schull has some remains of what appear to be an oratory and hut built in drystone, and something of the same appears to be present at Kilmackowen in Beara. Excavation of a site like Kilmackowen, which seems to have had no medieval structures and only the later superficial childrens' burials, might yield interesting results. At Ballyvourney M. J. O'Kelly excavated a site known as St Gobnet's Kitchen close to her grave and holy well. It turned out to be a drystone-built round house, and very probably belonged to St Gobnet's nunnery. The roof would have been thatched.

Cork has a whole series of later, Irish Romanesque churches in ruins, as well as a couple of round towers. But the country was densely wooded and the easiest material for building was timber. Most of a monastery's huts and churches are likely to have been of wood, and it is thought that the projecting antae at the corners of the older churches are simply a translation into stone of the massive tree trunks which would stand there in a timber building. The big, straight-across, lintel slab of many ancient doorways is good stonemasonry, but it is also a builder in timber's method. The gable finial, mere ornament in a stone oratory, is derived from the essential cross main timbers of a gable end in a wooden house. Wooden churches are recorded both in the *Annals* and in some items of Irish art; excavation at some of the bigger ancient sites may yet reveal their post-holes and their size.

E. M. Fahy believed the old church on the West Skeames in Roaring Water Bay to be of 9th century date. Built of drystone, the west end has a solid door with splayed jambs and a massive lintel, and on either hand antae which extend 20.5 inches beyond the end of the church. Internally, the church is 12 feet 7 inches wide and the length at the time of Fahy's survey (1961) was 17 feet 6 inches, but the east end had already fallen into the sea and erosion was continuing. Recent excavation and conservation work dates the church as probably 10th century and, as there are burials underneath its foundations, it is likely to be on the site of an earlier one. From the air, the rocky bones below water of the original single island are obvious, and it is very unlikely that this old church with its surrounding graveyard was built on a cliff edge – rather it was built in the middle of an island.

In north-east Cork there is a group of early churches – Ardskeagh, Killeenemer, Labbamolagga, Ballyhay, Britway, Coole – which are all built in the beautiful red sandstone, merging into a conglomerate, which seems to have been the favourite stone of the time. A similar red sandstone is, for example, used in Ratass and Ardfert in County Kerry. The later, medieval churches are either of limestone, when that is available, or of the local flagstones.

Labbamolagga
St Molagga

Labbamolagga lies in pleasant country between the Galtee and Ballyhoura Mountains, four miles north-west of Mitchelstown. Little is known of St Molagga. He probably is early 7th century in date and was born at Shanballymore, according to local tradition. He made three foundations in north Cork; the first, identified by Canon Patrick Power, is Tulach Mhin, 'an almost forgotten *cillín* on the summit of Bawnanooneeny Hill' which stands midway between Ahacross and Labbamolagga, his other sites. He was also the founder of a monastery at Timoleague (Molagga's House) but this site is now entirely covered by the later Franciscan friary. Labbamolagga had a very large enclosure, clearly visible from the air but only partly from the ground, and the present church ruins and graveyard occupy only a small portion of it. The oldest building, Molagga's *leaba*, or burial place, is a solidly built structure with antae at both east and west ends, of carefully squared sandstone blocks, 13 feet 1 inch x 9 feet 5 inches. The walls are 2 feet 3 inches thick. At the west end is the massive doorway, 4 feet 11 inches high, built of two big uprights and a lintel stone, with a suggestion of an architrave decoration around their edges. Molagga's grave is marked inside by a stone bearing a double ring with two lines running from it – rather like a penannular brooch. Grave digging has brought to light some early cross-inscribed stones, some of which have been appropriated for more recent graves; the designs include the typical 'Celtic' cross with the halo round it, of which there are two examples.

Alongside this very ancient oratory is a larger and somewhat later church, of which only the base of the walls survive. Externally it measures 39 feet 7 inches x 24 feet and its walls are 3 feet 2 inches thick. Canon Power thought it represented the *eidhneán,* the ivy-covered church of Molagga mentioned in the *Life.*

Killeenemer

Killeenemer, like Labbamolagga, has a very large enclosure around it, though hardly visible at ground level. The site is near Glanworth above the Funshion River valley. It is another Romanesque church, 27 feet x 18 feet 8 inches internally, with walls nearly three feet thick. There are massive antae. The stone is, again, the beautiful red sandstone, a dune deposit, the crossing dune bedding clearly visible in many of the masonry blocks. A round-headed window cut from a single block has been set in the south wall for preservation; a rather crudely cut Maltese cross slab is set on the west wall. On the altar used to be a collection of old quern fragments, made of the red sandstone and associated conglomerate, now mostly taken away. The place commands a splendid view to the Galtee Mountains.

On lower ground, in the Blackwater valley, is another very old church of the same sort at Coole Abbey, which is supposed once to have been custodian of St Patrick's tooth. Further south is Britway, presently in poor and ivy-grown condition (Coole, Killeenemer, Ardskeagh and Labbamolagga are all in State care). Here is a fine west door with a simple decoration on the relieving arch above the lintel. There is a small round-headed window in the north wall in imminent danger of collapse. Ballyhay, between Buttevant and Rathluirc (Charleville), is likewise in poor condition. It has a plain Romanesque arched doorway in the south wall, with two projecting heads sculpted above it on the outside, and a projecting, decorated architrave on the inside. The door is now blocked up and the wall in which it stands is heavily mortared. Ardskeagh is only about a mile from Ballyhay. Its simple

Coole Abbey
Britway

Ballyhay

Ardskeagh

Labbamolagga near Mitchelstown, showing outline of the monastic enclosure

Romanesque west door survives virtually intact and the top of a round-headed window cut from a massive block of red sandstone has been secured on top of the south wall.

Round towers

The round towers, as uniquely Irish as the raths, are generally dated from the 10th to the 12th century, though some would put them earlier. How many there were in Cork we do not know. Two survive, minus their caps, at Castletown Kinneigh and at Cloyne. Charles Smith in his 1750 account of Cork says there was one just inside the Cork border at Nohavel Daly near Rathmore and, as this area was thickly settled with raths, it is quite likely that there was a large monastery there as well. The tower at St Findchu's (Fanahan), Brigown (Mitchelstown) only fell in 1720. Rosscarbery had a very fine tall tower likewise. The Cork round tower was at the present Church of Ireland cathedral site, and is represented on the base of a monstrance belonging to the Dominicans of Cork, dated 1669. It is probable that there were others. They served several purposes; they were bell-towers (*cloig teach)* and they could also be look-outs. Stone built, with the entrance reached by a ladder which could then be pulled up, they were safe refuges (unless attackers managed to set them alight) and here a monastery could store books and valuables of all kinds. Most of the wooden buildings of the monastery could be easily fired in a raid. It is of interest to note that the *Annals* record more raids by neighbouring tribes on monasteries than by the much maligned Vikings. The slender tower was visible for many miles around and the traveller would see it from far off and know the destination was, at least remotely, in sight.

Cloyne

Cloyne's round tower is very elegantly built of large flagstones shaped to the curve of the building using a chisel-pointed hammer. The stone, a

Kinneigh round tower

Kilcatherine

brownish sandstone, was obtained from a quarry between Cloyne and the coast; only later did people begin to use the abundant local limestone for building. The Castletown Kinneigh tower is unique in having an hexagonal base which, about 20 feet up, becomes the typical cylindrical structure. It is believed to be a very late example. The saint of the Kinneigh site is St Mocolmog, of whom nothing seems to be known.

No high crosses survive at any of the old Celtic church sites in County Cork. Many of the crosses which stood about a monastery or marked the boundaries of its lands may have been of wood. But a number of cross-inscribed stones and slabs occur at some of the Cork sites – those at Labbamolagga have already been noted. At Bawnatemple, ploughing turned up a boulder with a Maltese (Greek, equal armed) cross cut on it. Some sites have a cross roughly cut out of solid stone, for instance Kilcatherine and Kilmackowen in the Beara peninsula. At the small *cillín* at Ballymacrown near Baltimore a haloed Celtic cross is roughly cut from a flake of rock.

Best known is the Bantry pillar stone, from Cill Ruan (Kilnaruane). Of St Ruan little or nothing seems to be known, but the site was large, commanding a wide view of Bantry Bay, and the slender pillar, much weathered, is rich in Christian symbolism. Here is a ship, the ship of the Church, sailing heavenwards in a sea of crosses. Here is a person standing in the ancient attitude of prayer (the *orante*) with hands outstretched, raised to heaven.

Castletown
Kinneigh

St Mocolmog

Cross slabs

Bawnatemple

Kilcatherine
Kilmackowen
Ballymacrown

Bantry

Kilnaruane carved pillar

And here are the two old men, St Anthony the first monk and St Paul the first hermit, meeting in the desert, and a bird flying down from heaven with a loaf of bread, as they had nothing to eat; the bread from heaven, symbol of the Eucharist.

Ballyvourney

North of the Sullane, across the valley from St Gobnet's site at Ballyvourney, was a *cillín* which was destroyed by the local landlord long ago. Even its actual site is unknown today, but a cross-inscribed slab was moved to another site by the local people to preserve it. Recently it has been moved again, into the Ballyvourney museum. On either side is a beautifully carved Greek cross set in a circle, and on one side a small figure holding a *bachul* (crozier) stands on top of the circled cross. Françoise Henry thought it could date to the second half of the 7th century.

Tullylease
St Berchert

Much more sophisticated is the art of the Berchert slab at Tullylease in north Cork. St Berchert (Berikert), 'St Ben' in local speech, was one of a number of saintly Englishmen who came to settle in Ireland. One tradition makes him a brother of St Gerald who settled in Mayo ('Mayo of the Saxons') which would date Berchert to the early 8th century. At Tullylease, fixed to the wall of the later church is a splendidly and elaborately carved cross slab, inscribed QUI CUM QUAE HUNC TITULU LEGERIT ORET PRO BERECHTUINE (who reads this inscription, pray for Berchert). The style of the slab, which must have marked the saint's tomb, has been compared to the art of the Lindisfarne Gospels, and there is the suggestion that Berchert brought with him his native art form and some skilled artists. Berchert's Day is 18 February, and he is still venerated locally.

At Tullylease near the site of Berchert's monastery is a limestone boulder with a hollow in it, a bullaun stone. The hollow has a hole in it, and the story goes that when the church was being built a deer came every day to the stone and milked herself into it, so providing milk for the workmen. But one of them spied on her while she was doing this and in a rage she kicked a hole through the basin and never returned. Boulders with basins worn in them, bullaun stones, are a very common feature of early Irish monastic sites; curative powers may be attributed to the water that collects in them, or legends told like that of the Tullylease hind.

Bullauns

The truth about the bullauns is more prosaic. It seems fairly certain that they were used with a wooden or iron-shod pestle to bruise furze (an excellent animal feed), husk oatmeal or barley, or indeed crush anything one wanted broken up or pulped. (The modern equivalent is the liquidiser and its various accessories!) Such simple mortars are still in use by primitive people in other parts of the world, and they were reported in use in Scotland and Ireland until fairly recently. In 1883 in Donegal such bullauns were being used to crush oats for poteen making.

Clondrohid

A very famous and large bullaun is that outside the old graveyard in Clondrohid near Macroom; it is a massive basin in an upright stone and stands surrounded by a cluster of quartz boulders. Until motorised hearses made things too streamlined, nobody was considered properly buried at Clondro-hid unless the coffin had been carried the appropriate number of *deiseal* (sunwise, right-handed) circuits of the bullaun.

Not all hollows in rocks are man-made. Equally 'artificial' looking ones are potholes, produced by stones swirling round in them in a stream, or by differential weathering of the rock – for instance a clay nodule being weathered from a harder sandstone. Many of these natural hollows look like hand or knee prints, or hoof marks, and appropriate legends of saint or soldier or horse have been made to explain them. In fact, people seem fascinated by rainwater collecting in any sort of hollow in a rock and Cork has a number of 'wart stones', natural hollows in rocks which collect water believed to be a cure for warts. One such wart stone is in the forest park at Castlefreke.

Saints

Of the saints of Cork personally we know very little, for the most of the *Lives* of Irish saints are amalgams of legends only written down centuries after their subjects lived. We do know quite a bit about how they lived and that the monastic life was then, as it still is in the Orthodox Church, unspecialised and idiorhythmic. Most people were simply monks or nuns; only a few men were priests. If the legends make the saints seem gigantic, powerful and opinionated personalities, they were most likely just that. Modern holy men tend to show the same characteristics, especially when their followers come to venerate them. The cynic may ponder how they manage to combine the Christian virtue of humility with the arrogance of feeling that they have a hotline to heaven!

St Finbar

St Finbar is the tutelary saint of Cork. He lived in the second half of the 6th century, probably dying early in the 7th. He was born at or near Garranes rath, where his father, Amargin, was the chief metal-worker of the local king, Tighernach. Blonde, he was called Finbar, meaning 'Fair Crest'. After visiting various monasteries as a young man, he set himself up as a hermit in Gougane Barra, the corrie lake that is the source of the river Lee.

Gougane Barra

Mononagh bullaun

Bullaun at Clondrohid near Macroom

Kilbarry

Cork

From there he eventually moved downriver, making various foundations en route (Kilbarry in present place-names) and ended up in the great marsh of Munster where he settled himself permanently, most likely on the dry land where St Finbarre's Cathedral (Church of Ireland) now stands. Later, when the Vikings came to Cork, they would build some sort of a town near by on the same dry land above the marsh and its intertwining waterways. Around this Cork foundation a great monastery grew and became the core and origin of the present city. Finbar, known in the shortened form of Barr, was much venerated in Scotland. The Outer Hebridean island Barra is named for him and there was, until well into the 19th century, a big pilgrimage held in his honour there, everyone riding on horseback three times round St Barr's church, where at one time there was a wooden statue of the saint. It is quite possible that Finbar, like so many other Irish saints, visited the Western Islands.

His feast day is 25 September and a well-attended diocesan pilgrimage to Gougane Barra takes place on the Sunday nearest that date. This pilgrimage

Gougane Barra

is possibly old, but its main development seems due to a Carmelite priest, Denis O'Mahony, who lived there as a hermit and is registered as parish priest of Iveleary in 1704. He petitioned Rome for indulgences for the pilgrims visiting Gougane, obtaining the same as for visiting the seven churches of Rome. He erected the present square with its pilgrim stations, and is himself buried just off St Finbar's hermitage islet, on the hillside.

Denis O'Mahony

The traditional pilgrimage took place at midsummer, with blazing St John's Eve fires, and again in September, and with the prayers and penance went all the jollifications of high festival. The Roman Catholic clergy in the 19th century had little use for such Celtic (and indeed Catholic) exuberance, and did all they could to end many pilgrimages that had survived the similar attempts of Protestant extremists. Around 1800 the Bishop of Cork excommunicated all who went on the Gougane pilgrimage. But the pilgrimage went on, and is today led by the bishop.

Finbar's soul friend, his confessor, is said to have been St Olan of Aghabulloge in the Lee valley near Coachford. Again, we know next to nothing of Olan. At his old church site is an ogham-inscribed pillar on top of which was perched a quartz boulder. This was called St Olan's Cap and people made rounds with it on their heads; it was a specific for help in childbirth and could cure a headache if worn on the head for three rounds of the church. The parish priest in the mid-19th century tried to stop this 'superstition' by removing the stone, but another was quickly found. The present 'cap' has been recently cemented on to the ogham stone. Some way off is St Olan's well, with a fine beehive corbelled stone covering to it, and a tall ogham-inscribed gallaun, which was found forming a footbridge across a stream and was then set up by the well. Olan's Day is 5 September and the parish celebrates it with devotions at the holy well, which is very well maintained.

St Olan
Aghabulloge

The other great patron of Cork is St Colman of Cloyne. The county is unusual in that it contains several dioceses – Cork, Cloyne, Ross (amalgamated with Cork) and some parts of Kerry. Colman was born, according to the *Annals of Inisfallen*, in 530 AD and died in 606. His was a late vocation; he had been a professional bard, and is said to have met St Brendan of Clonfert (the navigator) who advised him to give up poetry for the Church. Colman Mac Lenin seems to have been born in Muskerry, but he made his principal foundation at Cloyne in east Cork. He had another important foundation at Kilmaclenin (Cill Mac Lenin) between Mallow and Liscarroll. His feast day is 24 November.

St Colman
Cloyne

Fachtna (Fachanan), whose day is 14 August, was the founding saint of Rosscarbery (Ross Ailither, Ross of the Pilgrims) and virtually nothing is known about him; he may have died *c.* 600. Ross became a large and important monastery; just outside of the present town on the old road to Cork are the remains of a small church and a holy well dedicated to Fachtna. Bishop Pococke, visiting Ross in July 1758, says this little church was 'rebuilt by a Protestant, who made a vow on recovery from sickness'.

St Fachtna
Rosscarbery

St Findchu
Brigown

Devotion to St Findchu ('White Hound' or Fanahan) of Brigown at Mitchelstown is still alive, and a modern statue of him was lately erected at the Garda station. His parents are said to have been from Ulster and were living in exile in Munster when he was born. Findchu is said to have gone north to Bangor to study but his great monastic foundation was Brigown, where he died in 664 or 665 AD. As late as 1750, Brigown had the saint's crozier, the *baculus Finechani*, on which people used to swear oaths. His feast day is 25 November. Local devotion to St Laichtin of Donoughmore (*Domnach mór* – the great church) seems to have long died away but the beautifully decorated shrine of St Laichtin's arm is in the National Museum.

St Laichtin
Donoughmore

St Gobnet
Ballyvourney

Undoubtedly of all the Celtic saints of Cork the one to whom devotion is most alive, indeed possibly growing, is St Gobnet of Ballyvourney. Gobnet, who perhaps belongs to the 6th century, is said to have come from Clare, gone to Inisheer in the Aran Islands to escape an enemy, and there had a vision of an angel. The angel told her that 'the place of her resurrection', where she would make her final and greatest foundation, was where she would come on nine white deer grazing. So Gobnet set off across Ireland, meeting up with three white deer at Clondrohid, six at Ballymakeera and finally, across the Sullane, on the higher slopes, nine. Here she founded a convent and lived for the rest of her life. She kept bees, which on one occasion she very successfully loosed on some robbers who were driving off her cattle. Abban is said to have been associated with Gobnet at Ballyvourney and the cairn and its ogham stones to be his grave – the original 'round' of Ballyvourney included it. Several Abbans existed but there is no hard information about them. At Killeagh in east Cork the Church of Ireland church is supposed to be on the site of a nunnery founded by a St Abban, but this is not necessarily the Ballyvourney man.

St Abban

Killeagh

St Gobnet

Devotion to St Gobnet is very much alive. People come from considerable distances to make the long round at her grave, well, the old medieval church ruin, the 'kitchen' or hut excavated by M. J. O'Kelly and the fine statue by Seumas Murphy with its traditional Irish prayer to the saint and sculpted bees. In the parish church, the statue of Gobnet, one of the few surviving medieval wooden statues of a saint, is preserved. Even today Cork people turn to Gobnet, not only for ordinary requests but when all other help, medical included, has failed.

Holy wells

Cork has numerous holy wells, though only a few are now regularly frequented, and only St Gobnet's has moved with the times to the extent of having a pipe and tap for ease in filling mugs and bottles of water. It is likely that devotion to wells is as old as humanity, for water is essential to life. Christianity, baptising by immersion, and with a rich symbolism of water, readily took over the cult.

Holy wells in Cork mostly have dedications to local Cork saints, but a good number are named for the Mother of God, Mary. It may be that these Marian dedications came later than the basic series of Celtic saints, together with those to St Michael the archangel. Associated with the continental religious Orders are St Bernard's well for the Cistercians at Fermoy and St Dominic's for the Dominicans at Glanworth. The maps mark a St Valentine's well in the Knockraha district, and at Clonmult is the well-kept one of St Laurence, one presumes Laurence O'Toole of Dublin. Both Patrick and Brigid have wells dedicated to them, though neither Patrick nor Brigid of Kildare were ever in Cork. There was a well of St Brigid on Rabbit Island off the coast between Glandore and Myross, and people used to go out on the evening of the vigil of the feast. However, when a boat capsized on the way back one February, the pilgrimage was transferred to the mainland and a well at Squince. The St John the Baptist wells, visited at midsummer, have already been noted; also the one dedicated to the Trinity near Newmarket which is the seepage of water at the trough site in the middle of an old *fulacht fiadh* mound.

Fermoy
Glanworth
Knockraha
Clonmult

Rabbit Island

Newmarket

Holy well, Lough Hyne

VII

The Castles

WITH THE ARRIVAL of the Anglo-Normans in Ireland in 1170 a revolution in building came about. As invaders they needed strong defensive positions in which to maintain themselves, so they began to construct castles. The first Viking landings had been made in Cork around 820, and a permanent fortified settlement had been established in 846, but although the Norse introduced towns to Ireland, it was only after the coming of the Anglo-Normans that the compact walled city developed, itself a kind of enlarged castle, and brought about a sharp dichotomy between town and country.

If there had been no Anglo-Norman invasion, it is certain that these changes would still have come about, though in a different and more peaceful way. Already the reform movement in the Irish Church with which St Malachy was involved had, by his efforts, introduced two continental religious Orders, the Canons Regular of St Augustine and the Cistercians, and they were bringing a new kind of plan and building for their monasteries as against the native Celtic Church layouts and the strong elegance of the Irish Romanesque. And when castles and walled cities were being built in continental Europe and in Britain, the Irish would undoubtedly have followed suit. Indeed, as the tide of the Anglo-Norman invasion receded, most of the later Cork castles did belong to Irish families.

Motte and bailey

The first strongpoints built by the Anglo-Normans were of the quickly constructed 'motte and bailey' type, consisting of an earthen mound on which a wooden castle and stockade wall (the bailey) were set. The temporary wooden structures were later replaced with stone-built ones. Castles on

Inchiquin

these early mottes in County Cork include a fine example just south of Mallow, Barrett's Castle (also known as Castle More) and another at Kilmaclenin. Barrett's Castle belonged to the De Cogans, and dates back to the 13th century though the actual ruins date from a later stage of construction, after it had been taken over by the Earl of Desmond. Possibly the oldest castle in the county is Inchiquin, a round tower of local limestone set on the banks of the Dissour river estuary near Youghal. Certainly it is claimed as the first castle erected in this part of Cork. It is about 170 feet in circumference, and has easy access to the sea by the river estuary. Like Barrett's Castle, it was a stronghold of the Earls of Desmond; later it withstood the cannon fire of Cromwell's forces until, so the story goes, a servant girl hung out a white handkerchief to indicate the weakest part of the structure.

In some cases, castles replaced old Celtic raths and dúns, as at Liscarroll, Dungourney and Crookstown (Castle More – not to be confused with Barrett's Castle also known by this name). Castles were sited on old promontory forts, on rocks and crags where nature could aid their defences, or simply in the fields, where their security depended entirely on the strength of their walls. Today it is difficult to realise how strong they were when attackers were only armed with sword and bow, or if they were lucky a missile-throwing engine that worked on the principle of the catapult.

County Cork is crowded with castles, but most of them are of comparatively late date (15th or 16th century); very early castles are rare, but the county has some storybook examples. Ballincollig Castle, set on a limestone bluff, is one such. Its curtain wall runs around the edge of the rock on which it stands, and inside is a slender central keep. It is believed to date from the time of King Edward III. Liscarroll Castle in north Cork is the third largest Anglo-Norman fortification in Ireland. Its central keep buildings have

Barrett's Castle

Earl of Desmond
Inchiquin

Dungourney
Crookstown

Ballincollig

Liscarroll

Ballinvard

Castlederry

vanished, but a huge walled rectangle remains virtually intact, with a great gatehouse tower, in which the portcullis ran, facing the village street. A square tower marks the south-west corner (the gate is in the south wall), but that in the south-east is gone. There are round towers at the north-west and north-east angles and another square one, matching the gatehouse, in the middle of the north wall. Behind is a meadow, the tournament field, in which one can just trace from the air the outline of the earlier rath on the site. Liscarroll was well settled in early times: there are many more raths, some of them ploughed out, in the immediate vicinity. The castle was probably built in the late 13th century and it may have belonged to the De Barrys.

Dromsicane

Dromsicane, just north of Millstreet, is very much in the Liscarroll style, featuring a great curtain wall on a rectangular plan with round towers at the angles. However, about half of it is destroyed and the remainder is now part of a farmyard. The O'Keeffe castle of Dromagh, further east along the

Dromagh

Carrigadrohid

Blackwater valley from Dromsicane, has been much altered and ruined, but is said to have been another ancient square stronghold with circular towers at the angles. The Roche's stronghold at Glanworth, on the Funshion, a tributary of the Blackwater, is in fairly good repair compared to Dromsicane; a keep and curtain wall sit on a limestone cliff above the river. It has been recently excavated and conservation work has been undertaken by the Office of Public Works.

Some old castles were pulled down to make room for newer and more convenient Big Houses. Kilbrittain was one such: it is said to have had a castle inside a large bawn defended by six towers along its walls. Robert de Marisco built a castle at Rostellan on the east side of Cork Harbour at the time of the Anglo-Norman invasion. That was later pulled down and rebuilt, and the Big House that replaced it is gone, too.

While the powerful lords built themselves castles, their followers needed less expensive but defendable homesteads. They constructed moated granges: rectangular enclosures with, if possible, a shallow moat outside the wall of earth and stone, and their houses set inside. Cork had a goodly number of these moated sites even at the time of the first Ordnance Survey maps (*c.* 1840) in the areas of Anglo-Norman influence – around Cork city and in the rich lands of the Blackwater by Mallow and Fermoy. However, a large number of the moated sites that still survived in the 1840s have now been ploughed out, a destruction more extensive than that of ring forts which were protected to some extent by being believed to be 'fairy forts', unlucky to meddle with. A few examples survive, including a fine one at Millstreet, between the town and Drishane, and others still show up as crop marks. One moated site was excavated at Riggsdale near Ballinhassig, but without yielding any significant finds.

Most typical of Cork are the later tower-houses, most of them small and compact, each storey being a single large room with the topmost, the great chamber, being the best room. Built around the same time (replacing older structures) are the much larger castles of Blarney, Barryscourt and Castle More (Crookstown).

Meantime, gunpowder and fire-arms had come onto the scene and would ultimately revolutionize the whole theory of castle building. Gunpowder seems to have been first used in Europe to fire a cannonball early in the 14th century. By the 1330s, cannons were being used quite widely, even being loaded onto ships and used at sea. But cannons were heavy and awkward to transport, and it is unlikely that the ordinary castle owner in Cork would ever expect to be bombarded by them, at least until the wars of Elizabeth I and Cromwell. What was useful to him was to have a small cannon and some muskets inside his tower-house. Thus you will quite often come on a small round opening in the castle wall, through which a little cannon could fire, and a long cylindrical passage at the castle door in which a musket could be inserted and fired straight into the face of anyone stand-

Glanworth

Kilbrittain

Rostellan

Millstreet
Riggsdale

Tower-houses

ing outside. Both devices are crude in that they did not allow you to swing the gun around to cover a wide field of fire, though the castle owner could also fire from windows and other shot holes or from the castle battlements. Certainly the narrow passage for the musket in the stone jamb of some castle doors is well worn, as if frequently used or, at least, the long slender barrel frequently inserted. But this was really only trying to adapt an old castle design to make use of the new technology. Only with structures like Charles and James Forts came the complete innovation, building to make the best use of the now powerful cannon.

Ballynacarriga

Of County Cork's very numerous tower-houses (325 at the least) the most perfect is Ballynacarriga near Dunmanway. Beautifully built in the local flag-stone, set on a glaciated ridge of rock above a lake, the tower shows the whole series of rooms, from the dark stone vaulted bottom storey to the great chamber at the top, with its big windows surrounded by elaborate carvings. The top floor was both the safest and the most pleasant place to be in such a castle, and was therefore the 'best room', where the owners lived in some comfort. The decorations include foliage and abstract designs together with a crucifixion and emblems of the passion. A cock perched on a pot is featured with the latter – the cock that is so familiar on late 18th- and 19th-century tombstones. The legend is that, after the crucifixion, someone remarked at dinner that Jesus would no more rise from the dead than the boiled fowl in the dish in front of them. Whereupon the fowl rose up and crowed.

The stairs leading from one floor to another in a tower-house may be straight flights or in a spiral and are usually very well made, but they are very narrow and one must suppose that any large furniture must have been constructed *in situ* in the rooms. The Ballynacarriga carvings (and the ornate chimney-piece in the MacSwiney tower-house at Crookstown) can only suggest how pleasant some of the rooms must have been. The sculptures

*Ballynacarriga,
near Dunmanway*

were probably painted; there would be rich hangings and maybe a fine set of plates to dine on.

The normal construction features a massive vaulted base-room, where often the wicker covering of the wooden supports on which the stone arches were built and left to set remains marked in the mortar. Then stone and wooden floors alternate. Atop was a steeply pitched roof with a parapet walk around it. The towers have a graceful batter (an inward slope to the walls) and elegant cut-stone work around their Gothic arched doors and ogee windows, often limestone with trim peckings in a pleasing but simple design. Very often the cut-stone work around window and door has been robbed for later buildings, as at the rather interesting little Kilmeedy Castle, which stood guard in the pass between Millstreet and Macroom, where a local farmer took it all. Most of them have good fireplaces, at least on the top floor, but Carrigaphooca on its *roche moutonnée* (up which the Office of Public Works have run an inelegant set of cemented steps) has no built fireplaces at all. Water must always have been fetched from outside, unless the run-off was collected from the roof.

Sanitation was by way of a privy, jakes or gong, to use the names that go back to the Middle Ages, though most writers on castles use the Norman-French word, garderobe. In the tower-house, the jakes were in a small room off the stair, with a stone seat or seats which fed into a stone-covered chute down the castle wall. Garderobe, which is merely a translation of wardrobe, really means the little room leading into the actual privy, in which clothes could be kept.

Outstanding tower-houses in Cork include the very tall, elegant and well preserved Conna Castle on its rock overlooking the east Cork river Bride; Conna

Carrigaphooca

Castle Richard
Dunmanus
Kilcoe
Rossmore
Kilcrea

Old Head of
Kinsale
Three Castles
Downeen

Ardintenant

Castle
Widenham
Leamcon
Lohort

Blarney
MacCarthy More

Castle Richard near Castlemartyr; Dunmanus Castle in the Mizen peninsula; Kilcoe Castle on a little islet linked to the mainland by a bridge, near Bally-dehob; Rossmore south of Ballynacarriga; and Kilcrea Castle close to Kilcrea Friary, where the remains of the bawn as well as the castle still stand and round which was once a large circular moat, the outline of which is visible from the air.

Castles, consisting of tower-house plus turrets and wall, which cut off promontory fort areas, are the De Courcy one at the Old Head of Kinsale and the O'Mahony 'Three Castles' on the Mizen. As already noted, there are other tower-houses on promontory-fort sites, and one, Downeen, is entirely insulated by the sea as the linking neck of headland has collapsed. Downeen is at Rosscarbery. A few were sited inside older ring forts like Ardintenant near Schull.

Some tower-houses have been restored or were incorporated into later houses – like the tower at Castle Widenham at Castletownroche. Leamcon, on an islet linked to the mainland by a bridge, on the Mizen peninsula, has been recently restored. Lohort, near Mallow, was restored in the early 18th century by Lord Egmont. Lewis wrote of it in his *Topographical Dictionary* (1830s): 'Here was formerly an armoury for 100 cavalry, well furnished with broadswords, bayonets, pistols, carbines and other weapons, among which was the sword of Sir Alex McDonald who was treacherously killed by a soldier after the battle of Knockinoss; these arms have been deposited at Charles Fort for security.'

Of the bigger castles contemporary with the tower-houses, Blarney is the best known in all Ireland. It belonged to the MacCarthy More, and Cormac Láider of that ilk is said to have built the 85-foot-high tower, in which a stone is said to read CORMAC MCCARTHY FORTIS ME FIERI FECIT A.D. 1446 (Cormac McCarthy More had me made 1466). To this was later added a large rectangular keep topped with crenellated battlements. How the legend that kissing a certain stone high on the castle walls would bring the gift of eloquence was invented, nobody knows for certain. However, one of the earlier writers about the legend gave a different version, saying that it conferred the ability

Kilcoe   *Dunmanus*

to lie without blushing.

Barryscourt Castle near Carrigtwohill is another massive and complex fortress, in which it is quite easy to become confused as to which stairway leads where! It is a rebuilding on an older fortress site; an inscription on a fireplace in one of the upper rooms reads Aᴼ Dʼo 1588 ɪʜs ᴅ ʙ ᴇᴛ ᴇ ʀ ᴍᴇ ꜰɪᴇʀᴇ ꜰᴇᴄᴇʀᴠᴛ (ᴀᴅ 1558. IHS. D.B. and E.R. had me made), the initials referring to David Fitzjames Barry and his wife, Ellen Roche. Ellen was the younger daughter of David, Viscount Fermoy. Barryscourt has a spacious and well preserved chapel. It is presently undergoing extensive restoration.

The Crookstown Castle More is the next largest castle in the county after Blarney but is virtually wrecked. Originally there was an outstanding rock of limestone here, on which was Dún Draighneáin, one of the raths in the orbit of Rath Raithlean, Garranes. The De Cogans built a castle on the rock, but the Blarney MacCarthys subsequently got hold of it. There was, it appears, a curtain wall around the rock with the main castle, rebuilt at various dates, inside. But this is a valley of limestone working and the whole rock, bar an outcrop or two carrying the actual castle ruins, has been cut away, so that the remains, such as they are, survive in the middle of a large and busy quarry.

Apart from the very elegant treatment of castle windows and doorways – windows with ogee heads and sometimes decorative curlicues in the angles – two strange sorts of sculpture that sometimes turn up on Cork's tower-houses need to be mentioned.

On some of them – Ballynacarriga has a good example – are the curious figures known as sheela-na-gigs. Sheela-na-gigs are normally female figures, erotically stressing their sexuality, and they continue to puzzle historians. Are they fertility figures from some remote cult, or good-luck symbols, or charms to avert the evil eye? They occur not only on castle walls but on

Downeen

Ballyvourney
Aghadoe Castle

churches: one is built into the wall over a window in the medieval church ruin at Ballyvourney. Aghadoe Castle at Killeagh is totally destroyed but its sheela, a huge and splendidly carved one in limestone, was set in the outside wall of the dovecote, perhaps taken there from the old castle. Temporarily removed from the dovecote to the present house, it is now kept as a detached slab.

Perhaps even more mysterious than the sex symbol, which makes some sense in the way of fertility or pleasure, are the human heads. Some Cork castles, Kilcrea among them, have a human head, an ordinary portrait in relief, sculpted on one of the blocks of their walls. Kilcrea's is about 30 feet up, on the north side of the north-east angle and quite hard to pick out from the ground below. Who do these heads represent: the master-mason, the lord of the castle …? We simply do not know.

In Italy in about 1530 a quite new style of fortress building appeared, designed specifically for defence by cannon and resistance to artillery attack. Where the idea originated is uncertain, and it is even possible that the English worked out the same idea themselves without reference to the continental forts. It is certain, however, that one Micheli Sanmichele devised a new sort of bastion at Verona in the period 1530-40. The new bastion was very solid, an angled projection from the equally substantial curtain wall of a fort, and it was designed as a platform for cannon which could fire from it over a wide field. The 'star fort' was thus born in which angular bastions jut from the intervening fortress walls like the points of a star. A book on fortifications by one Zanchi, published in 1554, goes into full detail about the new design and gives many sample plans. Yet the first two printed books on fortifications (Valle, 1521 and Albrecht Dürer, 1527) make no mention of star forts. The new idea spread rapidly in Europe among fort builders.

Star forts

Sheela-na-gig from destroyed Aghadoe Castle, Killeagh

James Fort

James Fort at Kinsale is a perfect example of a star fort. This was built to defend the town and harbour of Kinsale and its construction was begun at Castlepark immediately after the battle of Kinsale in 1601. The architect was Paul Ives and it took four years to build. It is quite typical, with a central keep and massive bastioned walls around it, surviving more or less unchanged in plan from the time of its building, as it was quickly superceded by an even bigger and more magnificent star fort, Charles Fort, on the opposite side of the harbour entrance. Charles Fort, now being carefully restored by the Office of Public Works, is far more complex, as it remained in military occupation till the 1920s, with all the changes and additions so long a period of use involves.

James Fort

Construction of Charles Fort began in 1677 on the site of an earlier castle called Ringcurran. The architect was Sir William Robinson, superintendant of fortifications in Ireland. The new fortress had five bastions (Charles, Devil's, North, Flagstaff, Corkpit) and mounted 100 brass cannon. Men working on building the fort got six pence per day for a 72-hour week. Most of the stone for the fort was quarried locally, but the special dressed limestone used on the gun emplacements must have come around from Cork Harbour by ship. The lime used came from Kilcrea in the West Cork Bride

Charles Fort

Charles Fort

valley and cost 1s 9d (about 9p) per barrel. Whatever about the 100 brass cannon that Charles Fort is said to have mounted, there were certainly others around of cast-iron there later on, typical old muzzle loaders. These old cannons had delightful names, many of hawks: the falcon and the smaller falconet, the minion and the saker. The biggest cannon of the period around which James and Charles Forts were built was the Basilisc, which was 11.5 feet long, weighed 9,000 lbs and fired an 8.75 inch diameter ball.

Charles Fort has a very interesting magazine, built entirely of brick with a steeply pitched brick roof like that of an early Christian oratory, for storing gunpowder and ammunition for its weaponry. Brick was supposed to absorb the blast from an explosion, whereas stone would splinter and fragments fly in all directions. Alongside is a massive baffle wall, as an additional precaution to control the effects of an explosion. Flagstaff bastion was intended to be a final citadel if attackers gained entry and to be a self-contained unit with some of its guns facing into the fort.

Dunboy

While James and Charles Forts are the county's, indeed Ireland's most magnificent star forts, Cork has a number of other lesser ones. Best known is Dunboy, the 'Yellow Fort', which stands on a promontory in Castletown Berehaven which belonged to O'Sullivan Beare. At the time of the Battle of Kinsale there was a Spanish garrison here as well as in castles in Baltimore and Castletownsend. When Kinsale was lost, O'Sullivan Beare made his final stand at Dunboy in 1602, with Carew and 4,000 men attacking. They fought to the last man, Carew saying that 'so obstinate and resolved a defence had not been seen within the Kingdom'. Dunboy has been excavated. There was, it appears, a tower-house of probably 15th century date with a bawn round it, and it was this that Carew attacked, cannonballs and rubble marking his assault. Afterwards the castle was re-roofed and a small star fort built around it. This later fell into ruin, the Puxley gardens and mansion (built with the profits of the Allihies copper mines) adding to the destruction.

In the excavation a great deal of pottery was found, dated mostly to the late 15th, 16th and 17th centuries and all imported – from France, Spain,

Castle Donovan, Drimoleague

Dunboy Castle

Portugal, Italy, Germany, Holland, England and, most surprisingly, China. The Spanish garrison was in Dunboy for about six months and the Spanish fragments include pieces of olive jars. The Chinese fragments are four small pieces of late 16th or early 17th century Ming china. Once again we are aware of the sea along the Cork coast as a wide open highway to the rest of the world.

Other 17th-century star forts in the county include Bantry, at Newtown, which had a garrison of 100 men in 1659, and Castletownsend, built by Colonel Richard Townsend around 1650 and intended as a defendable house. This latter is on the height above the present 'castle' Townshend, hidden in trees, a pocket-sized star fort and only big enough one would think to contain the smallest of cannon. At Crookhaven Sir Thomas Roper built a star fort in 1622, which was listed as having 30 men in 1659; at Rosscarbery, Captain Robert Gookin built a fort in the period 1641-52 for 100 horses and foot. Its remains survived till early in the last century.

There was another fort on Sherkin but the site is now lost; it could have been at a place called the Garrison at Barrack Point. The site is also lost of the star fort at Newmarket. Mallow (1659) and Fermoy (1690) Forts are also gone. Cork city has Elizabeth Fort (of which the walls remain, with a modern police station inside them), and long gone Shandon Castle. Youghal had some sort of star fort which jutted out into the harbour and was linked to the town by a causeway. There were also the Cork Harbour defences – Carlisle Fort appears on maps around 1600 but the present Carlisle and Camden and Spike Island Forts, though maintaining star plans, are all 19th century.

Bantry
Castletownsend

Crookhaven
Rosscarbery

Sherkin

Elizabeth Fort

Youghal

Carlisle Fort
Carlisle
Camden
Spike Island

O'Donovan Castle, Raheen, Castletownsend

Three Castles Head

VIII

The Medieval Monasteries

EAST AND WEST went their separate ways in the development of the monastic life. In the East, monks have remained quite simply monks to this day, with the hermit life seen as their peak of achievement. Celtic monasticism worked on the same principle. Yet it was flexible enough to encompass the hermit on an islet or in a forest, and allow for adventurous voyages at least as far as Iceland, an apostolate across Europe and into northern Italy, as well as serving the local religious needs of Ireland.

St Benedict

St Benedict came out of that ancient monastic tradition that had its roots in the desert, but his Rule began to codify and legislate in a new way. He dropped some of the violent asceticism of the desert, but he lost some of its ancient freedoms, too. The monk began to be a person who could do this but not that, and the road opened to the tremendous diversification and specialisation of the western religious Orders and congregations. Although to the outsider they all appear to be 'monks and nuns', western canon law restricts these names to only a few of them, the rest being friars or brothers and sisters, or even secular clergy living in community.

St Malachy

St Malachy, who was deeply involved in a great reform movement in the Irish Church, was responsible for introducing the first of the new continental Orders to Ireland. The one which took over so many of the old Celtic Church foundations and carried on their work of serving the local people were the Canons Regular of St Augustine and they were, in fact, secular clergy living in community according to a monastic type rule. The other Order that Malachy introduced were true monks, the Cistercians, a reform of the Benedictines. Malachy himself had met and loved St Bernard, who was the great saint and inspiration of the Cistercian way of life.

Augustinian Canons
Gill Abbey

Ballybeg
Bridgetown

In Cork the Augustinian Canons had three houses. In Cork city there was Gill Abbey, also known as the Cave, situated not far from St Finbar's monastic foundation. It appears there was some ancient cave shrine there. The Canons came there around 1134, but nothing remains today of their foundation. There are, however, considerable remains at their other two Cork houses, Ballybeg near Buttevant, and Bridgetown near Castletownroche. Both places are set in pleasant meadow-land, the latter in the Blackwater valley. While the king of Desmond, Cormac MacCarthy, is said to have been the founder of Gill Abbey, it was the Norman, Philip de Barry, who founded Ballybeg in 1229. Like many of the Canons' establishments, it was very large, though today the remains, with an outlying tower and the shattered walls of the great church, give only a partial impression of how extensive it was. But the round dovecote with its stone-built nesting boxes remains intact; pigeons for meat and eggs seem to have been important both to castle and monastery – even as late as the 18th century, the Dominican friars of Drogheda were buying peas for the pigeons. At Killeagh in east Cork, as already mentioned, Aghadoe Castle is long gone but its round, stone-built dovecote survives.

The ruins at Bridgetown have recently been cleaned up and are now easy of access. Alexander FitzHugh is said to have been the founder, sometime in King John's reign. The powerful Roche family of the district also supported the foundation.

Whereas most of the religious Orders in Ireland survived the Reformation, continued to work from 'houses of refuge' in the areas of their ancient foundations or, like the Cistercians, made a comeback when times were easier, the Canons Regular, with their 116 Irish medieval houses, died out completely, and are not now represented in Ireland.

The Cistercians are contemplative monks, engaging solely in prayer and normally taking no part in the active apostolate. They, like all the newer Orders, made a division between the 'lay brothers', who did most of the work on their extensive farms, and the 'choir monks', who were normally priests and largely occupied with the celebration of the Divine Office in church. Although this meant that anyone, without much education, could follow a monastic vocation, it did introduce a class barrier into the original brotherhood of the monastery.

Cistercians

Bridgetown Friary

Fermoy

Cork is not really Cistercian country, and little remains of their foundations there. Donal Mor O'Brien founded *Castrum Dei* (all the Cistercian houses had charming Latin names) at Fermoy in 1170. It seems to have been a centre of rebellion against the central Cistercian authority for a long time. Unlike the typical Cistercian house, the church served as the local parish one. At the time of the dissolution of the monasteries in 1541, the Fermoy monks owned two castles, a mill and over a thousand acres of land. Nothing survives above ground of this foundation, though carved stones and old walls and graves have turned up in various building excavations in Fermoy town. Nothing is left either of *Chorus S. Benedicti*, the Midleton house founded in 1180 and, like Fermoy, involved in rebellion against the Cistercian Chapter General. Again, the church served as the parish one; the monks' property included a water-mill and a salmon weir. Officially suppressed in 1543, the monks were still there in 1548.

Midleton

Tracton

Tracton, *Albus Tractus*, was founded from Wales in 1225 by, it seems, Maurice MacCarthy, and the church served the parish. The monks had a relic of the True Cross and there were many pilgrims in Holy Week to venerate it. Nothing is left above ground of church or monastery, but carved fragments are fairly widely distributed in various people's houses around, and the farmer on the actual site has unearthed, among other things, a very fine tombstone with a floriated cross on it.

Abbeymahon

Fons Vivus, Abbeymahon, halfway between Timoleague and Courtmacsherry, is the only Cork Cistercian house to have any walls still standing, and they only an overgrown and fragmentary bit of walling. *Fons Vivus* was, it appears, founded from Baltinglass in 1172 by Dermot MacCormac MacCarthy at Aghamanister, a few miles away from Abbeymahon, in the Seven Heads peninsula. It was shifted to its present location sometime before 1278. Abbeystrowry seems to have been a cell of Abbeymahon, never succeeding in being an independent monastery.

Abbeystrowry

Abbeymahon, abbey gate and old parish church

The Cistercians died out in Ireland after the dissolution of the monasteries, only returning in 1831, with the resulting foundation of Mount Melleray in County Waterford. They actually came via Cobh, where 64 Cistercians, refugees from France, arrived in December 1831 and took up temporary residence in a house near Rathmore on the border of Cork with Kerry, from which, as it was quite unsuitable for them, they moved as soon as possible to the site on the Knockmealdown Mountains.

By the time that St Malachy was encouraging Canons Regular and Cistercians to come to Ireland, Cistercians rather than Benedictines were the popular Order of monks, and the Benedictines were never very numerous or successful in Ireland. In Cork the main Benedictine house was Rosscarbery, founded from St James of Wurzburg early in the 13th century. By the time of the dissolution, its church and conventual buildings were all described as being in ruins.

In Cork city there was a small Benedictine cell with a hospital attached to it, depending on a parent monastery in Bath. Both monks and nuns formed the community, which was in existence in the late 12th century, and suppressed in 1536. In 1484, there was a complaint that the monk in charge had no Irish, could not therefore hear confessions, and yet would not appoint an Irish-speaking deputy. Youghal also had a small Benedictine cell, founded in 1185: of this, a neat Gothic doorway in the main street and a massive stone passage-way beyond is all that remains. As in Cork, the monks looked after a hospital for lepers, situated on the hill above the town.

Skin diseases were prevalent in medieval times and not all 'lepers' had leprosy as modern medicine defines that disease. It was, however, amongst the diseases of the time. There were a number of leper hospitals in County Cork, looked after by religious; several in Cork city and others at Aghada, Midleton, Cloyne and Kinsale, as well as Youghal. Remains of the Midleton lazer house were still standing by the river in 1750 but are long gone; there are still ruins (signposted) of the leper hospital outside Timoleague. Both the Cistercians of Abbeymahon and the Franciscans of Timoleague are said to have served the place.

There are many 'spittle' names in the county – like Ballinspittle (Hospital Town) – and these mark the locations of hospitals or hospices maintained for poor travellers rather than hospitals in the modern sense of the word. Hospitality to travellers, the poor and the sick, has always been a part of the monastic tradition everywhere.

The Knights Hospitallers were that curious medieval concept, a fighting Order of men who were at once knights and warriors, and religious. They were originally founded to care for pilgrims to Jerusalem, and to fight if need be. Their monasteries had the character of castles and in Ireland they seem to have assisted in the Anglo-Norman conquest; they came to have 21 houses here. In Cork they had only one house, at Mourne, south of Mallow, at which some very ruined buildings mark the spot where in 1335 Brother

Benedictines

Rosscarbery

Cork city

Youghal

Lazer houses
Cork city
Aghada
Midleton
Cloyne
Kinsale
Youghal
Timoleague
Abbeymahon

Hospices

Knights Hospitallers

Mourne

Kilshanig

John Fitzrichard was told to build a strong and fortified tower. Just outside Mallow, at the Church of Ireland church of Kilshanig, beside Newberry House, a tombstone of one of the Mourne Knights is fixed in the church-yard wall.

St Dominic
St Francis

With St Dominic and St Francis, and their Orders of Dominicans (Friars Preachers) and Franciscans, a new concept was injected into the western monastic tradition. The Benedictine or Cistercian monk was bound not only by the traditional vows of poverty, chastity and obedience, but was also tied to his monastery. Francis and Dominic invented the idea of the friar, a man who lived like a monk but took the world for his pillow, as the saying goes, and was free to range widely, preaching and teaching. Friaries were normally outside the walls of medieval towns, because the friars did not want to be tied down to the hours at which the gates were shut for the night. Their churches were built, not for themselves with occasional and abnormal use as parish ones, as with the Cistercians, but as big preaching halls for the reception of large crowds of people. Dominic's men were essentially well-trained scholars who were dedicated to preaching; Francis laid more stress on poverty and a certain joyous view of life, though his friars would often be as learned as Friars Preachers. And while the Reformation brought about the end of Cistercian and Benedictine houses, the friars stayed on and were to a large extent responsible for the survival of the Roman Catholic faith in Ireland.

Dominicans

St Dominic died in 1221; the first Dominicans arrived in Ireland three years later and made a foundation in Dublin. In Cork there were certainly three foundations: Cork city (1229), Youghal (1268) and Glanworth (1475), and probably another at Castlelyons.

Cork city

In Cork, the Dominican priory was founded by Philip de Barry and they selected an islet in the marsh close to but outside the walled city on its island. It was called St Mary's of the Isle. The Franciscan house was on dry ground, out of the marsh, in the present North Mall, north of the city, while the Augustinians had a site south of the various channels of the river Lee. St Mary's was very close to the walled city and in 1317 the friars were granted a charter by which the mayor, bailiffs and other trusty men were to have charge of the town gate nearest the priory and grant free passage in and out to the friars and, for their sake, to other good citizens. Nothing now remains of the old priory, though a map of 1602 shows the church with an east window divided into three lancets. It was built of locally quarried limestone. At various times – when pits were being dug for tanning in 1842 at St Dominick's Mills and earlier in the construction of Walker's Distillery in 1804 – quantities of human bones and some medieval tombstones were turned up. One stone coffin, known as 'King O'Falvey's', had its carved lid given to Father Russell OP, who took a keen interest in Dominican history at the time: it was of imported English freestone. Medieval Irish churches accessible by sea and short land routes often have some of the more elaborate of their carvings in imported stone. Cork had a wooden statue of St Dominic which was publicly burned in 1578, to the great distress of the people.

The dissolution of the monasteries did not shift the Dominicans out of Cork. With the ups and downs of Catholic hopes, they were first still in and then out of their island priory. During penal times they had a chapel in Dominick Street, while they themselves lived in a house in Mallow Lane (now Shandon Street). When Catholic Emancipation came in 1829, the religious were officially excluded, though in the event this meant very little. Cork was suffering a recession at the time, cholera was rampant, poverty increasing, and two Roman Catholic churches already planned. Yet the friars pushed ahead and successfully built their great church on Pope's Quay, the foundation stone being laid in 1832, with the solemn dedication on 20 October 1839, to the general rejoicing of the people of Cork, including many Protestants. But it was not until 10 August 1851 that Father Russell preached publicly in his Dominican habit, the first time it had been seen in Cork since the time of James II; the friars waited until 1854 before venturing on the public singing of the beautiful Dominican version of Compline.

Dominick Street
Mallow Lane

Pope's Quay

What was once known to Cork people as 'the chapel on the Sand Quay' has a very fine collection of old chalices of 17th century date and the already mentioned monstrance with the figure of St Finbar and of the round tower of Cork. Here, too, is the tiny ivory plaque of Our Lady of Graces from the priory in Youghal.

Youghal

Of the Youghal priory, the 'North Abbey', just north of the Youghal walls, little remains but some finely sculpted fragmentary walls of the church. It was founded by Thomas FitzMaurice and dedicated to the Holy Cross, later changed to Our Lady of Graces. The Youghal friars fell into financial difficulties, and all or several of them dreamed that Our Lady told them all would be well if they opened the tomb of Maurice O'Carroll (archbishop of Cashel from 1303 to 1316) who had died at their priory in Youghal and was buried there. They were to recover the little ivory plaque (probably made *c.* 1300) which had belonged to the archbishop and been buried with him. This they did, and it immediately became the centre of devotion and pilgrimage and miracles were ascribed to it: the priory's troubles were at an end. Originally painted and gilt, the much-worn ivory has a figure of Our Lady and Child; an enlarged sculpture of it by Seumas Murphy now stands in Youghal. The ivory itself is displayed at Our Lady's altar in the Cork Dominican church.

As in Cork, the graveyard around the old Youghal church has yielded up stone coffins with fleur-de-lis crosses and traces of Norman-French inscriptions, as well as two full-length freestone effigies of knights in armour. All the Orders of friars held on to the titles of their medieval houses as long as they could, appointing men to them, most of whom worked in the area, though the last titular prior of Youghal, Gerald Stack (dead by 1812) worked in Kerry. Reduced numbers of friars meant that eventually many of the old foundations were let go: mostly around the 1800s.

Glanworth

Glanworth was founded by the Roches in about 1475 and dedicated like Youghal to the Holy Cross. Today only the bare walls and typical squat Dominican-style tower survive, together with St Dominic's well on the river-bank below. The well seems to have been much visited at least until the early 19th century. The last friar was John G. Nugent, parish priest of Mitchelstown, who was dead by 1815.

Castlelyons

In James II's time there are said to have been documents in existence proving an old Dominican foundation at Castlelyons. At this period the friars moved back there briefly; in fact, the last Dominican to be attached to Castlelyons was Patrick Lonergan who died in 1819. There do seem to be two friary ruins in Castlelyons. One is the extensive remains of the friary and church of the Carmelites. The other, at the old Church of Ireland church site with the Barry Mausoleum, is a curious place, for the Church of Ireland church (now itself in ruins) was built inside a much larger medieval church with a tower of friary type. The Church of Ireland appropriated a fine lime-stone cut-stone Gothic doorway for their west door. The older building would fit exactly into the general design of a Dominican church and very probably was just that.

Franciscans

The Franciscans have always been the most numerous and most popular of the Orders of friars in Ireland and the remains of their friaries with their tall and elegant towers (as against the low squat ones favoured by the Dominicans and Carmelites) are frequently well preserved. In County Cork

Head, Youghal church

the Franciscans had houses at Youghal, Cork, Buttevant, Timoleague, Bantry, Sherkin, Kilcrea, and possibly at Goleen in the Mizen peninsula; and there are extensive remains of both church and friary at Timoleague, Sherkin and Kilcrea. Thus anyone wanting to study the architecture and plans of County Cork monasteries will do best to explore these more or less extant Franciscan remains first, and then be able to fit the fragmentary portions of the others into their proper context.

Nothing survives of Youghal, traditionally claimed as the first Franciscan house in Ireland, founded by Maurice Fitzgerald in 1224. Youghal was then an important seaport and a natural point of entry for anyone coming from England or Wales. There is a doubt about the 1224 date, other sources putting it at 1231, and indeed a doubt, give or take a few years, about many of the Franciscan foundation dates. There is a tradition that the friars came to Ireland during St Francis's lifetime, and he died in 1226. The Youghal house stood to the south of the town walls, near a windmill as shown in a picture map of 1600. The site is built over by the Presentation convent and the Devonshire Arms hotel. The friars continued to work in the area after they lost their friary, and indeed continued to maintain the title to the old foundations far longer than the Dominicans were able to do. The last guardian (equivalent to prior) was James Burke, appointed in 1872.

It seems that people often used the friaries as places to deposit goods for safe-keeping, and indeed the buildings, outside the security of the town walls, were strongly built and not too easy to raid. However, in 1290 John le Juvene, who owned the *Rodship*, which sailed out of Waterford, and who had deposited a box containing jewels and other valuables and muniments (documents) with the Youghal friars, complained that the sheriff of Youghal and his men had broken into the vestry and made off with them.

From Youghal, too, comes the only surviving catalogue of a medieval Irish Franciscan library. In 1491 it listed about 150 volumes; 30 more by 1523. These included liturgical books. The catalogue is now in Berlin in the Prussische Staatsbibliothek.

Of the Cork house, founded *c.* 1229-31, no remains are standing. It appears, with its tower, on picture maps of 1585 and 1600. The friars maintained a continuous presence in Cork, ending up with a much loved but decrepit church in Broad Lane, which was replaced in 1953 by an immense church and friary in pseudo-Byzantine style.

Kilcrea was originally a Celtic Church foundation of St Crea; the Franciscan house was dedicated to St Brigid and founded by Cormac MacCarthy in 1465, for the Observant reform. Both Dominicans and Franciscans experienced a reform and renewal movement at this time, and many new Observant houses of both Orders were founded in Ireland, particularly in the Gaelic west of the country. The friars, who had arrived with the Anglo-Normans, came to identify themselves more and more with the Irish nation, and at the attempted dissolution of the monasteries they were in the

Youghal

Cork city

Broad Lane

Kilcrea

very forefront of Irish and Catholic resistance.

Kilcrea, in the valley of the West Cork river Bride, is today so well cared for that it is difficult to realise that when the Commissioners of Public Works took it over in the 1890s the burials and bodies were so piled up and so thinly covered that their workmen could not be sent there in hot weather.

Like other friaries, it had a library, and Brother Michael O'Clery of the Four Masters copied manuscripts there. Its east window is said to have had beautiful stained glass. Much cut stone was taken for other buildings, and there is a tradition that a church was built from Kilcrea stones. The friars were in and out of the place after the Reformation: so were Cromwellian troops who made it into a stronghold for themselves in 1650. Kilcrea is beautifully built in the local limestone with occasional insets of red sandstone, the walls elegantly battered and the tower rising to a height of 71 feet. The stone steps leading to the tower parapet are intact.

Friary churches to begin with were plain: a choir in which the friars sang the Divine Office, separated from a long nave by a screen. This nave was meant to hold as many people as possible, for the church's services and to listen to the friars' preaching. While the friars' domestic buildings, grouped like those of the monks around a rectangular cloister with covered walk, are normally to the north of the church, monks like the Cistercians preferred to place their buildings on the sunny south side. After all, they were mostly 'at home', whereas the friars were meant to be out on the mission. When more room was needed for the public, the church was extended by throwing out a transept to the south, if the cloister lay on the north side. Towers were added in the 15th and early 16th century, at the same time that tower-houses were being built. Most of them are central, near the transept/nave crossing and over the screen between choir and nave. They were bell-towers, but they had several roomy chambers, like the tower-house ones, and these could well have been places to store valuables for the friars or other people.

Thatch seems to have been a common and cheap roofing material.

Kilcrea

However, in ploughing around Kilcrea, fragments of a local red slatey sandstone with peg-holes turn up, and it would appear that at least part of the pale grey limestone buildings had red slated roofs. Before they became as broken as the remains are now, the Kilcrea slates are said to have been of two sizes, 10 x 8 and 7 x 5 inches. Wooden pegs would have been pushed through the slate and over the laths of the roof, so that the slate hung from the lath. M. J. O'Kelly saw this sort of roof in an old building in West Cork.

Kilcrea, then, is a long, narrow church with the tower at the division between nave and choir. The church was extended to the south by a transept and an aisle, with an elegant line of arches on massive round limestone pillars. From the choir a door led to the sacristy on the north side; over this a well-lit room is thought to have been the library and scriptorium, where the friars could read and copy manuscripts. The door on the north side under the tower led into the cloister. At ground-floor level, the east rooms were a common room to the north and the chapter room against the church wall. The kitchen and refectory were in the north range and there were cellars in the south range. Dormitories were upstairs. Sanitation was usually fairly well planned in the monasteries; Kilcrea's latrines are off the common room and the dormitory above it, and upstairs, again off the south dormitory. The friars and monks arranged to bring a piped supply of water into their premises, though the remains of these systems only survive at a few places.

Timoleague, like Kilcrea, is on the site of an older Celtic establishment, that of St Molagga. The date of its foundation as a Franciscan house is disputed, the Four Masters claiming 1240 by MacCarthy Reagh, but Smith (*History of Cork,* 1750) saying it was founded in the 14th century for the Observant reform. Rather it seems that the house became Observant then. The tower is very roughly, even crudely, inserted into the older church. It is 76 feet 6 inches tall, and was built by the Bishop of Ross, Edmund Courcy, who was a Franciscan. He died in 1518, and he is also credited with building a dormitory, the infirmary and the library at Timoleague. However roughly the tower is built into the church, the effect from outside is magnificent, with the old buildings and their elegant tower rising from the water, in which they are often seen reflected. Timoleague is in fact a seaport town, though today the estuary is heavily silted up. But when the friars lived in their monastery, ships would have come right up under their walls.

The cloister is again on the north side of the church. In the east range is the chapter room, with the refectory to its north, and beyond that the infirmary for the sick. There was a dormitory over the refectory and another over the kitchen in the west range. The library was the upstairs room in the north range. Timoleague is unusual in that as well as its cloister it has a large courtyard to the west of the kitchen range. Again the church is enlarged by an aisle and a transept to the south; the most peculiar feature is a kind of passage in the east wall of the church, which actually crosses the east window

Timoleague

behind the high altar. It has been compared to a triforium passage of bigger cathedral churches, yet it seems to have no obvious purpose and one suggestion is that it was taken over from some part of a castle which is said to have stood on the same site before the church was built. In one of the refectory windows is a beautiful slab with fossil ripple prints, perhaps deliberately selected as an ornament. When the tide is out, one can look from ripples of Carboniferous age to modern ones on the Timoleague sands and mud.

Both in Kilcrea and Timoleague, the friars remained in the area. The last titular guardians were appointed in 1872, which seems to have marked the end of such appointments for all the Cork houses. Kilcrea's guardian was Francis Chambers and Timoleague's Patrick Carey. There is a strange story from Cape Clear about some friars from Timoleague. A fisherman came on a drifting boat with two dead friars in it and a third just alive. The latter was nursed back to health on Cape Clear and, before he left, gave his hosts a black box to keep till he returned. But he never did. Sometime in the 1850s the parish priest, Father Leader, was holding a Station Mass on the island and was told of this box, left from so long ago. He opened it and found

Franciscan Friary, Timoleague

some decayed vestments and a chalice, of which FRU MIN CONV DE THIMOLAGGI (Friars Minor of the Convent of Timoleague) was readable in the inscription. It is said that a bell of Timoleague was carried to Bandon to serve Kilbrogan (Church of Ireland) there.

The friary on Sherkin Island was founded for the Observant reform by Fineen O'Driscoll who obtained a papal licence for it in 1449; however, it does not seem to have been built until about 1460. The O'Driscolls are said to have built the adjacent and now much ruined castle to defend the friary. They, the O'Driscolls, had a running feud with the men of Waterford, who indeed burned the friary in a raid on the district in 1537. The friars were back on the island in 1627 and trying to repair their house. The building is small and compact, snuggled in amongst the rocky ridges of the island, just up from the present landing place. The tower is 48 feet 6 inches high. The church is not exactly orientated east/west, but about 30 degrees to the north of true east – so, it is thought, that it could fit most conveniently into the available ground between the rocky ridges. The place has undergone quite a lot of rebuilding and the tower is thought to have been built after the Waterford people's burning. There is a transept to the south, divided into two chapels. The refectory was in the north range of the cloister. The Office of Public Works has lately carried out excavation and extensive conservation work on the buildings.

The last titular guardian of Sherkin was Francis Beggs, and of Bantry, Patrick Fidelis Kavanagh. Virtually nothing survives of the Bantry foundation (at the old graveyard outside the town). It seems to have been founded in the 15th century, and the Observants introduced there in 1482. The friars

Sherkin

Bantry

Sherkin Friary and harbour

Sherkin Friary

Gahannyh

Goleen

Castlelyons

Buttevant

remained in the house even when it had been supposedly dissolved; two of them were killed when it was occupied by the English in 1580. The Order maintained the title until 1872, but they did not keep up a succession for the rather mysterious Gahannyh. The only record of this house is from 1442 when the pope granted an indulgence for those who helped to repair the house of St Francis at Gahannyh in the diocese of Cork. It had been founded by Donald Oscolly of the Order, who had collected money for its construction in the first place. It is thought that Gahannyh is Goleen in the Mizen peninsula, where there is a tradition of a monastery (dedicated to St Brendan) in Lissygriffin townland, and O'Scully is a local name. The Franciscans did keep up a claim to Castlelyons and appointed guardians to it, though in fact they had no medieval house there at all.

At Buttevant, the church remains, minus its tower which fell in 1814. The building is very unusual in having a crypt, in fact two crypts, one above the other. From the air in particular, it is obvious why these crypts under the choir were needed, for the building juts out over the steep bank of the Awbeg River and had to be built up from below. There is some fine carving on the capitals of the arches supporting the crypt vaults. When the remains were taken over by the Commissioners for Public Works in the 1890s they noted that 'the floor of the upper crypt is at present heaped with human bones and skulls; at one time the apartment was closely packed to the roof with them, but they are rapidly diminishing; visitors from a distance are said to be eager to take them away as specimens.' They are all gone now. The east window of the church was originally three lancets; these were filled in and replaced with three smaller, decorated ones. A most peculiar feature is a second tower, now attached to the Roman Catholic church, called Caisleán Caoimhín. It could have been a defensive tower attached to the friary, but its real purpose remains obscure. Buttevant's last titular guardian was Anthony White.

Carmelites

Castlelyons

The Carmelite friars came to Ireland sometime between 1265 and 1272 and made their first foundation on the river highway of the Barrow at Leighlinbridge in County Carlow. In Cork their first foundation was Castlelyons, given to them by John de Barry, *c.* 1300. Here are extensive

Capital of pillar in the upper crypt, Buttevant

remains of the church and partial ruins of the cloister and conventual buildings on the south side of the church – all in the local limestone. They held on to the place after the Reformation and re-established themselves there around 1737. But they were not able to continue at Castlelyons and today the only house of the Calced Carmelites is in Kinsale, where their house of St Mary's was founded in 1334. Their vicar general, Thomas Courcy, was hanged at Kinsale in 1577. There are no ruins of the medieval priory in Kinsale.

Kinsale

The Discalced Carmelites are also represented today in Cork, where they have a college at the old 'stately home' of Castlemartyr. The Discalced are the reform begun by St Teresa of Avila and St John of the Cross; when they arrived in Ireland in 1625, they had some dispute with the Calced branch of the Order as to who had the right to the medieval foundations. Perhaps the most evocative item of Cork Carmelite history is the Carmelite hermit of Gougane Barra, Denis O'Mahony, and his promotion of the pilgrimage there.

Castlemartyr

Gougane Barra

The Augustinian friars (not to be confused with the Augustinian Canons), had only one house in County Cork, in the city of Cork. This was the Red Abbey, though the tower, all that survives, is of grey limestone, and was dedicated to St Augustine. It was founded *c.* 1300. The Augustinians seem to have been able to remain at the Red Abbey until 1641. Their only present church is in Washington Street – within the confines of the old walled city, outside of which the Red Abbey stood.

Augustinian friars
Red Abbey

The Red Abbey tower, Cork

Kilcatherine doorway and carved head

As to women religious, very little of their medieval history has survived. There seem to have been far fewer women 'in religion' than men. It is much later, from the end of the 18th century on, and with Cork's Nano Nagle, that they came to dominate the religious scene and play such a large part in education and nursing and on the missions. Most of the medieval nuns seem to have been Canonesses of St Augustine, but in Cork city one Order of women was Benedictine, associated with the hospital and Benedictine cell of men. The other, apparently Augustinian, formed the convent of St John the Baptist in John Street in the Cork suburbs; founded as a result of a petition, approved in 1297, of Agnes de Hareford who was living as a recluse with other like-minded women.

In Youghal the convent was dedicated to St Anne and is said to have been founded in the time of Henry II; it was suppressed in 1543. It seems to have become Franciscan (Poor Clares) in the course of its history; the most interesting item preserved about it is that the nuns were responsible for keeping the beacon light, Youghal's lighthouse, going.

Ballymacadane, to the west of Cork airport, is marked by an overgrown ruined church, small and simple, in a field. It is said to have been founded for Augustinian Canonesses around 1450 or 1472 by Cormac MacCarthy MacTiege. Its first abbess was Honor Ní Carthaigh, but the house did not flourish and the buildings passed to some men of the Third Order Regular of St Francis (Tertiaries living in community), or so it is said, for there seems considerable doubt over all its history; the nuns could even have been still there at the time of the Reformation and the friars could have taken over later again.

Merely summarising the history and the surviving ruins of Cork's monasteries tells very little of their life. The churches were plastered and painted inside; there were statues and lights and shrines, and the glory of the Liturgy. We are looking back on the lives of hundreds of religious, who were trying to live up to very high ideals, sometimes not very successfully, and to communicate those ideals to the rest of the world. We are looking back, too, on all the days of persecution and penal anti-Catholic legislation, when youngsters slunk out of Cork ports bound for the Continent to complete their religious training and came back, most of them, to Ireland, to live roughly enough among the people they served, dressing like everyone else and being addressed as plain 'Mr'. There is a lot of history and heartbreak and adventure behind the modern Franciscan, once again able to walk in habit and sandals along the streets of Cork.

IX

Town and Village

THE HISTORY OF the town in Ireland involves the introduction of something alien. Like the Irish, the Icelanders lived dispersed, all on their own farms or estates, and went on doing so till the present century: 'We're only now learning to live in towns.' The Irish, however, had the town introduced by the Northmen, and then fully developed by the Anglo-Normans. The first generation of towns in County Cork are those settled by the Anglo-Normans. There was a second generation of walled towns after the Tudor reconquest with, for instance, Bandon being founded by the Great Earl of Cork. The people within the walls of the first series of towns tended to be Anglo-Norman, of the second to be aggressively Protestant. More towns were founded in the 17th and early 18th century, but now in more peaceful style: towns for the linen industry; towns and villages, such as Mitchelstown and Doneraile, laid out by the big estate owners. It does not seem to have been a very difficult thing to do. 'Sir James intended to have built a village here, which would have done great good. A village is like a heart to a country. It produces a perpetual circulation, and gives the country people an opportunity to make profit of eggs and many little things which would otherwise be in good measure lost.' (Boswell's *Tour of the Hebrides*, when at Portree in Skye, 12 September 1773.)

Yet other small settlements must simply have grown from all sorts of nuclei: a port, a big fair, a crossroads, a Big House with its need for many workers. Today we forget how important fairs were, and how nearly every

Glanmire

St Fin Barre's Cathedral, Cork

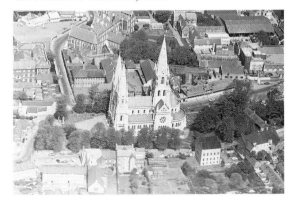

hamlet had its fair green and its fair, annual or quarterly or monthly, at which beasts were bought and sold and people met and exchanged news. Streets were crowded with cattle, splashed with dung, and populated by haggling men. Auction marts and motor transport have put paid to these bustling, colourful occasions, except for one or two historic survivors like the big Cahirmee horse fair, held in the streets of Buttevant each July.

Cork city

The roots of the city of Cork are in Finbar's monastery and then in the Viking settlement alongside it. So far no excavations have revealed Viking Cork, nor do we know its exact limits and location. Diarmaid MacCarthy surrendered Cork to Henry II and he, while granting all the 'kingdom of Cork' to Robert Fitzstephen and Milo de Cogan (1177), kept the city for himself. The city's first charter came from Prince John in 1185, and gave it the same privileges as the city of Bristol.

It was an extraordinary concept, this marsh that was Cork. It was a walled island among a number of islands through which the channels of the Lee threaded and the tide rose and fell. It measured 690 x 240 yards and had one straight street through the length of it, the present Main Street, with a North Gate Bridge at one end and a South Gate Bridge at the other. The bridges are still there, though the gates have gone. Round it was a substantial wall of limestone blocks, which is exposed at intervals when construction work is done along its line. Where the Queen's Old Castle now stands was a Water Gate, so that ships could actually be berthed inside the city walls. The picture map in *Pacata Hibernia* (1595) gives a vivid impression of this little walled island town, and shows that some development was taking place. Shandon (the Old Castle), for instance, is to be seen on the steep slopes rising from the marsh.

The extraordinary thing about Cork was that not only did it spread up the dry hillsides but its people went on to colonise the other islands in the marsh. These islands were drained as far as possible and built upon. The first was the area between Patrick Street and Emmett Place and Lavitt's Quay, work which began in the 16th century and was completed by 1750.

Castletownsend

Rosscarbery

Between the South Mall and Patrick Street was Dunscomb's Marsh, reclaimed 1690-1759, followed by Morrison's Island, reclaimed between 1700 and 1750. The city was now a sort of Venice, with waterways for streets and steps leading up over arched boathouses to the merchants' front doors, a number of which still survive. But this did not content the ambitious people of Cork, who next set about the dehydration of their waterways, by the construction, as it were, of continuous bridges, turning them into the present broad streets of the city. Grattan Street dates to 1778; Sheare's Street, 1795; Grand Parade (where an old cannon which served as a mooring bollard for ships still stands at the corner of Tuckey Street), *c.* 1780; Patrick Street *c.* 1783; and the South Mall *c.* 1800-30. This work was an immense and very successful engineering feat, but the water is still underneath and given high tides, an easterly wind and a lot of water coming down the Lee, it can flood up through the drains and spread over the lower portions of the 'flat of the city'. The hydro-electric scheme on the Lee has helped to control flooding; what it was sometimes like in the past is indicated by the steps up to the modern Franciscan church which clear the highest flood level recorded.

At the end of the 17th century Cork was listed as fifth in importance of Irish cities; by the 18th century it had moved up to second place. It had always done a considerable amount of trade with England, particularly through Bristol, and with the Continent; in the 18th century it developed an enormous provisioning business. Vast herds of cattle were slaughtered (it was known as 'the shambles of Ireland') and the meat was salted and barrelled to be sold not only to British ships but to foreign fleets that called to Cork to stock up before proceeding across the Atlantic. A very successful export market in butter was developed as well. And although Cork has never been a manufacturing city as such, it had a remarkable variety of industries: brewing and distilling, glass-making, silversmith work, iron-founding and the making of steam-engines, sail-making (in Douglas village), tanning, even, during the 18th century only, refining West Indian sugar.

The Mayor of Cork's jurisdiction extended out to sea, ending at a line across from Cork Head to Power Head, and he went out each year to throw a dart into the sea to maintain his claim to his territory – a custom recently revived. Likewise the Sovereign (mayor) of Kinsale ruled some part of the sea as well as the land; the small Sovereign Islands are so called from marking one of its limits.

To begin with, Youghal or Kinsale were as likely as Cork to have become the major port of the south. While the harbour of Cork is one of the world's finest, the actual approach up to the city wharfs is not. Big ships had to unload downriver and have their cargoes brought up on lighters; the PS *Sirius*, which made the first scheduled transatlantic steam crossing, used to complete her loading at Passage, owing to the shallowness of the river in the city. Today, regular dredging makes it possible for fairly large freighters to come right up to the city.

Kinsale

Kinsale (Cionn tSáile, the head of the sea) was a walled city and naval base, latterly defended by the massive James Fort and the even more massive Charles Fort. The sea used to come further into the little town than it does now – the area around the post office, beyond the Court House has been reclaimed from the sea. But nothing remains of its ancient walls, though some if its old charters are on display in its museum. Its first charter, as a city, was granted in 1334 by Edward III. The actual document no longer exists, but its terms and privileges are repeated in a charter of Elizabeth I, which is to be seen in the museum. Although its walls no longer stand, Kinsale wears its history on its sleeve, with the great star forts, the 'gift houses' (alms houses) of *c.* 1680, the medieval St Multose church, the old Court House and the Desmond Castle.

Youghal

On the other hand, Youghal (place of yews) is, apart from its 1771 Clock Tower and arch over the main street, not immediately impressive as an ancient town. Yet it was a very important port, not only a harbour but the entry to the river Blackwater and its inland waterway into the fertile hinter-

Kinsale

land. Youghal's old walls are still there, part recently renovated, and records of grants for their repair go back to 1275 and Edward I's time. There is a water gate fronting the quays, a very ruined tower-house in the main street and, close by, alms houses (1613 or 1634) erected by the Great Earl of Cork, and the medieval church with its great polychrome memorial of the aforesaid earl, Richard Boyle. It is in the old church that the great age and importance of Youghal will begin to impress itself upon the visitor. Even as late as the 1880s the port was still quite busy with some 50 ships registered there, sailing not only to Britain and continental Europe, but to Newfoundland, Canada, the Channel Islands and the Baltic. Figures for the period 1678-9 of the various ships owned by the three ancient walled seaport towns of County Cork, remind us how important Youghal was and how immensely Cork has grown at the expense of every other port along these coasts.

Youghal, showing medieval wall with towers, collegiate church of St Mary, and Sir Walter Raleigh's house

	Vessels	Tons	Crew
Youghal	33	1,778	355
Cork	24	1,130	200
Kinsale	22	757	151
Baltimore	2	50	10

Cloyne
Buttevant
Kilmaclennan
Kilworth
Mourne

Other medieval towns of County Cork include Cloyne whose charter dates to 1251; Buttevant, which received £105 in 1317 toward building its walls; Kilmaclennan; Kilworth; and Mourne, where there is said to have been an ancient walled town that was destroyed in the time of Edward IV. Of towns that the Anglo-Normans founded or tried to found, some faded away like Kilmaclennan (Kilmaclenin) and others never really got going at all. There are several deserted medieval village and town sites in the county of which nothing now survives to mark where they were.

Bandon

Richard Boyle, the 'Great Earl', was the founder of Bandon. He came to Ireland in about 1588 with £27 8s in his pockets and rose to being Earl of Cork and one of the richest men in Ireland or England. He bought Sir Walter Raleigh's estate (42,000 acres) for £1,000 and, basing himself at his

Clonakilty

new castle at Lismore, developed industries – iron-smelting and fishing – and built towns. He obtained a charter for Bandon (Droichead na Banndan, Bandon Bridge) from James I in 1613. This appointed the houses 'on both sides of the waters running under the bridge to be one entire and free borough and henceforth to be called the borough of Bandon Bridge'. There are still remains of one section of the walls on the west side of the town. They enclosed 27 acres and there were four gates. Boyle had a strike on his hands during the building of the walls. The masons got $2\frac{1}{2}$d (about 1p) a day and demanded 3d; the Earl had to concede the rise. It is further related that when the men returned to work they killed the one fellow who had not joined the strike and interred his body in the wall.

To this day 'Bandon, where even the pigs are Protestant' has remained as a saying, even though the modern town is fully ecumenical in outlook. In 1750 Charles Smith said there was not one Popish inhabitant in Bandon, nor 'will the townsmen suffer one to dwell in it, nor a piper to play in the place' – because this was the Irish martial music. Bandon could then raise 1,000 armed men, many of whom would appear in their volunteer regimentals of red, faced with black.

Dunmanway

Richard Boyle founded three other towns in West Cork – Enniskean, Castletown Kinneigh and Clonakilty – of which only the latter really developed. Clonakilty, like Bandon, was meant to be a Protestant town, and a centre of the linen industry. It was founded in 1614, and used to have its Sovereign and burgesses, as an important manufacturing town and seaport – though bigger ships had to tie up at nearby Ring, owing to the shallowness of the estuary on which the town stands. The family of Cox were responsible for founding another linen town, Dunmanway, which was Ireland's tidiest town in 1982.

Dunmanway has two triangular 'squares'. The triangular 'square' (another fine example is Dromcolliher, in County Limerick, just over the Cork border) is a feature of these early 17th-century towns and was intended to be defensive; the houses along the three sides forming a convenient bastion against attack. Normally the 'square' was used for the markets; Dunmanway's second one might be more in the nature of simple ornament.

All this West Cork country was engaged in linen manufacturing, in addition to the county's considerable production of wool and woollen cloth. In 1696 Irish linen was allowed into England duty free and in 1711 a Linen Board was established, which set about upgrading standards of manufacture. A great many people were engaged in production – growing the flax, retting it in ponds before it was scutched and cleaned and spun; weaving it into various grades of cloth – and it was very much a cottage industry. Power looms ended most of this and Irish linen manufacture became concentrated in the north, so that by the time West Cork was so severely hit by the Famine, the linen industry, which could have kept many people alive, had disappeared.

At Blarney there were a few mud cabins outside the old castle and the Big House, but its owner Mr S. J. Jeffreys began to build a model manufacturing village in 1765, which ten years later had 90 houses. It was to produce linen, stockings, woollens and leather. The original project, in fact, faded out, only to rise again as large woollen mills.

Know-how was introduced by 'foreign' workers from the north of Ireland coming to Dunmanway and to Adderleys' Inishannon – to which, in about 1760, French Huguenot refugees came as well and attempted to start manufacturing silk. The silk scheme failed, though Inishannon still remembers the 'mulberry field' where the trees whose leaves were to feed the silkworms

were grown. In Dunmanway, memorials in Fanlobbus Church (built in 1812) and the graveyard round it carry many names suggestive of incomers to the district: Wagner, Jagoe, Shuldham, Bonar, Peyton, Norwood, Gillman, Deane, Welply, Levis, Lucas, Cox, Chambers, Clarke, Beamish, Swanton and Kingston.

The Kingston family laid out Mitchelstown beside their great house there, in the form of a big market square, in which the present lively open-air markets still take place, and beyond which is the Roman Catholic church. Back from this big market square is a most elegant vista from the shapely Church of Ireland church down a long straight road to the rectangular

Kingston College, alms houses for 'decayed Protestants'. Kingston College was built between 1771 and 1775 and designed by John Morrison of Midleton, and its beautiful old buildings still fulfil their original purpose. The church at the other end of the vista is early 19th century, by the Pain brothers of Cork city.

Fermoy on the Blackwater has undoubtedly the strangest history of any Cork town, for it was the brainchild of a keen-witted Scots businessman, John Anderson. Born in about 1747 at Portlong on the Solway Firth in Scotland, of quite poor parents, John received an ordinary but good Scots schooling, of which he was very proud. He began trading in Glasgow, doing well enough to remove himself to Cork in about 1780, where he prospered even more. Cork was then doing very well indeed in exporting provisions, and Anderson engaged in this profitable trade. He is said to have been the first person to build a house on Lapps Island in the marsh. Anderson's Quay, one of the city wharfs, is named after him.

Fermoy then consisted of a few houses, the ruins of the Cistercian abbey, and a bridge over the Blackwater. The bridge had 13 arches and had been built in 1689 at a cost of £7,500, a very considerable amount in those days. The village, such as it was, lay on the south side of the river, where the abbey

Fermoy

Mitchelstown

had been, and people used to say 'all on one side like Fermoy'. Anderson realised that it could become a nodal town, and managed to raise the money to purchase the Fermoy estate in 1791. He started the mail-coach service between Dublin and Cork and, with two other Corkmen (O'Donoghue and Fortescue), took on the repair and maintenance of the coach roads. He set up a repair shop for the mail-coaches themselves in Fermoy. He laid out the whole town and the big corn-mills just downstream from the bridge, which he had widened to carry all the new traffic (the present bridge is a rebuilt one of 1864), and he brought in the military. The soldiers came in 1797, before the two great barracks, the Old Barracks (1806) and the New Barracks (1809), were completed. Fermoy became known as the 'Irish Alder-shot'. Kilworth, which had been the medieval town of the area, declined as Fermoy blossomed, but the army eventually moved up on to the Kilworth uplands to make itself a firing range in 1896; the wife of General Fryer, officer commanding in the Cork area, fired the first shot and scored a bull.

Kilworth

Eighteenth and 19th-century Ireland was heavily garrisoned, with many army and police barracks and the coastguard stations as well. In a place like Fermoy social life must have been dominated and enlivened by the military presence.

Ballincollig

Ballincollig, now a rapidly growing satellite of Cork city, was until the 1970s simply a broad street of houses which had grown up against the barracks (still used by the Irish army) and the gunpowder mills. Lewis in his *Topographical Dictionary* (1830s) describes Ballincollig's 'Artillery Barracks [which] form a quadrangular pile of buildings, having in the eastern range the officers' apartments, and on the western side a hospital, and a neat church built in 1814, in which divine service is regularly performed by a resident chaplain. The buildings contain accommodation for 18 officers and 242 non-commissioned officers and privates and are adapted to receive eight field batteries, though at present only one is stationed there, to which are attached 95 men and 44 horses; in the centre of the quadrangle eight gun sheds are placed in two parallel lines, and near them are the stables and offices; within the walls is also a large and commodious schoolroom.' Ballincollig would later become a cavalry barracks with space for 450 horses.

Buttevant

Buttevant had a barracks covering 23 acres, two squares separated from one another by a range of buildings through which was an archway topped by a cupola. Mallow's troops were eventually moved to Fermoy.

Some idea of how many troops were stationed in the whole of Ireland can be gained from figures for 1759, when no rising or disturbance was taking place. The country then had four cavalry regiments, six regiments of dragoons and twelve of infantry. At the time of the Union, it was estimated that Ireland had between 30,000 and 50,000 soldiers, plus about 21,000 in the volunteer bands of yeomanry and militia.

Mallow

If Fermoy was the Irish Aldershot, Mallow was the Irish Bath. Its origins were houses around the castle, and the bridge over the Blackwater. For a long while this was the first bridge upriver from the sea. On 3 April 1666 Lord Orrery, then at Charleville, wrote to the Duke of Ormond about the Mallow bridge that 'there is but one bridge over the Blackwater, which is 40 miles navigable for boats. This bridge is at Mallow, where there is a castle of good strength if it had a little reparation, and is one of the greatest passes and thoroughfares in this province, and if seized on by an enemy would, in effect, divide the country into two parts.'

Mallow grew, getting its barracks and ironworks, and then benefitting from the fame of its warm spring. The maps mark quite a number of spas – mineralised springs – around County Cork, but Mallow's is the only warm one (though not the only warm spring in Ireland) and the only one which became fashionable. Arthur Young was there in 1776, and was not very impressed: 'I walked to the spring in the town to drink the water, to which so many people have long resorted; it resembles that of Bristol, prescribed for the same cases and with great success. In the season, there are two assemblies a week, lodgings are 5 shillings (25p) a week each room, and these seemed to be miserably bad. Board, 13 shillings (65p) a week. These prices, in so cheap a country, amazed me, and would, I should fear, prevent Mallow from being so considerable, as more reasonable rates might make it, unless accommodations proportionable were provided. There is a small canal, with walks on each side, leading to the spring, under cover of some very noble poplars. If a double row of good lodgings were erected here, with public rooms, in an elegant style, Mallow would probably become a place for amusement, as well as health.'

Despite Arthur Young's strictures, most writers were enthusiastic about its attractions and amusements. The warm spring had been 'discovered' as a curative one in 1724, and the town was able to cash in on it for over a hundred years. Charles Smith in 1750: 'Near the Spa there are pleasant walks, agreeably planted; and on each side are canals and cascades for the amusement and exercise of the company, who have music on their walks. There is also a long room where assemblies are held for dancing, card playing, etc.'

Castletownroche

A Spa House was built, with the hot spring enclosed in a cut-limestone basin with a flight of limestone steps circling elegantly down to it. This house is now privately owned and not open to the public. There was a Mallow Club, whose reading room was open to visitors; a public subscription news room; the fine Duhallow Hunt which met at Mallow; and a race-meeting in September (Mallow's races are still going strong). There was plenty of fun for the Rakes of Mallow and anyone else:

> Beauing, belling, dancing, drinking,
> Breaking windows, damning, sinking,
> Ever raking, never thinking
> Live the rakes of Mallow.
>
> Spending faster than it comes,
> Beating waiters, bailiffs, duns,
> Bacchus' true begotten sons,
> Live the rakes of Mallow.
>
> Living short but merry lives,
> Going where the devil drives,
> Having sweethearts but no wives,
> Live the rakes of Mallow.

For those who could not afford to go to Mallow, the water could be bought in Cork, bottled. The *Corke Journal* of 25 December 1858 carried the following advertisement: 'Richard O'Kelly offers for sale in Cork, Mallow Spa Water. It is remarkable for curing decay of the lungs and loss of appetite. Besides it is the best water in Europe for making tea or brewery punch. Also for drawing fine tinctures for apothecaries. It will be sold fresh every day at Richard O'Kelly's house in Kitt's Lane near Tuckey's Quay.'

Cobh Cobh, departure point for so many Irish emigrants, and the point at which the great transatlantic liners used to make their first and last European calls on the crossing, has quite a short history. It was only a small village in 1786, but grew fast with the increasing amount of shipping putting into Cork Harbour, and with the development of the naval base on Haulbowline Island close by. During the wars with the French, the British used to sail their merchant fleets in convoys for safety, and these great musterings often took place in Cork Harbour. It is said that sometimes as many as 600 merchant ships were moored off Cobh and 400 would leave in their various convoys in a single day.

But Cobh could be as gay as Mallow. The old building of the yacht club (now based at Crosshaven) still stands on the seafront. Here was founded the first yacht club in the world: the Water Club in 1720, later the Royal Cork Yacht Club. The old building dates from 1855. The Water Club members (and it included the ladies, with their own version of the men's yachting uniform) used to go out to Haulbowline Island and the old fort there, before it was turned into a naval base. Thus on 14 July 1785: 'The boat races at Haulbowline commenced; the day was fine, a brilliant concourse of people were assembled. The island having previously been taken possession of by William Lombard, who was styled governor for the day, a platform was erected and surrounded with picquet lines to reserve the space within for the nobility and gentry. The governor's tents were pitched and his tables being covered with a cold collation, a large band of music was in attendance, and the batteries of cannon were mounted on the most advantageous ground in the island. The governor was dressed in a fancy habit, resembling a highland chieftain's dress. On the river were a great number of yachts and boats, all filled with various parties vying with each other in gaiety of dress and cheerfulness of appearance.' (Tuckey's *Remembrancer.*)

Cobh

Ballydesmond   One of the most recently founded Cork towns is Ballydesmond, right on the border with Kerry, north of Rathmore, which celebrated its 150th anniversary in 1983. Founded as King William's Town, it was planned as a model village to work the land round about and raise the standard of living of ordinary people: what today would be called a pilot scheme. It seems to have been doing quite well until the disaster of the potato famine threw the whole countryside into chaos.

In all the Cork towns there were, of course, two worlds: that of elegance, of ball and assembly and plenty, and that of extreme poverty. It was into this

Nano Nagle   second world that Nano (Honora) Nagle (1718-1784) ventured and started an educational project that ended in the foundation of the Presentation Sisters. Nano was born in a Big House, Ballygriffin, in the Blackwater valley, and from that background was to get to know well the stews of Cork city.

Daniel Corkery   Much later, Daniel Corkery would give an intimate glimpse of the life lived in the crowded lanes and tenements of Cork in the stories in his *Munster Twilight*. Most of those buildings where so many people lived so poorly are now gone, replaced by the widespread, largely post-World War II, new housing estates, which ride up from the 'flat of the city' far over its surrounding ridges and uplands.

Gyleen in mid-1950s

X

The Big House

TUDOR ENGLAND WAS, by and large, a peaceful place in which to live. Wealthy and powerful people did not need to live in castles, with all their inconveniences, but could build themselves large and comfortable houses, surrounded by pleasant gardens. The same situation did not exist in Ireland, and whether you were an Irish lord or an incoming English adventurer, you needed a place that could, at a pinch, be defended against attack. The tower-house was very strong, but its style and way of life was going out of fashion. People no longer wanted to pile one room above another; it was much more pleasant and comfortable to expand laterally – the way most houses are today. So in Ireland, the comfortable Tudor house idea was adapted and turned into a very good looking but fortified dwelling. County Cork has an exceptional number of these early 17th-century fortified houses, and it also has the only surviving intact unfortified 16th-century house – Myrtle Grove in Youghal. This did not need to be fortified, because it was snuggled in under the massive protection of the town's walls, beside the collegiate church. It belonged to Sir Walter Raleigh during the period of his Irish adventure, and it is here that he is said to have been smoking when a servant threw water over him, thinking he was on fire. Although it has undergone some later modifications Myrtle Grove remains, at heart, Raleigh's Tudor house.

Myrtle Grove

Another solution was, as at Castle Widenham, to build on to an existing tower or part of an old castle. But many completely new houses were built with big windows and ornate chimneys, yet with machicolations, openings for guns to fire through, and plans that allowed the defenders to command all the walls, that made them truly defendable. The surviving examples in County Cork include Kanturk (*c.* 1609), Mallow (before 1603), Dromaneen, Mount Long (1631), Monkstown (*c.* 1636), Coppinger's Court (before 1641), Ightermurragh (1641), Castle Warren, Ballyannan, Kilmaclennan (*c.* 1641), Castlelyons, Durrus Court and Reenadisert Court. Ronayne's Court, between Douglas and Passage West, was built in 1624 and demolished in 1969, its dated and elaborately carved stone fireplace being removed to Blackrock Castle.

Kanturk Castle is the most castle-like of these fortified houses and stands, in the Blackwater valley, almost as complete as when MacDonogh MacCarthy built it in 1609 or thereabouts. It is said to be the biggest house ever built by

Kanturk

an Irish chieftain – but MacCarthy never finished it. Jealous neighbours reported the work to the English Privy Council, who demanded that the building be stopped, on account that 'it was much too large for a subject'. Though it is difficult to believe that London's edict could be enforced at so great a distance, the work was halted, and the infuriated MacCarthy threw away the special glass tiles he had had made for the roof. There is an area south of Kanturk called 'Bluepool', and a field next to the castle beside the river, the Glassford, which seem to tie up with the story of the special glass tiles. But another version says that MacCarthy's servants were bringing the glass from Cork when they got the news, at Assolas, the ford of light, and dumped them there, so that the place was given a longer name, *Atha soluis na gloinne*, the ford of light of the glass.

Whatever about the glass to be used in the roof, the Kanturk Castle house was very strong. It consists of a rectangular central block, the house proper as it were, but with a massive tower at each of its four corners for its defence. External string courses, marking the floor levels, lighten the exterior effect. The house stairs were in one of the flanker towers, reminding one of the situation in the Burren, where a fortified house was built onto a tower-house at Leamanagh, and the tower-house stairs served the whole block. Most of the 17th-century fortified houses had the stairs where one would expect them today, in the core of the house itself.

The Blackwater, which in the early days of Irish tourism was called the 'Irish Rhine', is so rich a valley that all along its length were and are castles, fortified houses, and the Big Houses and estates that followed them. Downriver from Kanturk is the O'Callaghan's fortified house of Droman-

Dromaneen

Mallow

een, set on a limestone rock above the river and constructed of that same stone, with some fine bits of cut-stone work still surviving. A little further on is Mallow 'Castle', successor to a ring fort and a medieval castle at the river crossing. Sir Thomas Norris, or Norrey, got a grant of 6,000 acres in Munster in 1588 and built this great house there sometime before 1603, the year he died. His daughter Elizabeth was a godchild of Elizabeth I of England, and the latter gave her a pair of white bucks from which the present herd of

Kanturk

white fallow deer at Mallow Castle is said to be descended. The deer graze alongside the old fortified house, which withstood an attack by Lord Mount Garrett in 1642, but fell to Lord Castlehaven in 1645. The family moved into the stables, abandoning their house, and from these stables gradually evolved the present, very extensive, mansion house.

The Mallow plan is rather different from Kanturk's; it is much more house than flanker tower, and its defensive tower projections are much smaller – the central porch, one at each corner either side of it, and one only at the back of the house which contained the stairs.

Coppinger's Court and Ightermurragh have a fairy-tale quality about them, for both are elegant buildings in idyllic settings: Coppinger's Court in a beautiful little valley running down to the sea near Rosscarbery, and Ightermurragh, grey limestone walls set in green meadows near Lady's Bridge in east Cork. Coppinger's Court was built around 1620 or 1640 by Sir William Coppinger, a Cork merchant, originally of English origin but hostile to the English settlement at Baltimore, which he was trying to terminate. He planned to build a village in the little sun-drenched valley by his great house, but the troubles of 1641 put an end to the scheme. Coppinger's Court, with its tall chimneys, at first sight simply a very beautiful house, has, like Mallow, two flanker wings on its east side and one on the north, which allowed its defenders to bring their guns to bear effectively on any attacker.

Ightermurragh was built of limestone, quarried from the rock on which it stands, by Edmund Supple and his wife in 1641. Evidently they meant to keep warm: there are 12 fireplaces, some of them finely carved. The main rooms were on the first floor and, in the principal one, an inscription over the fireplace reads: EDMVNDUS SUPPEL DOMINVS MARGRITA QVEGERALD HANC STRVXERE DOMVMQVO SLIGAT VNVS AMOR. 1641 (Edmund Supple and Margaret Gerald whom love binds in one, built this house in 1641).

An immense kitchen chimney rises at the west end of the long rectangular

Coppinger's
Court

Ightermurragh

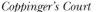
Coppinger's Court

Ighterrmurragh

building. It has a brick-lined baking oven at one side of the great fireplace. This would be filled with faggots, and when these had burned to ash, the ash would be swept out and the loaves put in to bake in the gentle residual heat. Ighterrmurragh has 44 windows, and its 12 fires vented into seven chimneys, one of which has fallen. Its five storeys are, again, marked externally by string courses.

Monkstown

Monkstown Castle and Mount Long, the one in the environs of Cork, the other by the sea in Oyster Haven near Kinsale, are so alike that it seems they must have had the same architect. Both are on the same plan as Kanturk, a rectangular house with four flanker towers at the corners. Monkstown was kept in repair until quite recently, ending as the clubhouse of the Monkstown Golf Club, but is now, sadly, being allowed to decay. It was, so the story goes, built for a groat – 4d (less than 2p) – by Anastasia Goold, wife of John Archdekin. This lady built it for her husband while he was fighting with the Spanish army. She insisted the workmen buy all their provisions from herself, a transaction on which she made so much profit that at the end the total outlay for the great house was just four pence. Mount Long is in far more ruinous condition but appears to have been inhabited until the early 19th century. At that time the date of 1631 was visible cut in the wall, and elsewhere another inscription read, JOHANNES LONGE DE MOUNTE LONGE, GENEROSIS. John Long was its builder.

Mount Long

The 17th-century Durrus Court, with fine curly chimneys, is hidden away behind the more modern but still old Durrus Court near Durrus village, at the head of Dunmanus Bay. Not far off, at Ballylickey on Bantry Bay, is Reenadisert, falling into decay after fairly recent habitation. Castle Warren, near Ringaskiddy on Cork Harbour, is incorporated into a farmyard.

Durrus Court

Reenadisert
Castle Warren

Broderick's Castle,
Ballyannan

Durrus Court

Kilmaclennan is fairly ruined, while the Barrys' great house at Castlelyons appears even taller and more ragged than it ever was, due to the fact that most of the rock on which it stands has since been quarried for limestone, so that, like the much older Castle More at Crookstown, the remains are perched upon surviving pinnacles of a once extensive rocky hillock. The kitchen has big brick-lined baking ovens and one can still make out, around about, suggestions of the ornamental grounds. Bringing water to a high house on a limestone rock was something of a problem and according to Charles Smith (1750) the kitchen was 'watered by an aqueduct contrived by a common Irish miller; a celebrated undertaker from England having failed in an attempt to bring this water by another course, after a good sum was expended thereon'. Castlelyons was burned down on 22 July 1771, and it is said that the estate workers let it burn, hoping to gain more by rebuilding the whole. But it was never rebuilt. Kilmaclennan
Castlelyons

Ballyannan, or Broderick's Castle, is on the shore of the estuary of Cork Harbour that runs up to Midleton. It is apparently unique in the county, a fortified house on the 'Scotch' Z plan, in which two defensive flanker wings form the two ends of the house. Sir James Broderick, who lived in the old house, added to it in about 1641; it is now still striking but much ruined. Field outlines and a beautiful little brick gazebo or summer house recall its once extensive pleasure grounds. The house itself, with its two circular flankers and its tall chimneys, is of limestone and brick. The statues and fountains of Ballyannan's grounds were eventually moved to Blarney, and it is of them that Milliken sang in his 'Groves of Blarney'. Ballyannan

As things did become more peaceful in Ireland, it became possible to build what we now think of as the Big House, the lordly mansion geared entirely to peaceful purposes, set in its extensive grounds, breathing of power, money and fashionable taste. True, there were some attacks by Whiteboys, Fenians and the like, and in some old houses you will find massive bars to the doors and behind the window shutters. But this was more a matter of passing local disturbance: the Big House was no longer its owner's castle in the true sense of the word.

Palladio's ideas seem to have been known in England around the beginning of the 17th century, but their effect was seen in Ireland a century later. He sought symmetry and balance above all, and the result was the Big House with two wings, perhaps linked to the central structure by graceful and colonnaded arms. Kilshannig near Rathcormack is one such house, the kitchen (now ruined) upon the one wing, and the stables upon the other. Moving the kitchen out of the main house meant moving out cooking smells and fire risks – it seems it is only quite recently that people have developed a mania for having the food served to them at near boiling point. Later, the house plan would become more formal, though Ireland has a great number of box-like Georgian houses, with a big central hall and stairway, and two big rooms balanced either side of it, upstairs, downstairs, back and front: a very *Palladio*

Kilshannig

livable plan. The early 19th century saw the Gothic revival, in which churches went in for pointed arches and spires, and houses for battlements and turrets. Pugin, who designed so many neo-Gothic churches, and seems to have linked salvation with the pointed arch, saw something of the humour of it and wrote a parody of a modern (19th century) castellated mansion, with its drawbridges that would not lift and its conservatory at the back: 'Who would hammer against nailed portals when he could kick his way in through the greenhouse?'

County Cork has quite an exceptional assemblage of Big Houses, showing the entire development from the fortified house to the present day. Even if many of the Big Houses have been totally destroyed or now stand in ruin, what remains is still a massive number, and really far too extensive for brief description. Brian de Breffny and Rosemary Ffolliott in their volume on *The Houses of Ireland* (1975) aptly describe the houses around Cork Harbour as 'a microcosm of Irish domestic building. Above the trees is the massive Monkstown Castle, built for a groat before Cromwell came to Ireland; near Glanmire a bevy of Georgian seats, including the elegant Lotas of Ducart and Hargeave, and the solid Neo-Classsical Dunkettle; on its lovely island is Fota, altered by Morrison, just masking from view the old tower-house of Belvelly; high on a distant cliff gleams the white facade of Ringabella House facing across the mouth of the Harbour to the crescent of Regency coastguard cottages at Roches Point; and on Great Island are the steeply rising Victorian terraces of Cobh and the Edwardian villas of Rushbrookes.'

Cork city and Kinsale have a very special shape of house, the 'roundy' house, swelling bow-fronted on the street and sometimes weather slated. In the wet driving winds and rains of Cork, weather slating walls proved an ideal method of countering damp and is a feature of many old houses and churches. Houses built of limestone tend to be damp, and owners tried to keep the inside walls dry by wood panelling (Tudor panelling still exists in Walter Raleigh's house in Youghal) and, rather later, by a brick lining. Brick lining in Ireland dates from the mid-17th century. Bricks were used, too, to

Monkstown
Lotas
Dunkettle
Fota
Ringabella

Kilshannig

line the high walls of the Big Houses' gardens, on which fruit trees were trained, as they would absorb the sun's heat and bring on peach and plum and pear and apple more quickly. Bricks were produced on a large scale in the county, but they also came into the seaports as ballast in ships come to load cargoes. Combining brightly coloured brick with local flagstones or cut limestone, a brick surround to a window or door is often used decoratively in outbuildings, like the ruined stables at Mount Leader (Millstreet), or in old industrial premises. Cork city, in particular, uses its red sandstone and pale grey limestone in checkerboard patterns in many buildings. Usually local stone was used – Kilshannig can point to the quarry alongside – but sometimes it might be imported, for some special purpose or building.

If today people complain that modern buildings of glass and steel and concrete do not blend well with the existing landscape, the same must have been equally true for the Big Houses. It could be argued that Ireland has had no truly native architecture since the Irish Romanesque, though she had adapted incoming styles to her own liking. The plans behind the Big Houses were all as foreign as a modern skyscraper to native tradition; it is by virtue of their being there, and by their own virtues, that they have become part of the cultural heritage of the Irish nation.

The Sardinian Daviso de Arcort, anglicised to Davis Ducart, worked in Cork between 1765 and 1770 and was responsible for Lota, the Mayor's house in Cork city (now the core of the Mercy Hospital) and for Kilshannig. Kilshannig has a most elegant staircase of imported Portland stone which circles upward, supported on its basal steps alone. It is said to be the only stairway of its type surviving in Ireland. All the principal rooms have the most splendid stucco work by the Francini brothers. Kilshannig was originally built by a wealthy Cork banker, Abraham Devonsher, but when it was bought by Commander Merry in 1962 was being used as a grain store and fast falling to ruin. Just in time, the Merrys were able to rescue it and restore the great feature to something of its former splendour. *Ducart*

Kilshannig

Very elaborate stucco work by the Francinis is the great feature of the early 18th-century Riverstown House, near Glanmire; this was falling into ruin and was rescued at the last moment in 1965 by the new owner John Dooley, aided by the Irish Georgian Society. Riverstown is open to the public, as is Fota, which incorporates a new safari park. It appears that the Barrys, when they ceased to live in Barryscourt Castle, had a hunting lodge on Fota Island; this was enlarged in the 1820s to Sir Richard Morrison's plans. Again the principal rooms have elaborate stucco work, some of which has recently fallen. Today one may wonder whether it would be pleasant to live with classical figures, foliage and fowls surrounding one in plaster 24 hours a day, but this stucco work was obviously very popular at one time, and even the most modest Georgian house is likely to have at least a stucco roundel of foliage as the ceiling centre-piece of its hall, if it has not already fallen with age and damp. Riverstown House

Fota

Vernon Mount   Vernon Mount, just outside Cork city, has been saved by becoming the headquarters of the Munster Motor Cycle and Car Club. It was built by Henry Hayes in about 1784 and is on an oval plan with curved end bows, so that it has been called 'a study in curves'. It has a very early central-heating

Assolas   system. Assolas, near Kanturk in north-west Cork, has the most wonderful wide eaves and sweeping curved roof lines, as well as very beautiful grounds with an ornamental lake. Assolas differs widely from such creations as Vernon Mount or Kilshannig, built at one time to a very definite design, for it began life as a tower-house. A house was added to this in the late 17th century, more was attached in the 18th century, while the whole got its present spectacular roof in the early 19th century. Yet the result is a unified and beautiful house.

Pembrook   Pembrook House, near Passage West, was recently demolished, but a
House   manuscript history of it and the family who lived there was written by Anne Boland sometime in the mid-19th century. She gives a vivid picture of how an old house could grow and change. 'The first house that was built at Pembrook was what was afterwards the coach-house, a high building very strong, with an old-fashioned fireplace that people could sit in. Then there was a house built in the Elizabethan style, the walls very thick; it is more than 300 years old. There has been one storey taken off it by some of my ancestors and the woodwork that was outside the windows, and it was new roofed, so that anyone to look at it now would never suppose it was built in the Elizabethan style. My great-great-grandfather, Adam Parsons, built the front

Bridestown Towers

Assolas, Kanturk

house at Pembrook more than 120 years ago of red brick cemented with bullocks' blood; it is in the Roman style of architecture. It is a very stately and imposing-looking front, and very like an old English house. The rooms are all 25 x 18 feet. He intended to throw down the back house and to build a house which would be the counterpart of the front; but got into such grief at the death of his only son, that he never finished it but joined the new and the old house together by a cross stair.'

Between Rathcormack and Glenville is Bridestown Towers and a sudden jerk into the very alien world of French chateaux. Bridestown has two French-looking towers and a fine range of farm buildings running back from them toward the later house. The tradition is that the towers were built by a Cork merchant, Jonathan Morgan, for his French wife. Morgan traded in Bordeaux wines and there met the girl he married – one story says he took her from a convent. The towers are from 1790, but the original house was burned and replaced by a later, very typical, Georgian one. In the garden is a 1635 sundial, and beyond the stables a tall folly tower.

Bridestown Towers

Macroom Castle, of which very little is now left, began life in the 15th century when it belonged to the MacCarthys. Later, it was held for a short while by Admiral Sir William Penn, father of Penn of Pennsylvania, and went thereafter through a whole series of rebuildings and modernisations, into which a couple of its original towers were incorporated. An advertisement in the *Corke Journal* of 2 August 1758 describes what it was then like, and gives a good idea of how self-sufficient and self-supporting the Big House on its big estate was. 'To be let from March 25th, 1759, for 15 years, the castle of Macroom, with its outoffices, garden and improvements, with from 10-100 acres of meadowing. The castle is as spacious, good and convenient a mansion house as there is in Ireland. It has a room 36 feet long, 26 broad and 20 feet high. It has a noble drawing-room, overlooking a beautiful river; several large bed-chambers, with closets. There is a parlour, kitchen, servants' hall and fine vaulted cellars. The outoffices comprise three large stables, large barn, coach-house, brew-house, turf-house, servants' apartments, granaries, fine fruit and kitchen gardens, a bowling green, and a well-walled-in orchard. The castle grounds overhang a serpentine river in which salmon and trout abound. They are enclosed with fine groves and double ditches, and are situated in the most beautiful and wholesome country in Ireland. They are in the vicinity of a fine Spa, much esteemed for its curative effects.'

Macroom

Life in some of the Big Houses could be idyllic. Anne Boland wrote of Pembrook in about 1800: 'When Grandmama reigned mistress of Pembrook, it was the period of the good old times when the houses were thatched with pancakes, and the streets paved with penny loaves. Grandmama kept open house for all-comers. She used to rise at six o' clock in the morning regularly and ring a bell and call up all the servants. She used to have her own corn ground, send it to the mill, bake her own bread, churn her own butter, make large casks of cider. There were no foreign productions in her house, but tea, sugar and wine, and even of that she used to make casks. There were no shops in the town of Passage in those days: the first shop set up there was a baker's, Kirklands, they were people that Grandmama brought to Passage and patronised. ... Grandmama kept house on a large scale. On every hook in Pembrook kitchen, which is large, hung a ham. The large oven was always full of bread, plum cakes and biscuits, and in her storeroom were two immense crocks full of every description of cakes, the other full of biscuits, while a larger one outside was filled with loaves of bread, and pans full of butter on the shelves. She also used to brew her own beer, and as was usual with ladies of the period, she understood how to cure every kind of disease by various kinds of herbs which she used to make into medicines, and the cures she performed were something surprising; she was idolized by the poor people.'

Things could be great fun. 'There were soldiers quartered in Monkstown Castle, and the officers lived in the house near the castle. One evening as Grandmama and her friends were at tea, a knock at the hall door, followed by another and another and so on, the door was opened and an officer came in followed by another until there was a good number; they each had a portmanteau with their dancing pumps. They said they were invited to a ball at Pembrook but when they found out it was a hoax, they wanted to go away; but Grandmama would not hear of it; she told her brother, Richard Parker, who was present, to put his back to the hall door to prevent their leaving, and then she sent word to all the young ladies in the neighbourhood to come to her at once which they accordingly did with great glee, and there was an impromptu ball – everyone said it was the pleasantest they were ever at.'

Bantry House

Many of the Big Houses became storehouses of works of art. The wealthier owners made the Grand Tour, travelled widely on the Continent and brought back loads of beautiful and valuable things. Bantry House (the first house in the Irish Republic to be regularly open to the public) is still a treasure house of such things, with its CAVE CANEM mosaics from Pompeii in its entrance hall. It stands in perhaps the most splendid location of a Big House in all Cork, on high ground overlooking Bantry Bay, with sward and a ring of old cannon in front of the house, facing out to sea; behind, gardens rise in terraces behind the Big House and a paved garden with wisteria in a blue mist over its trellises. The house was begun in about 1740 and enlarged in about 1770. At this time the Whites bought it from the original owners, the Hutchinsons. They were created Earls of Bantry after the 1796 attempted French invasion, of which they sent early notification and took immediate action for the country's defence. The house was further reconstructed in 1845. Of the Big Houses in County Cork regularly open to the public, this is the only one still occupied by the descendants of the family who built and adorned it.

Of the Gothic castles in County Cork the outstanding example was

Mitchelstown Castle, a rebuilding of the Kingstons' old house there. The commission was given to the Cork architects George and James Pain in 1823: to build a castle bigger then any other in Ireland and suitable to entertain the King (George IV) when he came to Ireland. The project cost £100,000 and was completed in two years, and, to judge from the pictures, it looked every inch a medieval castle, inside and out. But though its life began with lavish entertaining the Kingstons fell on hard times, and at the end the poverty of their entertaining seems to have been a byword. Finally, in 1922, the castle was burned and its cut-limestone walls stood in ruin until removed to build the new church of Mount Melleray, an unfortunate choice as limestone subjected to heat becomes the most unstable of materials. Mitchelstown Castle's beautiful old stables still stand and house Mitchelstown Creamery's fine stud of bulls for artificial insemination, while the same company makes powdered milk on the site of the Kingstons' grandiose dreams. Between the powdered milk towers and the stables is a small graveyard, relic of a much larger one, and it seems likely that the Kingstons' house was built on the site of an ancient hilltop church. It is said that some of the tombstones from the old churchyard were used by the Kingstons to pave a lily pond.

Castle Freke, between Rosscarbery and Clonakilty, is another Gothic fantasia. The Freke family, later Lords Carbery, lived at Rathbarry but moved out of this old house to build a new one near by at the end of the 18th century. At Rathbarry there are still the extensive remains of very fine stables with beautiful cobbled floors and yard. The new house was, by the owner's commission, 'thrown into the character of a castle' to Richard Morrison's plans in about 1820. It was only finally abandoned to fall into ruin in 1952.

Cor Castle at Inishannon is a compact little Gothic castle, lacking only its roof. It was burned in the Troubles like a number of Big Houses in the Bandon valley. One man recalled seeing seven Big Houses burning there at one time, though overall the number destroyed in this fashion in Ireland is not so great – for the whole country between one and two hundred out of a total of 2,000. Burning them was not a mere matter of hate or class prejudice; the Big Houses with their solid walls, their walled orchards and stables, were natural strongpoints in which British forces would for the most part be

Mitchelstown

Castle Freke

Cor Castle

Castle Freke

welcome to establish themselves. Much more destruction has resulted from owners' inability to maintain them, a costly business today; their removing the roofs in the days that one had still to pay rates on every roofed building; their letting the structures merely fall down; or actively demolishing them. Elizabeth Bowen's house, Bowen's Court was, for example, pulled down by the new owner when he bought the estate from her.

Life in the Big House was not as comfortable as it might appear. They were cold: central-heating, bar such attempts as Vernon Mount's, was a thing of the future. The big fires kept the area round them warm, but not the whole house. They were dark. Wax candles in crystal candelabra sound attractive and look well, but in the heel of the hunt give little light. They were replaced by oil-lamps and later some Big Houses made their own gas or, later still, bought an engine to generate electricity. Water supplies and plumbing could be difficult. Sanitary arrangements might be worse than in a medieval Irish monastery. It was only in 1778 that the first really workable water-closet was patented by Joseph Bramah. Judging from the 1840 Ordnance Survey maps, a reservoir on a stream and a hydraulic ram was a common method of getting water into the Big House.

Little could be done for illness, accident or difficult childbirth. Grand-mama Boland's herb remedies were your safest bet, for medical aid could be worse than the disease and very likely to kill the patient.

Visitors to Ireland sometimes complained that the Big Houses were often in poor condition, that lavish hospitality and high living were combined with a neglect of neatness and cleanliness: the custom of mending household rat-holes by nailing a bit of tin over them has a long history! In fact, as late as the time of Edith Somerville and Martin Ross, the poverty of the ordinary people of West Cork kicked back on Big House life; servants were so ignorant of cookery or hygiene that dirt and its attendant rats were a constant problem. The Somervilles in Drishane House, at Castletownsend, had sometimes to evacuate their dining-room when a rat died under the floorboards. Yet it was a good life. At the age of 83, Canon Claude Chevasse, who had lived at Castletownsend, talked to Kevin Myers: 'It was a very happy community with no quarrels. We'd our own pack of hounds, we'd got our own private telephone service, we'd got our own golf clubs. ... We were perfectly confident, we thought we would go on forever. Now we've pretty well all died out.' (*Irish Times*, 10 January 1980.)

The Big House stood, according to its size and importance, in its own grounds or landscaped park. The entrance gates had, and many still have, elaborately sculpted pillars with heraldic beasts or the owner's crest, and beside them was the gate-lodge. The gate-lodges are works of art in themselves, very small (the lodge-keeper's family had not much room to move, but more than other folk in mud cabins) but usually of striking design outside. There was a lodge to each of the several gates into a big estate, and a high wall around the whole. Some of these great park walls, and the follies

Somerville and Ross

inside them, were built to relieve the poverty of ordinary people by providing them with work. Caesar Otway in his *Tour of Connaught* (1839) writes that to call such buildings 'follies' only 'argues poor taste and sense in those who bestow them. Would that there were many such evidences that the rich cared for the poor.'

From the gate the drive swept up to the front of the great house. This approach would be carefully landscaped. At Manor, at Glenville, there are two approaches, the main one sweeping up through the park with its specimen trees to the front of the house. A back drive leads to the stableyard, with a branch to the house running through a very long avenue of beech trees which meet overhead and form a long green tunnel. A number of other such avenues still survive leading up to Big Houses in the county.

Gardens have taken a far greater knocking than the houses to which they belonged. In Ireland, with its mild climate and fertile soil, it needs a daily army of gardeners to maintain a big garden and prevent it from reverting to jungle almost in a matter of months. The earliest gardens were formal ones, laid out in geometric patterns with clipped yew and box hedges. Palace Anne, on the north bank of the Bandon River, between Bandon and Enniskean, was a supreme example of this style. Its ruins were finally demolished, bar one section of the facade, in the 1950s, and of the gardens only an old cedar remains.

Palace Anne has been described as 'the most beautiful example of the Queen Anne style of architecture in Ireland'. Lieutenant Arthur Bernard, born in 1666, married Anne Power of Mount Eglantine, County Waterford, and called their new house after her. It was built of brick with freestone quoins. At the house-warming, an ox was roasted whole and a carving of its head in oak was set up in the hall, ever after called the Bullock's Hall. Although the family were Protestant, they included a priest's hole in the new house, and later a wanted priest was successfully sheltered in it.

Joseph Cooper Walker wrote in 1790 that the Palace Anne grounds were of 14 acres with a high wall around them. Two acres were given over to a nut grove. 'It had a large fish pond, a bathing house, monstrous high yew hedges and some laurel ones; these were cut into fantastical forms, obscuring the rays of the sun. Here were also large green plants in various figures.' The *Dublin Penny Journal*, 15 February 1834, gives a fuller account, describing Palace Anne as having a front 140 feet long 'consisting of a centre and wings; the centre rises into three ornamental gables in the old French style. Before the house there is a large pleasure garden in which the clipped yews and hollies and old parterres have been scrupulously preserved in the taste of past ages. To the rear ascends a broad, high hill, clothed with fine old oak and walnut trees.' By 1875, however, Palace Anne was in ruins.

Two wonderful examples of formal layout survive, with magnificent clipped beech hedges bordering the principal walks at Manor and at Castle Hyde on the Blackwater. Castle Hyde is situated on the north bank of the

Gardens

Palace Anne

Castle Hyde

Blackwater just west of Fermoy and is a magnificent house, built in about 1801, fronting on to the river. On either side of the massive central block are bow-fronted pavilions, which are linked to the main building by corridors; the land rises steeply behind it and the gardens sweep up the slope to the line of the main Fermoy-Mallow road. The formal hedges lead the eye from river and house up to the Gothic church on the main road, now in sad decay. The house was built by the Hyde family, though it was sold in the mid-19th century, not so long after it was built. Douglas Hyde, first President of Ireland, belonged to this family. Castle Hyde's second owner was William Wrixon-Becher, a dedicated fox hunter and a sailor, who took his cutter across the Atlantic and back in 1856.

Manor

Manor is a very fine late 18th-century house, with extensive old stables behind it and a walled garden through which runs a great clipped beech hedge. Beyond, the land falls to a deep glen and tumbling stream, developed as a wild garden by the present owner, with many beautiful rhododendrons and azaleas. The original owners were a family of Hudsons, one of whom was the William Elliott Hudson who wrote the music of the song 'Who Fears to Speak of '98' and was a collector of traditional music.

The formal garden lent itself not only to sundials and fountains but to the garden gnome syndrome. In the early 1700s John Daly, marble mason of Cork, advertised that he had just imported from London 'a large quantity of ornaments of Stone and Lead, such as Statues, Urns, Flower-Potts, Vases, Pines, Lions, Eagles, Foxes, Hares, Rabetts, and Sun Dial Pedestals, which goods he will sell cheaper than any gentleman can import'.

Castle Bernard

Castle Bernard at Bandon, whose first version was a brick house built in 1715, had a garden on three sides of the house with fountains, statues and 'other decorations'. This house was treated to a Gothic reconstruction and its stables, which still stand, were made to look like a church; the house itself was burned in 1921.

Meantime, the opening up of the New World – the Americas, Australia, New Zealand – was to bring new colour and a host of new species to European gardens. Plant collectors travelled the world and sent back carefully packaged roots and seeds on the long sailing-ship voyages. Enough survived to revolutionise gardening. The risks were not only that the plants might die, but that the ship they were travelling on would be taken by a privateer and the specimens tossed overboard, or that a British ship would be captured by a French or Spanish man o' war.

In that latter case a way round the problem was found, for science and the love of new plants rose superior to mere wars. One of the earliest and most outstanding of plant collectors, John Bartram (born 1699) would put an alternative address on his packages: Antoine de Jussieu at the royal gardens in Paris. For, he said, though the French are 'what is commonly called our enemies, yet if they make proper use of what I have laboured for, let them enjoy it with the blessing of God'. And the scheme worked; ships' captains did see the captured plants safe to Paris and, with the coming of peace, de Jussieu would send them on, keeping back some items for himself first.

The great age of Irish gardening is said to have coincided with that of Grattan's Parliament, the last 20 years of the 18th century. Not only were all these new species arriving almost daily and being propagated and sold, but formality was being replaced by landscape gardening and the theories of 'Capability' Brown. This 'improver' got his nickname from his habit of remarking, when brought to any property, 'I perceive that your estate has great capabilities.' Straight lines were no longer to be tolerated; avenues were cut down or reduced to clumps of trees, and since vistas must not be broken by fences or walls, the sunken trench or ha-ha was devised to take their place. (It is said that the name comes from one's surprise on finding the way blocked by one of these steep-sided and deep trenches!) The white fallow deer of Mallow are still kept in their deer park by one such ha-ha between them and the Big House.

Doneraile Park, now in the care of the Forest and Wildlife Division, its 18th-century Big House maintained by the Georgian Society and used for local events, is a fine example of such landscaping. From the Big House one looks over rolling expanses of grassy parkland broken by clumps and clusters of trees, water flowing from lake to lake with gracious bridges over the stream and the invisible deep ha-has. It still has its deer and remains of the duck decoy.

Charles Smith described Doneraile in 1750: 'In the front court, on a pedestal, stands the statue of a gladiator, with other lesser figures. The out-offices are large and regularly built; the gardens well laid out and of a very considerable extent. In them is a wilderness and a labyrinth; and toward the foot of the gardens is a canal of 370 yards long and 140 broad, well stocked with fish. The water is constantly supplied by a large wheel that casts up a part of the river Awbeg into a reservoir, which is conveyed underground into the canal and returns back over a cascade into the road. On the other side of the river are pleasant lawns, and an extensive deer park, well planted and enclosed; and to the east of the house is a fine decoy.'

Smith gives a good idea of how vistas were laid down in his account of Dromore House about two miles from Mallow on the Clyda River, where Sir Matthew Deane had just built a house: 'The improvements are situated on the west side of a sweet romantic glen, formed by the above mentioned river, whose sides are embroidered with delightful groves of timber trees and evergreens. On the west side of the river, which is here confined so as to form a noble canal, is a high terrace walk. To the north and south of the house are beautiful plantations, and all the valley is shaded with full grown woods, through which three vistas are cut: the first terminates on the north, in a view of the pleasant mount of Woodfort; the second with a Roman temple; and the middle one commands a prospect of a waterfall cascading over a rude rock. Another waterfall is also designed on the east side. The vistas to

Doneraile Park

Dromore House

the south guide the eye to the neat church and the steeple of Temple Michael, and another to the ruins of Castlemore.'

In these big estates gazebos were common – the one at Ballyannan has already been noted. Here the gentry could sit and take tea and look at the vistas and views. There is a well-preserved gazebo on Currabinny Hill near Carrigaline, overlooking Cork Harbour (now a Forest Park with nature trail). Currabinny was a late development, toward the end of the 19th century, laid out with a Carriage Drive (for the indolent), the Middle Walk and the Water and Cliff Walk. It then belonged to James Lane of Myrtleville, grandfather of Sir Hugh Lane, the art collector, who was drowned when the *Lusitania* was sunk in 1915.

Currabinny

A hundred years earlier the pond at Pembrook had an island on which, as Anne Boland wrote, was 'a Chinese Pagoda that they used to drink tea in on a summer evening, it was nicely ornamented inside with Shells; they used to row out in the Indian Skiff and invite some friends with them always. A weeping willow hung over the pond. There was a pair of beautiful white swans swimming in it.' Collecting shells and ornamenting little summer houses with them seems to have been very popular at one time.

Bishop Berkeley of Cloyne, the famous philosopher, was a keen gardener. During the time he lived at Cloyne (1734-1753) he maintained a 400-acre farm and a four-acre garden in which he planted shrubs and laid out walks, 'one of which was lined with myrtles, whose roots he personally covered with large balls of tar, as he believed in its horticultural efficacy'. Not far off, at Castlemartyr, from 1721, Henry Boyle was working hard laying out a canal and a twisting river with cascades and fine trees. But by the early 19th century the Boyles had become absentees and the gardens began to run down, though the magnolias and camellias, arbutus, Chinese roses and myrtles still flourished. (The tower-house and Big House and part of the Castlemartyr estate are now a Discalced Carmelite college; another part of the estate is a Forest Park.)

Cloyne

Castlemartyr

Of the shrubs so adventurously collected and precariously carried halfway across the world, and so carefully tended here at first, the rhododendron and the fuchsia were to spread like forest fire and rapidly become typical members of the Irish flora. The New Zealand flax, which is not a flax at all but which was used by the Maoris for fibres to weave cloth, was brought in with the hope of using it industrially here. The proposed new industry withered before it was born, but the New Zealand flax is now a familiar plant of the coast of West Cork and provides an excellent shelter belt. The Boggeragh Mountains have showy hedges of olearia, the daisy bush from Australia and New Zealand, which survives the occasional snowfalls on their heights. Eucalyptus trees tower over Glengarriff and their silvery branches out-top all the other trees around the wrecked mansion of Hoddersfield near Crosshaven. Mimosa flowers happily in early spring on warm southern walls in many places in the county.

New Zealand

Olearia

Eucalyptus

Mimosa

In 1883 William Robinson, who came from Ireland, published his *English Flower Garden* and began a real return to nature, reacting against the rigid rules of landscaping. Gardens were now to look natural. Annes Grove near Castletownroche in north Cork is in the Robinson manner. (Its gardens are open daily to the public.) The house itself dates to 1740 and there is a formal walled garden but the major part of the grounds, the creation of their owner Richard Grove Annesley in the first half of the present century, represent the Robinson ideal of plants and shrubs growing in their normal and natural disorder. Rhododendrons and azaleas are the speciality, from seed collected in Tibet and Nepal which Mr Annesley germinated here in north Cork. The grounds drop steeply to the river and on an island is a water garden, with species from South America and Australia.

The best-known garden in County Cork is that on Ilnacullin, Garinish Island, in Bantry Bay off Glengarriff; it is a creation of the present century. Once shelter belts had been grown to provide protection from the salt-laden gales, the mild climate allowed the construction and planting of this extraordinary oasis, part in 'natural' style, part formal, with its almost endless catalogue of plants from all over the world, set against the dramatic backdrop of the Sugar Loaf mountain. (The estate was donated to the nation and is open daily.)

The owners of the big estates planted trees in all manner of ways. Clumps and 'tree rings' (whose enclosing earthen or stone banks may be mistaken for ring forts), to enhance vistas from the house or its walks, are common. Longueville House, just west of Mallow, a gracious early 19th-century house with a Victorian conservatory, now a country house hotel, had specimen trees planted on the parkland in front of it to show the positions of the troops at Waterloo. Other owners set ordinary commercial stands or made collections of tree species in arboreta. That at Fota is claimed as possibly the finest in Europe. It is especially beautiful in autumn, when from the air one can see a brilliant patchwork of many-coloured leaves. Blarney Castle has a considerable collection of trees and, since no tree lives for ever, the mid-

Annes Grove

Rhododendrons Azaleas

Garinish

Longueville House

Fota

Blarney

Annes Grove House, Castletownroche

1970s saw extensive new planting of a varied collection of trees and shrubs in the park around the Big House.

Walled kitchen gardens and orchards provided the main sources of fruit for the Big Houses. Cider-making went on all over the more fertile parts of the county; Ballymaloe House (now a country house hotel) was famous for it and there were cider orchards all along the Blackwater valley. Smith (1750) says that 'the Burlington crab or Earl of Cork's pippin, and a harsh austere apple called the Kekagee, with a mixture of golden pippins, are most esteemed in this country for making the best and strongest cider'.

Peaches were commonly grown. Anne Boland tells a story from Pembrook at the end of the 18th century. 'When Miss Anne Parker was courting Col. John (Boland), the Col. put her up to a joke which was to steal the peaches, and how to get over the garden wall as the garden was kept locked. So he found some empty wine barrels about the house and placed one over the other by which means Miss Anne and the Col. got over the garden wall and stole all the peaches. They hid them away in one of the empty wine barrels and put it where it wouldn't be looked for. Grandpapa was about to give a large party and when all the arrangements were completed, he went into his garden to look for his peaches, but they were all gone, so that he was in great consternation and thought to send an especial messenger elsewhere for them, but the messenger was privately stopped by the Col. and they waited till the day the party was to be given, and then they gave up the peaches to Grandpapa who was delighted at recovering his lost treasures.'

Mount Uniacke (now totally destroyed) in east Cork, north of Killeagh, was successfully growing and ripening oranges in Charles Smith's time. The ruins of the early 18th-century Garretstown House, close to the sea and just west of the Old Head of Kinsale, include a fine brick-built orangery for the cultivation of such exotica. In the 1790s the Garretstown fields were described as being surrounded by high walls and towers, with a pyramid in the middle as a scratching place for cows. There was an enclosed rabbit warren so designed that dogs sent in could round up the rabbits easily.

Sport, of course, played a considerable part in the amusements of the time. Hunting had passed long ago from a necessity to a pastime. The animals pursued were numerous in the old days. In the 16th century (when in Bantry Sir Owen O'Sullivan was bound to provide food for the hounds of Donal MacCarthy More) they included deer, wild boar and wolf and, among lesser creatures, hare and pine-marten. As wolves and wild pigs became extinct, the list narrowed to deer, and a new object of pursuit, the fox. The deer in the deer parks (the whole of Whiddy Island in Bantry Bay was once used as a deer park) were let out to be hunted and, when captured, returned in safety to their park. It is possible that the Duhallows, the

foxhounds based near Mallow, were the first to hunt the fox in Ireland – they were certainly doing it by 1745. From a manuscript from Mallow of 30 July 1679 comes the music of various hunting horn calls, different sets of notes for the fox, the hare, the buck and the stag. Coverts, of furze or trees, were set aside for the comfort of the fox. Decoys tempted wild duck to their destruction, and the sportsmen walked the bogs after snipe and carefully preserved pheasants. They also turned their guns on each other – dueling was a part of life until more accurate pistols made it too dangerous – and a man was judged not worth much unless he had stood fire. It was illegal, of course, but magistrates had themselves fought in affairs of honour and were generally unwilling to convict a victor.

Another amusement was horse-racing and steeplechasing. The first recorded steeplechase took place in north Cork in 1752, from the steeple of Buttevant to that of the church on St Leger's Doneraile estate, four and a half miles. Another account claims that it was the steeple of Ballyclough from which they rode, not very far from Buttevant but giving a longer chase to Doneraile.

In Bantry House hangs the little red pennant flag of the Bantry cavalry, and these volunteer 'Home Guard' bodies of militia must have given occupation, and very occasionally action, to many gentlemen. The Bantry

Bantry

The Puxley Mansion, Dunboy

Volunteers were founded on 12 July 1779, though the Duhallow cavalry only came into being in 1822. They devised very colourful uniforms for themselves: Bantry wore scarlet with black facings and white edgings; the Imokilly Horse wore white edged with scarlet; and the Mitchelstown Independents scarlet, faced with black.

While some landlords were absentees, most were not. For Ireland as a whole, the proportion of absentees fell from a quarter to one-eighth of their total number between 1720 and 1770. Then, when the Irish Parliament was abolished at the Act of Union, people tended more and more to stay at home. Dublin was no longer a centre of government and gaiety; London was too far away. Many landowners did their best for their people and their estates according to their lights. They would build another folly to give employment, but, though they heard it regularly read in church, the injunction to sell all they possessed and give it to the poor might as well never have been proclaimed.

Follies
East Grove

Several of the Cork 'follies' deserve special mention. There is what can only be described as a complex of them at the beautiful house of East Grove, set in its lovely gardens on Great Island which slope down to East Ferry. The house is early 19th century and was built by Dorcas Bagwell, who was married to Benjamin Bousfield, on land that belonged to the nearby and now destroyed Big House of Belgrove. The Bagwell family came to inherit both East Grove and later Belgrove. The style of Dorcas's house is described as 'Cottage Gothic' and it ran to two towers, one being part of the house (the Wellington Tower) and containing the dining-room; a second, tall and slender, formed part of the yard buildings. Then on a neighbouring height is the solidly built Waterloo Tower, up whose steps you can ascend to the top and view the surrounding country. It bears a limestone slab inscribed WATER-LOO 1815, and below that a bigger one with a more lengthy inscription. This says, giving the date 1809, that the adjacent cottage (i.e. East Ferry house) was commenced by William Bagwell of Marlfield, County Tipperary, who employed his leisure hours laying out the grounds, and who died 4 November 1826.

> The Almighty Protector carries off
> The Immortal Spirit
> Unhurt by the fall of its earthly tabernacle
> To place it in a better Mansion.
>   Blair
> A memorial to perpetuate the taste of her ever lamented nephew
> This tablet is erected by Dorcas Bousfield.

Rostellan

Not far away, across the waters of the harbour, was the enormous Rostellan (finally demolished in 1944) of the Inchiquins, whose 5th earl was a great admirer of the actress Mrs Siddons. She paid a visit to Rostellan and he built a tower on the seashore in her honour; this still stands in ruins, as does an ornamental pillar a little further along the coast. Rostellan ran to a Gothic-style terrace with cannons mounted along it.

The Father Matthew Tower near Glanmire was erected in honour of a very different person, the Capuchin Fr Matthew, Cork's and Ireland's apostle of temperance. It was erected by a Cork merchant, William O'Connell, to mark the friar's return from a preaching mission in England in 1843. It is actually a pair of towers joined to each other, a thick one and a thin one, with large windows with Gothic tracery executed in wood. A statue of Fr Matthew, and some other (now wrecked) figures stood outside it on a little ornamental terrace. The architect is said to have been George Pain but he was dead by this time, so it would appear that an existing plan for a folly type tower of his must have been adapted to this particular purpose.

Fr Matthew

XI

The Churches

IN IRELAND, THE medieval churches, with few exceptions, are small and broken ruins, and the normal place of worship dates from the late 18th or the 19th centuries. In addition there is a scatter of modern churches, none of them representing an indigenous style of architecture, but rather a borrowing from overseas examples that appealed either to the architects or the clergy who commissioned them.

In England the monasteries were dissolved, the monks and friars were successfully evicted not only from their buildings but from the whole country, and their buildings fell in ruins. But the parish and cathedral churches were not destroyed; they were robbed of their decorations and statues of the saints, paintings on the walls were whitewashed over, and so on, but the structures stood and continued in ordinary regular parish use. And although the language of the liturgy was changed from rolling, sonorous Latin to equally beautiful English, and one no longer spoke of Mass but of Holy Communion or the Lord's Supper, the fact that the services went on in the old building and with a resident parson must have helped to give people the feeling that nothing essential had changed. When in the 19th century the Oxford Movement began to restore Catholic ceremony as well as theology to the Church of England, the old buildings blossomed again; the statues and the colour and the banners came creeping back, small boys swung censers, the clergy garbed themselves in splendid vestments and the critics would remark that it was 'higher than the Pope'. The Roman Catholic Church, laboriously re-establishing itself in England, could historically and theologically lay claim to having built the historic churches of English parishes, but had to struggle on in such new premises as it could afford to construct.

The Irish situation was entirely different. The monasteries declined gradually, not in one single act as in Britain; the friars stayed on, first sneaking back to their old buildings when they could, then in 'houses of refuge' in the country or in city back-streets. The Mass went on, at the risk of the priest's life, at Mass rock or cabin or back-street room. But the parish churches and most of the cathedrals were abandoned and fell into ruin. Men were indeed appointed to them, and collected their tithes, but one man might be rector of a half-dozen ruins and let them stay that way. It was only during the 18th century that the established church, the Church of

Ireland, set about building a whole series of new churches, very often on the ancient sites, and a little later, as anti-Catholic laws and feelings relaxed, that the Roman Catholic Church set about the same task.

Neither party had the means or inclination to build something very big and splendid like the great medieval English 'wool churches', which had been built with the profits from English fleeces. The Roman Catholic Church was concerned to get a roof over its big congregations, so that as many as possible could attend Mass in some comfort. The Church of Ireland was concerned to assert its presence, which it did very effectively, for you cannot travel many miles without coming on one of its churches, even though it must be doubtful if there were ever congregations to fill them properly. Artistically it laboured under the disadvantage of having to show itself as not being Catholic. It is only within recent decades that the Church of Ireland has allowed so basic a Christian symbol as the cross on its altars. It remained Low Church in thought, liturgy and decorations, so that the interiors of its charming little country churches tend to be very plain. Only occasionally does this change: Burgess's cathedral of St Fin Barre has the pure spirit of fun of medieval Gothic. Meantime the Roman Catholic Church was decorating its churches at a bad period for church art, with wedding-cake reredoses to its altars and statues that debased the very idea of sanctity. But many of these things were paid for by the pennies of very poor people, and they do represent a period of church art whatever the modern opinion of it may be. It is, in many ways, a shame that so much has been ruthlessly thrown out in the re-arrangements required by the new liturgy.

Drinagh West

Tracton Abbey

Looking back to medieval Ireland, it seems that the ordinary parish church was normally quite a small structure, and that the monastic and friary church must have stood out against it in cathedral-like proportions. Judging by the existing ruins, parish churches lacked towers and spires, at least out in the country. Inside they would have been well enough furnished and decorated. Cork county is fortunate in that it does possess four ancient churches: St Multose in Kinsale, the collegiate church in Youghal and the cathedral churches of Cloyne and Ross.

St Multose, Kinsale

The beautiful old parish church of St Multose stands on the original site chosen by the 6th-century St Eltin (*Mo Eltin Óg*, my young Eltin, anglicised to Multose) and, as already noted, a trace of the original circular monastic enclosure survives in the curve of the churchyard wall. The present building dates from the early 13th century and, although like all the Cork medieval churches it is much altered, it retains its basic plan: chancel and nave with aisles and a north transept. There is a noble oak roof, below which hang a fine series of five 18th-century hatchments (memorial tablets hung up on the individual's house at the time of the occupant's death and showing his or her coat of arms, which were later brought into the church). From late medieval times comes the great carved slab now on the south wall showing the crucifixion, thought to have been the reredos – behind the altar – in the now roofless Galway chapel. The old and massive font is believed to be very ancient, too. The tower was raised another storey in 1760, and the slated spire erected later still. The fish weathercock is a memorial to Mrs Eileen Marguerite Hill (†1930), given by her husband. Over the west door is a small carved figure in imported stone, of an ecclesiastic, believed to represent St Multose. There is a beautiful wrought-iron gate into the surrounding churchyard, and both the surrounds and the church have many interesting monuments.

St Mary's Collegiate, Youghal

Youghal graveyard, too, contains many fine ancient headstones and climbs up the slope from the church to the town's walls. St Mary's Collegiate Church is slightly later in date than St Multose, being mid-13th century. It is the second biggest medieval parish church in Ireland still in use. The plan is cruciform – the chancel was enlarged in the 15th century. Again, there has been much ruin and restoration, and at the present time there are old pictures in the church showing it in partial ruin. Its appearance now is spoiled by a massive silver screen which cuts off the chancel from the rest of the church to make a snug enclosure for the present reduced congregations. The vast polychrome monument of the great Earl of Cork, already referred to, has figures of his three wives and sixteen children – including the Boyle of Boyle's Law. The children lying down in the long row are those who died young.

Cloyne

Cloyne cathedral is dated to the 1270s and is a simple cruciform building. Its nave is 120 feet in length, and it is thought there was a tower at the intersection of nave and transepts that was later taken down – as were the massive battlements along the nave roof. Its most striking monument is the alabaster, life-size figure of Bishop Berkeley (1685-1753), the philosopher, who was bishop here. Outside are the slight remains of what may have been a chapel of the earlier monastery of St Colman and, just across the road, the round tower.

Rosscarbery stands on a very beautiful site overlooking the sea inlet, but the church has undergone much rebuilding and reconstruction. An arch survives from the older church. The present 1806 spire of cut limestone is a later addition to the old 1696 tower built in local flagstones; the limestone was probably shipped in from Cork. The church has many memorials of the Castle Freke family and a very fine Royal Coat of Arms in brightly painted wood. Church of Ireland churches all had these Royal Arms, and usually the Ten Commandments at the back of the altar; St Multose still retains them. Rosscarbery church has some carved fragments from Inchydoney church – the 'Island', which it was until joined to the mainland by a causeway constructed during Famine times. Island church was intact in 1615 but in ruins by 1642.

The first Church of Ireland church to be built *de novo* is claimed to be Bandon's Kilbrogan, St Brogan's Church, now secularised. It is placed on an upstanding knob, possibly once a ring-fort site, overlooking the river Bandon. The new church was begun in 1610 by Henry Beecher but not completed till the Earl of Cork took it in hand in 1625. Its attractive tower and spire only date from 1829. The present Church of Ireland church in use in Bandon is Ballymodan, on the other side of the river, only completed in 1849. It now houses some of the furnishings from Kilbrogan. The original Ballymodan was some distance off, where there is still a small graveyard and traces of an earlier monastic enclosure, south of Bandon town.

The main thrust of Church of Ireland building began in the 18th century and intensified with a great burst of activity from 1800, financed mainly by the Board of First Fruits and from 1834 by the Ecclesiastical Commissioners. The 19th century must have been full of optimism for the Church of Ireland because they then quite often abandoned their comparatively recently built

Rosscarbery

Church of Ireland
Kilbrogan

Ballymodan

Kilbrogan, Bandon

and pleasant little churches for newer and more ambitious structures. The earlier churches tend to be small, compact, with neat towers; the later ones bigger, more exhuberantly Gothic, and with spires. A common early plan in Cork was to have a semicircular apse at the east end of the chancel. Farahy, Elizabeth Bowen's parish church, now secularised, has this plan and dates from 1721; so does Templemichael (1707) and the old ruined church at Inishannon, which was replaced by the big, spired edifice at the other end of the village.

Mourne Abbey (1717) has been rescued by the Cork Preservation Society from total decay. It is near the remains of the old Mourne Abbey, and is dedicated to St Michael. Charles Smith, writing in 1750, described it as 'the neatest country church in the county. ... The altar-piece is composed of six fluted pilasters of the Corinthian order, with carved cherubims, neatly gilded, between them. On the panels are the Lord's prayer, creed and commandments in gold letters. At the west end is a handsome gallery erected at the charge of the late Sir Matthew Deane for the charity children. The pulpit and sounding board are neatly carved and gilded, as is the cover of the font, the basin in which is marble.'

Some of the churches were part and parcel of an estate plan. Castle Hyde was one such, a highly ornate Gothic chapel set at one end of the clipped beech walk up from the Big House below. It is now abandoned. In many of the churches the Big House family would have their own private gallery in which to sit. A fine example is the gallery for the Jeffreys family in Blarney church, which has its own separate entrance and steps up to the gallery with its fireplace and cushioned seats. A 'laird's loft' of this sort not only isolated the nobility and gentry from the common herd in the nave below, but must have given great opportunity for sleep or card playing during sermon time. You cannot see into these galleries from below and outside.

The crowning glory of Church of Ireland buildings in County Cork is the French Gothic fantasia of St Fin Barre's Cathedral. Designed by William Burgess, it replaced an 18th-century church, which in turn replaced the medieval one; it was completed by 1880 and by day, or floodlit at night, is the eye-catcher of Cork city, its elegant spires dramatising every vista and skyline. Its principal spire is 240 feet high and the building itself is only 163 feet in length. Externally this makes for a very pleasing composition; internally it is less successful as the church is far too lofty for its size and the acoustics are poor. The exterior repays long and detailed study, with its great collection of carvings from the Bible, from the activities of daily life and from the rich and Gothic imagination of William Burgess. St Fin Barre's Cathedral has a noble peal of bells and an expert team of change ringers, a rarity in Ireland.

Cork's Archives are now housed in Christ Church, a classical building of 1726, on the main street of the old city; but St Anne's Shandon, with its famous carillon of bells, still functions as a place of worship. It was built

---

Margin notes:

Farahy
Templemichael

Inishannon

Mourne Abbey

Castle Hyde

Blarney

St Fin Barre's
William Burgess

Christ Church
St Anne's
Shandon

between 1722 and 1726, but the bell-tower dates to 1749; two of its walls are of red sandstone and two of grey limestone. The carillon chimes out the hours and whatever else visitors may play on it.

Looking at the Church of Ireland churches is a matter of tuning in to their style: the beauty of a pinnacle on a tower, of good masonry work, the occasional carved head – as on Burgess's Crosshaven church. Fermoy's church, built in 1802, was designed by Abraham Hargrave and is very big, for it served a garrison as well as a parish. People say its doors are lofty enough for the troops to march in without dipping their flags too low.

Fermoy

The Pain brothers are responsible for many of the later churches; for the Gothic ornamentation of Castle Hyde; for Midleton's spire added to a First Fruits church, which was blown down in 1905; for the beautiful Castletown-roche (1825) on its rocky bluff above the river; for the spired Buttevant (1826 – now disused) and probably for the fine cut-stone Carrigaline.

James and George Pain, Englishmen brought to Ireland to assist in the building of Lough Cutra Castle in Galway in 1811, settled in Cork city, where they were first asked to build the new jail in 1818. All that remains of this today is its portico, preserved by the university when it extended its own buildings over the cleared prison complex. The Pains designed churches, courthouses, country houses – the huge Dromoland Castle in Clare is their work. Settled in Cork, they seem to have been readily assimilated into Cork society. Cork businessman James Beale, deeply involved in the pioneering of steam in ships, wrote to Captain Roberts, while the latter was at Port Glasgow fitting out the *British Queen,* telling him of George Pain's death. Writing from Cork on 26 March 1839, shocked by the death 'this morning of our friend George R. Pain: he died about two hours since of fever. I really can scarcely bring myself to believe it possible he was in my office with me apparently well last Saturday week and I never heard of his being unwell till Thursday or Friday last, since when he has rapidly declined. Dr Woodruffe was called in on yesterday week and afterwards J. Phipps; I met the latter yesterday and walked down the new mall with him, he gave me a very unfavourable account of poor G.R. Pain and this morning has realised my

James and George Pain

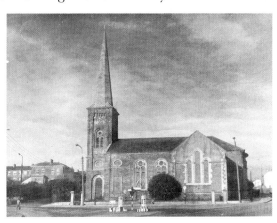

Garrison church, Fermoy

worst apprehensions.' And in a later letter, Beale goes on: 'I feel Pain's loss exceedingly as I never met a person so companionable to my taste in many respects. Turn which way you will here, you see monuments of his great genius. You cannot believe the blank felt here even among those who were unfriendly to him.'

Presbyterians seem to have had a liking for the Gothic, too: witness their church in Cobh, now the town's museum, and that in Clonakilty, with its gargoyles, now the post office. Methodism, however, ran to plain preaching halls and these were built in many Cork towns. Charles Wesley was preaching in Cork in 1748, and his brother John in the following year; both of them came to the very Protestant Bandon and its first chapel was built in 1760, though the present building, the third, was completed in 1822. Bandon seems to have been the centre from which Methodism spread over West Cork to Kinsale and Clonakilty, Ballineen, Dunmanway and Skibbereen, Ballydehob, Schull and Bantry.

Far fewer were the Quakers. They had a substantial, neatly built meeting house, which still stands in Gratton Street in Cork, and it is said that it was here that William Penn of Pennsylvania was converted. The Quakers did great work – partly because people trusted them – in the Famine, and it was from this old building that their Cork relief work was organised.

Meantime the church of the majority, the Roman Catholic Church, chose, when it was able to begin to build, to turn not to the Gothic but to the classical and baroque styles. The typical country church of the late 18th or early 19th century was T shaped, with galleries in each arm of the T, so that as many people as possible could be accommodated and have a view of the altar. Quite a number of these T shaped churches still survive around the

county; a very fine example is the one at Kilworth near Fermoy. This is located well outside the village, while the Church of Ireland church (now used for exhibitions, etc.) dominates the pretty little village centre. Similarly at Castletownsend (home of Edith Somerville of Somerville and Ross fame)

St Barrahan's Church is set on the hillside commanding the village, a lovely building of brown sandstone shipped in from Horse Island, while the Catholic church is about a mile away. The servants of the Big Houses would have had a long walk of it to Sunday Mass before getting the gentry's breakfasts or lunches – and in those days there were no evening Masses.

Some owners of big estates were more ecumenical in their outlook and their spending. Mr Leader of Dromagh Castle and Dromagh colliery in north Cork gave both the site and a sum of money for the new Catholic church at Coolclogh in 1830, and did likewise for the Church of Ireland. At about the same time the Jephsons of Mallow Castle gave the sites for both Catholic and Church of Ireland churches there.

Coolclogh is officially Dromtarriff church but is not on the old Dromtarriff church site and graveyard, which is some distance away. Aided by Mr Leader's £150, it was built as a plain barn-like structure, but its parish priest, Rev John Barry, was obviously caught up in the current passion for the Gothic and engaged a local sculptor, Charles O'Connell, to work on it. A spire and pinnacles were added, and the west front was lavishly decorated even to the extent of a stone clock-face. Heads of St Peter and St Paul, the papal arms of Pope Gregory XVI, and a *Memento Mori* (Remember Death) panel with skull and crossbones were included, together with the Leader crest and an inscription recording its bearer's generosity. Charles O'Connell's Gothic is very different from the later work of Burgess. He tends to be gloomy and serious where a medieval artist would be gay, and Peter and Paul are more like classical busts than gargoyles. Little seems to be known about O'Connell but his work turns up in churches (Dernagree and Kanturk – now part of the convent) and in monuments in graveyards – Mallow, Kanturk, Clonfert (Newmarket), Kilbrin (which also has a fine classical holy water font), and there are some more items by him at Glanworth and Castlelyons. However, the lavish decoration of Coolclogh and Dernagree are unusual in early 19th-century Roman Catholic churches. Many more of them had the plain simplicity of the recently beautifully restored Rockchapel.

Charles O'Connell

In Cork city the classical flowered in St Mary's, Pope's Quay (of the Dominicans) with its baroque interior, and in George Pain's St Patrick's Church. The later SS Peter and Paul (completed in 1868) is a Gothic design of Pugin's. Cork city has no Roman Catholic cathedral properly speaking, rather a 'pro-cathedral'. This dates from 1808 and has been added to and altered over the years from George Pain's time to the present day. Cloyne diocese achieved a magnificent cut-stone cathedral on a new site at Cobh, set high above the sea and dominating the town and harbour. This is a Gothic design of E. W. Pugin and G. O. Ashlin and it took a long time to

St Mary's,
Pope's Quay
St Patrick's
SS Peter and
Paul

Cobh

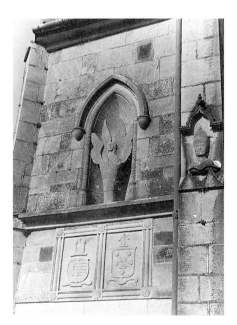

Coolclogh: work of Charles O'Connell

build – and to collect the necessary funds. Work began in 1868, but there was a long period during which the church was finished but the spire had yet to be built. Ultimately all was completed in 1919. The final pinnacle of the spire is of Meelin limestone from north Cork, so that emigrants from that area were said to glimpse their last view of Meelin as they sailed out of Cork Harbour.

Skibbereen

The Diocese of Ross has (under protest) been amalgamated with that of Cork; it does have a solidly built little cathedral church of its own at Skibbereen. Cork county actually contains three whole dioceses – Cork, Cloyne and Ross – and in the Millstreet area a small portion of Kerry.

The graveyards around all the old churches boast a rich variety of often much lichened headstones and monuments. Cork's magnificent limestone provided sculptors in reach of it with a splendid medium in which to work. Away from the limestone areas and into the poorer districts the monuments are naturally rougher. They range from large mausoleums of the great families through flat-topped or elegant table-legged, table-top tombs, to ordinary upright headstones. In east Cork it is possible to extract really enormous slabs of limestone for headstones, and some of them are up to seven feet in height and broad in proportion.

Kilcredan

Such enormous headstones can be seen at, among other places, Conna and Kilcredan, in east Cork. The church at Kilcredan was built for the Church of Ireland in 1636 by Sir Robert Tynte of Ballycrenane Castle. Inside it was erected his great monument of imported stone: Sir Richard in Elizabethan dress lying down and the kneeling figures, equally beautifully dressed, of his wives (one of whom was Elizabeth Boyle, the widow of

Remnants of the 17th-century Tynte monument in Kilcredan

Templebreedy, Crosshaven

Edmund Spenser). Unhappily, the Church of Ireland abandoned and un-roofed the church in the latter part of the last century, so that this remark-able Tynte monument survives today only in a very wrecked condition, though recently given some covering.

Hardly any graveyard headstones go back as far as the 17th century. Kilbrogan in Bandon has the tomb of Thomas Harrison who died in 1674. At Templebreedy above Crosshaven the oldest monument noted is 1711 and 1714, the dates of death of John and Elizabeth Darney. Another is of William Shea, who died in 1729. The vast majority of Cork headstones are from the mid-18th century on to the present day. Some graveyards have a division between Church of Ireland and Roman Catholic burials. Neither Church could employ stonemasons with a continuous live tradition of art on which to draw, but distinctive styles and symbols seem to have been quickly developed. Stone carving was a family trade; in Aherla, the Hickeys have been stone-cutters for five generations and their work ranges from a signed 18th-century headstone in Kilcrea Abbey to the noble grey granite cross in Bantry graveyard commemorating the dead of the *Betelgeuse* disaster at the Whiddy oil terminal in 1979. Anyone exploring Cork graveyards will soon find that different districts employ different styles and symbols, presumably coinciding with local tastes and the traditions of local masons. In the south of the county the cock and pot is very common; in the north-west a very fat sheep, the Lamb of God, though looking far more like the inn sign of the Golden Fleece.

Rockchapel's graveyard, in north-west Cork, is a little forest of tall pinnacle

Kilbrogan
Templebreedy

Aherla

Rockchapel

Dunmanway church

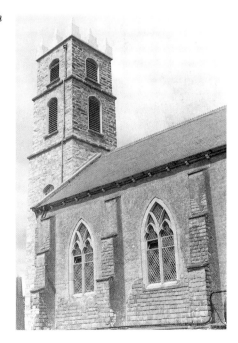

Hickey of Aherla signature on
18th-century headstone, Kilcrea

monuments, mostly dating from the end of the last century to the 1920s, and bearing national emblems, for this was a strongly nationalist district. Here are the round tower, the Irish wolfhound, the shamrock, the harp and the rising sun of freedom. Pinnacle-type monuments, fairly common in this whole district, occur scattered about elsewhere.

The lettering is usually very beautifully incised into the stone, but less frequently (and much more laboriously in the cutting) it is raised up in high relief. Matehy, north of Blarney, has several such stones of early 19th century date, and one is signed by its sculptor, Tim Cripps of Crookstown. Mostly the stones do not bear the masons' names, though the Hickeys did sign some, as on a big slab at Kilcrea – D. Hickey, Aherla. It is also rare to find any symbol of the deceased's occupation on the slabs, though a plough does appear on one at Carrigtwohill.

There seem to be two main strands in the carvings on the headstones: one tending to the classical and probably derived from the artworks in the Big Houses, the stucco work and the instructions to the masons of their employers. The other runs rather to the Irish traditional story of the cock, which frequently appears as a symmetrical pair very splendidly carved. Above are the cross and the monogram IHS and various designs of foliage or geometric pattern, including little ornamental roundels and sunflowers. The cock story has many versions and it is a symbol of the Resurrection. In one version Mary Magdalene comes to talk to the guards at the tomb. In Douglas Hyde's translation from the Irish, the Roman soldier tells her:

> 'I've a nice little cock which boils in my pot
> While the Camp looks on and sees us,
> And until the cock rises out of the pot,
> He never shall rise, your Jesus.'

Whereupon the cock rises up out of the pot and flaps its wings and crows.

The corners of the design are very often filled with angels and cherubs of varying degrees of beauty or grotesqueness. In east Cork in particular, there is a liking for very lightly incised and very delicate foliage designs – easily wiped out by over-enthusiastic 'cleaning' of the slab. The old graveyard of Clonfert at Newmarket, still with the rings to which to tie the mourners' horses along its wall, has a very remarkable headstone of 1828, with a Crucifixion scene in the style of the penal crosses. On one side is a Roman soldier on foot, and on the other a second soldier on a splendid prancing horse. The same graveyard has, at the opposite extreme, a classical monument of 1869 with a great *Memento Mori* skull and crossbones on it, the skull shown in great and exact detail, even down to missing teeth. The same graveyard has many headstones with the inscription set in an oval medallion which would seem to relate directly to some of the Big House ornamentation.

The gentry might bury their dead not in single ornate tombs, but in a family vault or in a mausoleum, the vault being sunk into the ground, the

[margin notes]
Matehy

Carrigtwohill

Clonfert,
Newmarket

mausoleum or ornate little house rising above the burial vault below. There are the remains of a whole cluster of small mausoleums at the now disused Church of Ireland church at Ballyclough; very fine examples, of the Broderick family at Midleton (Church of Ireland) graveyard and the immense one of the Barrymore family at Castlelyons (Kill St Anne, the possible Dominican site and later Church of Ireland one).

Ballyclough
Midleton
Castlelyons

The material of these monuments is normally limestone, but with some unexpected use of other materials. Cast-iron headstones turn up at intervals, for instance in the graveyard round St Fin Barre's Cathedral and at Coole Abbey. The beautiful Valentia slate makes an occasional appearance, as over one grave in Bantry cemetery.

For a kind of fantasia in carving on Cork limestone one should visit the old part (once the Botanic Garden) of St Joseph's cemetery in Cork city. Yet here there is so much that the impact is lost, and in some ways it is less impressive than the more scattered stones of country graveyards.

St Joseph's
cemetery,
Cork

Charles O'Connell created some solid four-square pillar-like monuments, one complete with the figure of Fr Barry who commissioned him to do the decoration of Coolclogh church. Most Irish headstones do not go beyond the formula of 'Here lies the body of …' with a 'Requiescat in Pace' if they are Catholic, but O'Connell sculpted long eulogies on the Barry monument at Coolclogh. On the front of the monument, with the Barry crest:

Charles O'Connell

This Monument was erected by the parishioners of Dromtariffe to the memory of the Revd John Barry, their parish priest who died August 23rd, 1836. Aged 38 years. Pray for him.

On the panels on opposite sides of the monument, surrounded by lightly incised floral designs:

> To this cold mournful marble we entrust
> Oh sacred priest thy venerated dust
> Lamented Barry, Pastor, Father, Friend'
> Thy flock bereav'd deplore thy early end
> Oh could thy people's prayers avert thy doom
> This weeping verse ne'er marked thy silent tomb'

> Here lie beneath this Monument's base
> A saintly priest he sleeps alone at ease
> His flock he Rul'd with true paternal mind
> His thoughts were pure, to the poor was always kind
> He was gentle, generous and refin'd
> In learning, wit and wisdom he outshin'd
> All who knew him will long his loss deplore
> His name JOHN BARRY alas he is no more

O'Connell worked on another rather similar monument, behind Mallow

Mallow

Catholic church, to James Curtin (died 1833) and Robert Shee (died 1834). Here he carved an exhortation to the reader to kneel and recite the Lord's Prayer which is given in full, and on a second panel, a lengthy prayer for the dead. This monument is signed *Carolus O'Connelli faciebat* (Charles O'Connell made this).

Ballygarvan

Epitaphs of this sort and length are not common but there is another, rather attractive one in the old graveyard at Ballygarvan near Cork airport.

> Lamented Busteed what tho short thy date
> Virtue not rolling Sun the mind matures
> That Life is long which answers Life's great end
> The time that bears no fruit deserves no name
> The Man of Wisdom is the Man of Years
> When kindred forms have mingled into kindred dust
> Congenial spirits meet to part no more
> ELIZA'S gone to join the early partner of her choice
> To Heaven's high will submissive
> Lured from a sinful world disowning death's controul
> Her body to Earth to Christ her ransomed Soul

Passage West
Captain Richard Roberts

At Passage West is the great flat-topped empty tomb of Captain Richard Roberts, RN, the son of the village who pioneered steam and was lost in March 1841 when the PS *President* disappeared on the run back from New York to England. His young wife Jane, with their son ('the little Captain') and aided by her friends, erected this monument, with four ships that he

Raised lettering on limestone headstone, Matehy

Newmarket headstone, 1828

had commanded on its four sides – *Black Joke, Sirius, British Queen* and *President* – and a lengthy inscription in which the mason got the date wrong, putting 1840 for 1841.

This stone commemorates in the churchyard of his native parish the merits and the premature death of the first officer under whose command a steam vessel ever crossed the Atlantic ocean. Undaunted bravery exhibited in the suppression of the slave traffic in the African seas, a character unequalled for enterprise and consummate skill in all the details of his profession recommended for this arduous service Lieutenant Richard Roberts, R.N. In accomplishing it he surpassed not only the wildest visions of former days but even the warmest anticipations of the present: gave to science triumphs she had not dared to hope: and created an epoch for ever memorable in the history of his country and of navigation.

The thousands that shall follow on his track must not forget who it was that first taught the world to traverse with such marvellous rapidity the highway of the oceans and who by thus connecting by a voyage of a few days the eastern and the western hemispheres has for ever linked his name with the greatest achievement of navigation since Columbus first revealed Europe and America to each other.

God, having permitted him this high distinction was pleased to decree that the leader of this great enterprise should also be its martyr. Lieutenant Roberts perished with all on board his ship 'The President' when on her voyage from America to England, she was lost in the month of March A.D. 1840.

Coachford

Gateway and church, Glandore

As the gallant seaman under whose guidance was accomplished an undertaking the results of which centuries will not exhaust it is for his country – for the world to remember to him.

His widow who erects this melancholy memorial may be forgiven if to her even these claims are lost in the recollection of that devotedness of attachment that uprightness and kindness of spirit which – for alas! – but three brief years formed the light and joy of her existence.

Unlike many memorials which are little less than carved lies about the deceased, the Roberts one happens to be true. He was a real pioneer of steam, and his letters to his wife, which have survived, show how very much in love the two of them were.

Very many Irishmen from Cork, and some Irish women in more recent conflicts, served in the British forces. Long lists of the dead of World Wars I and II are to be found in many Church of Ireland churches, and the neat little cut-stone headstones with their appropriate crests appear in country graveyards with brief and telling inscriptions of how men died:

M. O'Brien Chief Stoker HMS *Brontosaurus*. 2 March 1946 aged 38
His brother Joseph, stoker 1st class, was lost at sea, 13.6.1941 age 22 (Ovens)
T. Wingett, Chief Cook SS *Minehaha* 7 Sept. 1917 (Baltimore)
J. Driscol, A/C petty officer HMS *Vivid* 30 Nov. 1915 (Baltimore)
T. McCarthy 3rd Air Mech. Royal Flying Corps 16 March 1918 (Kinneigh)

Inside the churches there are more memorials where the terrible loss of war is honed down to one family's tragedy, the young lad who had gone off so gaily in his new uniform: 'Edward Charles Ellis, Lieut. 1st Royal Munster Fusilliers, Gallipoli, in action, 7 August 1915 aged 26' (Blarney Church of Ireland church).

In the pretty little Church of Ireland Rathclaren (the only church in the county to have a lychgate) is a magnificent memorial set up to a warrior whose career spanned battles from Walcheren to Waterloo and who survived to come home to Cork to die of old age. Flanked by two figures of lancers, the memorial (made by T. Gaffin of 63 Regent Street, London) reads:

In memory of Colonel Sampson Stawell who commanded the XIIth Royal Lancers for XX years and served in that regiment for upwards of XL. He died August 21st 1849 in the 64th year of his age.

This monument was erected by his brother officers as a mark of their esteem for his worth as a gentleman, an officer and a friend. AD MDCCCL.

And below they list his battles: Walcheren, Ciudad Rodrigo, Badajoz, Llerena, Almora, Vittoria, St Sebastian, Nivelle, Nive, Waterloo.

At the other end of the social scale are the Famine pits where the victims were hastily interred. Bantry has a big cross at their site in its cemetery; Macroom has signposted its separate Famine graveyard, off the road from Macroom to Millstreet.

Famine graves

Finally, holy wells sometimes have carved slabs showing the crucifixion, rather in the penal cross style, and in general more in the style of 'folk art' than most of that on the headstones. One such slab is set at Our Lady's well near Carrignavar; another at a Marian well near Farran. Meantime Tully-lease has, now preserved on the wall of the old church, the 'Dancing Master', a figure of St Berchert shown in contemporary, 18th-century costume.

Folk art slab at holy well

XII

Power and Industry

ONE OF THE great turning points in human history was when people thought of harnessing natural energy to work for them. Cork has coal, offshore gas and possibly oil, but until the coming of the steam-engine, water power was the energy resource in general use. There were a few windmills in the county, including one at Youghal shown in early picture maps and on the first edition of the six inch Ordnance maps (1840). Cork city has a Windmill Road, and Liscarroll a Windmill Hill, but these windmills were of little significance in the development of industry in the area.

The water-wheel, the mill-wheel, did nothing but grind grain for centuries. Only gradually was it seen as as source of power to work all kinds of machinery, just as only gradually did people develop the technology to construct more machines to work them. The industrial revolution began on water power, with steam-engines edging in as back-ups, to the extent that 'mill' became the universal term for a factory irrespective of what it produced.

Pounding and grinding in the preparation of food for humans and animals are as old as the art of cookery itself. Boulders with well-worn holes in them, bullaun stones, are very commonly found at early monastic sites and seem, with a wooden or stone pestle, to have been simple mortars for crushing. The earliest quern for grinding was the saddle quern, in which the grain was spread on a smoothed, curved stone and rubbed down with a second stone; the common rotary quern followed it and remained in use from prehistoric times to the present day. Old hand querns are found frequently, especially in the more 'mountainy' parts of the country, where people went on using them to grind small amounts of grain for making bread. The London-based Society for the Encouragement of Arts and Commerce offered, in 1759, among many other prizes, £20 to any parish in whose 'workhouse the greatest quantity of wheat shall be ground into meal, with handmills worked by the poor, in proportion to the number maintained therein, which meal shall be consumed in the said workhouse, or sold out to other persons'. There were second and third prizes of £15 and £10.

But very early on, someone – perhaps the woman of the house tired of the hard effort of working a rotary quern? – saw all the energy and force of the steam going to waste, and the powered quern, the horizontal mill, was born. The wooden mill-wheel, quite small, is fixed horizontally in the flow of water

Bullaun

Quern

and its shaft goes straight up to the pair of millstones immediately above it in the little mill house built over the stream. No gearing is required, and a simple lever allows adjustment of the coarseness or fineness of the meal. It has been suggested that the horizontal mill was invented in China; the first written reference seems to be one by Strabo, *c.* 65 BC, who mentions one in the city of the king of Pontus, Mithridates, on the southern shore of the Black Sea. It is thought that they were introduced to Ireland more or less with Christianity, and dendrochronology (tree-ring dating) has shown a great concentration of the mills with wooden mill houses and flumes to be of the period 770-870 AD. County Cork has produced, and continues to produce, a large number of horizontal mill sites and millstones. In the Cork City Museum, there is a working model of one such early Christian mill, excavated by E. Fahy when the Lee valley was about to be flooded by the hydro-electric scheme.

The mill house was rectangular, with massive timbers from the great trees of the Irish woods, and had a thatched roof. The water was directed, either straight from the stream or by a mill lead, on to the scoop-shaped paddles – about 20 of them normally – of the water-wheel by a flume, a timber channel. These flumes, dug out of the bogs, have sometimes been mistaken for primitive boats or even 'giants' coffins'! The wheel could be stopped by diverting the water from the flumes by sluices in the lead above it. The grain would be fed into the stones by hand, or in the later, more sophisticated versions of the mill, by a hopper, jiggled by a block of wood in the upper stone, to keep the grain moving down.

Horizontal mills of this sort worked in the Scottish Hebrides until the end of the 19th century; the one of Tamnavay in the island of Lewis worked up to the 1890s. Its mill house was built of drystone masonry as many in Ireland may have been in the stonier parts of the country. They continued in use in the west of Ireland to around the same period. At the present time there are no recent dates for the Cork examples. An enormous amount of timber turned up in 1979 at Little Island in Cork Harbour during development work for the industrial estate there, and was dated to the 7th century. It is thought that it represents several mills rather than a single one, and that there could have been a tide-mill. Tide-mills work by letting the sea fill the millpond at high tide and then controlling the outflow of the full pond by sluices to the mill lead.

Very massive and complete timbers of a mill house were found long ago at Aghabulloge near Coachford. Other Cork sites include Keelaraheen and Farranmareen (both found in the 1970s) and Desert south of Castlelyons. Some seven horizontal millstones are scattered about the forest beside the old church site of Desert; the timbers which turned up during the forestry planting seem to have been lost. One of the stones is a large erratic of Galway granite. Choice of the right rock for millstones is important. People might fetch stones from some specially suitable quarry at a distance, though

Horizontal mill

Aghabulloge
Keelaraheen
Farranmareen
Desert

in the early days they must have used what was locally available, pouncing on such a lucky find as a big boulder of granite. In Cork, sandstones and conglomerates appear frequently in the old millstones. Skulls of people who ate bread from flour ground by millstones often show the teeth well worn down by the grit from the stone that inevitably got into the flour. Choice of a sufficiently hard, fine-grained, non-friable millstone eliminates this unwanted gritty material completely. The 1,323-feet-high Carrigeenamronety in the Ballyhoura mountains, just over the Limerick border from north Cork, was one quarry for millstones of conglomerate and coarse sandstone; many half finished or broken stones are still lying there today.

Vertical mill

The more familiar type of mill is the big one with the vertical wheel and a system of gearing from its shaft to the millstones in the mill house alongside. This mill was first described by a Roman engineer called Vitruvius, between 20 and 11 BC, and it is possible that he invented the system. The use of this new mill spread slowly across Europe, reaching England in the 8th century or thereabouts and probably being introduced to Ireland by the continental religious Orders and the Anglo-Normans. Very many of the medieval monasteries owned mills: the Dominicans in Cork, the Canons Regular in Bridgetown, the Cistercians in Midleton and Fermoy all had one each, and the Cork Augustinian friars had a share in two. In 1590 William Lyons, Church of Ireland Bishop of Ross, was short of iron for a mill he was constructing and so took it from the Franciscans' mill at Timoleague, together with, it appears, the millstones. However, it is said that he had his trouble for nothing, as the river rose in spate and destroyed his new mill!

Industrial revolution

The industrial revolution produced an enormous improvement in mill-wheel technology and power. The first cast-iron water-wheel shaft came in 1769; between 1820 and 1850, mill-wheels generating 100 hp were being made. And this in the early days of steam: a steam-engine might even be used to pump the water up to work a water-wheel! With new powerful water-wheels, a whole series of millstones could be operated in one mill, and the typical very tall building began to appear, up to six stories high.

In Cork, the building of new big mills dates from the second half of the 18th century and it goes hand in hand with expanding and improving

Pavement of old millstones found in excavation of Glanworth Castle

agriculture. The big landowners developed their estates, grew bigger and better crops of grain on the large, fenced fields, and the mills bought it, dried it, ground it and sold it. The medieval mill had ground local people's grain for them; the new mills were engaged in commerce and mass production. All along the Cork rivers and even on quite small streams, stand the remains and ruins of great mills, often with very ingenious systems for leading water from the stream to the mill-wheel.

An account book of Leader's Mill (the property of Mr Leader, of the family that owned much of the land in the Banteer/Millstreet district of north-west Cork) survives for the period 16 September 1837 to 28 September 1838. Mill workers seem to have been paid about 5s (25p) per week. The book records amounts paid out:

Value of wheat purchased	£4,812.0.0
Paid out to William Leader	£3,262.0.0
Mill wages	£152.0.0
Running expenses, sundry wages etc.	£162.8.9
	£8,388.8.9

Rineen, beautifully situated at the head of the sea inlet of Castlehaven in West Cork, is probably the oldest Cork mill still working. Owned by R. Good and Sons at the present time, it is said that it goes back to the 17th century, though the present building would be 18th century. Externally it was originally weather slated; inside, the structure is of massive timbers of great age, one immense beam is at least 50 feet long. To be of that size at that period it is likely that all the timber was imported. Water came from a local stream in a long, carefully built lead, which is still extant, and worked the second largest water-wheel in all Ireland. In its later days, at least, the wheel was of iron with wooden paddles. In 1924 the wheel was replaced by a turbine, a more efficient way of using water power, which generated 24 hp. This was again replaced by a petrol/paraffin engine, an anthracite gas producer engine generating 56 hp and finally a Crossley of Manchester diesel engine

Rineen

Rineen mill, from an old postcard showing what was the biggest water-wheel in Ireland

of 66 hp with a flywheel weighing three tons – these last two engines still survive in the mill. The Crossley, as well as working the mill, generated electricity for the mill and the mill house alongside (now a restaurant) at 110 volts. Finally the mill went over to the national, ESB, supply of electricity. It presently makes a variety of animal feeds.

In the old days of grinding corn, the grain came in from as far off as Timoleague. 'Yellow meal' – maize – was also ground. Boats came into the estuary as far as the deep pool (the Poul Gorm) at its head, where the grain was unloaded by wooden buckets into lighters. These were then poled up from the Poul Gorm over the shallows, at the top of the tide, to the wharf and hoist of the mill. When maize first came into Cork as part of the Famine relief programme, the Cork mills had difficulty in grinding this very hard grain and had to run it through the millstones twice.

Crookstown

At Crookstown, Howard's Mills ('One Way' flour) are the only millers in Cork to continue to use the old-fashioned millstones to grind the wheat. The result has a special flavour and texture which the modern roller mills are quite unable to copy. The stones have to be taken down and refaced every three to six months. The grooves on the two faces run in opposite directions, so that the grain encounters a cutting action as the stones revolve. The Howards' millstones were imported from England.

The original mill seems to have been further upriver. The Howards owned a number of mills in Cork and eventually concentrated on this one, which still has its foundation stone dated 1810, though it is possible there was an older, earlier building on the site. A mile of carefully built lead brought water from the West Cork river Bride to a mill-wheel which was later

Old mill, Schull

Old corn-mills, Shannon Vale near Clonakilty

replaced by a powerful turbine. Sluices allowed the water to be cut off from the mill intake at night by diverting the water back into the river at two points. On one of these it cascaded down in a waterfall to a pool and in the morning the man going to open the sluice gate again might find a salmon in the pool. The turbine was replaced by a steam-engine, then from 1926 to 1958 by a diesel one, after which the mills switched to electricity. The buildings have been steadily added to and enlarged; animal feeds are made as well as flour for human consumption. The first weighbridge was installed in 1955; before then each sack was individually weighed and, in the days of the Macroom-Cork railway, brought up to the mill from the station in horse-drawn carts. Howards are a closely knit firm in which people tend to work all their lives and there is no fixed retirement age.

In Macroom, Creedon's Mills still use millstones for the production of Macroom Oatmeal. The old mill building had a long lead from the Sullane River, and had a turbine generating up to 35 hp. Here, too, water power has been replaced by electricity.

By far the most ingenious use of water power in Cork was, and is, that of the city's water supply. Above the city, on the river Lee, the Duke of Devonshire had a corn-mill and a weir to control its water supply, which also served as a salmon weir. The first proposal for a public water supply for Cork city came in 1761; the act establishing the Cork Pipe Water Company was passed in 1762, and permission was then sought from the duke to erect a water-wheel at his weir for pumping water. The idea was for a sort of perpetual motion: the river would turn the wheel and pump up its own water to a reservoir about 80 feet above the hillside, from which it would run down under gravity to the customers' houses. The foundation stone, dated 1768, is still in the present turbine house. At that time, it was not possible to cast iron pipes to carry the water and wooden ones were used, each log about 20 feet long and hollowed out to carry the water, giving a channel about two and a half to three inches in diameter. Each log was carefully socketed into the next and there were iron straps round the joins. These timbers have turned up in road work in Cork city, notably in the South Terrace in 1970, and examples are on display in the City Museum. The City Library has a list

Macroom

Cork city

Water supply

Original wooden water pipes preserved
in Cork City Museum

of all houses being supplied in 1809.

As the city grew, so did the water works. The original water-wheel was replaced by powerful turbines; in 1863 Cornish beam engines were added, to assist when the water level was low and power lacking. More and higher reservoirs were constructed, at 196 feet at Shanakiel in 1858, and then at Hollyhill at 386 feet above sea level. More beam engines appeared in 1869; the water mains were running out as far as Blackrock and iron pipes were being laid. (Iron pipes had been cast in England as early as 1846.) Ordinary river water was supplied until the first filter tunnel was installed in 1879.

In 1888 the weir was rebuilt, and the turbine house and new pumps and turbines were installed in 1890. Much of the ironwork for the turbines was done in Cork by two iron-founders: Perrott, of Hive Ironworks, and Merrick. The plant still has some of the wooden patterns of the different parts needed to be cast: cogs, pipes and so on. These had to be very carefully fashioned, so that the new cast-iron part would be an exact fit.

Engine and turbine houses, Cork city water works

By 1901 the original Cornish engine was on its last legs and the others were showing signs of wear; they were replaced by a new steam plant, erected in 1905. This new plant, consisting of three triple expansion marine type engines, worked continuously until 1938 and thereafter as needed intermittently until some time after World War II. The first diesel, a Blackstone, was installed in 1927, and in 1938 the first electric pumps arrived. Today the whole complex, opposite the County Hall at the western entrance to the city, forms an enchanting sight, reflected in the calm river water above the weir: the turbine house, in which the turbines still work away; the now empty engine-house of the old beam engine; the second house with its tall chimney in which the later steam-engines are conserved; and at low level the present group of electric pumps and filter plant. The old buildings are beautifully constructed in the red and grey checker of Cork: grey limestone, red sandstone and red brick. The whole represents a remarkable piece of industrial archaeology still at work. Reservoir levels have, of course, gone higher still, and with the growth of Cork's new industrial estates a second water supply plant has been built at Inniscarra higher on the Lee.

In the earlier days of operation, salmon were often taken by the men working in the turbine house. However, while this was accepted as a regular 'perk', there were limits. In July 1896 J. Tobin was dismissed as nightwatchman for aiding and abetting poachers in stroke-hauling in the tailrace of the turbines. At this period men worked at the plant six days a week from 7 a.m. to 6 p.m., but finishing at 2 p.m. on Saturdays. Further work – the pumping plant had to be manned continuously, seven days a week – counted as overtime.

It may be of interest to note how much water was being used by Cork city at that period, when by no means all the houses were connected up, and those who did have it used less than we do today. For the period 1 to 7 January 1894 the engines pumped as follows:

Pumped by steam	14,010,000 gallons:
Horizontal beam engine	12,260,000
West Beam engine	270,000
East Beam engine	1,480,000
Pumped by water	27,740,000 gallons:
New turbine	11,100,000
North turbine	8,300,000
South turbine	8,340,000

The famous Dripsey Woollen Mills in the Lee valley started life as a corn-mill. The Dripsey River, a tributary of the Lee, was dammed back to form a large reservoir lake – today forming a lovely ornamental feature to Dripsey House and the old tower-house of Carrignamuck. From the reservoir, a long

Dripsey

lead brought the water to the corn-mill lower down. The mill was turned over to woollen manufacture in about 1860, and its character entirely changed as new buildings began to spread from the original site. A water-wheel powering a factory requires quite a complex system of drive-shafts, running the length of the long buildings, from which belts take the power to the individual machines below. Later, water was replaced by steam (the old furnace chimney still stands) and then by electricity.

Dripsey was the only wool-mill left in Munster until, unhappily, it closed in 1989. Wool was bought both locally and from all over the world, and they worked the coarse fibres of the Kerry sheep and the very fine ones of the Australian – the drier the climate the finer the wool. They used the natural browns and greys of Scandinavian sheep, which is popular for hand-knitting. The mills carried out the entire process from the arrival of the raw wool, through carding, spinning and weaving, producing everything from blankets and heavy tweeds to the finest of light wool materials.

Blarney, harnessing the water of the Shournagh River, was, on the other hand, conceived as an industrial estate producing woollens and linens. The Jeffreys of Blarney Castle, aided by the Royal Dublin Society and the Irish Linen Board, laid it out in 1750, with the workers' houses built of stone with slate roofs and set around a square. There were four new bridges, a church, and a market house. When Arthur Young was travelling Ireland at the end of the century he found Blarney producing linen, woollen, stockings and leather: 130 looms were at work and 300 people employed (see Appendix IV). English competition killed the project and when Crofton Croker visited Blarney in 1821 the square was grass-grown and some of the houses roofless. But this was not the end of the Blarney story, for the woollen mills were revived and by 1890 Martin Mahony was employing 750 people. Like Dripsey, the Blarney mills carried out the whole process from raw wool to finished product – this was quite exceptional in the late 19th century. Water power again gave way to steam (first coal-fired and, towards the end, oil-fired) and then electricity. The mill closed in the mid-1970s and the old

Blarney

Blarney mill complex

buildings, displaying many photos of its past activities, have been sensitively converted into a hotel.

Midleton, on the other hand, had a mill built in 1796 for the woollen industry but it never functioned and the building was used for a while as a barracks. Soldiers scratched their names on the walls before embarking for Waterloo, for Midleton is on an inlet of Cork Harbour and had its own little port at Ballynacorra. Then in 1825 the brothers Murphy turned the place into a distillery, and today, alongside the carefully conserved old buildings, Irish Distillers have one of the most modern plants in Europe, producing nearly all the Irish brands of spirit – whisky, gin and vodka.

The old buildings are of cut limestone (Midleton is in a limestone district) with red brick facings, and there is a gracious house and garden built for the distillery manager. Irish Distillers conserve the old buildings, the great water-wheel – said to be the largest in Ireland – and the 1825 steam beam engine. The lead for the water-wheel took water to two more mills downstream and was known as the 'golden stream'. An elderly worker recalled to me how, at the age of four, he would be taken by his father after Mass to watch him stoke up the furnace for the beam engine. It was used to back up the water-wheel when the water level was low. The engine has a massive flywheel, ornate fluted columns to support the frame around it and decorated iron panels on the sides. In the old buildings, too, is the world's largest pot-still, which held 31,648 gallons of the once much-loved Midleton whisky. In the attractively landscaped plant alongside, both pot-stills and column-stills are in use for the production of the various spirits and brands.

Water power was harnessed everywhere in Cork, from the enormous

Millstones for grinding barytes, Schull

Wool-mill chimney, Reenascreena

barrack-like mills on the Blackwater, Awbeg and Funshion, to the tiny little mill at Schull, the last mill on the Mizen peninsula, and over to which the islanders from the islands in Roaring Water Bay would sail with their grain to be ground. There were starch-mills (making starch from potatoes), paper-mills, tuck-mills (shrinking woollens after weaving), shovel-mills and powder-mills. One extraordinary concentration is the series of old mills and mill sites along the little stream that comes down to the harbour at Glanmire, some two dozen in all. Quite a small stream was here skilfully used to produce the maximum power; the site was a very favourable one, in easy reach of Cork city and of the harbour (small boats used to come right up to Glanmire village) and the valley has many pleasant locations on which mill-owners and merchants could build their homes.

The principal stream at Glanmire is the Glashaboy, but it is joined by the Butlerstown River coming in from the east at Riverstown. The total of mills for these two streams appears to be seven corn-mills, one flax-mill, four woollen mills, one linen, one cotton, one starch, four paper-mills, and two shovel-mills making spades. There was a tannery, the first mill in Ireland to make pearl barley, and the Copper Alley mill which bottled spring water. Of the shovel-mills, that at Templemichael, high up in the northern section of the Glashaboy, is important in that, until it closed sometime in the 1950s, the shaft of its mill-wheel was that of the PS *Sirius,* salvaged after the famous ship was wrecked on one of her ordinary cross-Channel trips, at Ballycotton. The shaft is now preserved at Passage West.

Templemichael

Beside the little corn-mill at Schull was another that ground barytes ('heavy spar', barium sulphate) mined in the adjacent hills of West Cork and then shipped out. Another barytes mill was at the Falls of Dunamark at the head of Bantry Bay, where there are still quite extensive remains of the old buildings below the waterfalls .

Schull

Dunamark

A most unusual transport system operated at Glandalane Mill, downstream on the Blackwater from Fermoy. Here the old mill (now ruined and partly dismantled) was set on the river-bank with the ground rising steeply to the south behind it. A water-wheel was used, later replaced by a turbine, and everything was worked by water power. That included the aerial ropeway, set on derricks, which ran up from the mill, over the fields south of it and up to the station on the (now closed) Fermoy-Waterford railway line. Thus farmers brought their grain to the station: it went down the aerial ropeway to the mill and the sacks of flour came back up to the railway.

Glandalane

In what was then Douglas village, water power was used by the Huguenot family of Besnard to start a linen industry which was said to be the first in Ireland to operate power-driven spindles. It produced sailcloth and was established in 1726. The material was excellent and was widely used for sails by the British navy. The industry fell into decline with the coming of peace in 1815. In that year, between January and August 1815, Douglas produced 78,426 yards of sailcloth and 37,752 yards of raven, duck and light canvas.

Douglas

Around that time, some 1,000 people were employed in making sails and, under the same owners, ropes, at nearby Donnybrook.

Although Cork no longer spins flax and weaves linen cloth, it does provide yachtsmen with some of the world's most skilfully designed sails. John MacWilliam, with a background of flying in the RAF as well as in sailing, has applied the principles of aerodynamics to the business of sail-making, with great success. It is a curious fact that only after the study of the lift-producing forces acting on an airplane's wings has come the realisation of how the same forces act on a sail, and therefore how best to use it to propel a ship. MacWilliam's sail-making business is in the old mill at Hoddersfield near Crosshaven, sensitively restored and adapted. This was a small mill, mainly for the Big House (now ruined) alongside and, being high up on the hillside, water was allowed to drain from the land into a pond to provide sufficient head to work the mill intermittently. *Sail-making*

Of the shovel-mills, those at Monard near Blarney were the most extensive and interesting; they only closed in 1960. Unhappily the opportunity to conserve this very important piece of industrial archaeology was not then taken, but the present owner is working hard to preserve what remains. *Shovel-mills*

Monard (the high bog) is a wonderful example of the 'gleg e'en' (sharp eye) in the Scots phrase, of a person looking for a place to site an industry and harness water power. The Blarney River, a small stream in its headwaters, plunges into a deep, narrow glen. By throwing a series of dams across this valley and creating three reservoirs, a considerable amount of water power could be fed to the works which, with some of the workers' cottages, were built in the floor of the little valley. About 100 men worked in Monard in the four factories powered by the three reservoirs. Each of the four had its own manager; in the final years of the shovel-mills they all sold the finished products to Scotts of Cork city. They made not only shovels but forks, gates, fencing – almost anything in metal. And they made shovels (spades) and slanes (for cutting turf) for virtually the whole of Ireland. Every parish and district had its chosen shape for a spade and a slane and Monad had all their different patterns, supplying the right one for each place when ordered. Cork City Museum holds a set of all these different *Monard*

Monard shovel-mill machinery

spades and slanes for the different parts of the country.

The iron billets for the spades and slanes were heated red-hot in furnaces (the workers got free coal, too, and the narrow little valley must have been constantly overhung by a cloud of smoke) and then were hammered into shape by the big trip-hammers. The trip-hammers were powered by very large and massive wooden water-wheels. More delicate wheels, of iron with wooden paddles, provided power for the rest of the machinery, with over-head drive-shafts and belting. In a dry season when water ran low the high-est mill, with the biggest trip-hammer, had to shut down temporarily; when it was working, people in the vicinity felt its every thump transmitted through the ground. In its later days, Monard used diesel and petrol engines as well for power. A list of their power sources for 12 August 1952 reads:

1	. . .	0.5 hp motor
2	. . .	1 hp motor
2	. . .	2.5 hp motor
4	. . .	3 hp motor
5	. . .	5 hp motor
2	. . .	25 hp Deizel (sic) Engines
3	'Metal' water-wheels, approx 2.5-3 hp each	
5	'Timber' water-wheels, approx 12 hp each	

Ballincollig Gunpowder Mills

While the Monard shovel-mills are contained within the narrow confines of a tiny glen, the Ballincollig Gunpowder Mills sprawl over many level acres of land beside the Lee. A weir across the whole river directed some of its water into a series of canals which not only provided water transport (avoid-ing fire danger from road transport with its risk of sparks) but power for the actual mills. Lewis in his *Topographical Dictionary* gives a vivid description of the Powder Mills as they were in the 1830s: 'occupying a space nearly four miles in extent, are the Gunpowder Mills, 16 in number. At convenient distances are the different establishments for granulating and drying the gunpowder, making charcoal, refining sulphur and saltpetre, and making casks and hoops, and the various machinery connected with the works; the whole communicating with each other and with the mills, by means of small canals constructed for facility of carriage, and for preventing such accidents as might occur from other modes of conveyance. In appropriate situations, and near these establishments, are the residences of the different persons superintending the works; and at the eastern extremity of the ground, but at a considerable distance from the mills, are two ranges of comfortable cottages for a portion of the work people, now tenanted by 54 families who obtain a comfortable livelihood. The number of persons employed is about 200, and the quantity of gunpowder manufactured annually is about 16,000 barrels.'

Thus the entire process was carried out on the 400-acre site at Ballincollig, making charcoal from locally grown alder, willow, hazel and dogwood (different kinds of gunpowder require different woods); purifying the imported Sicilian sulphur and the saltpetre which came from the East Indies; and making the casks in which the finished product would be exported. The actual mills have enormous limestone millstones, a soft rock suitable for the gentle grinding required for gunpowder. They are set in line with baffle walls between them to limit the effect of an explosion, the canal carrying the water on one side, with branches from it through each mill and its water-wheel, and an outlet beyond into the Lee. The big stones revolved on their edges, not face to face as with ordinary mills, in a circular channel, and were used to crush the actual gunpowder mix, which varied in composition with the use to which it would be put.

The *Cork Advertiser* of 15 May 1856 described the whole process at Ballin-collig in detail, including mention of the big 16 hp turbine lately constructed by Perrott's of Cork to operate the saws making the casks. At this time 500 men, women and children were employed, and a family might earn 'upwards of three guineas [£3.15] a week'; in addition, their houses were rent free. The writer of the article, after describing the canal system, goes on to remark: 'this canal is continually enlivened by the passage to and fro of numbers of large boats, by which sulphur, saltpetre, charcoal and gun-powder in various stages of completion, are transferred from place to place'.

The Ballincollig mills worked from 1794 right through the 19th century and seem to have been reasonably free of serious explosions, though one bad explosion did occur just before they closed. Serious danger was, however, posed by smuggling out powder for sale to quarrymen. Thus on 3 November 1810 three houses in Brandy Lane (now St Finbar's Road) were blown up, with a number of people killed and injured. In August of 1803 a load of gunpowder going through Cork had a leak from one of its barrels in George's Street, which a spark from a horse's hoof set alight, resulting in an exploding trail down the road, which caused much alarm but no damage. In 1806, not unreasonably, the city magistrates got the government to agree to stop all carrying of powder through the city and its storage at Charlotte Quay, and that it should be routed around the town to 'Blackrock or some place equally distant'.

In the Catholic church in Ballincollig a tablet records that: 'In honour of St Joseph, patron of the universal Church, this altar has been erected by the men of the Powder Mills, Ballincollig. AD 1879.' Today the remains of the old mills are being conserved and the wide area over which the works were distributed beside the river Lee is a public park.

Just east of Macroom was a large corn-mill, with Macroom Engineering Works alongside, and in 1898 a small water-driven generator was set up at the mills. This provided Macroom with electric light, making it one of the first Irish towns to have its streets so lit. In 1906 the mill-owner, Mr Looney, asked that he should not be required to provide power on the two nights

Macroom

after the full moon, when it might be expected that moonlight would suffice.

In 1952 the Electricity Supply Board began work to harness the waters of the Lee and of its tributary the Sullane, which flows through Macroom, and produce not a little trickle of power that needs to be conserved on moonlit nights but, in a year of average rainfall, no less than 77 million units. The work involved the construction of a very large dam (800 feet long and 350 feet high) at Inniscarra, and a smaller one at Carrigadrohid (140 feet long and 70 feet high), each with its own power station and turbines. The whole of the Lee valley above Inniscarra, and back even as far as the Gearagh, was flooded and the district's roads re-routed. As an amenity, the new valley lake is an improvement, a very attractive stretch of water, and one on which boating and water-skiing are popular. Passes allow salmon to get round the dams. The dams and the two power stations have been well landscaped and blend with the new face of the Lee valley. They began producing power in 1957.

Gas drilling

In 1970 Marathon's first drilling ship began to explore the undersea resources off the coast of Cork. It brought a whole new dimension to the maritime scene in Cork: new sorts of vessels and platforms, specialised ships to serve them, and the regular scurrying back and forth of helicopters from Cork airport to the rigs. I flew out over some 30 miles of sea to look at the first drilling ship, out of sight of land, and found her securely anchored, at work investigating the rocks of the Continental Shelf some 300 feet below her. In 1971 the first finds of gas were made and further drilling went on to estimate its potential. The result was a commercial find of exceptionally pure methane gas in a quantity estimated at the time to equal 40 million tons of coal, in the Cretaceous-Wealden sandstones at a depth of over 3,000 feet. Two drilling platforms, Alpha and Bravo, were erected to work the gasfield, and a pipeline was laid from them to the Cork coast at Inch, a distance of 38 miles. (The pipe itself was of steel, from a Japanese firm, but its cladding was made by the Cork firm of John A. Wood.) At Inch the petroleum company hands over the supply to Bórd Gais Éireann. The first delivery of natural gas came on 1 October 1978.

Marino

Aghada

It was piped to Cork, to the NET fertiliser plant at Marino Point in the harbour, and to the ESB, where it is used both in the Marino plant in Cork city and at the new Aghada power station in Cork Harbour, close to the old World War I American seaplane base. Aghada is a striking building, the steam generator plant some 50 metres high, and the slender chimney rising far above it with its bright red bands and plume of steam. It was built to utilise Kinsale gas and completed in 1980. Its main unit generates 270 megawatts. The whole sophisticated plant is controlled from a room resembling a modern ship's bridge with its wide view over the harbour and arrays of instruments, lights and TV. It is a world away from old-style industrial activity, in which men worked alongside machines all the time, engaged in continual manual effort. Now the machines do the work alone and men sit

In the left margin:
Inniscarra
Carrigadrohid

at monitoring control panels.

A pipeline was laid for 138 miles from Cork to Dublin to bring natural gas to the capital city, where it arrived in December 1982. From the air, the route of the pipeline showed as a broad track, different in colour and texture from the surrounding land even though carefully landscaped back after the pipe was laid. The archaeology department of University College, Cork, carried out exploration and excavation of all the archaeological sites along the route which the pipeline would destroy. Spur lines to Limerick, Mallow and Waterford were added in 1986 and further archaeological discoveries were made along their routes.

Gas pipeline

Within Cork's university complex at the Maltings is the National Micro-electronics Research Centre where Cork-born Gerry Wrixton was responsible for harnessing solar energy at Fota estate. Here 40,000 solar cells, each measuring 10 cms x 10 cms, trapped the sun's energy and generated enough power to run the farm's milking machine for 250 cows, refrigeration plant and lights. With the sale of Fota, this installation shut down. The university has in addition, in its engineering department, a unit investigating wave power and how it could be harnessed. Out on the Bull Rock with its lighthouse off the coast of West Cork, they have been experimenting with the cave that runs through the rock. There is a blowhole through the roof of the cave and the investigation is concerned with whether the air being forced through this, as the waves surge into the cave, can be utilised to drive a turbine which could heat the lighthouse.

Energy research

XIII

Riches from the Earth, Mines and Quarries

COUNTY CORK TODAY has the appearance of a pastoral rather than a mining county, but a whole litany of minerals have, in fact, been found and exploited in it. Copper, iron, lead, manganese, barytes, coal, some small amounts of silver and traces of gold occur here.

Bronze Age Mount Gabriel

The history of Cork mining begins in the south-west in the Bronze Age. On the southern slopes of Mount Gabriel above Schull are some 30 small mines, little tunnels dug into the mountainside, from which the ore was extracted by fire setting: lighting a fire and then throwing water on the hot rocks so that they split off. Beach boulders were carried up from the shore to use as mauls; some of them have a groove to hold a thong binding the stone to a handle. Oak, hazel and willow were used for the fire setting, and for making the charcoal to smelt the ore. In 1985 Dr William O'Brien carried out a very full excavation of some of the Mount Gabriel mines. Their special interest lies in that they were covered up by a massive peat growth, now being eroded away, and so they remained untouched since the miners of the early Bronze Age abandoned them. Dr O'Brien writes that his work has 'confirmed that the Mount Gabriel workings are the oldest radiocarbon-dated copper mines in north-west Europe, and as such, a unique part of the Irish archaeological landscape. A major feature of these mines is the quality of preservation, in particular on Mount Gabriel which was spared the ravages of post-medieval mineral exploitation and mining seen elsewhere in the region.'

Derrycarhoon

At Derrycarhoon, about five miles north-east of Mount Gabriel, peat cover was 14 feet thick. Under it were found wooden and stone tools, a curved tube of oak and a primitive ladder – just an oak pole with steps cut in it. There are other probable early mines in West Cork but only if they have this protective peat cover can one be sure they are ancient – later trial pits would look very similar.

The concentration of the early copper mines in the districts with numerous wedge-tombs has led to the suggestion that the miners and tomb builders were one and the same people. As there is no tin in Ireland, and copper needs to be alloyed with it to make serviceable bronze tools, they must have imported tin from Cornwall.

In Cork there is then a sudden jump from the early Bronze Age mining to the 19th-century workings, when the Industrial Revolution required huge quantities of copper. So, in the 19th century, copper mines sprang up everywhere: at Allihies; down the Sheep's Head peninsula; on the Mizen in a whole series – between Ballydehob and Schull, at Brow Head and out on Horse Island and Long Island. Allihies was the biggest and most profitable and working went on there until 1908 with brief re-openings (1918-20 and 1927-30). Can-Erin explored again in 1956 with extensive drilling and in the mid-1970s the Argosy Mining Corporation of Canada found traces of uranium.

Allihies, on the Beara peninsula, shows a hillside scarred and pocked by workings; old engine-houses standing dramatically against the skyline. The deposits were discovered in 1812 and exploited by the Puxley family, whose (now ruined) grandiose mansion at Dunboy was built from the profits. Meantime, Castletownbere developed as a town and harbour to service the mines. Cornish miners were brought in as the technical experts and lived in their own Cornish village, of which some ruins remain. The chimneys for the mine steam-engines are the typical Cornish ones, stone-built below with the top of the chimney in brick. There is a very fine example of a Cornish chimney at Cappaghglass near Ballydehob.

Allihies

Lady Chatterton, author of *Rambles in the South of Ireland during the Year 1838*, visited Allihies bearing a letter of introduction to the Protestant (Church of Ireland) chaplain of the mines. At that time about 1,000 were employed. Girls, washing ore, got 3½d (just over 1½p), boys 6d (2½p), men 1s (5p) to 1s 4d a day. The higher paid men were those who handled the gunpowder for blasting the rock. The actual miners seem to have worked by 'task work', a gang undertaking to produce so much ore at so much per ton. Steam-engines were at work throughout the mines, operating all the machines, including crushers and pounders, and pumping water from the deep workings. One engine was sited 160 feet down in a working, with a long vent for its smoke coming up to the surface. The chaplain was a steam

Lady Chatterton

Allihies

Copper mining village ruins, Horse Island

enthusiast, and led Lady Chatterton around to visit all five of the Allihies engines: 'Our reverend guide was extremely polite, but I thought rather too fond of steam-engines, of the construction of which I must confess myself very ignorant, although I can not help seeing the revolution they are effecting everywhere and in everything,' she wrote afterwards.

Lewis
Cappaghglass

Lewis, in *A Topographical Dictionary of Ireland*, describes the Cappaghglass mines and those on Horse Island just off the coast there, at about the same date. 'Some very extensive mines have been opened on the summit of Cappach hill by the proprietor, Lord Audley; they were subsequently worked by the Irish Mining Company, but are now rented by the West Cork Mining Company, who have for a time suspended their operations here while they are working the mines in Horse Island, about 1½ miles distant; the ore found at Cappach and Horse Island is very pure.'

Horse Island

Borlin

There are some other small copper workings in the Borlin valley up from the head of Bantry Bay. A local tradition in Borlin is of an English company who were cheated by the local managers, living well and drinking whisky, not by the bottle but by the keg, and now and again sending a small consignment of copper ore over to England to encourage their employers.

Somerville and Ross

The West Cork mining companies seem to have had a passion for litigation, preferring to take their rivals to court rather than get on with the business of extracting copper! Somerville and Ross's story 'Harrington's', in the *Irish R.M.* series, gives a vivid picture of an unsuccessful West Cork mine.

Iron

Returning to prehistory, bronze gave way to iron; a curious development in some ways, since it is not as hard, rusts easily and is more difficult to smelt. Iron ores need to be roasted first, then smelted, a more difficult process and at higher temperatures than are needed for copper. Bronze can be cast at about 950 degrees celcius but 1,500 degrees celcius are needed to melt iron. The early furnaces could only get up to 1,200 degrees celcius, so the process was very laborious – smelting the ore with charcoal to end up with a spongy mass of iron bloom, which needed to be hammered, reheated and hammered again – to get a small mass of metal. Some of the carbon from the charcoal remained in the iron and made it harder, though it was only in the 18th century that scientists worked out that carbon hardened iron to steel. Professor M. J. O'Kelly of University College, Cork, was the first modern person to set up a primitive furnace and actually get it to produce a small amount of iron. While he used a thermo-couple to check on temperature, people long ago had only their senses and experience to work from, but seem to have managed well enough. Iron slag is a common find at early Irish excavations, and most ring fort owners probably smelted iron as it was required. Some iron ore was mined, and it is likely that the frequently occurring bog ore provided a ready source of supply.

There seems a considerable gap in the historical record of iron-smelting in the county between the small, temporary furnace sites of the ring fort dwellers and the large-scale ironworks of the 17th century. Vast forests attracted the iron masters as an enormous source of charcoal for smelting; both in Ireland and the Scottish Highlands, the native forests were clean-felled and destroyed, whereas in the iron-smelting districts of England, they were coppiced and allowed to shoot up again for further felling. In 1709 the Quaker Abraham Darby (1667-1717) showed that coke could be used for smelting, but the new process had to wait until the 1760s to come into general use, when steam-engines were available to boost the furnace blast.

Oak, one of the native forest trees of Ireland, was specially suitable for making charcoal for smelting. Two and a quarter tons of charcoal was needed to make a ton of bar-iron, so vast amounts of timber were needed. For the most part the iron ore came in by ship to the port nearest the forests, and if necessary then went inland on horseback. When the trees had all gone the ironworks closed. Thus Charles Smith (1750) wrote about the ironworks at Coomhola at the head of Bantry Bay (where a townland, Mill Little, is named for them): 'The iron furnaces at Comolin, have been in a thriving condition for some years past; but wood begins to grow very scarce'.

Eileen McCracken, in *The Irish Woods Since Tudor Times*, lists the following ironworks in County Cork – they are concentrated round Cork Harbour, and along the Blackwater in particular: Araglin (1625-1770), Adrigole, Awenbeg, Bantry (1684), Ballynetra (1606-38), Bandon (1642), Castle Martyr (1764), Clonmeen (1660-90), Coomhola (1701), Cork city (1740-97), Dunboy (1680), Dundaniel (1611-41), Fermoy, Glanmire (early 18th century), Glengarriff, Greenfield (mid-18th century), Kilmacow (1606-22), Macroom (early 17th century), Mogeely (1593), Roaring Water Bay (early 18th century), and Youghal (1607).

Richard Boyle, the Great Earl, was one of the chief iron masters of the early period, together with Sir William Petty, who had a number of iron-works in Kerry. Boyle set up ironworks on the Raleigh estates along the Blackwater. He had a double furnace at Cappoquin in County Waterford on that river, from which he could promise to sell Bristol a thousand tons of sow-iron a year at £5 a ton. English buyers, however, thought Irish iron was inferior to English, but Boyle then scouted around and in 1622 got a contract to supply the Dutch. He then improved his technology, moving from simple ingots of sow-iron to bar-iron, which sold at up to £13 per ton but needed a forge as well as a furnace to produce. By 1625 he was actually casting cannon at Cappoquin.

The blast furnace bellows were driven by a water-wheel, and a vast number of people were employed in such ironworks – to fell the timber, cart it, burn it for charcoal, cart the charcoal to the furnaces, and carry out the actual smelting and forging. The longest-lived of the ironworks started by Boyle are those on the lovely valley of the Araglin, a tributary of the Blackwater near Kilworth. Here a few walls of some of the old buildings still stand, and the local people used to use some of the surviving heaps of imported haematite, a reddish iron ore, to crush up and colour wash the walls of their houses in a

Coomhola

Ironworks

Richard Boyle

Araglin

mauve colour. It was some of this haematite from Araglin that Professor O'Kelly used in his successful experiments with a primitive iron furnace.

Just as Cornish people were brought in for the copper mines, English workers were brought over to work the iron furnaces. (For Irish slate quarries, Welsh experts were employed.) Sir William Petty brought over some 800 English people to his works. It was the East India Company which started an ironworks and shipbuilding dock at Dundaniel – on the Bandon River between Bandon and Inishannon, where the first edition six inch Ordnance map still marks 'iron mine' – but they are said to have left eventually owing to local opposition, though not before they had built two ships of 500 tons each. It is strange to think that the company occupied the old castle there as a strongpoint, when today it is a mere relic of a ruin. The Coomhola furnaces were worked by the Whites of Bantry House, but in 1701 they were taken over by a Mr Wallis. Working ceased in about 1760. Coomhola imported iron ore from Lancashire and mixed it with some obtained locally.

High up on the course of the Blackwater, at Clonmeen near Kanturk, Sir Richard Kyrle settled, set up furnaces and is said to have felled a great deal of timber to work them. Little today remains of any of these extensive works, though you may come on iron slag and the highly glazed stones of old furnaces. Perhaps their real monument is Ireland's absence of forest cover, though several other timber-using industries helped massively in its destruction.

As the Industrial Revolution got moving in Britain, and the supply of timber gave out, Cork ceased to smelt iron and began to import it. The city of Cork came to have a number of firms working in iron and making everything from turbines for the waterworks, steam-engines and heavy machinery, to the most delicate and elegant pieces of decorative ironwork: railings, ornamental lampposts and the fountain in the 'English' market with its birds and bullrushes. The old bollards along the quays (many lately removed with quay extension work) record some of their names – Steel, Perrott ('The Hive' with its beehive symbol) – and others appear on manhole covers – McBride, Merrick (the last to close, in the middle of the present century). The 'English' market fountain and the ornamental lampposts from the old Parnell Bridge, now set up alongside one another in the South Mall, bear the name of Harris. The Hive building was a very tall triangular one, facing like the prow of a ship into Washington Street. On its brick frontage the words 'Hive Ironworks' and 'Steam-Engine Manufactury' could till recently just be made out. A stone over a doorway at the rear bears the Hive symbol and the date 1822. Hive made farm machinery and some of it was exported as far afield as Australia.

Water-wheels, turbines, steam-engines – Perrott made them all, and some Perrott products keep turning up in unexpected places; for instance, on the iron pillars supporting the roof of the old coach-house (now the cafe) of

Muckross House in Kerry, with its Valentia slate paved floor. It was another Cork firm, R.J. Lecky, who made the machinery for the Valentia slate quarry which had extensive cutting and polishing equipment as well as steam-engines.

Casting items in iron is a highly skilled process. The exactly made pattern, such as still survives at the Cork Water Works – coated with graphite to prevent sticking – was packed into two boxes filled with specially selected sand. To help bind the sand, clay obtained from the Cloyne area was mixed with it. The pattern was removed and molten iron poured into the mould, from which, of course, openings were left for the escape of air.

Today, working in iron and steel in County Cork continues on Haulbowline Island, at Irish Steel. This operation began in 1938, and construction of a rolling mill started. World War II created a demand for iron in Ireland (for farm cartwheels among other things – the horse was still important) and supplies began to dry up. Irish Steel managed to get some billets to work – some even came from wrecks – but these sources eventually petered out. Operations began again after the war ended and have progressed well until the present over-production of steel in the EC which is putting so many steel plants in jeopardy. In 1970 Irish Steel got themselves a 30-tonne electric arc, then in 1978 a 90-tonne one, as part of a sophisticated, computer controlled 'mini-mill' which does the work of older and much bigger plants in small compass. The steel produced is for the construction industry. Steel today comes in many varieties and shapes, and mills specialise in one or more of the products required in the modern world.

Of the other minerals worked in County Cork, lead was mined at Ringabella on Cork Harbour, and manganese between Leap and Glandore,

Haulbowline

*Lead
Manganese*

Herons and bullrushes on fountain by Harris of Cork, in the now burned section of the 'English' market

Bollard by Perrott of Cork, cast at the Hive foundry in Washington Street

where there is a very well preserved engine-house for a beam engine. At the end of World War II there was a great demand for manganese, which is used in the steel industry in various alloys, and local farmers picked over the old mine spoil heaps and made considerable profit exporting the ore so collected.

Ringabella

Ringabella lead mines are extensive and relatively safe to explore, with quite lofty galleries cut in solid rock. The galena was, it is presumed, shipped from an adjacent jetty to Britain for smelting. Water trickling through the limestone in the rock sequence has set down some quite spectacular deposits of sparkling crystalline floors and cascades as well as hanging curtains of calcite in parts of the old workings.

Silver

Gold

Silver occurs in the county, associated with lead. When the railway line was being built from Bantry to Drimoleague, and cut into the old Scart lead mines about three miles out of Bantry, there was a good deal of excitement when a specimen with a high content of silver was found. Gold only occurs as traces in the gossan in the copper lodes, at Carrigacat, Crookhaven and at Kilcrohane in the Sheep's Head peninsula. Somerville and Ross refer to these finds in the story 'Harrington's': they had got 'Copper, and precious little of it, and they got some gold too – just enough to go to their heads and ruin them.'

Barytes

Barytes, 'heavy spar' or barium sulphate, has been mined in the Clonakilty area and in the Mizen peninsula and around the head of Bantry Bay. Its comparatively high density makes it useful in the production of high density drilling muds, and it is used in paper-making, in white paint, and in textiles. It is said that Cork was the place where it was first mined at depth. The old mills, where the stone was ground prior to being shipped out, have already been mentioned. The Lady's Well barytes mine near Clonakilty is a deep and extensive working, going down 400 feet, 300 feet below the adjacent sea level (it is on the cliff edge). Working began in the l9th century and ended in 1922, but was restarted in 1979 by Milchem. Mining was again halted in 1983, as a result of a general economic recession. Cork barytes had another

*Engine-house at the 19th-century
manganese mine between Leap
and Glandore*

use in the days when small sailing vessels frequented these coasts: As it is very heavy and compact, it was an ideal ballast, and little ships coming into ports near the mines would dump their existing ballast or unload their cargo and then head for the mine spoil-heaps for this particularly desirable rock.

The green and pastoral country between Millstreet and Kanturk in north-west Cork was once busy with a whole string of little collieries, and people still alive remember black dust on roadside grass. During World War II people used to go and gather coal from the old spoil heaps and mine entries, but these have now all been flattened or covered over; only occasionally a tractor wheel will go down through the roof of an old working. The Cork coal is of poor quality and difficult to work, as the rocks are highly folded. None of the 19th-century workings went deep because of the problem of water, though one is said to have used a water-wheel to pump itself dry. Culm, the lowest grade of coal produced, was used in lime burning. The Dromagh colliery had been working for about 100 years when Lewis mentioned it in his *Topographical Dictionary* of the 1830s; it closed in 1861.

There are six coal seams, and each of them had its own name – Morgan's Vein (shale, not worked), Finnane's Vein, Sweet Vein (the best, worked in four pits near Coolclogh), Rock Vein (culm and coal), Bulk Vein (culm), and Smith's or Harris's Bulk. It was at one time hoped to develop the mines on a much bigger scale and export the coal by water down the Blackwater. For this the first section of canal was built out of Mallow toward the coalfields which, however, it never reached. Only corn ever travelled on that short length of artificial waterway.

From the *Corke Journal* of 16 August 1759: 'Good coal may be had at the Earl of Egmont's colliery at Coolclough near Kanturk at 20 pence [9½p] per barrel of 4 bushels. Also culm for burning lime.'

Cork county has, too, a great wealth of excellent building stone. The red, brown and grey sandstones have been used very effectively in many old buildings. The beautiful Cork limestones show to perfection in Cork churches, courthouses and other public buildings like the Cork Savings Bank and the Provincial Bank with its wonderful sculptures on the South Mall. For roofing and for weather slating walls, the county produced excellent slates. (Slate started life as a mud, which in the course of intense folding and hardening has been given a 'slaty cleavage', allowing it to be split into thin laminae.) Slates were worked in an enormous quarry at Drinagh in West Cork until the 1950s; there was another very large working at Benduff near Rosscarbery, with some underground mining. The present new road out of Ross to Leap cuts through the great spoil heaps of Benduff and there is an old engine chimney at the actual working still standing. But slates were worked in many other places around the county, as they occurred and as they were needed.

It seems curious, with so much good stone at hand, that medieval Cork would import stone from England, but it actually did so. An oolitic limestone from Dundry near Bristol was popular for sculpture and examples of it turn up in the old churches of Youghal, Cloyne, Cork (13th-century fragments from the medieval cathedral) and Kinsale. The figure of St Multose in Kinsale is of Dundry stone. But Cork stones were also shipped around. Cape Clear in the 1780s shipped black freestone flagstones and hearthstones to Cork, while nearby Sherkin Island a hundred years later was shipping stone up the Ilen to Skibbereen in boats which carried 12 to 14 tons of it. The river was deepened by cutting through a rocky ledge to bring the stone-boats up easily. The Catholic church in Skibbereen was built with some of the Sherkin stone. The beautiful cut stone of the city quays (many now being replaced with repair and road widening work) came from the Little Island quarries, shipped upriver. There is still a jetty at Little Island with a tall, gallaun-like pillar of limestone set on it, which served as a bollard. Little Island also supplied rock for ballasting ships sailing empty out of Cork. If you come on unusual stones on a beach, never assume they got there by natural agency, as they could be ballast discarded when a ship was lading.

The famous limestone quarries of County Cork include Ballintemple (from which large blocks suitable for columns were obtained and used in such works as Cork's Savings Bank); Meelin; Carrigacrump; Castlemary; Broomfield; Gill Abbey; Sallyscross; Aherla; Ballyclough; Little Island and Copstown. Aherla produced well-bedded rock that could be split readily into slabs for chimney-pieces, flags and headstones. In 1845 it sold at 6d (2½p) per foot for plain work; 1s (5p) for window-sills, and at 1s to 1s 6d (5p to 7½p) for highly-finished work. Carrigacrump is a dark rock compared to the paler tints of quarries like Ballintemple. There are fairly dark limestones, too, at Meelin in north Cork, a little village that is surrounded by the

*Cape Clear
Sherkin*

Skibbereen

Little Island

Limestone

Coolbawn slate quarry

old quarries that are the reason for its existence. It supplied, as already noted, stone for the spire of Cobh cathedral, and quantities more for Killarney cathedral. Two loads of stone were got to Killarney in three days, with fresh horses for each journey, and the carters were paid 6s (30p) for each journey. A fine example of what can be done with Meelin limestone is the font in the village church, rock left grey and rough for the base, while the bowl, highly polished, takes on a deep glossy black. It is dated 1898.

At various places in the county (Little Island, Midleton, Buttevant) the limestone is coloured red or pink, and these 'Cork Reds' or marbles were used in decorative work. A charming example is the Church of Ireland church of St Lappin on Little Island. Here the main structure is the local grey limestone but with decorative bands and insets of the pink – both from the enormous old quarries nearby, which have now been engulfed by the golfcourse. Johnstown puce was compared by Cork sculptor Seamus Murphy to 'a yellow-hammer's egg, and if you use it with some of the dove from Beaumont, you get a grand contrast'. The Cork Reds were used in St Fin Barre's Cathedral and were sometimes exported, both to England and to America. Amethyst (purple-tinted quartz) turned up in a limestone quarry out at Blackrock in 1777, drawing such a crowd of people to see it and collect it that the owner had to call on the military for protection.

'Cork Reds'

Seamus Murphy

Everywhere in the county limestone was burned to make quicklime to spread on the land, except where shell-sand could be got from the coast and used instead. So all over the countryside there are old limekilns, large commercial ones near some of the big quarries, medium-sized ones at smaller quarries which would supply smaller districts, and very small, roughly-built ones up in the mountains just for the local fields. Until about the time of World War II it was necessary to burn the lime in order to get a powder fine enough to spread on the land. From the 1940s, it was found that very finely ground limestone – and the machinery to grind it to dust being easily available – was equally effective and cheaper and easier to handle and spread. All lime being spread today is ground limestone, calcium carbonate, and its preparation is concentrated in a few big quarries, from which it is trucked over the county to the farms.

Limekilns

Making quicklime was much more complicated. The broken rock, with layers of fuel – peat, furze, wood or culm – was packed into the kiln, which narrows at its base to a funnel closed by a slab called the 'eye'. It was set alight and kept burning till the process was complete, when the burned lime was withdrawn through the eye. The chemistry is straightforward – as the calcium carbonate is heated, it gives off carbon dioxide, leaving calcium oxide (quicklime): $CaCO_3 = CaO + CO_2$. The quicklime was then, ordinarily, 'slaked' by adding water, with which it combined to form calcium hydroxide, $Ca(OH)_2$, and the slaked lime was spread on the land.

Only two kilns are making quicklime in the Irish Republic today, and one of them is in Cork, J. A. Wood's quarry near Carrigtwohill. This is a very

Carrigtwohill

different structure from an old-style and relatively inefficient kiln, being a tall vertical kiln built in steel and fired by oil, the jets of flame being directed into the body of the kiln and the mass of limestone. The rate at which the quicklime is produced is controlled by varying the amount of oil fed to the burners. Some of the old kilns were quite ornate. Gothic ones were built down by the sea at Man o' War Cove and Nohavel Turrets, and up on the Leader estates near Millstreet very finely constructed kilns are still a feature of the countryside.

Charles Smith

Charles Smith (1750) gives an interesting account of lime burning in Muskerry barony (west of Cork city) in his time: 'There is no part of Ireland where so much lime is burned as in this south side of the barony of Muskerry. From the head of the vale of Castlemore, down below Kilcrea, on all the adjacent hills, there are great numbers of limekilns. It is not uncommon to see several on one farm, and some hundreds of them are constantly kept burning all the summer season, being mostly turf (peat) kilns, beside some of furze, which is here seldom used. The common labourers in this part of the country will set down their kilns, and burn them without the assistance of a mason. In one of them they commonly burn 200 barrels of rock-lime, which will make 500 barrels of slack. When it is burned, they take out the lime before it slacks, otherwise it would burst the kiln. They also use sea-sand for manuring, particularly in the south-east of this barony, it lying within two miles of the Bandon River, where it is navigable up to Inishannon. Several of the cottagers in this tract pay their rents by lime-burning and will often sell rock-lime, ten or fifteen miles from the kiln, at a shilling [5p] the barrel.'

Many of the old, small kilns were built in ring forts, the existing rath bank being used as a convenient ramp up which the loads of limestone and fuel could be carried to pack into the mouth of the kiln.

Arthur Young

Annes Grove

Arthur Young, in 1776, gave an account of the economics of large-scale lime burning by the bigger landowners, when he visited Annes Grove, north of Castletownroche. Richard Aldworth of Annes Grove, Young wrote, 'burns his lime in both running and standing kilns; in the former with culm (from Kanturk), and the expense to him is 8d [just over 3p] a barrel roach. In the standing kilns he burns without breaking the stones, 1,500 barrels at a time with faggots, and in this way, it is 6d [2½p] a barrel. These kilns, he remarks, should be built with very great strength, or the extreme heat of the fire bursts the masonry. His liming has been on so extensive a scale, that last year, he had seven kilns burning, two of these standing ones and burned in all 10,000 barrels, and as much this year, all for manuring his own farm.'

The Ice Age scoured vast quantities of rock off the surfaces over which the glaciers passed. The material ranges from huge boulders, now dropped as erratics, to the finest silt: anyone who has seen a big river coming from the snout of a glacier will be familiar with its turbid appearance, described as 'glacier milk', the water loaded with fine material. Cork has both the boulder clay, mixed silt and stones left by the melting ice, and the sands, clays and gravels sorted by melt-waters in the temporary lakes of the waning phases of the Ice Age. Enormous deposits of gravels are exploited at the present time in the valleys of the Bride and the Lee. In the past the clays were used for brick-making and pottery. The Ordnance Survey maps of the 1840s show a concentration of potteries around Youghal. At the present time, not very far off, Shanagarry uses local clay for its hand-made pottery. At Youghal there survive the extensive remains of a very large brickworks, on an inlet of the estuary north of the town.

One very tall chimney of the complex still stands beside the brick ovens. There was a wharf on the estuary to which shallow draft boats could come, and a small railway track to take loads about the works. The Youghal brickworks supplied the brick for the handsome brick-built Glanmire (Kent) railway station in Cork, and for very many other buildings. Two million Youghal bricks went into roofing the great railway tunnel leading into Glanmire station. Dublin builders were reported as saying that the Youghal bricks were 'the best in Ireland'.

Bricks were made in many other places including Cork city, where the works became such a nuisance that in 1778 an Act of Parliament was passed that 'no bricks shall be burned or any clamp of bricks set to be burned within two miles of English Statute measure, computed from the Exchange of the City of Cork'. Brick-making continued outside the city on the slobland at Douglas, using local clay, and being shipped upriver from there – most of these bricks were yellow but some were a bright grey. A few miles south from Cork airport was a big brickworks at Ballinphelic, which closed in 1912 and of which little now remains bar the old clay pits and the red bricks in local buildings. Ballinphelic had an overhead aerial ropeway to the railway station at Ballinhassig, on the Cork-Bantry line, to which bricks could thus be easily transported, and coal for fuel be brought back to the works. There was another brickworks at Belvelly on Great Island, another at Mallow (said to make rather inferior bricks) and various others about the county on a smaller scale, down to 'one-off' operations like that at Pembrook House at

Gravels
Clays

Potteries

Brickworks

Youghal

Cork city

Douglas

Ballinphelic

Belvelly
Mallow

Brickworks, Youghal

Passage, where the bricks were made just for that house, and the unsightly old clay pit turned into an ornamental pond afterwards.

Clay pipes

Cork city manufactured clay pipes for smoking tobacco for a long time, but here the clay used was not a local one but imported from England, though in earlier years a clay from County Clare is said to have been used.

Tiles

The most unusual clay product of Cork was the big red roofing tile produced by the Youghal brickworks, curved so that each big tile fits into the next and giving a roof reminiscent of those so often seen in Italy. Some of these old Youghal-tiled roofs survive in old, often ruined, houses and sheds in east Cork.

XIV

Road and Canal

ONE OF THE things that must strike any stranger to Ireland is the incredible number of its roads, a complex spider's web which leaves virtually no corner unroaded. But there is a notable absence of 'green roads', old trails long abandoned but still able to be followed. Early Ireland had a good system of roads and trails; the *Lives* of the saints describe them travelling in wheeled carts, and horse-drawn chariots appear on high crosses. But people continued to live, century after century, more or less in the same places, and so the ancient road became the modern one, ambling from farm to farm, the ford being replaced by a bridge. Or, if the old trail was no longer needed, it seems to have vanished without trace. The place-name 'Togher', in the south of Cork city and again out towards the Cousane Gap in West Cork, indicates a causeway over the bog, but of that, of course, all trace is long lost.

The story of Cork roads therefore is mostly one of improving, re-routing, surfacing and signposting. The 18th and early 19th centuries were times of great road-building activity. New lines were surveyed and built, like the Kerry Pike (turnpike, toll road) from Cork city to Kerry. The new routes often ran dead straight for many miles, and the stage- and mail-coaches travelled along them, with inns at intervals where horses could be changed and travellers refreshed. From the mid-18th century, the presentment system allowed improving landlords to lay down new roads; they 'presented'

Kerry Pike

*The c. 1600 bridge beside Glanworth castle and mill
is the oldest in use in the country*

Packhorse bridge, Mallow

detailed plans to the Grand Jury, and if approval was given the costs would be refunded to them out of the County Cess (tax). English travellers in Ireland commented on how good the roads were, better than those at home. Arthur Young wrote at the end of the century: 'I found it perfectly practicable to travel upon wheels by a map. I will go here: I will go there; I could trace a route as wild as fancy could dictate, and everywhere I found beautiful roads without break or hindrance.'

Arthur Young toured in Cork in 1776. Three years later, Taylor and Skinner surveyed the roads of Ireland for their magnificent book of *Maps of the Roads of Ireland.* They give all the main routes, with a number of pages covering Cork and showing very much the same lines as we have today, though naturally with some variations. The old Dublin road out of Cork, for instance, did not go by the then difficult coast route to Dunkettle, but struck out from Shandon over the hills to the north, and the Cork road out of Kinsale did likewise, taking a more northerly line out of the town. (Both these old main routes still exist as minor roads, and the old entry from the Dublin road to Cork is often worth using to avoid city traffic on the quays.) Travel was not cheap. At a time when a man might earn only a shilling (5p) or less per day a chaise and pair cost 1s 1d (just over 5p) per mile; a chaise with four horses 1s 8d per mile (8p), and a saddle horse 4d (2p).

Both mail-coaches and stage-coaches ran between the major towns, augmented in 1815 by the much cheaper 'cars' of Charles Bianconi. This remarkable man, who lectured in Cork to the British Association at its meeting there in August 1843 about his transport system, was quick to realise the potential of the railways when they appeared, and switched his routes to tie in with the new steam-trains.

Highway robbery, of course, existed. From 1790 there were armed guards on the Dublin–Cork mail-coach, and in 1808 a stage-coach advertised itself as bullet proof – it was copper-lined. And the weather then, as now, could be a hazard. Tuckey's *Remembrancer* for 31 January 1776 records that the Dublin post, which should have got to Cork on the 29th, did not arrive until 1 p.m. on the 31st, 'on account of the great fall of snow rendering the roads impassable'. The same source records on 10 December 1803 that the Dublin coach was blown over on Kilworth mountain but that nobody was hurt.

Tuckey reports, too, that the new road from Cork to Blarney, being part of the Kanturk main route, was opened in June of 1768, and that on 1 May 1816 the Limerick coach travelled the new road from Mallow to Cork for the first time with cheering crowds all along its route. (At the present time, yet another new and less twisting main road from Mallow to Cork is being constructed.) The 'Butter Road' was the name given to a route going west into Kerry from Cork, along which much of the butter for the Cork Butter Market came in little barrels on horse or human back. It ran by the Kerry Pike to Tower, Rylane, Millstreet and on to Killarney.

The only disused old roads of any significance which can still be readily followed are those over the county bounds. The original crossing from the head of Bantry Bay to the head of the Kenmare River (Glengarriff to Kenmare) was the Esk. This track may be easily followed as it climbs steeply up from the lower part of the present main road and drops down, even more steeply, on the Kerry side. This was the route in use when Arthur Young was travelling; the Priest's Leap road, to the east, was then still under construction. *(margin: Glengarriff–Kenmare)*

The Leap road goes up from Coomhola, to cross at about 1,000 feet into Kerry; it is in good repair with some pretty bridges, and commands very splendid views both back into Cork and then over the mountain lines of Kerry. Both the Esk and the Leap are easy routes for walkers and riders. They were replaced by the Tunnels road, which carries the present main road by a tunnel over the highest part of the county bounds mountain ridge. *(margin: Priest's Leap; Coomhola; Tunnels)*

Another old pass, a very steep one on the Cork side, is Lackabaun, which goes up over the hills back of Ballingeary and comes down to Morley's Bridge on the Kerry side. Again, it can readily be followed on foot. Meantime the road from Ballyvourney through Coolea over to Morley's Bridge, again crossing at about 1,000 feet above sea level, has been slightly changed, from the east to the west side of the little valley up which it climbs to the summit. The old, more easterly route, can be seen from the new one and followed on foot. *(margin: Lackabaun; Ballingeary; Ballyvourney; Coolea)*

The county has a number of very beautiful old bridges, ranging from the elegant cut-limestone ones in Cork city to the sturdy sandstone structures out in the country. The oldest bridge seems to be the 13-arch one at Glanworth on the Funshion River, built in 1600, though the delicate little packhorse bridge at Kilshannig (Newberry) outside Mallow could well be older, but is no longer in use. Another old and narrow and very fine bridge is that over the river Bride at Kilcrea Abbey. Sometimes, alongside an old ford, *(margin: Bridges; Kilcrea Abbey)*

Bridge on the Priest's Leap road

Clapper bridge, Rosalogha, Gougane Barra

**Ballingeary
Rossalocha**

stepping stones or a clapper bridge were set. A clapper bridge links the stepping stones with flat flagstones, to form a continuous, all-stone bridge. There are good examples at Ballingeary and Rossalocha, close to Gougane Barra.

In the 1950s Cork's byroads were mostly water-bound macadam – that is, they were untarred – and very often the bedrock would show through the grit as the road climbed steeply up a hill. In fact the Geological Survey mapped many rock outcrops in roads which are now covered with modern surfacing. From the 1950s on there was a massive programme of road improvement, so that now virtually no road in the county is untarred, and the majority of crossroads are signposted. From earlier days come some

Rostellan

rather pleasant cut-stone mileposts along the main roads, and at Rostellan a much earlier plaque of 1734 gives the distances in Irish miles (11 Irish miles to 14 English, according to Taylor & Skinner's road book) to all the neighbouring places.

Road metal in earlier times was obtained from roadside quarries, and a man breaking stones by the roadside was a familiar sight. But with modern machinery and transport, the production of chips for road-making – lime-

Carrigacliona

stone, sandstone and excellent non-skid ones from the volcanic plug of Carrigacliona near Mallow – is concentrated in a limited number of large quarries, equipped with the latest machinery.

Modern bridges, too, are replacing older ones, steel and concrete replacing stone. Big rivers, in the old days, were considerable barriers to cross in the absence of a bridge, and there must have been a number of ferry cross-

Milestone

Rostellan milestone

ings where they were too deep to ford. But rivers are also a very easy way into the country for a person with a boat, and the Blackwater, Lee and Bandon are all navigable in their lower reaches. When the 18th century realised the potential of water transport and the value of constructing canals, it was natural that people would think of extending the existing natural waterways in County Cork. The *Corke Journal* of 25 March 1756 reported: 'We hear that Parliament has devoted the sum of £2,000 to make the Lee navigable from Cork to Macroom, and £6,000 to make the Blackwater navigable from the coalpits of Dromagh and Desert, west of Mallow, to the bridge of Cappoquin in County Waterford.'

The Blackwater, 85 miles long and already readily navigable for a long stretch of its lower reaches, was the obvious baseline for a Cork canal system. Mallow was intended to be a kind of nodal point. The initial plans go back as far as 1715, when a whole series of canal projects was given parliamentary approval. A very interesting and imaginative route was proposed to link Cork with the Shannon estuary, which, if it had ever been built, would have been a most magnificent one to sail. The plan was to leave Cork by going up the Lee and then continue by its northern tributary to Blarney; then from Blarney up the Martin – into the valley utilised later by the railway for a fairly level run to Mallow. The valley climbs quite gently to the watershed, and by locks and a length of canal could be crossed to join the Clyda on the other side and so come down to Mallow. From Mallow, one route would go up the Blackwater to the coalfields, another down it to Cappoquin and the existing navigable section, while the Shannon branch would go north from the Blackwater at Killavullen by the deep rocky gorge of Castletownroche. From there, the Awbeg emerges at Buttevant and level plains, over which the canal would be carried to link with the Maigue and so down past Adare into the Shannon. There was also a plan to link Cork and Macroom and another to use the Bandon River to link Dunmanway with Kinsale. Dunmanway was then prospering with the linen industry and a canal there could

Blackwater

Mallow

Cork
Blarney

Killavullen
Castletownroche
Buttevant

Macroom
Dunmanway
Kinsale

Cromwell's bridge, Glengarriff

Stepping stones, Allihies

have been thought economically viable.

Despite all these wonderful plans, only five miles of canal ever came into actual existence. It runs west from **Mallow**, a damp trench along Navigation Road, and had two beautifully built, cut-limestone locks. It was completed in about 1761 at a cost of £11,000 and was used, briefly, to carry corn, not coal, for it never came in reach of the coal-pits. The lock at **Lombardstown**, below Longueville House, remained intact, even to the shell of the lock-keeper's cottage alongside, until very recently. Then reconstruction of the Mallow–Millstreet road cut into it and the engineers planned to make it into part of an underpass for cattle. Nearly too late, local historians became aware of what was happening and most of the lock, but not all, has been preserved. These Mallow locks were much larger then those constructed on other Irish canals, being about 127 feet by 22 feet, and the Longueville example is the sole survivor. (The Grand Canal had several of these large locks but soon reduced them by dividing the lock into two sections.)

Another short section of canal was built on the **Blackwater**, though in its brief excursion into County Waterford, not in Cork. This was the section from Cappoquin to Lismore, built at the expense of the Duke of Devonshire (whose seat Lismore Castle is) and open by 1814. It is a mile long with one lock. In 1844 it was described as carrying corn and flour out and bringing timber, iron and coal in; it survived in use until about 1925. The east Cork river Bride is navigable as far as Tallow – its final section all in County Water-ford – and people recall how strange it was to see a sail moving through the fields, the river itself hidden from distant view.

Even as late as 1844, when J. R. O'Flanagan published his book on the Blackwater, some people still thought canals a better bet than the railroad. Flanagan, a great proponent of canalising the Blackwater, wrote: 'I would recommend short canals, having a practical object, or deepening the bends of rivers between towns, so as to afford direct communication from the interior of the country to the sea, in preference to, and as a much safer speculation than any system of railroads in Ireland.'

(margin notes)
Mallow

Lombardstown

Blackwater

XV

The Iron Road

RAILWAY MANIA RAN riot in the 1840s. Plans were advanced to lay lines here, there and everywhere, and companies were formed to promote them. It was a unique phenomenon, for roads have always been with us and the automobile's early enthusiasts struggled on through the dust as best they could; nor did the coming of the aeroplane and its need for airfields bring anything like the enthusiasm, energy and often ruin of the early railroad men.

Railway growth in County Cork was rapid and within 15 or 16 years Cork city was linked to Dublin and an excellent series of lines operated through the county. Even though the terrain was not too difficult, this represented a great achievement in the planning and mapping of the projected routes and in the employment of very large numbers of men, and of carts and horses. Not only had earth to be shovelled (all by hand), rails to be manufactured, shipped in and laid, but stone had to be quarried and carted for the bridges and viaducts of which a good few still stand, witness to the skill of their builders. Stations were built, signals set up, and all at a time when communications were by horse traction on land, and by sail, or sail-assisted steam, at sea. Apart from the main line to Dublin, almost all of this immense effort has been thrown away by the scrapping of most of the lines in the county.

The railway brought not only rapid communications but a considerable change in the way of life along its routes: secure employment for those who worked on it, a centring of road communications on its stations, and the introduction of a sense of time. 'There was no time,' Mrs Mary O'Shea once told me on Valentia Island, speaking of the days before everyone had a watch and the radio brought constant time signals. People knew (as one still can) the approximate time by the sun, and at night some knew by the stars; but the Big House stable bell ringing for dinner break and knocking off time were necessary enough, and the midday and evening guns banged out the exact hour at Cork and Cobh. The train, however, running very regularly, brought exact time to everyone living along its line. The train could be something small and intimate: the Travers at the castle at Timoleague found the little Courtmacsherry train something quite pleasant to have crossing the end of the garden each day. Or it could be the very peak of the achievement of steam, the great *Maeve* pouring on the power and hauling a heavy load out of Cork's Glanmire Station up the severe incline through the tunnel and on to Blarney, for which it was mostly necessary to climb out double-headed.

Ireland was one of the pioneers of the railway age, the Dublin and Kingstown (Dún Laoghaire) line being opened on 17 December 1834. The Act of Incorporation of the Great Southern and Western Railway came ten years later, on 6 August 1844, with the plan to link Dublin and Cork by 165 miles of railroad. It was planned as a single unit from the start, not, as so often, piecemeal construction by various companies along the route, and it would be the longest inter-city line not only in Ireland but also, at the time, in Britain.

The Great Southern plan included a branch line from Kildare to Carlow, and this was completed by 1846. July 1848 saw them at Limerick Junction; March 1849 brought them to Mallow, where they crossed the Blackwater by a ten-arch bridge (blown up in the Civil War). Much work was needed on the final stretch into Cork city from Mallow, including a tunnel to bring the trains to the main station planned at Glanmire. While this was being excavated, a temporary station was built at Blackpool, and a directors' train steamed into it on 18 October 1849. These were, of course, the years of the Great Famine and railway construction must have given a great deal of much-needed employment. Many of the first engine drivers, however, were brought over from Britain, as Irish men needed to be trained to handle the new machines. They earned £2 a week, but a plate-layer working on the permanent way only got 12s (60p) or less.

The great tunnel to Penrose Quay and the new Glanmire Station was completed by 1855. It is 1,355 yards long, cut through the red sandstone ridge – the stone brought out of it being used to build many Cork houses. It is ventilated by shafts sunk vertically down and protected on the heights above by tall towers like truncated round towers. It was tunnelled out, working from both ends, and the two sides met with near spot-on accuracy in the middle. It was not cut without cost in death and injury to the workers, and a hut outside the tunnel mouth continued to be called the 'Dead House' for decades.

Margin notes:
Dublin–Cork

Mallow

Glanmire
Blackpool

Glanmire
Station

Cork–Mallow–Dublin railway and road bridges just north of the city

Glanmire is peculiar in that its platforms and roofs are gracefully curved; the railroad sweeps in on a wide arc. It is close to the quays and a series of short feeder lines ran out of them, so that the ships could unload direct into railway wagons. These wagons were propelled in and out of the station to the ships by an hydraulic system worked from a reservoir on the hills above at Kilbarry. The same system also opened and closed the road bridges over the Lee for ships to pass through. All these quayside rails have now been lifted, as well as those on the line from Glanmire through the town to the Albert Quay terminus, as they were no longer used and were a hazard to traffic, especially to cyclists.

At the present time the Youghal and the Cobh lines come into Glanmire Station, but this was not the original plan. In the 1840s there was a scheme to lay a railroad from Cork to Waterford, via Youghal and Dungarvan. It ended simply in a line from Cork to Youghal. Construction began at Dunkettle, several miles east of the city, and the line to Midleton was completed in 1859. Youghal was reached on 21 May 1860. Work then shifted to the other end of the line which was extended into Cork city to a station at Summerhill, which was reached in May 1861. Summerhill was a little higher than Glanmire, but it was eventually given up and the trains were brought into the main station.

The line to Cobh (then known as Queenstown) branched off the Youghal line at Cobh junction, and was completed in March 1862. Making it involved some rock cuttings along the cliffs in the narrows of Passage West and an extensive system of embankments and viaducts to get it out to the islands of Fota and Great Island (on which Cobh is sited). The Cork-Cobh line is a delightful experience of a kind of marine train journey (with close-up views of wading birds when the tide is out on the mud flats), venturing over the sea, plunging into the green and verdant Fota, and rattling along the cuttings overlooking Passage West. A condition of its construction allowing it to pass through Fota's grounds was that it would always stop there, whether there were passengers or no. Today, with Fota open to the public, the little station has come into its own as the most pleasant way out there is either by

Youghal
Dunkettle
Midleton

Summerhill

Cork–Cobh

Kilpatrick tunnel on the Cork–Bantry
line, the first tunnel cut in Ireland

the train or (some days during summer) by boat. Cobh is a busy line, the commuter route to Cork, and Cobh therefore, alone among Irish towns, has no bus service.

For sailing ships, beating up and down the English Channel was, if they left from London or the Channel ports, the biggest delay on a transatlantic crossing. The coming of steam began to make things easier, but there were many projects to make Ireland the real departure point for the New World. People could cross England by train, the Irish Channel by steam packet, and continue by rail again to a port on the west coast of Ireland. Galway, Valentia Island, Bantry and Crookhaven were all promoted, but the choice fell on Cobh. The transatlantic liners began making regular calls there in 1859, and once the Cobh to Cork rail link was completed, an American mail-train could run from there direct to Dublin.

The first American mail-train, with both letters and passengers for the USA, ran on Sunday 6 November 1859, leaving Dublin at 11.20 a.m. and arriving in Cork at 3.50 p.m. Passengers and mail then went on by boat to join their ship at Cobh. This final leg by ship ended, of course, when the railway was built to Cobh. For the liners to leave their mail at Cobh and let it go on by train and cross-channel packet represented, at that time, a considerable speeding up in the delivery of letters. But from 1900, with bigger, faster ships, the liners began to carry the mail on to Britain themselves, and the mail service through Ireland finally ended in 1914. The trains made very good times: the Dublin-Cork day mail-train took 7 hours in 1849, had cut this to 4 hours 5 minutes in 1884 and to 3 hours 55 minutes in 1897. At the end of the 19th century, letters leaving Cork by the 3.30 p.m. mail would be delivered in London the next morning.

For a brief period, 1950 to 1953, the *Enterprise* train ran straight through from Belfast to Dublin to Cork.

Looking back to the great days of rail and steam, it is interesting to see businessmen hiring a 'special' when today they would charter a plane. There was the case of Mr Piza, who set off from London on some very urgent business in the USA. He caught the train and packet successfully as far as Dublin, but missed the Cork train. So he hired a 'special', engine and carriage, which cost him £44 10s (£44.50) and got him from Dublin to Cobh in 3 hours 25 minutes. But the SS *Teutonic* was already steaming slowly out of the harbour. Not to be stopped at the last moment, Mr Piza hired a launch and set off in pursuit, overtaking the liner and climbing aboard to the cheers of the other passengers. The date was December 1892.

From Mallow the Great Southern built two other lines, one running east and the other west, along the Blackwater valley. The eastern one went by way of Fermoy to Cappoquin, Dungarvan and Waterford, with a branch line from Fermoy to Mitchelstown. The western one was to Killarney and Tralee, with branch lines to Reenard and Valentia Harbour (the most westerly railway station in Europe), and to Dingle by a light railway. All of these, except

Cobh

Mallow–
Waterford

Mallow–Tralee

the Killarney-Tralee line, are now closed.

Work on the Killarney line began as soon as the railway reached Mallow from Dublin; it was open as far as Millstreet in April 1853, and in Killarney by May of 1854. The now closed line to Fermoy, with some fine viaducts over the deep little tributary streams of the Blackwater, was finished in 1860 by the Great Southern, but the Lismore to Waterford section was the responsibility of the Waterford, Dungarvan and Lismore Railway and they did not finish their part of the work till 1878. The middle sector, Fermoy to Lismore, was built by the Fermoy and Lismore Railway, and completed in 1872. The Mitchelstown branch line was closed in 1953 and the whole route, Mallow-Waterford, in 1967.

Fermoy

The Mitchelstown branch line, 12 miles long and completed in 1891, had been intended to go on to Cahir but never did. Off the Killarney line was a branch going north to Banteer and Newmarket. It was built by the Kanturk and Newmarket Railway but was always operated by the Great Southern rolling stock. It is unusual in that its moving spirit was a woman, the wife of the chairman of the company, Colonel Aldworth, and it was therefore nicknamed 'Lady Mary's Railway'. In 1928 a steam rail-car, a Sentinel Cammall, was put on the line but was not successful; final closure came on 1 January 1963.

Mitchelstown

Kanturk
Newmarket

No fewer than five schemes were promoted, all at the same time, for a railway from Fermoy to Cork, and none of them came to anything. It was also planned to have an electric tramway from Fermoy to Kilworth Camp but again this never materialised. It is said locally that some construction work was actually carried out on the Fermoy-Cork route, and for a while fares from the Waterford side to Cork were calculated on the shorter mileage that such a line would have meant, rather than the true distance through Mallow.

Fermoy

When all these trains were running, and little paddle steamers plied the Blackwater, for 6s 6d (32½p), one could have a very pleasant day out. Leaving Cork by train, at Youghal ('the Irish Brighton') one embarked on a steamer which took one up the Blackwater ('the Irish Rhine') to Cappoquin. Here the train was rejoined, and one went on up the Blackwater to Mallow ('the Irish Bath') and so back to Cork. This lovely trip came to an end with World War I, and was not revived after it.

Blackwater

The Great Southern had several 'firsts'. It built Ireland's first railway hotel, in Killarney, and it ran Ireland's first dining-cars – on the Dublin–Cork mail-train – starting on 1 June 1898. Its concessionary tickets included one of a halfpenny per mile for the destitute going to the workhouse, and another of 10s (50p) from anywhere in Ireland for convicts going to prison on Spike Island in Cork Harbour.

Moving around Cork Harbour was much easier by sea than on land, and a variety of ferries and small boats – sail to begin with, steam later – plied back and forth. The railway to Passage West, and eventually Crosshaven, ran at

Cork Harbour

first in competition with some of these vessels, but eventually came to own a string of them, so that its trains connected with boats for Cobh or Whitegate or Monkstown.

Passage West

Plans for a railway from Cork to Passage West were being made as early as 1836, two years after the Dublin–Kingstown railway had got going, but it was not until 1845 that three companies put forward their individual plans for a Cork, Blackrock, Passage and Monkstown Railway – the Monkstown being dropped as the line got only as far as Passage at that time. That line was opened on 8 June 1850. It left Cork from the City Park Station (close to the then town racecourse, and at the junction of Victoria Quay and Victoria Road), but later the terminus was moved to Albert Street. The line swung out of the city on a wide curve, running deeply in a cutting over the estuarine lowlands to cross the Rochestown inlet by a viaduct. This closed the water upstream to shipping – old wharves still survive from the days when boats came right up close to Douglas. Then it hugged the shoreline so closely that a couple of small bays used (as they still are) for harbouring small boats were given access to the sea outside by little bridges, so that one could be rowing out under the line with the train thundering overhead. (This shore section of the old line is now developed as a seaside walk.) Ann Boland's manuscript gives an insight into the lobbying that went into the making of a railway: 'My father (Thomas Parsons Boland) got the Passage Railway Bill passed thro Parliament. The Directors sent him to London for that purpose; they having no interest at all, Papa overwhelming interest. The Lords of the Admiralty having opposed the Bill because they thought a railway so near the river would interfere with its navigation, Papa's friends and relations induced the Lords of the Admiralty to withdraw their opposition; Sir Byam Martin, Papa's cousin, being the particular friend of the First Lord

City Park Station

Rochestown

Douglas

Monard railway viaduct and ironworks in the valley

of the Admiralty. The others were Lord Dunrobin, Sir Charles Coote, Lord Monteagle, Lord and Lady Monteagle being most intimate friends of Papa's. So the Bill passed and the railway was made, but the Railway Company did not afterwards behave well to Papa, they only gave him £3,000 instead of the £5,000 agreed for his stand.'

As the line prospered, it was decided to carry it on to its logical conclusion, Crosshaven, via Monkstown and Carrigaline. The original line had been standard gauge, but it was to be narrow gauge out to Crosshaven, so the line was, unusually, converted to narrow gauge all the way. It reached Monkstown in 1902, Carrigaline in 1903, and on 30 May 1904 Crosshaven Station was formally opened. It must have been a charming route to travel, with it continuing to hug the shore from Passage to Monkstown and, between the two, a kind of arcaded tunnel under the present road but with wide arches on the seaward site framing the view to Rushbrooke. It then curved inland, crossing the river at Carrigaline on a high viaduct and then along the wooded shores past Drake's Pool to Crosshaven. Here there was the Glen to cross, a deep hollow, and red brick pillars survive of the viaduct there. Return tickets to Cork cost 2s (10p) first class, and 1s 6d (7½p) third. The line was always well maintained and the engines were fast, making speeds of up to 50 m.p.h.

During World War I the line carried troops to and from the two harbour forts at Crosshaven. The company found its fleet of steamers expensive to maintain and began to sell them off in the 1920s, the last going in 1927. Even with that economy ordinary rail traffic apparently was not enough to keep the line going, and it was closed in 1932: the Monkstown-Crosshaven section in May and the rest in September. Today, with massive suburban development in the whole area, the line, if it had survived, would be an invaluable commuter service.

West Cork came to be very well served by rail. The Cork-Bandon line was being built at the same time as the main route from Dublin to Cork and the Passage one. Its extension to Bantry came by way of projects from several companies – West Cork Railway, Ilen Valley Railway and Bantry Bay Extension Railway – whose sections linked up and were run as a unit.

The first section to be constructed was that from Bandon to Cork, beginning at the Bandon end. A survey to estimate likely traffic revealed that each day 687 people travelled the route by coach, carriage or cart, while 500 went on horseback or on foot. The proposed railroad was quite a difficult one, with one long and one short tunnel to bore, as well as a crossing of the Bandon River. The first sod was cut by the Earl of Bandon close to Dundaniel Castle on 16 September 1845, using a steel shovel made by Hogg of Patrick Street, Cork, and wheeling it away in a mahogany barrow made by Henright, one of the contractors for the railway work. Rails and the rest of the material needed came in by sea to Collier's Quay near Inishannon on the Bandon River. This starting point meant they could begin work nearest

Marginal notes:
Monkstown
Carrigaline
Crosshaven

Cork–Bandon

Collier's Quay

their source of supplies and later, as they moved away, the supplies were sent after them on the new track.

Edmund Leahy was the original planner of the route but, after a dispute with the company, was replaced by Charles Nixon. Nixon was a well-known English engineer and immediately changed Leahy's plan from a deep cutting into a tunnel at Kilpatrick. The tunnel, cut through solid rock, was £4,000 cheaper than a cutting, and was the first tunnel cut in Ireland: it is 170 yards long. Begun in August 1846, with workmen from the West Carbery mines who worked day and night shifts, the passage was cut through by the following August. On the Bandon side the tunnel opens straight onto a high viaduct crossing the Bandon River, of which today only the piers remain. On the other side the line crosses the Brinny by a substantial bridge. One can still scramble down from a minor road north of the Bandon River to the tunnel, walk through it and along the very overgrown line toward Upton.

Trains began to run on the line as soon as the track was completed from Bandon to Ballinhassig, passengers making the rest of the journey to Cork in horse omnibuses. There were five of these, each carrying 28 passengers, whom they set down in Cork at the Imperial Hotel. Meantime work went ahead on cutting the great tunnel through Goggin's Hill, which was 900 yards long with three 'round tower' ventilating shafts. As the rock was alternately hard and soft, the tunnel was partly cladded internally. On the Bandon side is Ballinhassig Station where the trains came out of the tunnel straight into the platform; on the Cork side the train ran in a long cutting before crossing the Chetwynd viaduct. This was designed by Nixon and had stone piers 70 feet high and a span of 110 feet in cast-iron. The skeleton of this magnificent structure in iron and limestone still stands. The terminus in Cork was at Albert Quay. The first train to make the complete run, Cork to Bandon, ran on 5 December 1851. The two tunnels on the Bandon line were therefore well ahead of the cutting and completion of the enormous one into Cork from Mallow.

The engines run on the Bandon line bore Irish names, the first being *Rith Tinneadh* (Running Fire) and *Sighe Gaoithe* (Whirlwind), two sandwich-framed tank engines, 0-2-2, and followed in 1850 by *Fág an Beallach* (Clear the Way). The line was the only one in Ireland ever to have American engines, two being bought from Philadelphia in 1900 when an English firm could not supply them. They had powerful hooters, which apparently annoyed people along the way and had to be replaced by whistles. The engines are described as of typical American design and were 0-6-2STs.

The next section, from Bandon to Dunmanway, was opened on 12 June 1866. It was a straightforward stretch of line following the Bandon River valley and turning into Dunmanway by a bridge over the river and through the marshy area there called the 'Island'. Going on for Bantry meant climbing up through the great wind-gap through which the road also goes, and then straight on, on a downhill run to the town. This final section was not

Kilpatrick

Bandon River

Upton

Bandon–
Ballinhassig

Goggin's Hill

Chetwynd
viaduct

Bandon–
Dunmanway

complete, however, until the route from Drimoleague (on the Bantry side of the wind-gap) to Skibbereen was finished. This was the Ilen Valley Railway section, and it was opened on 21 July 1877. The Bantry extension was finished by 1 July 1881. When the line from Bandon to Dunmanway was opened the two engines working it were named *Patience* and *Perseverance*!

Ilen Valley

Branching off from the basic Cork-Bandon line at Killeady Junction, was the Kinsale railway. It was opened to traffic on 16 June 1863 and closed in 1931, the first railway line in Ireland to be shut down. Curiously, its eleven-mile route still survives and stands out clearly from the air, when many lines closed far later have virtually disappeared. It has been ploughed out here and there, but even then you can see its traces from the air and follow its sinuous course, which picks the only fairly level passage through the gentle east-west undulations of the terrain. The station was on high ground above Kinsale; plans to bring it to the docks and the profitable loads of fish never materialised. Though from the air the curves look gentle enough, they were a problem to its first engine, an 0-4-0 Fairbairn saddle tank, which seems to have made a habit of becoming derailed.

Kinsale

Telegraph lines followed the convenient routes of the railway, and one was set along the Kinsale line and so out to the lighthouse on the Old Head.

From the line beyond Bandon, at Clonakilty Junction, a branch line went off to that town via Ballinascarthy. It was completed in August 1886. From Ballinascarthy the Courtmacsherry Light Railway ran to Timoleague and then along again, hugging the shore, to its terminus. From Skibbereen there were two more branch lines, to Baltimore and to Schull. The Baltimore Extension Railway took the line to Baltimore in 1893. Baltimore is an important shipbuilding and sailing centre, as well as the point of departure for the regular ferries to Cape Clear and Sherkin islands. Up to the time of the

Clonakilty
Courtmacsherry
Skibbereen
Baltimore

Section of old railway line to Kinsale

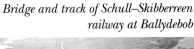

Bridge and track of Schull–Skibberreen railway at Ballydebob

closure of the whole Bantry system, on 31 March 1961, regular Sunday excursions were run from Cork to Baltimore.

Schull–
Skibbereen

The most romantic, and most unprofitable, of the Cork light railways, the Schull and Skibbereen Tramway, ran from Skibbereen to Schull via Bally-dehob, and was originally known as the West Carbery Tramway and Light Railway. Its chief monument is the very beautiful 12-arch stone viaduct over the estuary at Ballydehob; it was 15.5 miles long, with a three-foot gauge, and it opened on 9 September 1886 for passenger traffic. A pigs special had been run to Ballydehob three days earlier; local farmers were well pleased with it and said they had got better prices for their animals. On the day of the official opening, a monster sports meeting was held in Ballydehob. There were great hopes for the future of the railway – that it would open up the Mizen peninsula, maybe go on to Crookhaven which might become a calling point for transatlantic liners, and certainly carry ore from the West Cork copper mines. None of this happened. It was a loss-making line, though it could have now become a major tourist attraction, picking its way amongst rock and furze and heather and crossing the great viaduct.

Ballydehob

O. S. Nock describes the first three engines, 0-4-0s, writing that they 'were surely the queerest looking and most ineffective that have ever run in these islands'. They were supposed to be able to haul 30 tons up a 1-in-30 gradi-ent, but did nothing of the sort and had to be replaced within a month of the line's opening. The eventual 'stable' was of three 4-4-0 tank engines: *Erin* (1888), *Gabriel* (1906) and *Kent* (1914). At Schull the engine-house stood at right angles to the track and there was a turntable to get the engines into it. There was a short extension of track down the pier for the loading of fish and sand. Curiously for so remote a line, *Erin* was the first engine anywhere in Britain and Ireland to be fitted with a Belpaire firebox.

The line, which was badly damaged during the Troubles, closed owing to shortage of fuel during World War II, was re-activated on 11 December 1945, closed the following year when there was another fuel crisis, and never re-opened.

Somerville and
Ross

Maybe it was this little railway that Somerville and Ross had in mind in

On the closed Cork–Bantry line

'The Shooting of Shinroe', when the unsuccessful sportsmen were told they might be equally unsuccessful in catching the train home. 'She had a fashion of running early on Monday nights, and in any case if you'd want to catch that thrain, you should make like an amber-bush for her.'

Meantime, the main Cork to Bantry line liked to call itself the 'Prince of Wales Route'. In 1858 this was the way that the future Edward VII had followed on his visit to Ireland: Cork to Killarney via Glengarriff and Kenmare. You could take the train to Bantry, and go on by horse-drawn coach (supplied by Vickerys of Bantry) or embark on the *Lady Elsie* or the *Princess Beara* and get off at Glengarriff and then continue by road to Killarney. In the 1880s a single first-class ticket from Cork to Killarney by the Prince of Wales route cost 22s (£1.10). But you could also get a circular return ticket through the Cork Steam Packet Company from British ports to Cork, to Killarney via Bantry and back to Cork via Mallow.

Cork–Bantry

A railway was built between Cork and Macroom, following easy gradients out along the West Cork river Bride by Ballincollig, Killumney and Lissarda, where it made its way through the low gap in the ridges to Macroom. Much of the Macroom end of the line is now under the waters of the Lee reservoirs, though traces of it and its bridge can be seen when the water level is low.

Cork–Macroom

The Cork and Macroom Direct Railway was opened on 1 August 1861, sharing its Cork station with the Bandon line until the two companies had a dispute and Macroom set up its own station at Capwell. This was a handsome red brick building, now part of the Bus Éireann bus depot there. Capwell Station opened in 1879 but closed when the Macroom trains started running into the Albert Quay Station in the 1920s.

Capwell Station

Macroom railway carried troops to and from Ballincollig barracks, and took a daily basket of the barrack laundry to Clonmel for washing! Like all railways, it had its own ethos and tricks and jokes. Killumney (church of the cave) and Ovens (cave – both are close to a large limestone cavern) are about half a mile apart. Ovens is on the main Cork-Macroom road and today, with road transport, it is Ovens for Killumney. But Killumney was on the rail route, and when the trains ran, it was Killumney for Ovens. The track ran just behind the pub, with a climbing grade beyond it toward Macroom. On its return from Cork, it often proved convenient for the train to make a longer-than-scheduled halt at the back of the pub, the official excuse being that time was needed for the engine to build up enough steam to climb the gradient ahead! At the end of its days, the line only carried a cattle-train from Macroom market, and complete closure came in 1953.

Killumney
Ovens

Finally there was the interesting little Cork and Muskerry Light Railway, which ran out of the western end of the city along the Carrigrohane straight road and on to Blarney, with branches to Coachford and Donoughmore. A narrow-gauge line, the Cork to Blarney section opened on 8 August 1887; the Coachford section on 18 March 1888, and that to Donoughmore on 6 May 1893. The routes traversed were very pleasant rural ones through lovely

Muskerry

Coachford
Donoughmore

country and the little train was much loved by those who travelled on it. It ran more or less in the open and sported cow catchers and bells, and even once collided with a steamroller on the Carrigrohane straight road. The steamroller got the worst of the encounter, which did little damage to the train. Old pictures show the train, when the straight road was flooded, puffing its way through the water. The guard, checking tickets, used to swing himself from carriage to carriage while the train was in motion. Generally a beguiling little railway, it closed in 1934 but is remembered with pleasure by many who took the 'Muskerry tram' into the country of a Sunday.

In addition to the railways that carried passengers, there were various concerns which had short lengths of track for their own use and internal transport. On Haulbowline Island the British Admiralty docks had some track, as does Irish Steel today. Camden Fort, at Crosshaven, had an 18-inch-gauge railroad to move supplies around from pier to store, with little turntables made by G.R. Turner, Langley Mill, Notts, according to the inscription on it. There is a second length of track at a higher level, and a tradition that the fort had a small locomotive which was swung by a crane from the upper to the lower tracks as required. At Bandon a tramway linked Allman's Distillery with the mainline station, both track and locomotive on it being owned and maintained by the distillery. It was last used in 1929.

Meantime Cork city had a tramway system. There was a shortlived and unsuccessful attempt with horse-drawn trams from 1872 to 1874. Then in 1898 a good system of electric trams was laid down, covering the city and reaching out to what were then separate villages like Douglas. This tram system flourished until 1931 when it closed down in face of increasing competition from motor buses.

A very old steam-engine is preserved in Kent station, Cork. No. 36 stands on a length of the original rails of the system and is the sole survivor of a whole fleet of Bury Curtis and Kennedy engines owned by the Great Southern and Western; indeed, sole survivor of the type anywhere. All these engines were taken off the Great Southern's routes in the period 1869-79, but one was kept as a museum piece. It is a fine example, carefully restored, of what might be called a second generation railway engine.

Haulbowline
Camden Fort

Bandon

Trams

Old engines

No. 90 on Mallow platform

Engine 90 was built in Inchicore in 1875 by a famous engineer, Alexander McDonald. She is an 0-6-4T and cost £1,584. She was built for use on the Castleisland railway in Kerry but was transferred from there to the Fermoy-Mitchelstown route and ended up hauling beet for the sugar factory in Mallow from Courtmacsherry and Timoleague. She was 'retired' in 1961 and kept as another museum piece, first at Fermoy and then, from 1967, on Mallow station where she always attracted a lot of interest. But a few years ago, Iarnród Éireann gave the old engine to Westrail Ltd, a group of steam enthusiasts who set about restoring her to working order. In 1990, Engine 90 was back in action, hauling railway enthusiasts on excursions in County Galway where she and Westrail are based.

XVI

A County of Ships

CORK, THE *PARLIAMENTARY GAZETEER OF IRELAND* wrote in the mid-19th century, is 'a maritime county of Munster'; it went on to remark that the county's coastline was estimated at 200 miles but was actually much more. One might – say in Kanturk or Rathluirc – feel far from the ocean, but Cork's history is nevertheless very much a maritime one. The sea was the highway in and out of the county and for to-ing and fro-ing along it. That way came pirates and sometimes invaders. That way one might make a decent living by smuggling or by fishing, for Cork's rivers and seas teemed with fish

Galley Head

until recent times, when pollution and overfishing have destroyed so much of the stocks. And along the coast, even out on the islands, shipwrights built ships – big ships and little ships, wooden ships and iron ships – and they have been doing so since humans first came to Cork. As Thor Heyerdahl pointed out in *Early Man and the Ocean*, 'Man hoisted sail before he saddled a horse.'

The evidence is that early people came to Ireland by sea and not by a land bridge, about the existence of which (even for the coming of plants and animals earlier) there are some considerable geographical and geological difficulties. All the ideas and techniques of building the great stone tombs and stone circles came in by sea, as did Christianity later on. People sailed to Cornwall to get tin to make bronze in Ireland. Prehistoric Irish gold ornaments are littered all over Europe – ships carried them to the lands in which they have been found. The Irish saints were as much at home on water as on land. They used both wooden ships and skin-covered curraghs. (Out of Crosshaven boatyard went Tim Severin's skin-covered ship to retrace St Brendan's possible voyage to the Americas.) Into Cork's harbours and viks (bays) came the Viking longships, bringing more knowledge of first-class shipbuilding and navigation over long distances.

We forget how much easier sea travel often was than pushing through forest and bog, and how good navigation can be accomplished with very simple means and accurate observation. You can, for instance, get an approximate sun or star sight without even so primitive an instrument as a cross-staff, let alone an astrolabe or a sextant. 'By Jordan, if a man lies flat on the ground, raises his knee, places his fist upon it and then raises his thumb from his fist, he sees the Pole Star just so high and no higher.' In that way, an Icelandic pilgrim to the Holy Land in 1150 could explain to people at home where it lay, in latitude, relative to Iceland.

Early trade

Early trade between Cork and remote places has already been indicated in the finds which have turned up in excavations, such as the eastern Mediterranean amphorae of Garranes ring fort. Movement between Ireland and Britain and continental Europe has been a feature of life throughout human history here; it is the records that increase as we get nearer our own time.

Pottery

Excavation in the old city of Cork has turned up a great deal of pottery, 80% of which was imported. Dating from the mid-13th century to the early 14th century, these finds indicate extensive trade with south-western France and with England, where the principal port for ships was, and continued to be, Bristol. Import of Dundry stone, for special artwork, from Somerset has already been mentioned. Thirteenth-century Ireland was a time of improving farming and this made it possible to export quantities of wool and hides and corn. Cork city, of course, was not the only port in the county: Youghal, Kinsale and Rosscarbery were also very active. By the 14th century there was a decline in farm production and corn began to be imported. Fish exports – hake, herring and salmon – were important. Although ale was made at home, wine was not. Most of it came into Cork from Bordeaux; thus in 1497

Youghal

Kinsale
Baltimore

Cork

Fishing

J. Mahon of Youghal was importing wine and paying for it by exporting hake. In 1502 another Youghal merchant, Morice Donyth, was buying in wine for Kinsale, Waterford and Baltimore and paying for part of it with herring and other fish. Then in 1503 Richard Donnet, of the same town, paid for his wine cargo in cash plus herring, hake, leather and Irish cloaks. Cork was also buying wine and using fish cargoes for payment at the same period. Another record, of 1520, is of a group of merchants of Youghal, Bordeaux and Florence getting together to ship a big cargo of wine to Youghal in a Breton ship, to be paid for partly with hake. Fishing was a big industry in County Cork; in human terms, it means people building fishing boats, and people sailing them; people to make fishing nets, to process the fish for export by drying, smoking or salting, and to package it up for loading into the merchant ships.

As well as sea fishing, there was extensive river fishing. All the monasteries had salmon weirs. 'Fishing engines', fixed traps for catching fish, were set up in great numbers along all the Cork rivers, and a great deal is known about these 'engines' and where they were. The only surviving working example on the Cork rivers is actually just over the border in Waterford, at Molana Abbey to the north of Youghal. Called a 'sprat weir', it actually catches a variety of fish. Originally of stakes and wickerwork, it is now of wire mesh – a corral facing upstream so that, as the tide falls, fish in its wide mouth are trapped in the narrow downstream apex.

Salmon

Taking salmon coming up river in nets across the stream has been practised for centuries and still continues, but the more sporting form of hunting the salmon with spears has died out. Walter Scott gave a vivid account of this form of fishing in *Guy Mannering*, for it was carried out in Scotland, too. He says it could be done both by day and night, but was most often done at night, 'when the fish are discovered by means of torches'; and how 'by this light also were seen the figures in the boat, now holding high their weapons, now stooping to strike, now standing upright, bronzed by the same red glare, into a colour which might have befitted the regions of Pandemonium'. Three salmon spears from the river Lee are now in the National Museum. Today, when salmon are an expensive luxury, it is difficult to realise how common

Stencils, Baltimore

they once were, and how their excellent meat, both fresh and smoked, made a substantial contribution to ordinary people's diet. Eels are still very numerous in Cork rivers, and in the past there were many eel weirs.

Cork Harbour was very rich in oysters, and they were also fished in Kinsale, where the Corporation was at pains to conserve the stock for local use. On 3 October 1726, for instance, it decreed that 'whereas the bed of oysters lying up in the harbour or river of this town above Comeen Point and Ringrone Castle hath been preserved by this Corporation for some years past, to the end that the town may be served with oysters, and when they come to perfection and as we find that said oysters are carried by joulters in great parcels to Corke and other neighbouring towns at such time when no oysters can be had for money or otherwise in this town, we present that no joulter presume to carry any oysters dredged in this harbour to Corke or elsewhere before the town is first served'.

Commercial mussel farming is being practised in many parts of Cork today; in the past the river mussel of the Cork rivers was also sought for its pearls. The delicate 'moonlight' river pearls are still sometimes found in river mussels, though probably pollution has much reduced the numbers of the molluscs. Sir Richard Boyle, the Great Earl of Cork, often referred in his papers to the river pearls and to buying them. Thus, on 3 January 1635: 'Sir Randal Cleyton and his lady with my two daughters came to Lismore, and he brought me a very large rownde fine pearle, taken in the river of Bandon, which the poor woman that found it sould in Cork for 2s [10p] in money and 4d [under 2p] in beer and tabackoe; that partie sould it again for two cows, who sould it the third tyme for £12 to a merchant of Cork; and there my cozen Bardsey counselled Sir Randall Cleyton to buy it for me, who paid for it in ready gold £30 sterling, and I bestowed it for a new year's gift on my daughter Dongarvon.'

Sir Richard Boyle seems to have introduced the seine net to Ireland, bringing it to his Cork estates, while Sir William Petty carried its use further west into Kerry. It was, in fact, just over the county border at Ardmore in Waterford that Boyle first mentioned using the seine net, in 1616. It was an exciting method of fishing, two big rowing boats, leader and follower, spotting the shoal of fish (pilchards originally, mackerel later on) and working round them, with a net being paid out between the two boats. As they moved round the shoal and toward each other, the fish were trapped in the net. This method of fishing continued almost to the present day; Conor O'Brien (*Three Yachts*, 1928) gave a vivid description of watching it off Valentia Island, and recorded that 40,000 mackerel had been landed from one shot of the net. Seine-boat racing is still the highlight of Kerry regattas.

In the 17th century, pilchards were very abundant and their fishing very profitable. Bantry town seems to have greatly developed on the strength of this fishing. The catch was processed in the *pailís éisc*, anglicised to 'fish palace'. The process began with piling up the fish in heaps for a couple of weeks in winter, three in summer. For export to hot climates, the fish were next smoked (*fumados*). But most were packed in large hogshead barrels and pressed by means of a weighted beam pushing down on a movable lid on top of the barrel. As the oil oozed out and the fish were pressed down, more were added, until the cask could hold no more. The oil which ran out from the bottom of the barrels was carefully collected and sold (as 'train oil', from a middle Dutch word meaning a tear, an exudation). Train oil was used as a lubricant and in leather processing among other things. In yet another method, the pilchards were gutted and split and preserved in salt in barrels – the way mackerel would later be dealt with. Ballydehob used bracken for smoking pilchards as it was thought to improve the flavour.

Ballydehob

Richard Boyle

The pilchards were exported to Spain and Portugal and to Italy. Sir Richard Boyle wrote in 1616: 'Delivered to Captain William Hull, £20 as earnest money to buy casks for fumados, upon an agreement to have half his fish to be taken the next season at Crookhaven in which he and I are to be partners and Captain Hull is to advance £100 with me in my season's fishing at Ardmore.' The pilchards were shipped out of Crookhaven from that particular fishery. There are still fairly extensive ruins of a fish palace near by. The slots in the wall on which one end of the pressing beams pivoted can still be seen. Irish people did not seem to have any taste for pilchards, but the Cornish miners at Allihies bought them. The Cornish are still very fond of pilchards, but the shoals have deserted Ireland.

Whales

Much bigger sea creatures that come into Irish waters are the whales, and birdwatchers on Cape Clear observatory see them at intervals as they pass along the south-west on a regular migration route. The Faroe islanders still hunt pilot whales, circling them in boats as a dog herds a flock of sheep and

German sail trainer Gorch Fock *at Custom House Quay*

Asgard II off the Old Head of Kinsale

driving them on to a suitable strand, where they can be easily killed in the shallow water. In this way, in May 1844, 300 or so pilot whales were killed at Glengarriff and valued at £1,500. But regular whaling was never practised out of Cork ports, though various species of whales at various times have been stranded. Reported Cork strandings include the blue whale, the fin whale, the little Minke and the bottle-nosed whale. Occasionally a ship ran into trouble by hitting a whale. The Cunarder SS *Scythia,* en route Liverpool-Cobh-New York, hit a whale off Ballycotton. The impact was so violent that the passengers thought a rock had been hit; the sea ran red with blood. In Cobh it was found that one of the four blades of the propeller had been broken off and passengers, mail and cargo had to continue by another ship. Much worse was the experience, described in Tuckey's *Remembrancer,* of the *Charming Sally* of Bristol, sailing under the captain John Maddox, in June 1738, who 'when within 300 leagues westward of Ireland, struck against a grampus of enormous size; the ship gave a terrible bounce, and overset all the chests &c in the cabin and between decks. It was supposed that the fish was cut dreadfully, as the sea was stained with his blood; shortly afterwards the ship began to fill with water, and upon examination, it was found to have been much injured, and to prevent her sinking, the crew stuffed pieces of beef and pork between the planks, and by continual pumping kept her above water for five days, at the end of which period they met a sloop from Portugal bound for Cork, into which they went, and thus arrived safe in this city (Cork) in a few days.'

To return to more ordinary sorts of fishing, Richard Pococke, one of Ireland's earliest tourists, riding around the country and putting the beauties of Killarney on the map, wrote a vivid account from Sherkin Island on 24 July 1758. 'They are all fishermen both in this island (Sherkin) and Cape Clear; and they have on the coast, places for curing fish, commonly called fish palaces, and come to these parts from Cork and Kinsale, most especially about Crookhaven which abounds in fish, and make up little huts in which they live during the summer; most in time of peace the French come over here to fish; when the Pilchards came great fortunes were made by them: now they get chiefly Mackrel during the month of July and August, Herring also come in at that time; they catch likewise Hake, Ling and Cod, all which they salt and barrel up the Mackrel and Herring. The Mackrel sell well, as they give only half a Mackrel to the Negroes (on the American Plantations) which they call a fish with one eye. In Crookhaven they are out in the evening and as soon as they see the shoals by the motion in the water they draw their Sein nets across and enclose 'em, they take also Breme, Turbot, Plaice and John Dory; and in the season the people live on fish; they have great plenty of salmon, but it does not sell under a penny a pound. Lobsters, crayfish and crabs sell for pence a piece and are very good. Wild fowl are sold by the couple – Plover 2d, Partridge 3d, Teal 4d, Duck 8d, and they sell black cattle which at three years old sell for 10s [50p] and when fat weigh 300lbs.'

Contemporary Cork fishermen have to go farther and work harder for

Richard Pococke

Sherkin

their catches, now that this great plenty of local fish has been destroyed; naval vessels patrol to try to prevent further destruction of stock by foreign ships poaching in Irish waters. The poaching is nothing new – the Frenchmen mentioned by Pococke evidently should not have been there, for Tuckey, in May 1767, quotes a complaint in one of the Cork newspapers that 50 French ships were fishing for mackerel on the coast near Bantry Bay 'without interruption from the revenue cutters'.

Cork city
Meat exports

For the city of Cork, however, the great exports of the 18th and 19th centuries were meat and butter. Vast numbers of cattle were slaughtered and the meat salted down, not only to supply British ships and the Royal Navy, but also large numbers of foreign vessels which would put into Cork to stock up before heading out into the Atlantic. L.M. Cullen in *An Economic History of Ireland since 1660* writes that late 18th-century Cork was 'in fact, one of the major ports of the entire Atlantic economy' and that it was then the most cosmopolitan port in all Ireland. It seems to have taken over the meat exporting trade from Kinsale, which in the 1660s is reported to have been frequented by ships loading beef, hides, tallow and butter, to go to France and the West Indies. But it was Cork that became 'the ox slaying city', in Lord Orrery's words of 1736, and of course the meat trade involved not only killing cattle, but processing the meat and by-products and making the casks in which the 'salt horse', as sailors sometimes rudely called it, went out. Cork had, until comparatively recently, a large colony of coopers making casks for meat, butter and stout. They had a reputation for being hard drinkers!

There are detailed figures for the Cork provision trade: 10,000 cattle were being slaughtered each year, according to a 1688 account. The meat went out to the West Indies and to many European ports. By 1750 the figure for the annual kill of cattle was 100,000, and by the period 1771-78 Cork was exporting 112,789 barrels of meat – 56% of the total Irish export. By then the places to which Cork exports went ranged from Africa to Norway, from New Zealand to New York, from Italy to Nova Scotia. Meat and meat by-products – beef and pork, tallow and hides (Cork had 40 tanneries at one time) – and butter, together with fish, were the main cargoes.

Butter exports

Cork's butter exports go back to around 1633, when the Irish learned how

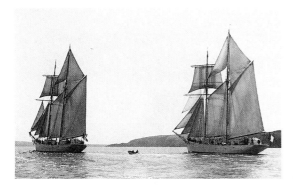

French sail trainers leave Kinsale

to barrel it so that it would travel. The first recorded butter export from Cork is 1636. The industry gathered momentum and in 1769 a committee of merchants was set up to manage the Butter Market. The actual market was near Shandon church, and to it came butter from all the neighbouring counties, where it was carefully checked, graded and packed, salted, for export. It gained a high reputation for quality control, coming to have no less than six different grades of butter. The annual export was around 109,367 barrels in the 1770s. It even succeeded in breaking into the Australian market, sending 60,000 firkins of butter there in 1858.

Butter Market

The end of the butter exports came when countries like Australia became self-supporting, and when Danish and Dutch butter edged into the English market. The whole scene began to change at the end of the 19th century; farmers no longer made butter at home but took milk to the new local creameries that were springing up. The development of refrigeration meant that it was no longer necessary to salt butter down to make it keep. Today Irish butter is mass-produced by the big creameries and exported under refrigeration.

The firkins (barrels) in which the Cork butter was packed were made of American oak. Earlier, timber for cask-making had been an important export from Cork and this had contributed, together with iron-smelting, to the destruction of Irish woods. Walter Raleigh, in his brief Irish adventure, started a cask-making industry for export – to the Azores among other places, for the wine trade. Since the Azores were Spanish, this was trading with the enemy and the English government stopped him. However, he began selling his 'pipe staves', as the barrel sections were called, to England. Apparently their export there, too, was prohibited but he got away with it for ten years. Richard Boyle, when he took over Raleigh's estates, went on with the pipe stave industry and produced some 4 million of them in the period 1616 to 1628 (equivalent to 500,000 cubic feet of timber). It was in this period that it was said that all French wines were casked in Irish wood. The chief timber

Timber

Walter Raleigh

Richard Boyle

*Cork city coat of arms
of Cork limestone*

Cobh graveyard

Baltimore,
Cork city
Kinsale
ports of County Cork were Baltimore, Cork city and Kinsale. Figures for the period 1683-86 give the following totals for their exports:

Baltimore: 1,958 hundreds of pipe staves; 160 tons of timber; 700 feet of planks
Cork: 266 hundreds of pipe staves; 56 tons of timber
Kinsale: 421 hundreds of pipe staves

But with the increasing destruction of the Irish woods, the trade changed. Timber was imported into Ireland in a steadily increasing stream from the early 18th century on. Wood for casks now came in, though they could still be hooped with Irish hazel or willow. The willows were grown in special plots which were regularly managed and harvested to provide withies for making baskets of all sorts and for such things as barrel hoops. The six inch Ordnance map of the 1840s marks many osieries ('sally gardens', willow beds) around the county.

Today it is difficult to picture all these little sailing ships coming and going with their imports and exports from so many little harbours along the coast of Cork. They were quite small and they were powered, of course, entirely by sail. But they made many journeys and carried a great deal of cargo. A number of them were built in Cork, and so helped use up more of the native timber. It is reckoned that a ton and a quarter of timber would go to making *Shipbuilders* a ton of wooden ship. Shipbuilders looked for oaks 100 years old when it came to building Britain's wooden walls, her naval vessels, and they reckoned it took 2,000 such oaks, 500 acres of woodland, to build a big warship. Shipwrights also looked for the natural arms and crooks of trees to fit into the actual design of the ship, as it would be far stronger than shaping cut timber for the purpose. (This has been done in building at least once in stone, when an anticline, a fold in the rocks at the quarry, was used for the arch of a doorway in Bantry workhouse.)

In County Cork, obviously, people had been building ships of native timber ever since they first settled there. Fishing boats were built near the little harbours from which they fished. As ships got bigger and their construction more specialised, they tended more and more to be built in one or two large yards near major ports. In 17th-century Cork, ships were
Youghal
Cork
Kinsale
Sherkin
Baltimore
built in Youghal, Cork and Kinsale, and on a smaller scale at many other places. Sherkin Island has a place called the 'Dock' and engaged in ship-building. This later shifted to the mainland at the adjacent Baltimore, where it was continued (up to large fishing boat size). It was in Baltimore that *Saoirse*, Conor O'Brien's yacht, the first to carry the Irish flag right around the world, was built by Tom Moynihan.

The county had some special designs of boat peculiar to itself. The design of the Kinsale hooker was said to be more seaworthy than that of the well-known Connemara hookers; as full plans exist, it would still be possible to build one. Probably it is the one described by J. Coleman in 1892: 'Cork

Harbour can boast of some very unique naval specimens in the safe and roomy, if not gracefully designed "hookers" which are always to be seen ploughing its waters, either trawling for fish or conveying cargo from one locality to another within its limits.' And he mentions another, striking visitor to the harbour: 'The small one-masted Norwegian craft, occasionally to be seen anchored near the Spit Lighthouse in Queenstown [Cobh] Harbour, laden with fish from Iceland en route to Spain, are said to resemble the kind of vessel in which the Danes of old invaded.' (The fish would have been dried cod.) Baltimore built, in the open on the shore, the distinctive Hare Island yawls, which sailed along the Cork coast, fishing. There was also a distinctive West Cork punt.

Major shipbuilding came to be concentrated in and around Cork Harbour, culminating in the very large dockyard at Rushbrooke of the present time. Earlier, ships were built at Passage West and in various small yards along the river running up into Cork itself, of which the Cork Harbour Commissioners' one is the sole survivor. Many of these small boatyards were done away with when the cut-limestone city quays were erected. **Rushbrooke**

The Anne Boland manuscript has an interesting account of the trials and tribulations of one shipbuilding yard at Passage West: 'Papa made another causeway in the town of Passage where the square is now, Paterson's house etc. and the Packet quay which he did not finish but let it on a lease to Mr Pike, the wealthy shipowner. Papa used to take great delight in the Docks and to be forever there building Yachts for his own amusement and Uncle John, who was equally fond of boats, built a small house there for captains of small merchant ships to stay when on shore. Papa who was alive to the important business position of the Docks, tried at that time to let them to an English company, but did not do so. He afterwards let them on a lease to Brown, a decent Protestant tradesman, with no capital whatever but his own industry. There was great planning before a proper gate was made to the Docks strong enough to keep out the tide. An English gentleman who was staying in Cork at the time told Papa that the gate Brown was intending to put there would keep out animals but not water. At this time, the anxiety of Brown's mind was so great that when he was asleep at night, he used to hear the waters rushing into the Dock and awake, thinking his prospects were ruined; so the gentleman I have mentioned and Papa put their heads together and advised Brown and the result was, a strong Iron Cassoon was made, resembling the stern of a ship and it answered the purpose and the Docks throve and prospered. But Papa had let them to Brown to encourage him as he was a very poor man. Papa also got Brown's father a lucrative contract for building boats for the coastguard, there was a great deal of smuggling going on at the time and the government were resolved to increase the number of revenue boats in order to put it down. In order to make money, Brown built a number of colliers and got those that had money to take shares in them, they were built of cheap green timber which would not last. Aunt Kitty lost £2,000 by taking shares in *Anne Boland* Passage West them, Grandmama lost a similar sum. And Grandmama Phipps, £1,500. She is the grandmama I am called after (Ann), and intended this money for me, one ship in particular, the John George Elphinstone, she had taken a great many shares in this ship. There was a good captain and crew on board her, but she went down off the coast at Kinsale and all on board her were drowned. Truly whoever built her, have a great deal to answer for! Mr Elphinstone lost a great deal of money by her, she was named after him. But for those Browns and their ships, Grandmama would have built a house for me on Toureen. I would have it now but for them. There were some other people in Passage engaged in boat building, the Barrys, the Peasleys and Jem Taylor – he had a dock near the Browns but did not get on, his dock is since absorbed in the Victoria Docks. I remember Papa giving directions to Jem Taylor how to raise a vessel that had been sunk. It was successful but Jem thought the proprietors did not give him enough of money, he was a rather stupid man.'

It was then very usual to invest money by taking shares in ships, so as to profit by their trading; the prudent spread the risk over many ships rather than taking large shares in just one or two. As it happens, Mr John George Elphinstone's will has survived, dated 13 December 1836. In this he leaves to 'my dearly beloved wife Catherine Elphinstone my share in the schooner *Nancy Dawson* also my share in the schooner *Jane* ...' Elphinstone died about three years later.

Passage then did not only build sailing schooners. It built the first steam paddle steamer to be constructed in Ireland. She was the *City of Cork*, launched 10 September 1815, and she was 86 feet long, 50 tons, with 18 hp engines by Boulton and Watt, giving her a speed of six knots. She survived to the 1850s but is said to have had so little power at the end of her life as to have been stopped by a shoal of jellyfish! She ran back and forth from Cork to Cobh. At Cork itself *Waterloo* was built in 1816, with a 50 hp engine by the Hive ironworks, thought to be the first marine engine built in Ireland. She was 88 feet long and survived until 1865.

Verolme
Dockyard

At Passage West today, a plaque still reads: QUEENSTOWN DRY DOCKS SHIP BUILDING AND ENGINEERING COMPANY LTD ESTABLISHED 1832, and goes on to say it was renamed the Royal Victoria Dockyard in honour of Queen Victoria's first visit to Ireland. Today the old Passage yard is occupied with ship-breaking; the building of big ships continued until recent years just across the narrow sound at Rushbrooke on Great Island. The 70-acre site of Verolme Cork Dockyard there includes an old dry dock of 1860, when shipbuilding started there, and which, falling out of use, sometimes served as a swimming pool for Cobh. It is now part of the Verolme complex, which dates from 1959 when the Dutch company purchased the site. Shipbuilding there was very remote from that of Passage West's first little wooden paddle steamers! Here are two slipways for the construction of ships of 73,000 and 35,000 tons dead weight; a dry dock in which ships up to 20,000 ton dead weight can be repaired, and two big floating docks as well. Verolme could design, build and fit out a ship from start to finish. They were also involved in the world of offshore gas and oil rigs, and had contracts for particular non-marine items – for example, the boilers for the Moneypoint (County Clare) electricity generating station. Unhappily, they had to close in 1984. In 1990 the yard was sold to the Dutch company, Damen Shipyards, and may now hope for revival.

Damen Shipyards Haulbowline

On Haulbowline Island, the British Admiralty established a victualling base for its fleet in the early 19th century, and later a large dry dock, completed in 1887. This naval dock was extended by work begun in 1907 to a total length of 608 feet, making it then the longest in Ireland. Today, Haulbowline is shared by the Irish navy with the steelworks, the old dock no longer functioning as such but used as a sheltered harbour for the naval corvettes. Meantime, the Crosshaven yard is the principal centre of yacht building and yacht repair in the county.

Crosshaven

It is difficult today to picture the sheer weight of shipping that once frequented the Cork seaways. There were the big British naval bases in Cork Harbour, Berehaven (Bantry Bay) and, in the old days, Kinsale. Until the coming of peace in 1815, there was the mustering of massive convoys in Cobh for the West Indies. The returning fleets would put into a Cork port. Richard Pococke wrote from Crookhaven in the Mizen peninsula on 25 July 1758: 'The West India fleet often puts in here, by contrary winds going or coming. When an East India fleet or indeed any other puts in here, it raises all provisions to an exorbitant price.' Sometimes when these big fleets were sighted off the coast too far out for identification, people were afraid they might be hostile. Tuckey's *Remembrancer* records several such alarms, as when on 24 September 1779 the ships turned out to be the Jamaica fleet homeward bound. On 22 September 1781 'great alarm' was caused when 137 sail of the Leeward Islands fleet were first sighted; they were accompanied by HMS *Triumph* and HMS *Panther*, each of 74 guns. Tuckey, too, records some departures. On 25 January 1778 the West India fleet of 64 ships left Cobh convoyed by HMS *Torbay* (74 guns) and a sloop called the *Camel*. On 24 September, another convoy for the West Indies left, of 'above 40 ships', convoyed by HMS *Winchelsea* and HMS *Lynx*.

Cork Harbour
Berehaven
Kinsale
Cobh
Crookhaven

Here, too, troops were mustered and put aboard transport. In December

Verolme

1807 there was a general order at Cobh that soldiers who died on board the transports there should be buried at sea in their hammocks and not brought ashore. From Cork Harbour convicts were loaded into the transports for shipment to the penal colonies in Australia. And at intervals the press-gangs rampaged ashore, seizing every able-bodied man, to so great an extent in 1803 that nobody was willing to work near the harbour until a ruling was made that year that only seamen were to be taken.

There were the people, then as now, who set out to do unusual things and then came sailing into Cork. Tuckey, in September 1741, records: 'Captain Chipps arrived in Cork from Danzic in 30 days in an open boat of 6 tons burthen, with only one boy. He had before made a voyage in a sloop from Barbados, with only one man.'

'Queenstown for orders.' In the days of sail, the ships, loaded up in Australia or America or wherever, left to get home as fast as they could, but without a fixed port for the unloading and sale of their cargo. They would then put into a British port, and it was often Cobh, to get in touch with the owners, who by then would know which was the best place to forward the cargo to. Since a ship, properly handled, is usually safe enough in the wide spaces of the ocean, it was very often on these coasting trips, from the port where she picked up her orders to the port where she would unload, that disaster struck and all was lost in a wreck on the dangerous shores.

It would undoubtedly be possible to compile a list, very long but incomplete, of the famous ships that came and went in Cork Harbour: men o' war, massive and wooden with muzzle-loading cannon, and a spread of sail; later the slinky iron ships of modern warfare; sailing merchant ships of all sorts and sizes, culminating in the great names of the last days of sail; transatlantic liners, from the days of sail through the early days of steam to the great days of the greyhounds of the ocean, until they were overtaken by air travel.

From Cobh the *Titanic* left for her fatal encounter with an iceberg. It was her last port of call; she spent one and a half hours lying off Roches Point to pick up the Irish passengers. The big ships did not linger very long; if there were only a few passengers, they would not even anchor but hove to while the tender came out and made the transfer in about 15 or 20 minutes. Transfer was always fast; even 6–700 bags of mail, and passengers and their baggage, would only take some two hours.

In 1897 there were some 400 calls by liners, going east or west, to Cobh.

Emigrants sailed to the New World by their thousands, in the Famine years and then continuing on and on, a steady drain of people looking for a better future across the sea. For many in the Famine years, Cobh was their last ever sight of land, for they died at sea. Hundreds more died on arrival in the New World of fevers which spread readily on the overcrowded, ill-found emigrant ships.

Eventually legislation was introduced to lay down some minimum standards for emigrant ships, but during 1847 one in nine of the passengers died on ships sailing from Cork. The worst of the emigrant ships were not those leaving from the big ports but the small ones going out from the little harbours, like the brig *Vista* which left Castletownbere with 'rotten rigging, uncaulked timbers, a leaking hull and a steerage which was a shambles'. While desperate and ignorant passengers might embark on such vessels, one wonders at the state of mind of the captain and crew, who must have been well aware of the small chance of their own survival. Carrying lifeboats, at least ones capable of making shore, was very much for the future; it was only the *Titanic* disaster that forced the Board of Trade to impose regulations. Her lifeboat capacity bore no relation to the numbers that would need them, if the ship were to be completely evacuated.

Cork Harbour was busy, as already mentioned, with small boats plying back and forth from one little coastal town to the other. There were ferries, fussy little paddle steamers. There were the pilot boats which went out to meet the big ships and bring them upriver, as there still are. In the 19th century, there were whale boats owned by Cork merchants who would go out, even as far as the Galley Head, to intercept the incoming big ships for orders. These whalers might be out for a week, and some did not return. In 1884 six Cobh men were drowned in one such boat, from which only one man, James Hayes, survived. Legislation was demanded to control their activities.

There were ships, too, that seemed almost indestructible relics of the past. At the little Cork Harbour port of Ballynacorra, by Midleton, Captain John Creenan owned a 106-ton schooner called *Brooklands*. She had been built in 1859 for the Azores fruit trade and she sailed on and on – she had no auxiliary engine – through World War II, and finally came to an end in 1953, when she was wrecked off the Wexford coast. Another elderly schooner was the 210-ton *Loch Ryan* (Captain James Nolan), registered at Skibbereen; she was bombed by three German aircraft on 16 August 1940, when she was carrying china clay from Cornwall to Arklow. No one was hurt but a good

Ballynacorra

Skibbereen

Kinsale Yacht Club

Old trawler, Bandon River

deal of damage was done to the ship, for which the Germans would not pay compensation, saying that she was in a blockaded area at the time of the incident. *Loch Ryan* survived until March 1942, when she was wrecked off the Donegal coast. During these same war years the infant Irish Shipping, having no facilities in Ireland for ship repair, bought and used the old dock-yard at Rushbrooke for this purpose.

To within living memory, small sailing ships travelled along the Cork coast carrying supplies here and there, together with larger steam vessels which called only at the bigger ports. The paddle steamer *South Western*, 143 feet long, built at Blackwall, began a service in the late 1850s from Cork to Dingle. There were calls, as required, at Schull, Castletownbere, Bantry, Kenmare, Sneem and Cahirciveen; the service was operated by the Clyde Shipping Company from 1876 until its end in 1905 (after the grant of £500 a year from the Congested Districts Board was withdrawn in 1904). Other steamers used on this route, which must have been a joy to travel, included *Rio Formosa*, *Skelligs* and *Valentia*; passengers paid 22s 6d for the round trip (£1.12^1/$_2$). It was at that time the easiest way to carry bulky cargoes along the south coast, for, apart from the routes served by the railways, carriage was a matter of horse-wagons on dirt roads.

Youghal was still busy, if declining, in the 1880s and owned some 50 vessels which traded with the Baltic, with St John's, Quebec and the Channel Islands, as well as Britain and continental Europe. Farm produce came down the Blackwater from Cappoquin and Mallow in little 'market boats', which re-turned with whatever goods were needed by the upriver communities. The island of Cape Clear had 43 fishing boats in 1920 – the catch was salted on the island – but the trade died out there, as elsewhere, at the end of the decade. Some of the Cape Clear boats engaged in the coasting trade and continued to do so until 1939. What appears to have been the first donkey-engine installed on a ship in Ireland was on one belonging to a Cape Clear man.

On Cork's ancient trading route to Bristol the new steam-assisted packet boats were very suitable for short or shortish cross-channel runs and able to maintain, if all went well with what the old accounts call 'the machinery', better schedules than sailing vessels. A group of businessmen of Cork, Dublin and Liverpool founded the St George Steam Packet Company in 1821. Its old offices, with a magnificent sculpture of St George and the dragon on its roof, still stand on the Cork quays. It began with the historic Cork-Bristol run, but was soon to add other routes: Liverpool, Glasgow, London, Dublin and the Isle of Man. By 1840 the company was operating 28 vessels, some of which it owned, while others were on charter. In 1843 it was reformed and reorganised as the Cork Steamship Company. That same year it placed an order for *Nimrod*, the first iron ship to be Cork owned. Thereafter the story is of more and bigger ships. The company later became the City of Cork Steam Packet Company, and in 1936 it was taken over by the B & I Line. Unhappily, recent decades have seen increasing contraction of

Cork–Dingle

Clyde Shipping Company

Youghal

Cape Clear

Cork–Bristol

St George Steam Packet Company

the route, Cork-Swansea and later Cork-Pembroke, ending with the complete withdrawal of B & I services from Cork in 1983, leaving the city, almost for the first time in its recorded history, without a direct shipping link to the Wales/Bristol area. This meant a considerable loss to tourism in the south-west, as visitors bringing their own cars had to drive all the way from Rosslare to reach the area. Happily in the last few years a new Cork-based company has run a Cork-Swansea car ferry during the summer period.

The other company operating various cross-channel routes out of Cork was the Clyde Shipping Company, which had ships working out of Cork from 1859 to 1962. They ran ships from Cork to Glasgow, with calls at Waterford and Dublin, as well as the aforementioned coasting service to Dingle.

Clyde Shipping Company

Undoubtedly the most famous Cork-owned ship to date was the *Sirius*, belonging to the St George Steam Packet Company. In 1838 she made the first steam scheduled run to New York, just beating Brunel's custom-built *Great Western* to it. The career of her captain, Richard Roberts, RN, to whose memorial in Passage reference has already been made, shows what an Irishman of that time might achieve. Born at 'Ardmore' (the house still stands) at Passage West in 1803, he joined the navy at the usual early age of the time and gained promotion to lieutenant by his gallantry in the capture of a slaver *El Almirante* off the West African coast in 1829. Roberts was then serving on the little *Black Joke*. (A popular tune of the day bore this name and Moore set words to it: 'Sublime was the warning which Liberty spoke'.) He was put in charge of the captured prize, and the log of his voyage on her to port is still extant. She was carrying 464 slaves and mounted 14 guns. Roberts was then transferred to HMS *Eden*; he came back to Britain from Sierra Leone in 1830, escorting some sick seamen home. Expecting to return at once to *Eden*, he found himself put on half pay and began a series of letters to the Admiralty asking for employment, pulling all the strings he could lay hold to. Eventually he turned to the local steamship company and a post on board the PS *Victory* of the St George outfit, becoming her captain

Sirius

Captain Roberts

Passage West

St George and the dragon on the offices of the St George Steam Packet

in 1834. *Victory,* built in Liverpool in 1832, was 154 feet long and, of course, a wooden ship. It was before he became captain that all the crew were dismissed for 'smuggling whiskey in their births' (a common way at the time of spelling 'berth'). *Victory* brought London papers to Cork via Bristol, 30 hours earlier than they would have arrived going via Holyhead. In February 1836 the *Cork Southern Reporter* gave Captain Roberts a silver box for carrying the express with the King's speech to them. Politely thanking them, Roberts wrote: 'I feel I only discharged my public duty as the Commander of that excellent Vessel, the Victory Steamer, whose superior power fully warranted the engagement entered into for that purpose.'

James Beale, Cork businessman and president of the Cork School of Art and Commerce, was involved with the St George Company and the development of steam navigation. Could a steamboat carry enough fuel to make it across the Atlantic? Some of the experts said firmly 'no'. Brunel was planning and building the *Great Western* and the British and American Steam Navigation Company the *British Queen* for that very purpose. Brunel was

ahead; the *Queen* was nowhere near ready. It was James Beale who suggested to the British and the Americans that they charter the St George's new cross-channel steamer *Sirius*, put Roberts in charge of her and get a jump on Brunel. *Sirius,* built at Leith by Robert Menzies and Son in 1837, had cost the company £27,000. She was schooner rigged with a beautiful dog figure-head (which still exists), 208 feet long and 26 feet broad, 700 tons, and she was, as the registration certificate says, 'propelled by steam with an engine room 57 feet in length'. The engine was built by J. Wingate and Co. of Glasgow; the cylinders were of 60 inches diameter with a piston stroke of six feet, and she had Hall's Patent Condensers, so that she used and re-used fresh water in her boilers. (Incredibly, the early marine steam-engines had used salt water.) The engines developed 320 hp.

So *Sirius* slipped her moorings at the Eastlane Stairs in London on 28 March 1838, and set off on the great adventure. She called into Passage West to top up her supplies of coal and was given a rousing send-off. She carried a crew of 38, including one stewardess, Margaret Lynch. Forty passengers had responded to the publicity and the posters advertising the passage: first class, 35 guineas including provisions and wines, five ladies and six men; second class, 20 guineas including provisions, five ladies and three men; third class/steerage, 8 guineas, one lady and twenty men. She had 450 tons of coal, 20 tons of water and 58 casks of resin, which they found made the furnace burn hotter. She was well provisioned with food, taking on the bulk of her groceries in London, but picking up £20 11s (£20.55) worth of Beamish and Crawford's Extra Stout in Cork and some tinned goodies from Cork's pioneer food canning firm, Gambles Provisions of Morrison's Quay. She ran into rough weather but the steam-engine continued to turn, and she paddled into New York to a tumultuous reception on 22 April 1838. Brunel's *Great Western,* delayed by a stupid accident, arrived less than 24 hours after *Sirius*, but nobody would look at her; it was all '*The Sirius: The Sirius: The Sirius*' of the banner headlines. In spite of receptions and crowds of visitors to the ship, Roberts found time to dash off a letter to his wife Jane Johnson of 'Rockingham', Passage West. He wrote: 'New York. 26 April 1838. My darling little Jane. What pleasure I write from this place where we arrived the 22nd after Eighteen days passage against very heavy Gales and strong breezes, we have performed wonders – our reception in New York is beyond all description – nothing that could not be done to compliment and welcome me as the first Steam Navigation to cross to their shores – deputation after deputation call with all the pomp and parade of the United States ... I will send papers they give a full description ... The "Great Western" arrived the day after, she had a passage of 16 days – she did not get the Heavy Gale that we encountered the third day after leaving Cork – I am classed here with the greatest men of the day – judge all for yourself by the papers. "Great Western" is scarcely noticed – they have not taken as well with the Yankeys as we have. My own little darling, how happy I shall be when I am once more in your company... I would not have lost being the first person in Steam for £500 – the "Sirius" is crowded all day scarcely less than three or four thousand every day – the Packet is just off – I am your affectionate and fond husband, Richd.'

Sirius steamed back to more celebrations. Captain Roberts was, naturally, particularly fêted in Cork and given the freedom of the city. *Sirius* made a second run to New York but under a different captain, for Roberts was sent off immediately to see to the fitting-out of the *British Queen*. This took an inordinate length of time but she finally got going on the New York run in

Cutty Sark Tall Ships Race 1991. Malcolm Miller *with her all girl crew, swings across river to berth at a Cork city quay*

1839 and, with Richard Roberts in command, made a number of very successful voyages. Her sister ship, *President*, was an unlucky ship. In appearance she lacked the grace of the *Queen* and did badly in three trips, each under a different captain. Roberts was transferred to her to try to improve her reputation; she was said already to be in poor condition. They made it to New York but disappeared without trace on the return voyage in March 1841. It is generally believed that she foundered in a severe storm, but an undated clipping from a Cork paper amongst the Roberts manuscripts relates a death-bed confession of a seaman who said he had been a pirate and that *President* had been taken by pirates, her company killed and the ship scuttled.

Cork Habour Commissioners

From *Sirius* and the pioneering of steam voyages to the present day, the Cork Habour Commissioners work hard to make the most of their great harbour. Many new industries and industrial estates, a number belonging to various multinationals, have sprung up around the harbour area, and more are hoped for.

Tivoli Industrial Estate
Dunkettle

Ringaskiddy

Very extensive reclamation work has been done downriver from Cork city, ending with the completion in 1976 of the 155-acre Tivoli Industrial Estate, with its roll-on roll-off facilities and container handling facilities. More reclamation is going on, further east, toward Dunkettle. Next, the Commissioners turned their attention to the outer harbour and the construction of a deep-water harbour at Ringaskiddy. This ties in with a plan to develop a new industrial estate in the Ringaskiddy area, based on the new harbour. Its construction involved much reclamation from the sea for the actual harbour and the deepening of the waterways leading to it. In 1984 Ringaskiddy was chosen as Ireland's first Free Port. In 1990 the completed deep-water terminal was opened by an Taoiseach Charles Haughey and the big Cunarder *Queen Elizabeth II* was able to dock there. She had already begun to call to Cork again as part of the 150th anniversary celebrations of the *Sirius* voyages in 1988.

Queen Elizabeth II

XVII

Attack and Defence

I
F THERE ARE some magnificent harbours along the coast of the county,
there are also many hazards. It is a dangerous coast; all coasts are, but
this one is fanged with jagged reefs and high, unforgiving cliffs. To warn
of its major hazards, the lighthouses, successors of ancient beacon lights,
flash their messages; to rescue those in trouble on the sea, the lifeboats are
always ready. But in the past there was also danger of seaborne raiders,
whether of local origin, foreign armies or professional pirates.

World strategies have changed so much that Ireland cannot be thought of

Mizen Head

now as the 'soft underbelly', in Churchill's wartime phrase, of England. But she was that, a place to which a Spanish or French fleet could sail, with any luck almost unobserved, and make a landing with the expectation of a friendly welcome from very many of the local people. It was for that reason that star forts sprang up all along the coast after the battle of Kinsale, and Martello and signal towers later when the French were feared.

O'Driscolls

One of the strangest sea conflicts, however, was that between the O'Driscolls, whose country lay west of Cork city around Baltimore and Sherkin, and the men of Waterford. Each raided the other by sea, in a conflict that went on for a long time. In 1368, the O'Driscolls teamed up with the Poers (Powers), whose terrain lay to the east of Cork Harbour (Power Head commemorates them) to raid Waterford. In 1413 the Waterford men retaliated by raiding Baltimore. More than a hundred years later the *Santa Maria*, en route from Lisbon to Waterford with 100 tons of wine, was foolish enough to shelter in Baltimore and was promptly seized by the doubtless thirsty O'Driscolls. Waterford came back with a massive raid, destroying Sherkin Friary, the castle on that island and another on the mainland at Baltimore, and rampaging over several other islands.

The O'Driscolls were very powerful in their own terrain and they made it expensive to fish there. They claimed, at the end of the 16th century, that 'every ship or boat that fishes within his [O'Driscoll Mor's] territory, viz, between the Fastnet Rock and the Stags Rocks is to pay 10s 2d [just over 50p], a barrel of flour, a barrel of salt, a hogshead of beer and of fish three times a week – and if they dry their fish in any part of the country, they are to pay 13s [65p] for the rocks'. (Fish were spread to dry on the coastal rocks in the sun.)

Baltimore

In 1631 came the famous Sack of Baltimore by Algerian pirates. These raiders seem to have been most excellent seamen, for they not only raided Ireland and carried off prisoners, but made their way as far north as Iceland, where they carried out a devastating raid on the Westman Islands, bearing off their inhabitants all the way back to Africa.

Richard Boyle

By this time Baltimore had been 'planted', like many other places in Cork, with a little colony of English settlers brought there by Sir Thomas Crooke, and it was these unfortunate English who were abducted. Richard Boyle, the Great Earl, sent a map of Baltimore to Viscount Dorchester, with a covering letter dated 19 February 1631 pointing out how best to fortify the place. He went on, 'for that I have received new intelligence that the Turks are preparing to infest these maritime parts of Munster. And my intelligence (whereto I give belief) importeth that they mean to attempt the forts of Cork and Kinsale – Halebolyes [Haulbowline] and Castle Park [James Fort]... such nests should not be left unguarded for Turks to lay eggs in.'

Algerian pirates

On 18 June 1631 two Turkish (Algerian) ships under the command of Captain Matthew Rice (a Dutchman and convert to Islam) came nosing along to Kinsale. They had already captured and sunk a Dartmouth ship, taking the crew prisoner. But off Kinsale they sighted two warships, so they turned west toward Baltimore. Off the Old Head of Kinsale they fell in with two Dungarvan boats and the captain of one of them, Thomas Hackett of Dungarvan, offered to pilot them to Baltimore. (One wonders if perhaps the old O'Driscoll-Waterford feud influenced his decision.) The two raiding ships came into Baltimore at midnight, landing at 2 a.m. on 21 June 1631. They sacked the town and carried off 119 prisoners. Not until 1646 did the English parliament send a man to Africa to try to redeem captives, at £30 a head. Of those that were brought back were two from Baltimore, John Brodbroke and Ellen Hawkins. Thomas Hackett remained in Ireland, but was caught and hanged in Cork two years after the raid.

The easiest way to raise an alarm in those days was by lighting beacon fires. *Beacons*
Lord President St Leger wrote to the Lords Justices of Ireland, on 27 March 1632, with the necessary details. 'I have ordered beacons to be set up on the following headlands and eminences: One at Dundeedy [Galley Head] and at Dunworley [Seven Heads] to alarm the inhabitants at Ibawne, who upon the firing of the beacons, are to assemble under arms at Cloghnakilty; so that if either Ross or Timoleague are attempted, they may relieve them. Castle-haven has not many inhabitants, and the harbour was secured by Mr Salmon, who raised a fort and mounted ordnance on it. I have ordered beacons to be erected on the promontory over Baltimore, on the island of Cape Clear, at Mizen Head, and one at Sheep's Head Point. Mr Daniel O'Sullivan has a house of reasonable strength at Ballygobbin: he promises to erect five beacons – one on the Dorseys, and four upon the Great Island [Bere Island]. I have directed O'Sullivan More who lives in the river of Kenmare, to take warning from the beacon erected on the promontory over the Dorseys.'

The Algerian pirates still posed a threat in 1636 when Stafford reported their actually getting into Cork Harbour. 'The Turks still annoy this coast, they came of late into Cork Harbour, took a boat which had eight fishermen in her, and gave chase to two more, who saved themselves among the rocks, the townsmen looking on at the same time, without means or power to save them.'

Less exotic pirates frequented the Irish coasts at the same time. In 1631 *Nut*
not only 'Turks' raided, but a certain man called Nut who both robbed at sea and on land. He had a little fleet of three ships: his own (20 guns, 300 tons), his second-in-command's which they had captured and which had belonged to St Malo (160 tons), and a third, another capture, originally belonging to Dieppe. Nut brought all this flotilla into Crookhaven and took up provisions and water. Apparently the government thought the best thing to do was to make friends with so formidable a freelancer, and sent him a pardon which, after an initial refusal, he condescended to accept.

As to the Spanish fleets, story has it that they gave chase to Sir Francis *Spanish fleets*
Drake in 1589 and he, with five ships, put into Cork Harbour and moved up *Sir Francis Drake*

Drake's Pool

Battle of Kinsale

French fleet

the river Owenboy estuary from Crosshaven. Now this estuary bends sharply and Drake went well up it, and when the Spaniards sailed into Cork Harbour, they could see no trace of him and went away again. Ever since, this particular reach of the river has been called Drake's Pool.

The big invasion of Cork waters by Spanish ships occurred, of course, at the time of the battle of Kinsale in the winter of 1601. Twenty-four Spanish ships brought men and material to Kinsale that October, and sailed away again after the battle was lost in the following January. Their commander, Don Juan del Aguila, surrendered on good terms, with safe conduct back to Spain. Earlier, in November 1601, a reinforcement of six ships and 2,000 men, led by Don Pedro de Zuiber, had fought a brisk engagement off Castlehaven against English ships, which got the worst of it. The Spaniards landed and made Castlehaven their base, putting garrisons in its castles. After the defeat at Kinsale they sailed back to Spain, Red Hugh O'Donnell travelling with them.

Then there was the war with France, and Irish hopes to free Ireland with French assistance. It seems that the Irish leaders overestimated the enthusiasm of ordinary Irish people for revolt: Cork certainly does not seem to have been filled with delight when a French fleet staggered into Bantry Bay. Under the young General Hoche, accompanied by Wolfe Tone, 43 ships had left Brest on 15 December 1796. They had 15,000 soldiers on board and all the necessary arms and equipment for such a force. Bad weather and poor navigation scattered this Armada – the weather fought for England – and the French fleet abandoned the whole project and trickled back to France. So the same motto, *Aflavit Deus et Dissipater*, that had been used at the time of the Spanish Armada was put on some commemorative medals issued to

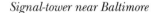

Signal-tower near Baltimore

Drake's Pool

the volunteers at Kilcrohane on the Sheep's Head peninsula, who had stood-to when invasion seemed imminent. Some of the French ships cut their cables in their haste to get away, and an anchor dredged up by a fishing boat in 1964 in the bay very possibly belonged to one of their ships. It is now displayed on a plinth on the road into Bantry from Cork.

Communications were slow and difficult as compared to the radio and aerial reconnaissance of today. Colonel White of Bantry House sent off a messenger to Cork, who rode the 42 Irish miles in four hours on a single horse. White was rewarded with a peerage. But Maurice O'Connell of Derrynane, uncle of the 'Liberator', seems to have seen the fleet two days before White did, and wrote with the news to Pelham on 20 December 1796. The difficult, scrappy way in which he picked up news is well indicated by Colonel White's letter of 30 December 1796. 'A lugger this day came to anchor back of Whiddy Island, full of men, eight of my tenants went on board with provisions, and were detained. An American brig came to anchor before the house this instant, she saw two French frigates, one of 20 guns, the larger at anchor near Bere Island, the frigates fired at her – they are at anchor with the lugger – they have a small English brig – no other ships in our bay – the rest must be disposed of: I went to Whiddy to see the lugger, she cannot be so mad as to land. 5 o'clock at night – what we thought were frigates are two sixty-fours, they appear as if they were in an engagement from the shattered condition of their bowsprits and rigging, and this from the report of our naval officer – they are at anchor at the north side of the island. This instant Admiral Elphinstone and Hull's dispatches are that a French 40 gun frigate, 346 seamen, with 230 soldiers on board, is wrecked at Barley Cove, only 7 saved. If Kingsmill could send any force to Elphinstone they would be taken, all the country people are prepared with pikes, spades &c and will do their best.'

Troops marching to Bantry from Cork were, it was reported, well received by the country people along the route, who gave them food. The invasion never came, but the fear that the French might return someday made the authorities eager to improve coastal defence and communications. Neither was 1796 the first time a French fleet had sailed into Bantry Bay. Lewis, in his *Topographical Dictionary* wrote that 'In 1689 a French Fleet entered the bay and being pursued by the English fleet under Admiral Herbert, bore down upon the latter in a line of 28 ships of war and five fire ships, when a brisk action ensued, in which the English stood to sea in order to gain some advantage by manoeuvring, and which terminated by the French Admiral's returning into the bay.'

Beacons

At the end of the 18th century the beacon fire was still the basic form of warning alarm. If the watchmen were quick, a signal fire lit on Dursey Island could, through a chain of beacon sites, alert Cork in minutes instead of the four hours that Colonel White's remarkable horse took. More sophisticated forms of long-distance communication were only slowly being invented and promoted. In 1782 the British navy had got its first signal book – a series of numbers each of which represented an instruction or word (the present day 'Q' code does the same thing with groups of letters). It was in this old number code that Nelson made his famous signal at Trafalgar. In Ireland, as far back as 1766, that somewhat eccentric mechanical genius Richard Lovell Edgeworth, Maria Edgeworth's father, had been working on a semaphore, in which arms or shutters in various positions are a code for the alphabet. Not until he learned of similar work being done in France did Edgeworth try to promote his semaphore as a system for military use, which he did in 1795. Nobody was interested, not even after the events of 1796, when in 1797 he published a pamphlet entitled *A Letter ... on the Tellograph and on the Defence of Ireland.* The French were more progressive and the Edgeworths on their first visit to Paris in October 1802 were thrilled to see the 'Telegraph at work'. Later on, massive semaphore masts were erected along the Irish coast, by means of which ships could signal their arrival and receive instructions.

Signal-towers

Meantime, government set about building a series of signal-towers along the coast. The work seems to have begun in the last days of 1803, when a Captain Maguire RN arrived in Cork to superintend the erection of the towers, and their building went on all through 1804. They are some of the most attractive and beautifully located of Irish monuments, looking, at first sight, exactly like the late medieval tower-house. They are built, and built very well, of local stone, with some use of brick inside and with Gothic battlements. Their walls were weather slated against the driving rain and mist that would beat upon them in their exposed position. A drystone wall seems to have been built round them and, in surviving examples, to have been semicircular in outline on the seaward side, but rectangular on the landward. This can be well seen at Ballylinchy (Baltimore) and at the Seven Heads tower.

They are all in sight of one another – obviously this was essential – and only one of the Cork series has been destroyed. In clear, fine weather, there

Signal-tower, Seven Heads

Beacon house, Old Head of Kinsale

is no better way to get to know the coast, and see the most splendid prospects, than to visit some of these old watch-towers – especially on Dursey Island, Sheep's Head (lately collapsed), Mizen Head, Ballylinchy (Baltimore), Seven Heads, the Old Head of Kinsale and Knockadoon. Frequently the visitor will find a small, modern look-out close to an old tower; this was for wartime coast-watchers at the time of the Second World War.

The tower locations follow fairly closely those chosen after the Algerian raids. The series begins in County Cork with the very well preserved tower on the tip of Dursey Island, at 832 feet. Next is one on Bere Island, at 600 feet, which has been struck by lightning. The Sheep's Head tower, at nearly 700 feet, was gloriously sited, well out on that long narrow peninsula. On the Mizen, the old tower looks down on the present lighthouse; it is about 400 feet above the sea, and was reached by a long track running inland northeast above the present Mizen road, and surviving as a 'green road'. Very near is a fine tower on Brow Head still with much of its weather slating. Yet another above Lowertown just west of Schull is now restored as a house. Beside the later, disused lighthouse on Cape Clear is that island's signal-tower, and then, on the mainland, Ballylinchy stands at about 300 feet, with great views over the Kedge Islands and along the coast, east and west, and out to Cape Clear.

Next along the coast is the tower on Toe Head, placed inland on the rising crest of that big headland. A dwelling-house was built on to this tower, but is now ruined. The Galley Head tower was not on the headland at all, but on the high ground inland, toward Clonakilty at Ardfield. Only the lower part of the tower survives. The Seven Heads tower is in good condition, as is the one on the Old Head of Kinsale. The missing tower in the sequence was on Barry's Head, east of Kinsale Harbour; it was pulled down only 25 years after its building and the stones used for a farmhouse. Next then is the tower on Robert's Head, and east of Cork Harbour, Roches Point, Churchtown (near Ballycotton, converted to a dwelling) and Knockadoon.

The towers were defendable, up to a point, but the second structure, erected at the same time, was supposed to be an immensely strong 'pill-box' to mount a massive muzzle-loading cannon, which could be trained to fire in any direction. This structure was the Martello tower, and Cork had six in Bantry Bay (four on Bere Island and one each on Whiddy and Garinish Islands) and five in Cork Harbour. The origin of the name and the design is interesting. In 1794 HMS *Juno* and HMS *Fortitude* were beaten off from the island of Corsica, which they were trying to capture, by the strong gunfire from a round tower at Mortella Point. Not to be beaten, the British came back, made a landing and took the tower, but it impressed them so much that they decided it was the ideal design for a strongpoint. Mortella means myrtle, which grew abundantly in the area, but the British contrived to misspell it Martello, and Martello towers they remain to this day. The design, with minor local modifications, is standard: circular or nearly circular, with

Dursey Island

Bere Island
Sheep's Head

Mizen

Brow Head
Lowertown

Cape Clear
Ballylinchy

Toe Head

Galley Head

Seven Heads
Old Head of Kinsale
Barry's Head
Robert's Head
Roches Point
Knockadoon

Martello towers

massive walls some eight feet thick. Entry was by a ladder to a door set about ten feet from the ground (later, ground-level doors might be added, when attack was no longer feared). On the ground floor was the store of gunpowder (in a wood-lined room fixed with wooden pegs to avoid any risk of sparks) and the store of cannonballs. There was also a water storage tank. Living quarters for the soldiers were on the next floor. On the very strong roof the big cannon was mounted, its carriage fixed to a central pivot, so that it could be swung around the full 360 degrees and trained to fire in any direction. At the Rosslague tower in Cork Harbour the central pivot still survives.

Whiddy
Garinish

The Whiddy Island tower, which was being built in October 1804, was particularly large, with an internal diameter of 240 feet. That on Garinish Island, in the middle of the beautiful and exotic garden, is said to have been the first Martello built in Ireland. Its gun carriage pivot appears to be an actual old cannon set into the roof. In Cork Harbour the Martellos are on

Haulbowline
Rosslague
Belvelly
Monning
Ringaskiddy

Haulbowline, at Rosslague and Belvelly and Monning (Fota), with a fine example at Ringaskiddy, back from the new harbour there, and enclosed with a circular, 'ring fort' style, earthwork. Monning is the only Irish Martello ever to have been attacked – on St Stephen's day 1867, by Captain Mackey and his Fenians. Taking the garrison by surprise, they were able to demand the keys of the magazine from which they bore off all its store of arms and ammunition. Nobody on either side was hurt, the raiders assuring the soldiers' wives and children that there was no need for alarm and they would not be killed!

It was not a false alarm that put all these and more structures up. Napoleon did intend to invade Britain and there were even schemes that he might attempt an airborne attack, by balloon. So Ireland went ahead, building harbour defences on either side of the entry to Cork Harbour. The

Camden fort
Carlisle fort

enormous structures that would become Forts Camden and Carlisle (now Dún Uí Mheachair and Dún an Dairbhisigh) were begun in 1804, together with those on Spike Island. Lesser but still massive structures went up on

Martello tower, Bere Island

Bere Island, in addition to the signal and Martello towers.

It is perhaps only from the air that these great harbour structures can be fully appreciated or an idea gained of the immense labour that must have been expended on them. Some 400 or 500 men were employed in 1804. The two massive and high headlands on either side of the entry to Cork Harbour, Ram's Head (Camden) on the Crosshaven side and King John's Fort (Carlisle) on the eastern one, were obvious defensive positions and there had been some fortifications on both of them for a long time. For some part of the work, convict labour was used, and additions and improvements went on all through the 19th century. The result is that these two natural bluffs have become fortresses in which the whole hillside has been remodelled for defence, deep-trenched around the landward side, and with gun emplacements at different levels, from the upper ones down to those in deep-cut passages for firing point-blank into passing shipping.

Spike Island had an old ruined fort and towards the end of the 18th century the government set up a battery of twenty-one 24-pounders and a magazine. In 1790 more extensive plans were made for a great fortress by Charles Vallencey, RE, FRS, soldier, antiquary and engineer, with Michael Shanahan as architect. The work pushed ahead after the French invasion attempt and the rising of 1798, and continued for decades. Convicts were used to build the wonderful star-plan fortress of limestone hewn from the island, and to scarp the island itself up to the great walls. Spike, after transportation for convicts was halted, served as a prison from 1847 to 1883. There is a graveyard on the island where those who died are buried, most with unmarked stones, a few with the prison number of the dead man on them. Among those imprisoned on Spike was John Mitchell, awaiting transportation, which was not ended for political prisoners until 1856.

Spike Island

Spike Island was being developed by the Irish navy, now that their quarters at Haulbowline are too cramped for their increasing numbers, but it is at

19th-century fortifications, Whiddy Island

Camden Fort, Cork Harbour

Charles Fort

present being used as a prison again. It also serves at intervals as a quarantine post for imported cattle. Carlisle and Camden and the lesser forts on Bere Island, as well as Charles Fort, were all used by the British forces until their withdrawal. With the exception of Charles Fort, the Irish army has maintained an occasional presence at the old strongholds. In 1989 Cork County Council took over Camden and it is being developed as a heritage centre.

Berehaven

Berehaven is an excellent harbour and was one of the British navy's bases. In the 1890s a tiny country post office at Waterfall, between Castletownberehaven and Ardrigole, had the honour or duty of receiving telegrams for the fleet 'except when the Flagship is connected by telegraph cable with that office'. 'That office' also got them the exact time at 13.00 hours, Greenwich time, which was 'passed on to the ship connected by Telegraph cable with the shore by the operator at Waterfall directly he observes the needle deflected'. Communications had improved a lot in the century, Valentia Island and Newfoundland linked by submarine cable, and the wires of the 'electric telegraph' strung along the railway lines everywhere. Crookhaven was soon to see, or rather hear, an even greater breakthrough.

Coastguards

Ruined coastguard houses may be found along all the coast. One has been very attractively restored and made into a beautiful house at Rosscarbery. They remind us that there was a large and active coastguard maintained with regular coastal patrols, providing a service which was not continued by the new Irish government. The coastguards did what they could when a ship was seen to be in difficulties but their principal purpose, with the revenue officers, was to prevent smuggling. Smuggling will always be with us, as long as

Smugglers

governments tax or prohibit certain imports, and it went on all along the coast of Cork, with general popular approval, and many families lived and thrived by it. Sometimes they worked with the Cornish smugglers. People like the Deasys of Abbeymahon in the Seven Heads area maintained a small fleet of ships running back and forth to France. The revenue officers were sometimes lucky in making a capture; sometimes they found it more prudent to turn a blind eye. Seizures when they took place were quite large; for example, 3,000 lbs of tobacco taken in January 1760 by Cliffe Tottenham, surveyor of Timoleague. The sloop *Margaret and Hanora* of Clonakilty was captured by the revenue cutter *Prince George* in June 1766 and found to be loaded with brandy from Nantes; and these are only a few examples from a number in a single district.

Tuckey's *Remembrancer* records on 7 January 1785 that 'Eight American vessels which sailed in company for the purpose of smuggling, appeared off the harbour of Castle Townsend, but being pursued by the *Bushe* cutter, an engagement took place within pistol shot, when the latter was overpowered by numbers: the smugglers then landed all their cargoes.' It is said, in fact, that early in the 18th century, privateers and pirates actually raided in Cork Harbour and carried off some of the customs officers 'to larn them to speak

French'. And Tuckey has a fine tale from 10 June 1776 of a woman outwitting the customs men: 'A woman who had been on board an East Indiaman then in this harbour [Cork], refusing to be searched by the revenue officers, was carried on board the quarantine vessel that lay near them, where she was obliged to strip to her shift, inside which she had a piece of handkerchief, which was immediately seized, to the poor woman's mortification, it being her all. Decency caused some persons present to direct that she should be accommodated with a private place to put on her clothes, in consequence of which she was ordered into the cabin, in which was a locker, where the different seizures, consisting of muslins, silks &c of considerable value, had been deposited; the key having remained in the locker, she closed the door and helped herself plentifully to the seizures, which she packed up in quantities, by way of reprisal, and left the ship.'

Ballyandreen, just west of Ballycotton, was one of many smuggling villages. A French ship used to call regularly. 'Watch the wall, my darling, as the gentlemen go by.' An elderly man in Ballyandreen told me that his father would sometimes find a box of cigars and a roll of tobacco left in the stern of his boat. It was said to be one of the places that tried to tempt ships in by putting out lights that could be mistaken for proper beacons, and so lure them on to the rocks where they could be wrecked and plundered – the Cornish did the same thing. For a long time Ballyandreen had a running fight with the coastguards over driftwood, which the people naturally wanted to gather but which was supposed to belong to the landlord alone.

To warn shipping of dangerous rocks, or the right route into a harbour, beacon lights and lighthouses were erected from very ancient times. Cork's oldest light still in action is that at Youghal, where it was maintained by the nuns in medieval times. St Anne's Tower, dating from the late 12th century, was intended to guide the Anglo-Norman ships into the harbour. It was about 24 feet high and ten feet in diameter, with spiral steps leading up inside to an upper chamber which had two big windows, one facing the

Ballyandreen (margin)

Lighthouses
Youghal (margin)

Early lighthouse, Old Head of Kinsale

Old lighthouse and signal-tower, Cape Clear

Old Head of Kinsale

middle of Youghal Bay and the other Capel Island. It was demolished in 1848 to make way for the new light to be placed there, which was lit for the first time in 1852. The present light is automatic, requiring neither nuns nor men for its tending. In fact, all Irish lights are being automated now.

The ancient beacon house still survives on the Old Head of Kinsale. The visitor may be confused by the number of monuments on the Old Head. In sequence, they begin with the signal-tower, on the higher point of the landward side of the narrow neck leading out to the headland. On the neck itself are the defensive walls and towers of the De Courcy castle, on the site of the defences of the ancient promontory fort of Downmacpatrick. (The maps mark the site of Duncarmna on the west side of the narrow neck of land at this point, which was perhaps a small promontory fort whose headland is now entirely eroded away.)

Beyond the narrow neck, the land rises steeply to the extensive headland. On the east side (thus facing into the entry to Kinsale Harbour), as the land levels out, are two old ruined buildings. The long, low, rectangular one on the west side of the lighthouse road is the old beacon house – the fire was kindled on its massive roof. There seems to be no record of when a beacon was first placed to mark the entry to Kinsale; it is probably very ancient like Youghal's. In November 1703 the Sovereign (mayor) of Kinsale successfully petitioned to get the lights going again on the Old Head – they must previously have been allowed to lapse for some reason. The old beacon house was eventually replaced with the early 19th century, conventional round lighthouse on the east side of the road, which is now in ruin. Finally, in the mid-19th century a new lighthouse was erected on the tip of the Old Head, right out on the rocks, so that its signals shine both east and west of the headland as well as out to sea. In the old days the lighthousekeepers got plots of land nearby to farm as part of their wages. Ruined buildings near the lighthouse are of a semaphore station and look-out. The present lighthouse has some

Snow on the Old Head of Kinsale

Old lighthouse, beacon house and ruined lightkeepers' house, Old Head of Kinsale

of the old candle reflectors from the earlier light. The original fog signal stood out on the tip of the headland; in the first period of the lighthouse's existence, it was (as elsewhere) an actual gun, with a gunner employed to fire it.

Very probably there was once a beacon at the entry to Cork Harbour, but there are no remains or site. As well as the present lighthouse and meteorological station at Roche's Point, at the harbour mouth today there are the remains of the signal-tower and of two round lighthouse towers. One of these must be the one mentioned by Tuckey, who records in June 1815 an order to value the land around Roche's Tower for the purpose of building a lighthouse there and, in June 1817, work on the lighthouse being started. Roche's Point is thus somewhat a headland of towers, as there is a folly tower, called Roche's Tower, on a small hill immediately east of the lighthouse ones. The foundations of the old semaphore on the point are still to be seen, too. Cork Harbour

A lightship was moored over the dangerous Daunt Rocks on the approach to Cork Harbour and has latterly been replaced by an automatic signal. A fog signal station was placed on Power Head to the east of the entry to Cork Harbour, but no longer functions as such. Having entered a big harbour, ships need to be warned of its internal dangers and of the proper navigational channels. Thus in Cork Harbour an automatic light was placed on the Spitbank, and inside Kinsale Harbour there is another on Charles Fort. The Charles Fort light is successor of another ancient beacon, as it and the Old Head must be the two sites referred to in 1660 when Charles II granted letters patent to Sir Richard Reading to erect six lighthouses in Ireland, of which two were to be at Kinsale.

Youghal's inner harbour beacon is the one originally tended by the nuns. The headland marking the outer limit of Youghal Bay is marked by Ballycotton lighthouse on its offshore island. It is unusual among lighthouses in being painted black. Two headlands of very similar appearance jut Ballycotton

Lighthouse that was never lit, Capel Island

Haulbowline, Cork Harbour

Knockadoon
Head

out into Youghal Bay, the outer one being Ballycotton with two offshore islets, on the outer of which is the light. The inner headland is Knockadoon Head with Capel Island just off it. Both sets of islets off their respective heads have very evidently been only recently severed from them by the sea. Ballycotton itself suffers from ongoing and severe coastal erosion.

Capel Island

The merchants of Youghal apparently first thought that Capel Island was the most suitable site for an outer harbour light and set about the building of one there. But though they got as far as building a slender tower, with adjacent living quarters for its keepers, it was never lit, as it was said that a light in such a position would be a danger, not a help, to shipping. The upshot was the present lighthouse on Ballycotton Island, and Capel, a beautiful green island now kept as a nature reserve, still has its blind lighthouse tower. It is built of the local flagstones but with the standard cut-granite stairs of lighthouse tradition inside – leading nowhere.

Galley Head
Mizen

West of the Old Head there are today lighthouses on all the prominent headlands. On the Galley Head, as on the Old Head, the lighthouse is inside an ancient promontory and later medieval fort. On the Mizen, the buildings are on a horseshoe-shaped islet linked to the mainland by an elegant suspension bridge over the narrow and precipitous gut. On the tip of the

Sheep's Head
Crookhaven
Fastnet
Bull Rock
Cape Clear

Sheep's Head peninsula an automatic light is positioned, and there is another one on the entry to Crookhaven. And out to sea are the island lights, on the Fastnet and on the Bull Rock.

The original Roaring Water Bay light was on Cape Clear, where the old buildings are still standing in fairly good condition beside the signal-tower. But the site, Foile Cahill, at 480 feet above the sea, was often covered with low cloud and the light rendered invisible. So plans were made to build a new lighthouse on the Fastnet Rock.

Fastnet

The Fastnet with its slender lighthouse looks today very much like a black swan sailing over the glittering expanse of ocean. Even before the lighthouse tower was built it must have had a somewhat similar appearance, for it was known at one time, in Irish, as 'the swan of the jet-black cairn bereft of light in the dark'. Tradition said that on Mayday morning the Fastnet Rock would sail around Dursey Island and visit the Bull, Cow, Calf and Heifer rocks. A Cape Clear version of its movements on Mayday claims that it then turns into a full-rigged sailing ship with spreading canvas and travels over to the Stags Rocks, to the east, and whispers to them. Perambulatory rocks are not unknown in folklore; there are many tales of standing stones going down to water to drink or even to wash, and sometimes doing this nightly. One stone in England at Banbury is even claimed to hear the church clock strike midnight, giving it the correct time to go down to the river Avon.

Work began on building a tower on the Fastnet in 1848; it was completed and lit early in the new year of 1854. This first Fastnet tower was of cast-iron and set over a cave, which it was feared might ultimately collapse. (Nor indeed was cast-iron found to be the most suitable of lighthouse building materials.) So in 1891 plans were made for a new light on a safer part of the rock. It was built of Cornish granite – some 4,000 tons of it – and each cut block dovetailed into its neighbour. To make sure of an exact fit, the whole was assembled on land before being shipped off to Fastnet; it was completed in 1906. The tower is placed on the 91-foot-high rock and its light, 160 feet above the sea, is visible for 19 miles. Perhaps today Fastnet is most associated in the public mind with the famous yacht race from the Isle of Wight to round Fastnet and back, but it is one of the great sea stations of the world. Here, in the old days, transatlantic shipping and the big liners would signal their safe arrival in home waters, and it is a great landmark on that ancient shipping route that took St Ciaran of Cape Clear to continental Europe to discover Christianity. The bearings from Cape Finisterre to Mizen and Cape Clear appear on the very first pilot book or *rutter* (*routier*, route book), which is perhaps of 14th century date.

Off the tip of the Beara peninsula and Dursey Island stand the Bull, Cow, Calf and Heifer rocks. If you fly out today over the Calf, you see a broken tower and some old buildings cemented like barnacles to the tiny rock, and you wonder at the audacity or the foolishness of the people who thought of building there. The first moves to do so were made in a letter of 10 March 1846 from a Captain J. Wolf, who urged the erection of lights on a number of sites, including the Bull Rock and Galley Head. This got the lighthouse authorities investigating sites and costs, but not moving very fast. The Bull, it was reported, was the first and last land sighted by ships going to or from America. But it was the Calf that they set their light on, architect George Halpin estimating a cost of £16,000 for a cast-iron tower with floors of

Calf Rock

Wrecked lighthouse, Calf Rock

Bull Rock lighthouse

Valentia slate. The contractors, Henry Grissell of London, queried the location of the light and pointed out that it must ultimately be destroyed by the sea, but they were not listened to. The tower was 102 feet high, of cast-iron plates bolted together; total cost, including shore dwellings for the keepers on the mainland, reached £30,463 16s 9d! It was completed in 1864 but only lit in midsummer 1866.

In a storm on 27 November 1881 the whole tower (which had, of course, by then suffered some corrosion) broke in half. The six men there were luckily in the buildings at its foot, and there they managed to survive and await rescue. HMS *Salamis* sailed past and saw them and what they had written in red paint on the rock: 'No one hurt. Want to leave the Rock.' But the weather would not allow that for nearly two weeks, when the regular relief boat together with HMS *Sea Horse* got them off. The normal lighthouse 'crew' is three; the other three were, it is thought, workmen set to work on a crack in the rock which it was intended to fill in and make secure. A temporary light was erected on Dursey Island, and work then went ahead to build

Bull Rock the present, safely located and much higher Bull Rock lighthouse which was lit on 1 January 1889. The Bull had, at one time, its own gas plant to make gas for the light. There is a gannetry on its sheer cliffs.

All these island lighthouse stations are now regularly serviced by helicopter and have their own helicopter pads. The station from which the helicopter flies to Fastnet and Bull, and to Tearaght and Skellig in Kerry, is at

Roancarrig Castletownberehaven – Roancarrig shore station. Roancarrig itself is a rock out in the entry to Berehaven with a small lighthouse on it; in wild weather the seas sweep high over the rock, so that it appears more like a small boat thrusting through the waves than an island. There are two automatic lights in Berehaven as well, a directional light at Castletown itself, and one on Bere Island at Ardnakinna Point.

In addition to these sophisticated aids of the Lighthouse Commissioners,

Baltimore there are along the coast the more primitive 'marks' for seamen, for
Schull instance, the white 'milk bottle' style ones at Baltimore and the entry to
Crookhaven Schull Harbour, and a clutch of tall towers at Crookhaven. One of these, the Coughlin Tower, 105 feet high, was demolished in 1965 to allow the building of a bungalow. It was the most useful of the three towers of Crookhaven as a

Horse Island sea mark. On Horse Island, at the entry of Castlehaven, Castletownsend, is another tower, built by Thomas Somerville, 'the merchant', as a mark for his ships coming home from the West Indies. (This Somerville was the founder of the family fortune.) Mariners, of course, have always used natural marks – hills and headlands and rocks – in order to line themselves on the safe approaches to harbours and anchorages.

Lighthouses and marks are the passive defences for the safety of shipping along the coast. The active side of the story is represented by the lifeboats

Lifeboats and, today, the air/sea rescue services. The lifeboat service, which has saved so many lives and is always ready for sea, is entirely voluntary and depends on the natural instincts of ordinary people to go to the rescue of those in trouble. Lifeboat volunteers are normally, but not essentially, people whose livelihood is with boats and the sea; they know their local seas and their lifeboat, and they will always answer a call for help. How desperate that need can be, one only realises when reading of shipwrecks in the days before any such voluntary service was available.

In County Cork lifeboats are stationed at Youghal, Ballycotton, Courtmacsherry and Baltimore. A lifeboat was based at Kinsale from some time before 1825, but was given up before 1892; Cobh's lifeboat station was established in 1866 and closed in 1920. Courtmacsherry's lifeboat station is the oldest, established in 1825, followed by Youghal (1839), Ballycotton (1858) and Baltimore (1919). The Courtmacsherry station's active life really dates from 1867, because the 1825 lifeboat had never been used and in the absence of a boathouse for it had decayed. Meantime, as the Royal National Lifeboat Institution was informed, 'the Coastguardsmen and boatmen here often run very great risk in rescuing by means of their own open boats the crews of wrecked vessels'. That report was made in July 1867, and a lifeboat and a boathouse, costing £170, were quickly supplied. Earlier generations of lifeboats were, of course, propelled by oars and sails and hauled, often enough, to the launching place by horses. In 1874 £15 compensation was paid to the owner of a horse at Courtmacsherry, after the animal was taken ill following a launch. Courtmacsherry's missions include work during the disastrous Fastnet race of 1979; and, back in January 1904, together with a local yawl, saving the entire crew of the Dunkirk registered barque *Faulconnier*, which stranded on the Seven Heads in very wild weather. Of 1,715 tons, *Faulconnier* was carrying grain from San Francisco to Cobh. The oldest French lifeboat station is that at Boulogne, and a survivor of the *Faulconnier*, M. de Garrec, became its president. In August 1968 one of his daughters arrived in Courtmacsherry to bring greetings to the only surviving member of the old lifeboat crew of the 1904 rescue, John Whelton.

Courtmacsherry

Youghal's lifeboat has, over the years, rescued people from a whole string of small ships, including three of the crew of the schooner *Annetta*, a Dungarvan ship which was bringing coal to Youghal in December 1905. *Annetta* contrived to run herself ashore in wild weather opposite Youghal's railway station, so close to the safety of the harbour. Two of her crew were drowned.

Youghal

But the most exciting action of a Cork lifeboat to date is Ballycotton's service to the Daunt lightship. On 7 February 1936 Ireland was ravaged by a freak storm, which by the 10th had developed hurricane-force winds. Trees and telephone wires were blown down, roads were blocked, and the Daunt lightship broke from her moorings. Ballycotton Harbour was in danger of losing all its boats as furious seas broke over the pier. The local Garda station rang R.H. Mahoney, the secretary of the Ballycotton lifeboat, to tell him that a messenger had just arrived (the telephone lines out of

Ballycotton

Ballycotton all being down) with the news that the Daunt lightship and her eight men were adrift. The secretary struggled through the wind to tell the coxswain, Patrick Sliney (there were no less than four Slineys in the crew). Patsy said nothing, and the secretary dared not order the lifeboat out in such weather. He went back to the harbour a little later, and there was the lifeboat heading out into what seemed impossible seas. At one point in that journey, the lifeboat fell from the top of a huge wave into the trough so violently that they thought the engines must go through her bottom. But the mechanic reported at once, 'All's well. After that she will go through anything.' But they could not find the lightship. So they went into Cobh and got her exact position and set out again.

The lightship had anchored a quarter of a mile from the Daunt Rock and HMS *Tenedos* (a destroyer) and the SS *Innisfallen* were both standing by. When the lifeboat arrived, the *Innisfallen*, the regular Cork-Fishguard boat, left. The lightship crew wished to remain on their boat, maintaining the warning lights that she was out of position. But their situation was very dangerous, if the new anchorage did not hold. With *Tenedos* still standing by, the lifeboat ran back to Cobh for fuel and food and a brief rest for the men. When they returned to the lightship they found *Isolda*, the lighthouse relief ship, was expected and *Tenedos* left. They stood by all day and all night, made a second run back to Cobh, and then joined *Isolda* watching the lightship. The latter's position was now very dangerous, for she was drifting closer and closer to the Daunt Rock. She was rolling violently and taking her crew off meant running close in to the plunging ship at full speed, checking for a second while a man jumped, and then speeding ahead again. All the eight men were taken off in this fashion though the last two were afraid to jump and had to be snatched from the lightship rails. The Ballycotton boat came back into Cobh at 11 p.m. on 13 February, having been at sea for 49 hours (and on service for 63). In all that time her crew had had only three hours sleep and were suffering from colds and from salt-water burns. Patrick Sliney was awarded the Lifeboat Institution gold medal; the second cox, John Walsh, and the mechanic, Thomas Sliney, silver medals; and the others,

Ballycotton lighthouse

Michael Walsh, Thomas Walsh, John Sliney and William Sliney, bronze medals. (There is a detailed account of this rescue by the secretary, R. H. Mahoney, in the *Irish Lifeboat* magazine for 1972, through which those of us lucky enough to have met him can hear his voice telling of that extraordinary weather and the Daunt rescue.)

Although the Baltimore station was only officially established in 1919, a lifeboat service with the Ven. Archdeacon J. H. H. Beecher as secretary had been functioning for some years previously. He played an active part in the rescue of 23 men (out of a crew of 40) when the SS *Alondra* ran on the Kedge Rocks in 1916, and again in January 1917 when the SS *Nestorian* ran ashore on Cape Clear.

Crookhaven and Brow Head must remain almost holy ground for anyone concerned with safety at sea or in the air, for here were some of the beginnings of radio. By the mid-19th century the old semaphore with its visual signals relaying messages from ship to shore or overland was, in the latter case, being replaced by the 'electric telegraph'. It was an old blind telegraphist who taught Marconi the Morse code and triggered his interest in such things. In 1901 Marconi, who had, by the way, an Irish mother and an Irish wife, transmitted three Morse dots (the letter S) from Poldhu in Cornwall and they were picked up in St John's, Newfoundland. Next year, 1902, he arrived in Crookhaven (where he is remembered as 'a small thin fellow who could speak good English') and set up a radio station there. But Crookhaven was too low down to get out a good signal and he moved up to the neighbouring heights of Brow Head, where there already was the old signal-tower and a station of Lloyds, with a submarine cable out to the Fastnet for monitoring the comings and goings of ships. The Brow Head radio station used the call sign GCK – G for Great Britain and CK for Crookhaven. In 1906 it was moved again, to a still better position for the transmission of radio messages on Valentia Island in Kerry, but Valentia Radio kept the old GCK call sign till as late as 1950.

Radio, together with aircraft and helicopters, has transformed the whole business of safety at sea and of letting someone know a ship is in trouble and where she is. Air/sea rescue for the south of Ireland is co-ordinated from Shannon and, for work far out on the ocean, has the willing assistance of RAF long-range aircraft and helicopters.

Baltimore

Crookhaven

Radio

Marconi

Brow Head

XVIII

Wreck

SHIPS ARE LIKE aircraft: it is the land that can hurt them. In the wide open spaces of the sky, in the one case, and of the ocean in the other, they are nearly always safe. It is in the approach to or departure from land that danger lies, and there was special danger in the old days when a ship, after a long and arduous but safe passage, approached the rocky cliffs of Ireland. If the weather was bad and visibility poor – and the crew usually a little unsure of their exact position – it was only too easy to make a mistake and for the cry 'Breakers ahead!' to come too late. Today, with powerful and reliable engines and a vast array of navigational aids available, the tally of disasters is much shorter and rescue much more certain, but the sea remains a dangerous place for anyone who does not learn to know and respect her many moods.

It would be impossible to list all the ships that have come to grief upon the coasts of County Cork. Such a list would have to begin with the vessels of the first settlers and the first traders and go on with lost cargoes for wealthy farmers in ring forts, with Viking longships, with medieval cargoes of wine for Cork and export loads of Irish skins, marten and otter, deer and wolf, as well as sheep and ox. It would go on through Armada times, though no Armada ships were wrecked in Cork as they were in Kerry. There is a report of one of the Algerian pirate ships being wrecked on the Seven Heads; and, as already mentioned, some of the Frenchmen of 1796 came to grief in Cork. From the 17th century on, there are many records of wrecks and these alone show that there is virtually no rock or beach in the county on which a ship has not been wrecked or stranded.

But the character of shipwrecks has changed dramatically in the last few decades. Modern bulk freighters and container ships will break up very differently from a wooden ship or a small iron one. When a wooden ship broke up, her cargo, often in handy casks and boxes, soon came tumbling ashore, ready for the eager beachcombers to salvage. A container ship is more likely just to sink, all within her remaining inaccessible. You are much more likely to be rescued from a modern disaster, but its results may be devastating with massive spills of oil or of toxic substances. Terrible explosions can occur, like that of the old tanker *Betelgeuse* at Bantry oil terminal with the loss of all her crew as well as of the men working on the Whiddy Island jetty.

Betelgeuse

In their story 'Holy Island', Somerville and Ross give a vivid description of a 'traditional' shipwreck, from which it appears they must either have seen such a wreck or had a first-hand account of one. The story tells of three days of fog on the West Cork coast, with 'the Fastnet gun hard at work' and how 'the sirens of the American liners uplifted their monstrous female voices as they felt their way along the coast of Cork'. As the fog lifted, a gale blew up, and with it came the report of a ship wrecked; 'it was rumoured the crew had got ashore' but the big news was that she was breaking up fast. Like the real *Politician* in World War II, wrecked with her glorious cargo of whisky between South Uist and Barra in the Hebrides, the ship in the story carried spirits – rum. 'The ship was, or had been, a three-masted barque; two of her masts were gone and her bows stood high out of the water on the reef that forms one of the shark-like jaws of the bay.' The strand was crowded with people, and as the shout 'She's gone!' finally went up the barrels of rum came tumbling ashore to a tussle between the enormous crowd and the small handful of police and coastguards. 'With the darkness came anarchy. The rising tide brought more and yet more booty; great spars came lunging in on the lap of the waves, mixed with cabin furniture, seamen's chests, and the black and slippery barrels, and the country people continued to flock in, and the drinking became more and more unbridled.'

That story is told from the point of view of the well-fed people in the Big House. For ordinary folk, a good wreck might be the difference between life and death. Back in the Famine years, 'Black '47', east Cork people would say: 'We'll starve for Christmas, or we might have a wreck and be full and plenty,' and the saying is still remembered there. There is also the tradition, known from other countries as well, that the sea must have its victim one way or another: 'There is always someone drowned when a wreck occurs.'

Wrecks were remembered. Nohaval, in the area between Cork Harbour and Kinsale, still recalls the memory of an old man known as 'Danny Fat Mate'. Danny was particularly fond of fat meat. 'Give me some fat mate,' he would say, 'and I'll sing you the wrecks.' Thus encouraged, he would chant in a monotone the long litany of shipwrecks on the local coastline, from the Old Head of Kinsale to Cork Harbour: 'and then there was the … and then there was the …' and so on. It was a long song.

In the summer of 1982 James Murray of Ballyandreen in east Cork related a similar list, though in prose. The only wreck he had actually seen was the *Joseph Michael* in 1950. She was carrying coal, struck the cliffs near Ballyandreen, backed off and sank in deep water. Nobody was lost but the village only got five or six tons of coal off her. James Murray's traditional list ran from Power Head to Ballycotton, and was, as is usual with such accounts, vague on dates. It included, as well as the famous *Sirius* and the *Ibis*, the *Coromandel* which struck east of Power Head with a cargo of paraffin. It was in barrels, but nobody knew what to do with it. At that time, they burned fish-oil in cruses with rush wicks for light. However, a customs man showed them that it would not explode.

The brigantine *Saga* struck under full sail in February 1883. There was nobody on board and traces of blood in a cabin suggested a mutiny. Her steering gear was gone but a rudder had been jury-rigged. She was copper-sheathed, and a woman threw a coastguard over the cliffs in a struggle to get at the copper. *Saga* carried musical instruments as part of her cargo, and a local nurse, Miss Kelly, got a violin out of her, on which she used to play. The *Eugenie* of Dublin, a full-rigged barque, struck off Ballylanders. She carried general cargo, including willow pattern ware, pig-iron, cutlery and nails. Ballyandreen used the willow pattern ware, as did other coastal hamlets, but in the end most of it was either broken or given away as souvenirs. Netting thread was another item in the manifest, and the Knockadoon women made a big seine net for Ballyandreen out of it.

The copper-coated brig *James Ducket* carried palm kernels and nobody except the local pigs knew what to do with them. The pigs would go out to the wreck at low tide and feed on them, and then swim the channel back as the tide rose. (Pigs in those days were a lot thinner and more agile than the modern variety.) *Cherub* was a three-masted schooner carrying coal, lost on a terrible night with all hands. Men gathering seaweed for manure would just push bodies back out to sea again rather than have the trouble of burying them. *Rosina's* captain was 'a Chinaman with a tail' (pigtail) who saved himself by climbing the mast to the top of the cliff on which the ship struck. *Cooleen* was a big steel ship, registered in Belfast, which had loaded wheat in the Río de la Plata and was headed for Cork for orders in 1894. *Cooleen* missed the entry to Cork Harbour and struck on the rocks at Ballytrasna, where she did not last an hour and broke into two halves. Most of the crew –

Ballylanders (margin note)

Ballytrasna (margin note)

Memorial, St Multose, Kinsale

ten men – were on the forecastle which drifted out to sea, and they were all lost. The poop, with the French second mate, two seamen and a boy, drifted into the land and were saved. The boy's name was Philip Ridgeway; his parents were dead, but he said that he had had a dream in which his father came to him, told him the ship would be wrecked, and, when she was, for him 'to go to the after-poop and take off my sea boots'.

The above, which is only part of one person's memory of wreck traditions for one part of the Cork coast, shows how often and in what varied forms ships have died on the county's rocks. There were ships that came to grief entering or leaving Youghal Harbour, like the Norwegian registered *Galatea* in February 1858. She was carrying Peruvian guano from Callao to 'Queenstown for orders', missed the entry to Cork Harbour, came into Youghal Bay and drove on to the dangerous sandbars on its western side. Two pilot boats and the lifeboat went out to help, but the weather was so bad that only the lifeboat was able to get up to her and rescue her crew of 16, the ship's dog being the only casualty.

The most famous ship lost off this part of the coast was, of course, *Sirius*, of transatlantic crossing fame. Nine years after her triumphant arrival in New York, she was temporarily off her normal Cork to London run and was doing the Cork-Dublin-Glasgow route, while *Ocean*, whose route the latter was, was being overhauled. *Sirius* was heading for Cork in thick fog on the night of January 15/16 1847. Her captain, Moffat, failed to keep her well out to sea and in the murk, at about 4 a.m., she ran against high cliffs, which may have been those of Capel Island. The crew had no idea where they were, but they backed the badly damaged ship off and hoped to reach Cork with the aid of the pumps. In about half an hour it was obvious that the water was gaining rapidly on them, and they turned back towards the land. With the last gasp of the engines as the water rose, they were flung onto a reef of rock jutting from the cliffs of Ballycotton. There were some 20 cabin passengers and 50 deck as well as the crew, and panic broke out. They could have remained on board till the tide ebbed and scrambled ashore, but in the dark and fog and wild seas they launched a boat on the seaward side into which 16 or 20 people scrambled. The boat, naturally, overturned and they were all drowned. Captain Archie Cameron, a passenger returning from Glasgow to Cork, where he was captain of the river steamer *Prince*, kept his head and managed to get a rope across the rocks to the cliff-side by which people were saved; with dawn came more help on foot and by boat from Ballycotton.

The *Cork Examiner* reporter was on the spot almost immediately, and that of the *Constitution* not long after. Both left detailed and vivid accounts of the wreck. James O'Mahony, sent to Ireland to make drawings of the Famine disaster (this was the terrible winter of 'Black '47'), sat on the cliffs and sketched *Sirius* high and dry on the reef at low tide; then breaking up at high tide and local people salvaging timber in the adjacent cove, called

Youghal

Sirius

Ballycotton

Ware Cove from another ship wrecked there. The *Illustrated London News* published both the drawings and a full account of the wreck together with a commemorative poem in their issues of January 20th and 27th 1847.

O'Mahony's drawings exactly match the present landscape of cliffs at Ballycotton and the newspaper accounts leave no doubt as to where the *Sirius* struck and what happened to her. Broadside on to the seas, a wooden ship, she broke up in a matter of days, leaving only her heavy ironwork perched on the reef. This was put up for auction in the summer of 1847 and bought by John George Gibbings who owned the shovel-mills at Temple-michael.

With some difficulty he got the *Sirius* mainshaft to Templemichael and used it in an old over-shot water-wheel. When the mill closed the shaft was taken to Passage West, where the Roberts family still live and from whence *Sirius* had departed for New York, and erected by the waterside. As part of the 150th celebrations of the *Sirius* crossing to America, the first steam all the way, scheduled service, the shaft was re-erected in the middle of Passage West with a commemorative plaque.

The *Sirius* wreck is one of the best documented and illustrated from the period, and it is incredible that *Gores General Advertiser* of Liverpool published a purely fictitous and perhaps anti-Irish account in which she was said to have struck once on the Smith's Rocks, out to sea, and that the survivors had come ashore in the ship's boats and had had their belongings plundered by the local people on arrival. Yet this story led Messers Ensor of Cobh, salvage contractors, to dive on what they believed was the *Sirius* wreck and bring up half a ton of scrap, surprised to find it in so good a condition from so old a ship! Presentation sections of the pump rod went to British royalty and admiralty, and the president of the United States as well as to the Roberts family! Yet in 1847 all *Sirius* metal-work had been sold and recycled! Even today, people dive on what they believe to be *Sirius*. Careful research through Cork newspapers would probably reveal what later paddle steamer did come to grief somewhere in the Ballycotton area and the area of the Smith's Rocks, and whose remains are now venerated as part of *Sirius*.

Passage West

Drive shaft of Sirius

Actual relics from *Sirius* include her beautifully carved clock case, which was in a London saleroom in 1988 with a price tag of £20,000; part of her saloon table, now in Derrynane Abbey; and her bible, now in Ballycotton Church of Ireland church. Her carved figurehead, a dog with a star in its paws, is in the Town Docks Museum in Hull – where the St George Company once had an office. At Ballycotton there survive some pieces of willow-pattern crockery and an earthenware jar for whiskey or rum, said to have come off *Sirius* general cargo, and at Ballyandreen a wooden bench said to have been on her. Her bell which went to a local church has been lost sight of. Ballyandreen has a tradition that everyone was drunk at the wreck from beer in *Sirius* cargo and that one person salvaged a jug of whiskey, sold it for six shillings (30p) and bought a pair of boots.

Ballyandreen

There is another tragic Roberts link with Ballycotton. When Captain Roberts took over command of the *President* and set out with her on her last journey to New York, three young people, children of a Church of Ireland rector of Aghabulloge by his first marriage (he married twice), went out in a small boat from Ballycotton to see her pass. The little boat was overset and they were all drowned.

Sirius' sister ship, called *Queen*, was involved in 1844 in the rescue of passengers from another cross-channel boat, the *Vanguard*. The latter belonged to the Dublin and Glasgow Steam Packet Company and went on to the rocks at Roche's Point. The previous year, 1843, the Cork company had ordered an iron ship, *Nimrod*, for their fleet, the first iron steamship to be owned in Cork. *Nimrod* was wrecked off St David's Head in 1860, as was their much more magnificent *Ibis* off Ballycroneen in east Cork, on what has ever since been known as the Ibis Rock. *Ibis* was launched the year *Nimrod* was lost, in April 1860. She was the biggest iron steamer to be built in Cork – for she was constructed there in the yard of George Robinson and Co. – 262 feet long, schooner-rigged, with a twin-screw engine. She could sail from Cork to Plymouth in 20 hours, very fast going for the time, and she was regarded as both fast and strongly built. Captain Richard Holland was returning from London to Cork with 16 passengers and 24 crew in December 1865 when, abeam Ballycroneen and making to round Power Head, the engines failed (a crank pin had sheared). The weather was bad and seas rough and they were not able to control her with her sails. Drifting toward the shore, they managed to anchor and fire distress signals which were answered by the coastguards. Captain Holland lowered a boat and got within hailing distance of the shore where he was told that the seas were too wild to attempt a landing. The story is then a long one of attempts at rescue: two others of the Cork steamship company's fleet, *Cormorant* and *Sabrina*, came to stand by and attempted and failed to get a line on to *Ibis*. Tugs were called up and an effort was made to tow her off the rocks, *Ibis* cutting her anchor cables in her haste. The tow rope broke and *Ibis* was thrown finally on to the rocks. The ship's boats were lowered, but the people were too

Ibis

Ballycroneen

afraid to jump into them, even when the captain tried to encourage them by leading the way. He had planned to make for *Sabrina* but the panicking crew headed the boat for the shore with disastrous results in the wild seas, though the captain was swept in safely, clutching an oar.

Ibis was now breaking up fast. The first officer James Pieron, who was French, took charge, though he could not prevent people rushing an improvised raft and capsizing it. He got the remainder on to the bow end of *Ibis*, which still floated. *City of London*, a liner of the Inman Line, now appeared round Power Head and was intercepted by the tug *Lord Clyde*. The liner provided a lifeboat which the tug towed back to the *Ibis* and into which the 21 survivors were gathered, and so on to the tug. Seventeen had been drowned.

Eugenie, with the varied cargo so well remembered in Ballyandreen, was wrecked in nearly the same spot in the same week. Again her distress was seen and great efforts made for a rescue but the conditions were terrible, and only eleven were saved, 14 including the captain being drowned. At both the *Ibis* and *Eugenie* wrecks the Ballycotton lifeboat was called – and came, but too late to render much assistance. In those days it was brought overland on a carrier drawn by horses to the nearest launching place to a wreck, a slow and often difficult process.

There has been a number of wrecks around the mouth of Cork Harbour, on the Daunt Rock (which is why the warning lightship was placed on it) and even inside the harbour itself. In 1980 a tanker carrying gas for the Calor Kosangas plant at Whitegate ran aground coming in, causing a major alert because of the risk of a very violent explosion. Fortunately she was safely refloated.

Chicago was not so lucky in 1868. She belonged to the transatlantic fleet of the Liverpool and Great Western Steam Packet Company, and had been launched at Jarrow in 1866. She was, for that period, very big – 682 feet long, 2,918 gross tonnage – with two brig-rigged masts to carry sail to assist her engines. She left New York on her regular transatlantic run on 2 January 1868, with a crew of 96, fifty-four passengers and a valuable cargo of cotton and grain. As was the usual custom, she signalled her arrival to the Fastnet, from which a message was sent to Cobh via Lloyds station on Brow Head for a pilot boat to go out to meet her and bring her into Cobh. But *Chicago* ran into thickening haze and missed her rendezvous with the company's pilot boat. The captain slowed down, edging forward; but in trying to keep well clear of the Daunt, he failed to see either that or the Roche's Point light and overshot the harbour entry. He ran on to a reef off Gyleen; how easy it was to do so is shown by the fact that the lead line was giving 15 fathoms when she struck – the depth of the water on either side of the rocks. *Chicago* was badly holed and lifeboats were immediately lowered, everyone getting safely ashore. A rocket line was fired and used to bring the passengers' luggage in, while marines stood guard against looting. The captain, William McNay,

Eugenie

Cork Harbour

Chicago

went back to retrieve the £60,000 *in specie* which she was carrying.

There were hopes that tugs might be able to pull *Chicago* free of the rocks for repairs, but a series of gales sprang up and she became a total loss. The shores were strewn with booty and people crowded to them with horses and carts to gather all they could. Marines and police tried to prevent them and one marine shot a young man who was carrying off a bundle of cotton and a bit of wood. The man survived, though he was very badly hurt; the marine was put in Midleton jail and charged, but the jury would not find against him, on the grounds of insufficient evidence.

In the same period of bad weather, a nitrate barque, *Vanda,* coming from Peru, was wrecked. The coastguards at Inch had lit a warning beacon fire, which *Vanda's* captain mistook for the light on Roche's Point. Accordingly he turned in for the harbour mouth, found himself suddenly in calm water in the shelter of Power Head, on whose rocks *Vanda* then ran. The ship was lost though the crew were all taken safely off by rocket line from Power Head.

From the air and from the shore, the entry to Cork Harbour may seem spacious, but it must have been tricky enough for a sailing ship labouring along in bad weather. If one stands at low tide on the shore at Fennel's Bay and looks along that rocky expanse to the harbour entry, it will then appear small and fringed with reefs. One of the reefs of Fennel's Bay is called the 'Dutchman' because a Dutch ship once got into trouble on it – but got off again safely. Several other ships have been less lucky than the Dutchman, including a big French barque, *Admiral Courbet,* which ran on to it in 1915 after the rope of her tow out of the harbour broke and left her drifting. The crew all escaped by their own lifeboat but the ship was a total loss – and many good things came ashore, including wine and bacon, to the people of Myrtleville and Fountainstown. The *Celtic* ran on to Roche's Point in 1928. When she was built, she was believed to be the biggest liner afloat. Again, all were safely got off her, but two men died during the subsequent salvage work.

Cork Harbour has known other marine accidents as well as wrecks. In February 1806 the *Britannia* of Liverpool blew up near Cobh, only two of her crew of 14 surviving. She must have been carrying gunpowder, one supposes. No damage was done on shore or to ships moored near her. In 1916 the German *Aud,* carrying arms for the Irish rising, was captured and was being brought into Cork Harbour when her crew scuttled her before she could be unloaded by British forces. Divers report that the sea floor round her remains is still littered with ammunition.

The litany of wrecks continues as one goes west from the harbour mouth, past Robert's Head, to Rocky Bay and Man o' War Cove, which takes its name from the wrecking of such a ship there long ago. Much more recently, a small tanker (by present day standards) *El Zorro* was torpedoed off the Old Head in 1915 and was beached in this beautiful little bay. Most of her (a few

Vanda

Admiral Courbet

Celtic

Britannia

Aud

Man o' War Cove

El Zorro

plates still lie around) was broken up for salvage by eight Chinese workers sent over by an English company of shipbreakers.

The open expanse of Rocky Bay, between Man o' War Cove and Robert's Head, part rocky reefs, part sandy strand, and much visited by Cork family parties in summer, was the scene of another tragedy when the Austrian

barque *Idumea* was wrecked there in October 1881. She had a crew of eleven and was carrying salt from Liverpool to Baltimore. The captain was newly wed to 23-year-old Christina, ten years his junior, and she was on board with them. They ran into gales and were badly damaged off the Daunt; the rudder was rendered useless and the ship ran on to the Sleeven Rocks in the entry to Rocky Bay. She was seen, and thought by those on shore to be in no great danger, as she appeared securely wedged at least for the moment; however, the coastguards with the rocket apparatus had misjudged where she would be driven in and gone to the wrong part of the cliffs. They were now doubling back, but it was too late, for the ship broke up with great rapidity. The captain, supporting his wife, was seen struggling through the seas; the coastguards fired their rocket at them and Christina reached for it. Her husband thought she had a firm grip on the line and let her go, only to see her swept away and drowned. The captain himself was saved by a second line and the quick action of a coastguard who rushed into the water and dragged him to the shore. A young man, son of a local farmer, plunged in after another man, a badly injured sailor who later recovered. He and the captain were the only survivors. The others – Austrians, a Bulgarian and an Englishman – are buried in Ballyfoyle graveyard, but Christina was buried in Cobh after a big funeral from the cathedral. The Mayor of Lasampiccols, Christina's home town, was later to write to the *Cork Examiner* to thank the Irish people for their help and sympathy in this tragedy.

People on shore were not always so gallant in rescue attempts. Tuckey's *Remembrancer* for 22 December 1775 tells the story of another wreck in this

part of the coast: 'About seven o'clock this night the "Marquis of Rockingham" transport, from Portsmouth, with three companies of the 32nd regiment and their baggage on board, besides women and children, was in a

heavy gale of wind driven into Robert's Cove, and at three the following morning, was dashed to pieces on the rocks, and every soul on board perished, except three officers and about 30 privates and two of the crew. The officers who perished were Lt Marsh and Ensign Sandiman, besides the wives of Lt Marsh and Dr Baker. The officers saved were Captain Glover, Lts Booth and Carter, and the doctor's mate. 'Tis impossible to paint the distress of the officers and soldiers who were saved, the greatest part of whom being cast on the rocks had their flesh torn in a shocking manner, and instead of receiving the least assistance from the inhabitants, were attacked by a great number of the common people, who carried off every

article that could be saved out of the wreck.'

Garretstown Strand west of the Old Head saw another troopship battered to pieces. A memorial in St Multose Church in Kinsale reads: 'Lieu^{ts} Edmund Davenport, Edwin Harding, Ass^t surgeon Henry Randolph Scott and his wife, eight sergeants, nine corporals, one hundred and forty privates, thirteen women and sixteen children of the 82^d Reg^t, who perished on board the *Boadicea* Transport wrecked on Garretstown Strand on the night of 30th Jany 1816.'

Boadicea

Other ships lost on Garretstown include *Gulf of Quebec, Pearl of Gloucester, Lord Melville* and *Conloughry,* and keels, ballast stones and the like from these ships are seen at low tide or by skindivers. In general, losses in British troop transports were high at the time of the *Boadicea* tragedy. *Blackwood's Magazine* for September 1817 records that 'out of 5,511 men, embarked for foreign service, 1,702, or nearly one third, perished through the transports being wrecked'; experiments were therefore being carried out with soldiers wearing an early form of life jacket, Mallison's Life Preserver. It was found that a non-swimmer could, wearing this, safely get ashore from deep water.

Two Cork wrecks, *Killarney* and *Sylvan* show the beginnings of the use of the rocket apparatus which has saved so many lives, and of the hope of aerial rescue which the helicopter would eventually make possible.

Killarney

Reenies Point is the headland west of Man o' War Cove, and westward from it are very steep and high cliffs with jagged fangs of rock offshore at their foot. *Killarney* was a small sail-assisted steamer carrying general cargo, some 600 pigs and 50 people – passengers and crew. In January 1838 she set out for Bristol from Cork but had to turn back to wait for better weather. When it seemed to be improving, she left again, only to run into a gale and

Reenies Point

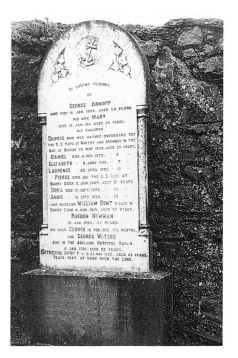

Headstone in Kinsale

fog – or, at least, very poor visibility, once she was beyond Roche's Point. The captain was uncertain of where he was and the crew seem to have been quickly demoralised. Big seas broke over her decks, sweeping away 160 pigs. Her sails were torn and her engines stopped. Whether more aggressive handling might have saved her we shall never know; as it was she drifted, position uncertain, sighting land only on the afternoon of the second day out. They did not know what land it was. She was driven into a narrow inlet of the cliffs west of Reenies Point (marked on the maps now as the Killarney Rock) and began to break up. The cliffs were a couple of hundred feet high; the ship was wedged in under them and there was no means of clambering up the steep cliff face. Some of the people on board managed to scramble from the ship on to a fang of rock alongside (now eroded away), which was the only hope of safety. It was a Saturday afternoon, and soon people got news of the wreck and began to crowd the cliffs to try to salvage some of the pigs as they were washed in. The pigs were very valuable to the poor people: an old man in Ballyandreen is remembered as having lived largely on limpets, which he used to corn (salt) against the days the weather was too bad to gather them fresh, and who was particularly delighted when a pig's carcase came in which could be salted away too. The dead pigs from the *Killarney* must have been coming in all along the shore at more accessible places than where the ship was grounded.

Not until the Sunday did 'some gentlemen' attempt to rescue the little group on the rock, whose numbers were gradually diminishing as people succumbed to exposure. They tried to throw a line out weighted with a stone, to fly it out attached to the leg of a duck or to fire it from a musket. One young man tried to swim out. It was all in vain. Finally they got a very long rope and slung it across the narrow inlet in which wreck and rock lay, letting it down on top of the rock. They said that only one survivor at a time was to attempt to get along this rope; two tried and the rope broke. On the Monday they tried again with a new rope, sending out first a basket of food and drink, and ultimately rescued the 14 people still alive, one of whom, the ship's carpenter, died immediately afterwards.

Sylvan

Oyster Haven

The *Sylvan*, on 11 November 1818, managed to run between the two Sovereign Islands off Oyster Haven and wreck herself there in wild weather. As she broke up, the sole survivor, a boy, was seen from the land clinging to her rigging. Next day, in spite of the high seas, an Oyster Haven boat rowed out, saw the boy now on one of the Sovereign Rocks, but was unable to take him off because of the weather. The Sovereign of Kinsale was notified and offered ten guineas (£10.50) to any boat that would rescue the boy.

One from Kinsale set off with warm wine in bladders, and two revenue officers from Oyster Haven went out in their boat as well, towing a punt. They got the punt alongside the rocks long enough to throw a line to the boy, but instead of tying himself to it for rescue he threw it away and went back up the cliffs. Night was coming on and the boy began gathering weed for a bed and herbs to eat. Mr Gibbons, in a whale boat, made an 11 p.m. attempt and another at dawn, but could not get near the rocks. In Kinsale the crew of an American ship, *Dayad,* which was being repaired in Gibbons and Co.'s dockyard there, said they would go out and not return if they did not make the rescue; before they went they successfully experimented with firing a musket-ball with a line attached to it. By this time a number of Oyster Haven boats were circling the rock, and finally Jack Carthy, who owned one of them, tied a rope round his own waist, plunged into the sea and scrambled on to the island. He tied the rope round the boy and had him pulled out to the waiting boat, meantime sitting himself peacefully on a rock waiting for the rope to be thrown back for his own return. He did not forget to make a bundle of his own and the boy's clothes, which he brought back to the boat. The American boat came up at this moment and gave three cheers for the rescuers; other boats included one with Lt Blackyen and Lt Desprang, RN, who had brought out geese and turkeys to which they intended to attach bread for them to fly it to the island.

Except for those of the *Betelgeuse* disaster in 1979, the most dramatic Cork wreck photographs are those of the *City of Chicago* in 1892. She was a big liner, steam with sails, on the transatlantic run. The day, 1 July 1892, was foggy. The tender which went out from Cobh failed to locate her and thought that, in the current weather conditions, she would run straight for Liverpool. In fact, she ran straight into the Barrell Rock on the west side of the Old Head of Kinsale (at the narrow neck) and anchored her bows securely in the cliffs. She fired distress rockets which the Courtmacsherry coastguards saw; they came quickly to the rescue, with rocket apparatus, and brought everyone safely up the cliffs, using a rope ladder. Big seas lashed the sides of the great ship wedged at right angles to the cliffs, and she broke clean in two, so that the stern lay at right angles to her bow. Before she broke up, salvage tugs tried to pull her clear but failed. Much of the ship was salvaged, Thomas Ensor and Son of Cobh dismantling and removing her machinery.

Courtmacsherry Bay, between the Old Head and the Seven Heads, was both a haven and a dangerous place for shipping. (Courtmacsherry itself had a little fleet of trading vessels in the recent past.) In fog a ship like the *City of Chicago* might mistake the entry to the bay for that into Kinsale or Cork Harbours. A sailing ship might get herself embayed and, like *Boadicea,* stranded on the rocks and sands of Garretstown, or thrown on to the hard black cliffs to its immediate west, as was *Albion.*

Albion was a Black Ball Line packet ship, en route from New York to Liverpool, and she was wrecked on the cliffs about a quarter of a mile from the point where the road from Ballinspittle comes down to the west end of Garretstown Strand. It was 22 April 1822. According to a local tradition, as the ship struck, a woman was seen in her bows holding up a bag, which was taken as meaning money for rescuing survivors. But of them there were very

City of Chicago

Old Head of Kinsale

Courtmacsherry

Albion

Garretstown

few – most of the passengers drowned. The mate identified the bodies as well as he could before they were buried in Templetrine graveyard. Among those who died were a well known Yale professor, Alexander Metcalf Fisher, and 44-year-old Major William Gough, who had served in Europe, Asia and America and fought under Wellington. Major Gough has a very fine table-top tomb in Templetrine graveyard. Inside the church is another memorial: 'Anne Powell, spinster, was a passenger on the ship "Albion" (wrecked on this coast 22 April 1822) and perished with many others, but her body being recovered from the sea, received from the charity of strangers Christian burial in the cemetery of this church, in grateful memory of which this marble is inscribed by W.D.P.'

The whole story of the wreck has been told by one of the few survivors, First Mate Henry Cammyer (*Southern Reporter* 8 June 1822). Stones to be found at low tide which are foreign to Cork are thought to be part of her ballast. She is said to have carried four tons of gold, and some gold coins at least have been recovered by present-day divers.

Seven Heads

The Seven Heads claimed more ships. The cargo of one grain ship lost there is said to have been blown many miles inland by the gale-force winds. At Dunworly, on the west side of the Seven Heads, not only was the Algerian pirate wrecked, but a British ship called *Thrush*, some of whose guns and trade goods (walrus tusks and beads) have been found. A wooden nitrate ship, *Ciampi*, was wrecked in about 1908 on Bird Island, a stack off the Heads, with the loss of all on board. One could continue with an almost rock-by-rock list of wrecks westward. And there was a German submarine,

Galley Head

sunk off the Galley Head on 13 March 1945, whose crew took to their rafts and rubber dinghys and were picked up by the Courtmacsherry lifeboat.

There were ships that had the devil's own luck, too. In about 1734 a ship

Betelgeuse *memorial*

inbound from the West Indies found herself in difficulties, with several feet of water in the hold. She had no idea of her exact position but steered toward a light and then dropped anchor near it. In the morning, she found herself snug in the southern harbour of Cape Clear, having come in on the light of a candle in one of its houses. But the wreck of a Portuguese ship on a rock known ever after as the Portuguese Rock, gave Cape Clear a proverbial saying. The ship was lost but the crew saved, and the captain declared he could have saved his ship, too, if he had had the big anchor that he had left at home. So, on appropriate occasions, Cape Clear people would say in their beautiful Irish: 'Ah, you left it at home like the Portuguese left the big anchor at home after him.'

Cape Clear people watched, unable to assist, the Irish collier *Kerry Head* bombed and sunk by a German aircraft on 22 October 1940, in sight of their island. There were no survivors. *Kerry Head* had previously survived a bombing off the Old Head of Kinsale on 1 August 1940. It had been the first Irish ship to be attacked in World War II, though it was by no means the last. Cork lost its regular cross-channel *Innisfallen* in a bombing raid on Liverpool on 20 December 1940. All on board were saved except two seamen and two cattlemen, who were killed.

Across Roaring Water Bay, Mizen Head, the extreme south-western tip of Ireland, has been a veritable graveyard of ships. So many have gone in, in Dunlough Bay between Mizen Head and Three Castles Head, that a diver said one could walk from wreck to wreck rather than surface between each. At least two ships have jammed themselves into the narrow gut between the tip of Mizen Head and the little islet just off it with the lighthouse station.

Irada had been built in Belfast in 1900: 5,334 tons, twin screw, steel hull, four masts. Her captain, Arthur Roberts, was highly experienced. She left Galveston, Texas, on 5 December 1910 with a crew of 69, a cargo of cotton and no passengers, bound for Liverpool. The ship ran into fog nearing the Irish coast but sighted the Bull Rock on 21 December and carried on by dead reckoning to pick up the Fastnet. But, pushed by the fast running tidal stream, *Irada* swung too close inshore and when the cry went up 'Breakers ahead!' it was too late to reverse engines and pull out. She piled up in the narrow Mizen passage and became a total loss. All the crew, bar the stewardess, who was swept off and fell between cliff and ship's side, managed to clamber off the ship on to the cliffs. Here they were found next morning by the workmen constructing the Mizen lighthouse station and rescued. The sea was awash with cotton bales, 22,000 of them (valued at £300,000). They moved like ice-floes into Bantry Bay, so thick that the lighthouse relief ship, *Ierne*, could not steam through them. A great number were salvaged, both by ships coming specially for the purpose and by local fishermen, who got £1 for each bale picked up. On shore, at Crookhaven, one could get 30s (£1.50) for each bale. The other big ship to go into the Mizen cliffs was the Spanish *Ibernia*, and her cargo was leather. This was of great value to the

Cape Clear

Kerry Head

Innisfallen

Mizen Head

Irada

Ibernia

local people who used it to make harness, and indeed some fragments may yet be found wedged into the cliffs.

Often a ballad would be written about some local event like a shipwreck. Joe Kerrigan gave me the text of a ballad about the *Memphis*, which he had collected from a local man, who said he had been responsible for her wrecking in Dunlough Bay. For that night (*c.* 1908) he had been born and the light in the little house where the birth was taking place lured the big ship in, and on to the high silvery gleaming cliffs under Three Castles Head. Today, with the coastline ablaze with electric lights and car headlights, it is hard to realise how dark it was at the turn of the century, when a single lamp could be mistaken for the Fastnet's. The *Memphis* ballad tells the whole story, and the captain's escape by way of one of the bullocks of her cargo is literally true.

Memphis

Dunlough Bay

> When the *Memphis* she left Montreal,
> The weather it was fine:
> Said the captain to her officers,
> 'We'll have a pleasant time.'
> But before she reached the Irish coast,
> There came a heavy fog,
> And the captain lost his reckoning
> By an error in his log.
>
> On the 14th of November,
> At eight o'clock at night,
> The lookout man at forecastle head
> He thought he saw a light:
> He took it for the Fastnet Rock,
> And sorry I'm to say,
> 'Twas by that fatal error,
> She was wrecked at Dunlough Bay.
>
> When the *Memphis* struck the rock that night,
> Our captain he did say,
> 'Brave boys, she'll go to pieces
> And we'll be cast away,
> So lower down the lifeboats
> And try your life to save,
> And I trust in God that none of us
> Will meet a watery grave.'
>
> We lowered our starboard lifeboat
> And she was full manned;
> But before she reached the waterline

The after-tackle jammed.
The forward one went by the one
And the boat she swung around,
The crew got in the water
And four of them were drowned.

We lowered our port lifeboat
And the painter was made fast.
The crew were getting into her
The captain was the last: –
But before he could do so,
A mighty sea came rolling in
And swept the boat away,
And left our captain to his fate
That night in Dunlough Bay.

The captain being a brave young man,
With courage stout and brave,
He sprang up for the rigging
His precious life to save.
But before he could do so
Another sea came on
And swept our captain overboard: –
We thought his end had come

The captain of the *Memphis* –
There was luck for him in store –
He got upon a bullock's back
And safely got ashore:
Where he was kindly treated by
The people there next day.
And that concludes my little song
Of that night in Dunlough Bay.

Animal cargoes that got ashore alive were, of course, very valuable to the local people. The Mizen peninsula got some fine horses that way.

And then there are the various mysteries of the sea. What ever became of *Lismore*, belonging to the Cork Steam Packet Company, which left Cork for Liverpool on her maiden voyage on 10 July 1924 and was never seen again? One survivor was found on the Wexford coast, but he was never able to give any account of what had actually happened to her. And what was the story behind the paragraph in the *Cork Advertiser* in 1867: 'The ship, "Czar" of Glasgow, was a few days ago found deserted off Cape Clear. She was loaded with iron and coal, and when picked up bore traces of having sustained a

Lismore

Czar

severe gale. Not a living creature was on board.'

Mary Celeste is by no means the only mystery of a crewless ship still sailing on! (Michael Fleming, of Youghal's *Dei Gratia* was, in fact, involved with that strange incident.) The account of the unmanned *Saga* being wrecked near Ballyandreen has already been given, and, curiously, Captain Roberts of Passage West and *Sirius* met with another on the maiden voyage of the *British Queen* from London to New York. Here is what Roberts wrote in the *Queen's* log for Friday 19 July 1839: '10.30 a.m. Stop'd Engines and sent the Boat with Chief Officer on board the Barque *Bethel* of Bideford, found her abandoned with all sails, running rigging, gone, Main Royal yards across with all other yards. Railroad iron in her hold with water nearly to lower deck beams – no boats – all Water, provisions & stores gone. Bulkheads broke. Cabin lockers broken – looks to have been plundered for everything – pump speers rigg'd appears to have worked with [illegible] which was not on board – in fact she appears to have been deserted without cause and plundered of everything removable.'

The most famous and, after recent researches, infamous sea disaster off the Cork coast, was the sinking of the SS *Lusitania* off the Old Head of Kinsale on 7 May 1915, with the loss of 1,201 lives. Colin Simpson's book, *Lusitania* (London, 1971), has carefully pieced together the whole sorry story – though she was carrying munitions, the British government was completely unscrupulous in its efforts to win the propaganda war, and distorted the facts surrounding the tragedy in order to edge the USA into World War I. The *Lusitania* sinking was excellent anti-German publicity and helped push the Americans along the road to a declaration of war.

Both *Mauretania* and *Lusitania* were government-subsidised ships, a condition being that they should be so designed as to be capable of travelling at 24/25 knots and carrying armament – that is, they could be readily converted to armed cruisers. *Lusitania* was launched on 7 June 1906 and made her maiden voyage from Liverpool to New York in 1907, leaving on 7 September. The design was necessarily curious, with the dual purpose in mind: there had to be very large engines and a big hold, with a luxury hotel atop them. The result was a very tall, relatively unstable ship. Coal, 6,600 tons of it, was stowed in longitudinal water-tight compartments, which formed the two sides of the ship, and were believed to cushion the effects of cannon shot. Too late, it was found that such compartments were absolutely fatal to a ship if it was torpedoed. (Among other things, the water-tight doors were also the ones to the coal holes and were difficult to close when thick in coal-dust and fragments.) In May of 1913 *Lusitania* was dry docked in Liverpool and had mountings for guns fitted.

When war broke out there were elaborate systems in America of 'front' companies to enable ships like *Lusitania* to carry contraband – munitions of war – under innocent listings in the manifests. The Germans in fact warned passengers that this was being done and that sailing on *Lusitania* was not

British Queen

Bethel

Lusitania
Old Head of
Kinsale

safe as she was a legitimate target. On her last voyage, some of her cargo was listed as munitions. Other items most probably were, too: 'cheese' may have been guncotton and the ship's big load of 'furs' is also suspect.

The southern and western shores of Ireland were patrolled by an elderly cruiser, *Juno* (also with dangerous longitudinal bunkers/compartments) and a few old yachts and fishing boats. The Admiralty had only just then realised that German submarines had the range to reach these waters by going round the north of Scotland; they had thought they could only take the direct route down the English Channel, and could not reach south-west Ireland. However, U-20's Kapitan Leutnant Walker Schwieger was cruising there that May, working up to St George's Channel. The war was still being conducted in a rather gentlemanly fashion. Sighting *Candidate*, the U-boat got her to heave to, let the crew take to the boats (they all escaped safely), failed to sink the ship with a torpedo and had to finish her off with gunfire. But they found that this apparently harmless merchant ship was armed and that meant danger to a submarine conducting conversations on the surface. So when they saw her sister ship *Centurion*, they simply torpedoed her. Again there was no loss of life, and they only managed to sink her by sending another torpedo into her at point-blank range.

Juno

Centurion

Kapitan Schwieger was now getting low on fuel and had only three torpedoes left. So he turned for home, conserving his fuel and his weaponry for the long run back. The Admiralty knew that he, or some U-boats, were in those waters and recalled old *Juno* to the safety of Cork Harbour. At this time *Lusitania* was steaming home, and received no special instructions and no radio-ed warning that U-boats were active off Cork. She was looking for *Juno* to escort her on the next leg of her journey. Some 35 miles off the Old Head of Kinsale, Kapitan Schwieger sighted *Lusitania* and fired one of his three remaining and not very powerful torpedoes at her. His log records his amazement at what happened. After the torpedo hit, the ship exploded; the whole superstructure and bridge were seen to be torn asunder by the blast.

Traditional ships' lifeboats can be launched easily from a stable ship in an upright position, but they can be worse than useless in wild seas with a listing ship. Now *Lusitania* was very big and very tall – her lifeboats hung 68 feet above water – and she plunged down, keeling over, and finally pivoting with her bows on the sea floor. Lifeboats that were slung out were torn by the rivets on the ship's side. One boat would fall on another. Panic had broken out and people who were not killed by the explosion or trapped below were to die in the lifeboat launching attempts or drown in the sea as the great ship sank in a mere 18 minutes. Rescue boats eventually came to help as fast as they could. *Juno* set out from Cobh and came in sight of the struggling survivors, only to be recalled because of the danger from the U-boat – which by then must have been high-tailing it home.

As some of the bodies showed evidence of the explosion, the government tried to get all of them brought into Cobh, where a proper selection could be made for the inquest. They tried to stop the Sovereign of Kinsale holding an inquest on the bodies brought there – but Kinsale held on to its rights, though the verdict was just what the government wanted. Sworn statements were taken from American survivors – and have never been seen since. Great efforts were made to blame *Lusitania's* Captain Turner for her loss (that he should have been zig-zagging, etc., etc.), but these failed. The propaganda victory was a very great one, however – the sinking without warning of an unarmed and innocent passenger liner, with brutal loss of life. Only in the 1930s did awkward questions begin to be asked, and modern research unearthed some of the terrible answers; divers to the wreck report how the explosion of her cargo blasted the metal of the ship's sides outward.

La Surveillante

Bantry

Just over ten years ago a Cork diver, Tony Balfe, located in the depths of Bantry Bay the quite well preserved French frigate *La Surveillante*. She was one of the ships of the 1796 French invasion attempt and it is hoped to recover a great deal of material from her and display it in Bantry. The 1796 French Armada Trust of Bantry has been formed to direct this undersea excavation. The frigate is about 100 feet below the surface and rests on her keel; her upper decks have collapsed and at the present time it is uncertain whether the lifting of any part of the actual vessel, as was done with the English *Mary Rose*, might be possible. Excavation and conservation on land of everything on her is possible and likely to make *La Surveillante* Cork's best known and most exciting wreck, offering an intimate picture of life on a French warship of 1796.

XIX

The Land

COUNTY CORK, SAYS an old account, has some of the best and some of the worst land in Ireland. A very large proportion of the county comprises excellent farmland – from Macroom, east to Youghal; along the Blackwater and northward to the borders of Limerick and Tipperary. But the west is mountainy with fertile plots of land between continual outcrops of rock, and a climate able to nurture the most exotic plants. The Nagles Mountains, too, break up north Cork. Here are heather moors and bogs, while in Beara the mountains are predominantly grassy and give feed to many sheep. It is therefore a land which attracted settlers, invaders, planters and land-grabbers generally, and where violence has often flared as people tried to regain some rights to their own country.

Over considerable areas of the better land, the 'traditional' view of Ireland, checkers of fairly small fields, has been obliterated in the last decade or so as field fences have been removed and enormous fields of prairie-like extent, mostly given over to pasture and subdivided by electric fences, have been created. Old field gates, often with attractive gateposts, have likewise been knocked to allow entry of modern gigantic farm machinery. Almost overnight, as it seems, the traditional stone-built and slated farmyard has vanished and concrete and galvanised-iron milking parlours, cattle sheds, factory farms of chickens and pigs, and silage pits have taken its place. This extensive restructuring and rebuilding and almost entire mechanisation of farming has, in Cork, been very largely a development from the late 1960s and through the 1970s. During the 1960s it was possible to see sickle, scythe, old-style reaper and binder and combine harvester, all in action within a few miles of each other in West Cork.

The 'traditional' checkerboard of fields enclosed by hedges and walls is not, however, more than 200 years old. It was in the mid-18th century that the big estate owners began a programme of agricultural improvement and land enclosure. The Royal Dublin Society gave grants for the planting of hedgerows (just as present governments have given grants to root them up), and Ireland got accordingly the lovely fences of hawthorn and furze which in early summer outline the fields with blossom – the cream of hawthorn and the gold of furze. Later, the fuchsia was widely used in hedges and in some places, including the Boggeragh Mountains, the olearia, the 'daisy bush' of Australia and New Zealand. Townsend's *Statistical Survey of Cork*

Enclosure

relates how, in the Fermoy/Glanworth area, 'the building of the three Rock mills on the Funshion in County Cork, resulted in the three adjacent baronies becoming enclosed, tilled and almost as full of inhabitants as the lands along the sea coast'. If this was true of this particular district, it was so generally. Both in England and in Ireland, enclosure meant taking land from people who had had common rights of grazing on it, and it resulted in violent protest. In the Scottish Highlands things were even worse as new landlords (after the forfeitures of the '45 rising) or impoverished old ones evicted their tenants with extreme cruelty, and changed the glens from populated districts raising black cattle to deserts with a shepherd or two and great flocks of sheep. Later, they would repeat the process to create more man-made deserts as deer forests for so-called sportsmen.

Farming, to be profitable, demands enclosure if crops are to be grown and protected while they mature. The old way of working the land was by infield and outfield, where a community would have communal arable land around its settlement and communal grazing on the outfield, often mountain land.

Barley Cove, Mizen peninsula in the mid-1950s

The infield would be fenced as a unit; in winter cattle were pastured on it, but in spring they were driven up to the summer grazings, and the people cultivated individual strips of the infield. In Switzerland, transhumance, going up to the high summer pastures (the Alps – high pastures, in the original usage of the word, not the actual rocky summits) still continues, and the cheese made up there can go to market by helicopter.

In the island of Lewis in the Scottish Hebrides the use of the shielings carried on, in a much diminished form, to the middle of the present century; in Ireland it is gone a hundred years or more, fading out last on Achill and on the Galtee Mountains. Shieling in Scotland was booley (from *buaile*, milking place) in Ireland. Some of the sites are still there on the Cork hills, green spots among the brown or purple of heather, a rickle of stones from a hut. On the spurs of Hungry Hill above Adrigole are many crude shelters built against rock faces and large boulders.

Booley

Richard Pococke wrote on 2 August 1758 of the Beara Mountains which have 'good pasturage on them, and they make huts and keep their cattle on the mountain in summer and live on new churn butter and milk'. The custom had an idyllic quality, going up to spend the long summer days with the cattle up on the hillsides, milking and making butter and cheese. Milk and milk products were vital sources of food in Gaelic Ireland, and continued to be so. (Cheese-making does not seem to have been as popular in Ireland as it was and is elsewhere, but it did occur, though it seems to have died out as the poverty of the general public increased.)

Yet it is not entirely accurate to attribute the checker of field fences to the 18th-century enclosures alone. Some of them are far older than that. Prehistoric field fences of the familiar shape were found at excavations at Cush in County Limerick, just over the border from Cork. On Beginish Island in Valentia Harbour in County Kerry, a settlement with small stone-fenced fields has been dated to the 11th century. Nobody flying over the Burren in County Clare can fail to be struck by the mosaic of very ancient and small stone-walled fields, with the modern and larger land divisions imposed upon them in newer walls. The strong impression is given that these old fields may well antedate the present soil erosion of the Burren; that they represent farming when there was more soil and cover on the limestone uplands there.

Old field fences

In Cork, in the mountain districts with good peat cover, old field fences under the peat, built before it formed, have yet to be traced, though they exist in some number in Kerry. Certainly some of the old 'stone heap' field fences in the west of the county may be very old – to cultivate the land, it had to be cleared of stones and the easiest way to dispose of them was in a circling wall. Other collections of gathered stones may be heaped on rocky outcrops in small mountainy fields, which, with those same fields gone back to grass, may give a strange impression of a cluster of cairns. The county's stone walls are a study in themselves. They range from cunningly balanced,

Stone walls

lace-like affairs on some hilly land to the massive stone-heap ones, which may be very wide indeed and are normally built with an outer facing of big stones and a fill of the smaller gatherings from the land. There are cleverly built walls of round boulders from beach or from boulder clay – for example at Kilcrohane, where the walls change as the land changes, they are built of angular fragments culled from the mountain and then, as the glacial morainic land is reached, of round boulders taken out of it. There are the solid walls that edge the road to the Old Head of Kinsale lighthouse built by the commissioners, which are mortared, as are the high walls built around the great demenses. There are drystone walls of small, thin slatey rocks, of thin bedded flagstone, fitted laboriously together in little pieces. There are walls of great stones, weighty to lift. There are walls with spaced, gallaun-like uprights, and walls of the lovely Cork limestone, splotched with golden crotal (lichen). Each one is craftsman-built and a work of art.

Most of Cork's hedges are not, like English hedges, planted on the flat, but decorate raised banks of earth or earth and stone. Hawthorn, black-thorn, bramble, wild rose, wild cherry, ash, fuchsia and more grow on them and form a massive barrier. This bank/hedge is at its widest and most diffi-cult to cross along townland boundaries, and today can be further defended by strands of barbed wire (often hidden in the vegetation) and another elec-trified fence set outside the main line. Cross-field walking is, because of the difficulty of getting through these great hedges, the most tiring form of pedestrian exercise in the country. That they occupy much land is one reason for their destruction today but they do provide very necessary shelter to both domestic and wild life, as well as juicy bites of assorted herbage absent from todays standardised pasture. Thus in England, after massive hedge clearance, a movement is beginning to replant some of them.

Farm animals

Horses, cattle, sheep, pigs and poultry have all changed profoundly over the centuries. Local breeds – agile 'greyhound' pigs, various sheep – have all died out, bar the Kerry cow; the Kerry horse, said to have been as remark-able as the cow, is long gone. Islands in particular, by their isolation, tend to have their own specific breeds and Cape Clear had its own small horses, cattle and sheep. 'The sheep on Cape Clear were formerly a peculiar variety,

Cape Clear

Old wall near Baltimore

small in size, the flesh very delicate in flavour; they had long depending, twisting horns; the wool was exceedingly fine, a fact attributed to the nature of the pasturage near the sea.' (D. Donovan: *Sketches in Carbery*, Dublin 1876.) Today, the farm animals in Cork are all of the internationally known varieties; the black-and-white Friesian is the predominant dairying breed with an increasing sprinkling of recently imported Continental breeds, Charolais, Blonde Aquitane, and so on.

The horse was still significant on Cork farms in the 1950s; it is now virtually extinct as a farm animal. It is, indeed, difficult to realise its vital role in transport and in all farm work, and how many trades depended on it: harness- and carriage-makers and cartwrights. The smithies were dotted thickly over the country, for everyone needed a smith within convenient horse-walking distance. Again, there were in the old days local fairs for the buying and selling of livestock at almost every village. These came to be replaced by fairs held in the streets of the county towns; with the early start to take cattle to market, the haggling, the striking of the bargain, the drinking in the pubs thereafter, they are still remembered vividly. Almost overnight, again, it seemed they were gone, replaced by the clinical atmosphere (and much fairer prices, if you were not good at haggling) of the auction marts. Two ancient horse fairs survive, in attenuated form so far as sales of horses are concerned, but extended by various carnival events: Buttevant's 'Cahirmee', held in July, originally at the site of the caher of Cahirmee, but now in the town; and Dunmanway's Ballabuidhe in August.

Sheep were, it seems, more valued in the old days for their wool than for their meat, which could not be salted down as well as beef or pork. Cork produced and produces a great deal of wool, but the Irish wool trade was hard hit by the 1699 English Wool Act which prohibited its export in order to protect the English industry. The Act was not repealed until 1779, but considerable quantities of wool seem to have been smuggled out to France – packed to look like barrels of butter and pork. Goats have always been kept, in the past very much as the poor man's cow; in recent years, however, their

Horses

Cahirmee
Ballabuidhe
Sheep

*Stones at Rathbarry forge for fitting
iron tyres on wooden cart-wheels*

Oxen

excellent and disease-free milk commands much higher prices than that of the cow.

It was less usual in Ireland to see oxen as a form of traction, either of carts or farm implement, but some of the big estates did use them in the 18th and 19th centuries. Slower than the horse, they have much greater pulling power. From the *Corke Journal* of 31 July 1760: 'To be sold by Mr Henry O'Brien of Kilcur, Castlelyons, light fresh young plough bullocks, well trained to wheeled carriage and field work. Also a carriage fitted for the drawing of limestone in which the said bullocks will draw five tons weight on any good road.'

Butter and milk

Cork's famous butter market has been mentioned – it was only finally closed in 1925. It stood for an entirely different way of life from today's on the farm. Each owner of milch cattle had a dairy, a churn and a set of crocks and tools with which to make butter. It was packed into firkins, the small barrels supplied by the Butter Market, and sent on horseback or cart or human back to that place, where it was carefully checked and graded. Cork had six grades, of which the lowest was known as the 'bishop', and the barrels were marked accordingly:

1st	2nd	3rd	4th	5th	6th
|	+	++	+++	+++	++++

The records of the Butter Market survive and show no diminution of supply or export during the years of the great Famine. Most of the suppliers were farmers above the poverty line, but one has the impression that the owners of the market were not greatly concerned for their well-being. In the minutes of a meeting held 5 January 1847, in a reply to a letter from Lord Bernard asking whether 'the prevailing distress had any effect on the Butter trade of Cork': 'It was resolved to inform his lordship that the Committee was not aware of any visible effect upon that trade which the Committee attributed to the admirable arrangements under which it was constructed.' In 1849 they protested loudly when the Collector of the Port would not issue bills of health on account of the outbreak of cholera. They claimed such action would injure the port's trade, and that the cholera was nothing to worry about; it was mild and confined to the workhouses. But cholera in Cork was no laughing matter – it was around this period that the Dominican fathers were exempted from their normal Monday and Wednesday abstinence to try to boost their health against its infection.

It was in the 1880s with the start of the co-operative movement of which Sir Horace Plunkett was the inspiration that the whole shape of the butter and milk market came to change. Local creameries (originally steam-engine powered) sprang up all over the country and milk was brought to them in churns to be made into butter. 'Going to the creamery' became a way of life and a social occasion. By donkey- and horse-cart, later by tractor and trailer, or trailer and car, churns were taken daily to the creamery and the men stood in a conversational group waiting their turn for its unloading and checking. It could occupy most of the morning hours. Then more and more amalgamation and centralisation of creameries took place, ending in Cork with three great processing plants at Rathluirc/Charleville (Golden Vale), Mallow (Ballyclough) and Mitchelstown. All the hard work, the skill of the farmer's wife in butter-making, the pulling and hauling, has gone. The cows are milked by machinery, the milk runs straight into a refrigerated tank on the farm, from which the bulk tanker pumps it out. It is then pumped from the tanker into the butter-making machinery of the great processing plants and from their sterile and mechanised maws pours out a golden stream of butter into the appropriate wrappings and packs, exactly weighed, wrapped, untouched by hand until you open it to spread on your bread.

Rathluirc/
Charleville
Mallow
Mitchelstown

This is not the place to go into the vast amount of traditional lore about the making of butter – how witchcraft or the evil eye were suspected when it would not come – or of how similar influences were believed to be the source of cattle disease. One of the more ornamental caterpillars seems to have been regarded as the cause of murrain in cattle, and a couple of silver charms, representing the *conach* (murrain caterpillar), with the markings on each side made to look like precious stones, have been dug up in the county, near Doneraile in 1834 and near Timoleague in 1843.

The cattle for slaughter converged, in great droves, on the north side of Cork city. It was a vast and messy industry, in which every bit of the animal was utilised. When Charles Smith wrote his account of Cork in 1750 he was told that 80,000 cattle were slaughtered annually but the number of pigs was beyond computation. Portuguese salt was preferred for meat, English for fish preserving. Normally the whole beef (about 400 lbs) was salted down into two barrels, so one got both the best and the worst of the joints. But if it was intended for the British navy, they left out the necks and other coarse pieces. 'They have a third sort which they call French beef, that is old cows and beeves, that are but half fat, which in time of peace they sell to the French. This sort of beef turns black and flabby, and almost to a jelly (no wonder sailors fed with this kind of meat, can't face our honest English tars, who have so much better and more substantial food in their bellies).' Smith was being optimistic here, as the poor food, often gone rotten, supplied by cheating victuallers and pursers, was a long-standing cause of complaint in the British navy.

Cattle
Cork City

He lists what happened to the rest of the animal. Tongues were barrelled and salted for the use of the ships' officers. The fat (tallow) was rendered down in Cork (with horrible smells, one presumes) and made into candles and soap; much was exported as well to Holland and to Bristol. Not all the hides were tanned in Cork; some were salted and sent to Holland. Most of the horns went to the same destination, though some were used in Cork. The hooves made glue and oil; the hair was used in plasterwork. They had been selling heads and kidneys to the poor till they found a way of boning the head and getting a good market for the meat. The poor of Cork were particularly angry when the hearts and skirts (a fringe of meat associated with the 'pluck' – heart, lungs, liver) began to be salted and packed off to Scotland. The round gut was salted and sent to Venice to make skins for Bologna sausage, and the small gut was made into catgut. The gall went to Bristol and the bladders likewise. The Dutch took the shank bones – 'a ship laden with them looks like a charnel house' – while the small bones of the feet were burned to make crucibles for extracting silver from lead: 'nothing stands the fire so well as ox bones'. The blood was fed to pigs, and was used, too, in that still traditional and well loved Cork food, *drisheen*, a gut-enclosed concoction related to the black and white pudding, and having the general appearance of a blonde snake. 'Skirt and kidney', the two cut up and stewed in a thick gravy, is another traditional Cork dish – and very good it is – while the city's continuing liking for tripe must also be related to the habits of the great days of its cattle killing.

The city indulged, to the annoyance of the upper classes, in bull baiting, taking a bull from a herd coming into the town and chasing it through the streets. Of the innumerable pigs, many were city bred and fed, scavenging in the dirty, unpaved streets. So numerous did they become that in 1804 a two-horse pig trap was put into circulation to try to round up some of them.

Efforts were, of course, made to remove some of the dirt from the streets and slaughterhouses, and it was loaded into small ships and sent downriver to Dunkettle and Glanmire to be spread on the land. Arthur Young at the end of the 18th century writes of 'Cork manure, of the richest kind, especially in the slaughter season' and that in the city you could buy slaughter dung at 8d (just over 3p) a horse load. The manure arriving at Glanmire went some four or five miles inland to the various farms in small carts pulled by a single horse.

Salt

By Arthur Young's time, the source of salt for the beef was still Portugal, shipped from Lisbon; salt for the butter came from both Irish and English saltworks, and for fish from Rochelle. The Cork people had become so expert in casking and preserving that they re-barrelled quantities of fish imported from Scotland, England and Sweden for re-export on the long-distance routes to American and the West Indies. The *Corke Journal* of 7 January 1760 had an advertisement for 'salmon cured in the New Cork manner, will keep for 12 months and stand the West Indies without tasting salty'.

Fertiliser

On the farm, farmyard manure, and city waste when it could be got easily as from Cork, was the only fertiliser. The development of farming on the big estates led to the extensive burning of lime, but near the coast people had already learned the value of shelly sand as a source of lime, and they both gathered and cut seaweed for manure. Smith (1740) says that the broken cockles of the sand of Red Sand (Dirk) Bay, just east of the Galley Head, were said to result in bigger crops of wheat and barley than any other and that it was carried 12 miles inland on horseback, presumably in creels or sacks. It was even worthwhile sending boats out to dredge up sea sand, as was done from Whitegate in Cork Harbour in the first half of the 19th century. As to weed control, now carried out almost exclusively by chemical means, the hoe and the hand were the only ways in the old days. The 19th century saw imports of guano and of Chilean nitrates coming in the big sailing ships, the start of the use of imported and ultimately synthetic fertilisers. Today, NET is occupied in fertiliser production. Its Marino Point in Cork Harbour is the largest Irish chemical plant and it began exporting ammonia and urea in 1979. The great cluster of modern structures on what was once the site of a Big House signposts how far Ireland has moved in recent decades, not only in the mechanisation of farming but in the perhaps excessive use of chemical aids.

Mechanisation

Mechanisation came only slowly to Ireland. In pre-Famine days there was plentiful and very cheap labour; it was only after the Famine that the sickle, that most laborious and back-breaking tool, was generally replaced by the far more efficient scythe for cutting hay and corn. The giant combines now do in hours what once took days and weeks. Though the scythe is still useful for cutting odd corners of grass and weeds, few of us today would like to face

Horse-drawn hay rake in a hayfield with a three-stone alignment

Threshing machine

a long day's work cutting corn with it. The cut had to be even and neither too big nor too little for the binders to pick it up into sheaves, which they then tied with a twist of corn stalks. Stooking was an art in itself, if the sheaves were not to fall in the wind; then came the leading in, the proper building of the stack. During winter came the arrival of the threshing machine, drawn by a thundering steam-engine, a time when all the neighbours helped and the farmer's wife made great feasts for the hungry army of workers. Earlier, threshing had been done by the flail, or by water-powered or sometimes horse-powered threshing machines. The horses walked round and round a spindle which was geared to the threshing machine. They could work a turnip cutter or whatever inside a barn on the same principle. Just as the quern stone for grinding small quantities of grain continued on and on in use in remote areas, so did the flail in the West Cork islands to the middle decades of the present century. In the 1950s people on Hare Island in Roaring Water Bay sometimes threshed by the even more primitive methods of 'slashing', hitting the heads of the grain against a stone set atop a barrel.

Reaper and binder

The horse-drawn and then tractor-drawn reaper and binder replaced the scythe. Hay was cut mechanically and could be tedded (tossed) by a machine, though you will still see people today in Cork hand-turning small amounts with hay forks. Cork now makes vast quantities of silage (with the accompanying danger to streams if it leaks into them) and much less hay, both straw and hay being picked up and baled by machinery.

So far as recent mechanisation goes, Ireland was about 20 years behind the rest of Europe. The 1950s saw its beginning, the 1970s its culmination. In 1975, most of County Cork had 10-15 tractors per 1,000 acres of arable land and pasture, but the Beara peninsula only five to 7.5. Much work is necessarily still done by hand in the small plots of land among the rocks of the west.

Lazy beds

Lazy beds, the digging of ridges on which to grow potatoes, remains widespread because it is an efficient method with easy weed control and good drainage. In the past, it was used for corn crops, too, and up all the mountainsides and along deserted stretches of coast, you will see the old patterns of ridges where people once laboriously won land from the moor and grew crops. Monard's continuing output of custom-made spades and slanes shows how widespread digging, quite apart from the cutting of turf for fuel, persisted into the present time. (It is recorded that, in the western 'Congested Districts', as late as 1891, some farmers had never seen a plough.)

Arthur Young

Arthur Young, travelling around Ireland in the 1770s, saw the beginning of the development of farming on the big estates. He saw other things, too, noting that the poor milked the sheep (ewe milk is excellent for cheese but there is no record of the Irish making it, apparently) and how in Mitchelstown and district 'Hogs are kept in such numbers that the little towns and villages swarm with them; pigs and children bask and roll about, and often resemble one another so much, that it is necessary to look twice before the *human face divine* is confessed.' What did delight him was how many Cork landowners were cultivating the turnip, of which Young was a most eager promoter. Lord Shannon of Castlemartyr and Richard Aldworth of Annes Grove were among those he praised for being enthusiastic turnip growers.

Arthur Young, just before the restrictions on the export of Irish wool were lifted, describes how it was being processed in north Cork. 'In the towns of Doneraile, Mitchelstown, Mallow, Kilworth, and Newmarket, are clothiers, who buy up the wool, employ combers in their houses who make considerable wages, and when combed, they have a day fixed for the poor to come and take it, in order to spin it into worsted, and pay them by the ball, by which they earn one penny three farthings to two pence a day [less than 1p]. The clothier exports this worsted from Cork to Bristol and Norwich. Of late they have worked a good deal of it into serges, which are sent to Dublin by land carriage and from there to the North, from where it is smuggled into England by way of Scotland. The poor people's wool is worked into friezes for the use of the men. The weavers who work these friezes and serges live about the country in the cabins. Immense quantities of raw wool are sent to Cork from all parts. Five hundred cars [i.e. light horse-drawn carts] have been seen in a line, and it is supposed to be sent in large quantities to France.'

Wool

Weavers

Along the coast and in West Cork, where wheeled carts were only coming into general use around the time of Arthur Young's visit, ships were used to transport farm produce. From around Clonakilty a group of farmers would get together to make up a load to sail around to Dublin. The cost was quite high, a 50/60 ton sloop, there and back, cost up to 40 guineas (£42), and prices might not be good when it got to the Dublin market.

Flax was widely grown. And as the population increased, more and more people were being crowded into less and less land in the poorer parts and becoming entirely dependent on the potato, which Walter Raleigh may well have first introduced to Youghal. Roads engineer Nimmo left his impression of Clonakilty in the early 1820s, which 'struck me as a very remarkable place, the whole peninsula around there all the way from Clonakilty to Courtmacsherry is cultivated as close as the bed of a garden – there is not a single bit of waste land, except a bog which we are going to drain for them, and all over Bandon the population is more numerous than in any parts I have seen in Ireland; and they are wonderfully quiet, but greatly in want of employment. The only thing they have is the linen trade, which is extending, and the cotton trade.'

Flax

Clonakilty

While on the big estates farming moved steadily forward with more crops, higher yields and the beginning of mechanisation, the ordinary person had a miserable life. The elegance of the 18th century, of the Georgian houses, was based on the affirmation of the rights of property and the denial of the rights of man. The ideals of the French Revolution and of human rights were regarded as godless, treasonable ideas to be crushed by every resource of the State. Democracy as Great Britain now knows it, and prides itself on, is no ancient right but something that her citizens fought and died for in the 18th and into the first half of the 19th centuries. In Ireland things were even worse, with a religious divide between the Catholicism of the masses and the Anglicanism of the establishment. Landlords had absolute rights to raise rents and evict. Violence was naturally met with violence. At the end of the *Whiteboys* 18th century the Whiteboys were active against landlordism and enclosures at the expense of the people. They threw down the enclosing walls just erected and resisted the payment of tithes to the Church of Ireland clergy. (The poor, who were struggling to live, were forced to pay this money to a cleric whose church they did not attend, and, as well, try to find something for the Roman Catholic priest, whose church they patronised.) The Attorney General reported in 1787, of the people in Munster: 'A poor man is obliged to pay £6 for an acre of potato ground, which £6 he is obliged to work out with his landlord for 5d [2p] a day.'

George Cornewall Lewis, writing about *Local Disturbances in Ireland* (London, 1836), said, very truly, that if every Irish labourer could earn 8d (just over 3p) a day, there would be no disturbances. He saw the Whiteboys as 'a vast trades union for the protection of the Irish peasantry'. They wanted to keep people in possession of their tiny holdings; they would kill without mercy if pushed to it, never for personal gain, but rather to bring about a better state of affairs in which people would be able 'to live by regular industry'. Visitors and strangers were never attacked; engineer and road builder Griffiths, living at Mallow, said he never took any security precautions and that he thought an Englishman coming in to start an industry would be welcome. But for the unjust, unpopular landlord, the situation was rather different. Lewis remarks on the 'levelling and democratic tendency' of the invention of gunpowder. 'A modern Irish landlord may barricade his house, and he is secure so long as he remains at home, but if he ventures in the open air, he is liable to be shot from a distance by a man who may have given his last farthing to purchase the powder and ball with which his stolen gun was loaded.' Old houses of the period have heavy wooden shutters to their windows and massive bars to hold them closed; other bars run in sockets behind the doors.

An increasing population, pushed more and more on to less and less land, became entirely dependent on the potato, which, when it does well, yields so big a crop from so small a piece of ground. Famine was always very near and if crops failed there were every so often quite serious ones. But the Famine, *Black '47* with a capital F, is that of 'Black '47', when potato blight ravaged the crops in 1846 and continued to do so in the following years. It had then no known cure; it remains endemic in Ireland and today's potato crops are only produced at the cost of regular spraying throughout the growing season.

Remote, overcrowded West Cork was particularly badly hit. It was from Skibbereen that the first terrible reports were sent to *The Times* of London. As late as 1974, Peter Somerville Large could write, in *The Coast of West Cork*: 'West Cork never recovered from the potato famine of 1847, and its effects linger like clouds of fall-out.' The story is too familiar to repeat in detail here: a starving, disease-ridden people, waiting, in a state of disaster and shock, for death; the mass burials; the rats and dogs fattening on the corpses; the overcrowded workhouses with the dying pressing in on the dead; the attempts at relief that were never enough. To start public works to give employment to people was a great idea, but in West Carbery and Bandon and elsewhere, men employed fell dead because their wages were weeks in arrears and they could not buy food to keep alive. Soup kitchens, the easiest way to make the minimum of food go the farthest, probably kept many alive. The great killers were the famine diseases – 'black fever' (lice-borne typhus), 'yellow fever' (relapsing fever), dysentry and scurvy – for the Indian meal brought in to provide a cheap alternative to the potato contained no vitamin C. People's bodies swelled with the 'famine dropsy', unhappily still to be seen in countries struck by famine today.

Malone: 'I know what I'm talking about. Me father died of starvation in Ireland in the black '47. Maybe you've heard of it.'
Violet: 'The Famine?'
Malone: (with smouldering passion) 'No, the starvation. When a country is full o' food and exporting it, there can be no famine. Me father was starved dead; and I was starved out to America in me mother's arms. English rule drove me and mine out of Ireland.'

(George Bernard Shaw, *Man and Superman*)

Shaw was right. There was no real famine, only the failure of the only food crop of the Catholic peasantry and a failure to take proper means to give them something else to eat; 8d a day dole would have saved them all.

Ireland was full of food. There were cattle, sheep, pigs, poultry, and deer in the deer parks. There was butter and milk. There were crops of oats and barley and wheat. There were orchards of both cider and eating apples, soft fruits, strawberries and peaches and plums. The seas and rivers were full of fish. Certain people had money aplenty – the 12 landowners in the Skibbereen area, the worst-hit district, had between them an annual income of £50,000, an immense sum at that time. Lord Carbery's share was £15,000, Sir William Wrixon-Becher's, the owner of Skibbereen town, £10,000, and the Rev. Stephen Townsend's, £8,000. In modern money, they would be getting up to the millionaire class. The Famine hit the rich a little – it reduced their rents as people died or left. Farmers gained as there was more land to apportion into more viable holdings. But disease was no respector of rank, and the better-off, especially those who engaged in relief work, died from disease like the poor.

In Cork city, Dr Callanan described what he saw: 'During the first six months of that dark period (1847) one-third of the daily population of our streets consisted of shadows and spectres, the impersonations of disease and famine, crowding in from the rural districts, and stalking along to the general doom – the grave – which appeared to await them at the distance of a few steps or a few short hours.' Someone had to make a profit by it; Cork's Patent Saw Mills had their 20 pairs of saws going almost non-stop, cutting up wood to make coffins, to make sheds as temporary fever 'hospitals' and to make berths for the ships intending to carry emigrants.

Today one must ask why nothing was done on a big enough scale to save the situation? The reason was the mentality of the time: that the right to eat must be earned by work, that the State had no obligation to give any kind of free hand-out or dole, that the ordinary processes of commerce must never be interfered with. If you had a contract to export grain from a starving country, government would not stop the ship in order to save lives at home. Scotland suffered, too, from the potato failure, but on a lesser scale because there were fewer people left there after the evictions. Whether the London government would have done more for a famine in England of the same sort must remain an open question; they were not particularly concerned at the misery of the millions crowded into the slums of the cities created by the industrial revolution.

There were some extraordinary incidents. The Americans sent two ships of war, the sloop *Jamestown* and the frigate *Macedonian*, with food and clothing for famine relief. *Jamestown* arrived in Cobh on 12 April 1847 and *Macedonian* on 28 July, where she was met by a welcoming party including the Capuchin Fr Matthew of temperance fame, and her dozen officers were given a sumptuous dinner which included every possible delicacy.

Many shipowners did well out of taking emigrants across the Atlantic. There was a big trade in timber from Canada, and no return cargo, so it was very profitable to ballast outward bound ships with emigrants instead of stones. John Ford, of Ballinascarthy, was among the thousands who left, and his wife one of the thousands who died on Grosse Island, waiting for permission to enter Canada. John himself moved to the United States and bought a farm near Detroit; his grandson was Henry of the Ford car. But not many of those who left and survived the voyage did so well for themselves so soon; most stayed in the towns and took what work they could find.

Emigration, of course, did not start with the mass exodus of the Famine years. Many people had already realised that the only hope of bettering themselves was to leave Ireland. 'There is scarcely any prospect of bettering one's condition in this country,' wrote James Huston of Bandon on 29 July 1827 to his uncle, Robert Eedy at Chaleur Bay, New Bandon, Nova Scotia. These were some of the Bandon weavers, and they were planning their emigration carefully, writing ahead for information about tools and so on they would need to bring. But from 1851 there was a great tide of people with no other hope but to leave, and they took with them abiding hatred for the British government that had brought them to this pass.

For those who remained there was a break-up of the old cultural patterns and traditions and a rapid loss of the Irish language. In 1843 County Cork was Irish-speaking, the language used by over 90% of the people. By 1883 it was down to 350 people in every thousand; today the Irish speaking districts are confined to the area around Ballyvourney, Coolea and Ballingeary, and Cape Clear Island. Poverty and want continued. For instance, the potato crop failed again badly in West Cork in 1890-91. Edith Somerville's diary for 30 January 1891 reads: 'Rode round the Toe Head country. Sickened and stunned by the misery. Hordes of women and children in the filthiest rags. Gave as many bread and tea tickets as we could, but felt perfectly helpless and despairing in the face of such hopeless poverty.' Yet that same year the Somervilles founded their West Carbery pack of hounds, of which Edith was sometime MFH. They had to shoot them all in 1897 when Cork suffered an outbreak of rabies and the hounds got it, but replaced the animals immediately so there was no break in their sport.

Irish language

Edith Somerville

Incidentally, Edith and her sister Hildegarde are claimed to have been the first to introduce Friesian cattle to Ireland, starting a dairy herd at Drishane, Castletownsend, around 1908, but gaining little profit by it.

Edith was much more successful in her horse trading, and perhaps she put something of herself in Bobby Bennett in the *Irish RM*. From the *Irish RM*, too, comes a vivid vignette of one of the small clusters of houses – clachans – set amongst the rocks of West Cork at the turn of the century. 'The bohireen dropped, with a sudden twist to the right, and revealed a fold in the hillside, containing a half-dozen or so of little fields, crooked and heavily walled, and nearly as many thatched cabins, flung about the hollows as indiscriminately as the boulders upon the wastes outside. A group of children rose in front of me like a flight of starlings, and scudded with barefooted nimbleness to the shelter of the houses, in a pattering, fluttering stampede.'

Clachans

Few of these ancient clachan settlements – houses in a friendly cluster, not a street – remain today except in ruin. You will come on their walls and old fields about the Cork hillsides – for instance, just below the signal-tower on the Sheep's Head, on the southern side.

Brave men and women were not wanting, however, to struggle for Irish freedom and for a just allocation of its land. The Famine years were followed by the rise of the Fenians, with their gallant attempt to win complete political freedom for Ireland, and in 1879 Michael Davitt's founding of the Land League. The Land League gave a powerful voice to the long-standing wrongs of the ordinary tenant, and put power into his/her hands by 'no rent' and boycott campaigns. One outstanding case of the latter method was that of William Bence-Jones of Lisselane between Clonakilty and Ballina-

Fenians

Land League

scarthy, who thought of himself as an excellent landlord but would not reduce any rents. People refused to pay any rent at all. All his Irish workmen left him, and he and his wife had to drive their own cattle to the station at Bandon at night. He had no easy passage thereafter to sell these same cattle, as the Land League was strong enough in the 1880s to have them boycotted in Cork, Dublin and Liverpool.

The British government moved at last, with land acts in 1881, 1887 and 1891, which reduced rents, gave tenants rights in their holdings and allowed the redistribution of land to farmers from the great estates. The Congested Districts Board moved into the most over-populated areas of the west and south-west, to report, administer and reorganise the tiny, chaotic holdings there. Its activities included building piers for some of the small communities along the coast, and with the people now gone from the more remote localities, you may sometimes come on a pier in the middle of nowhere, like Toor pier on the north side of the Mizen peninsula.

Men of County Cork were waiting for the share-out of *Aud's* arms in 1916, but she was captured on her way to them and, as already told, her ammunition lies on the sea floor in Cork Harbour. But when the struggle for Irish independence began nationwide, Cork's men and women took an extremely active and gallant part, figuring in many daring raids and ambushes. Crossbarry and Kilmichael are the most famous of the successful ambushes, but there were many others, including even a raid on the Bull Rock lighthouse, when a revolver, shotgun and some gelignite were carried off.

Congested Districts Board

War of Independence

XX

The Changing Face of Cork

ARTHUR YOUNG WOULD have been delighted at the present face of farming in Cork, with his beloved turnips widely grown, not to mention carrots and cabbages as field crops. But the blue flowers of the flax, so widely grown in the 18th and early 19th centuries, are gone, and so, with selective weedkillers, are the bright patches of scarlet poppies and golden corn marigolds in the cornfields. But the 1980s have seen brilliant colour return to whole fields with the golden flowers of oil-seed rape now being quite widely grown. Since 1925 sugar beet has been developed as a major crop in Ireland, making it self-supporting in sugar, and in County Cork vast quantities are processed each year at the Mallow factory. It is of interest that way back in the 18th century Ireland used to refine imported West Indian sugar – Cork city had a sugar refinery that is first mentioned in 1735 and continued till 1799 when it was abandoned after a fire.

Glandore, until recently, used to grow fields of violets, so that the passer-by got the scent of their leaves (the actual flowers were the big showy scentless ones) as one walked the roads. On the Sheep's Head peninsula, Kilcrohane has a very successful little co-operative producing daffodils for the early spring cut-flower trade. Yet it is not so much in the commercial growing of flowers and vegetables that Cork has seen a sudden and recent change, but in the development of gardens. Rack-renting and evictions meant that people in the past were slow to do anything to their homes which might give a landlord the idea that they were prospering. The habit lingered after the necessity was gone; 'garden' in Irish English actually meant a potato plot. Flying over the county, you could see old and established small gardens around houses in areas like Bandon, with its strong Protestant and monied tradition; none in any others. Then the 1970s brought more money, more prosperity, many new houses, and suddenly gardens blossomed, English style, with lawns and roses, swimming pools and greenhouses; the old-style seedsmen and nursery-men vanished and 'Garden Centres' selling everything from exotic shrubs to garden gnomes and rabbits in cement sprang up like mushrooms. The 'Tidy Towns' competition set people cleaning and painting, and adding little roadside gardens to their amenities. Colour came suddenly to street and garden in new paint and bright flowers.

The 'gallon' (a lidded tin of almost any capacity) in which one fetched milk from the farm has disappeared. Even farmers with large dairy herds

Cork city

Glandore

Kilcrohane

frequently use the pasteurised bottled or cartoned milk, distributed daily by truck over the whole country. Golden Vale and Mitchelstown co-operatives collect milk from Limerick and Tipperary as well as from Cork. Mitchelstown Co-operative Agricultural Society was founded in 1919 as a co-operative store; it began making cheese in 1932 and became the largest co-operative of its kind in Ireland, producing not only a great variety of cheese, dried milk powder, butter and pasteurised milk for daily consumption but also, under the Galtee brand name, a wide range of pigmeat products – bacon, ham, sausages, ham roll, black puddings etc. The Galtee foods factory was opened in Mitchelstown in 1967, near the main milk processing plant.

The Mallow-based Ballyclough started as a small co-operative in the neighbouring village of Ballyclough. It took over the Cleeves condensed milk plant at Mallow and added more and more amalgamations with local creameries – including, like Mitchelstown and Golden Vale, some outside Cork county – until it became Ireland's largest milk processor. Products include chocolate crumb for the Rathmore Rountree Mackintosh factory and butter oil for Saudi Arabia – where it is converted back into milk. Cheese-making at all these big processing plants is today a mechanised and standardised procedure, though originally they used the old hand-methods. Irish people had little taste for cheese and a massive marketing campaign only slowly got them to try and then to like it. Cheese uses a lot of milk and a lot of time and skill, so it is no wonder that, taking into account the historical background of Irish poverty and famines, it was not within reach of ordinary people. Happily today it seems to appear in some shape or form in most Cork homes. As well as the mass production of cheese, many individual families have turned to producing small quantities of high quality hand-made cheese – some outstanding examples come from Beara – but such work involves daily and skilful treatment of the product. Home cheese-making is far removed from the ten million gallons of milk that Rathduff process each year. 1990 saw Mitchelstown and Ballyclough merged to form a super co-op called Dairygold.

Ballyclough was the first place in Ireland to introduce artificial insemination and, in 1984, to pioneer a method of pregnancy testing for cows. Artificial insemination, bringing semen from the very best of bulls, has done a great deal to raise cattle standards (and reduce the risk of being chased by an angry bull when crossing a field!).

James J. R. Nagle was appointed to be the first veterinary director of Ireland's first AI station in 1945, and went over to Cambridge (enjoying VE day in London en route) to study the process. 'The biggest shock I got on my first morning observing collections was to see a four-foot-ten-inch Land Girl leading out an enormous prancing Friesian bull, managing to have him false mount the teaser several times, and then, with perfect timing, allowing him to serve into the artificial vagina.' Ballyclough, meantime, was building the new station at Ballyvorisheen, just east of Mallow, and went into action in 1946. Ireland's first artificial insemination was on the farm of Michael T. Barry, Ballyduff, Killavullen, using semen from a short-horn bull called Ballingurrane Benigh Count and resulting in a red roan bull calf. The inseminators ('the bull in a bowler hat') went around in the early years on bicycles, and were sometimes thought to be photographers with their bags of gear slung on their backs. Today, Ballyvorisheen has a splendid stud of bulls: Friesian, Hereford, Aberdeen Angus, Shorthorn, Simental, Limousin, Blonde D'Aquitane. As already mentioned, Mitchelstown has another very fine collection of bulls in the stables of the old castle; a third is at Bandon. All three are under the direction of the Munster Cattle Breeders Association.

Much malting barley is grown in Cork. Just as with milk and butter-making, so with distilling and brewery, and a multitude of small companies have given place to one or two centralised large ones. The first record of whiskey distilling in Cork is apparently that of 1618; how it came to be concentrated in Midleton has already been outlined. Illicit distillation, the making of poteen, continues on quite a large scale in West Cork. Brewing is centred in Cork city, in Beamish and Crawford's and in Murphy's breweries; in former times there were brewers in most towns of any size.

In Cork city itself there were at one time no less than 30 small breweries. Of the existing two large firms, Beamish and Crawford are the older, going back to 1792 when the Cork Porter Brewery was founded by William Beamish, William Crawford, Digby O'Brien and Richard Barrett. Beamish and Crawford have remained on their original 18th-century site on the South Main Street, with convenient access, in the days of water transport, to a wharf on a branch of the Lee. But the use of the site for brewing is older than Beamish and Crawford's settling there; a record of 1669 records a George Gamble having a malt house and brewery in the same place. The original Beamish and Crawford site was only about a third of its present size – old photographs show the glass tower of the adjacent Cork Glass Company whose land they acquired, pulling down the tower for their own new buildings. (Cork had three companies making glass: the Hanover Street Cork Glass Company, established 1783; the Waterloo Glass Company, Wandesford Quay, 1815; and the Terrace Glass Company of the South Terrace, 1818; all now defunct.)

Porter used to be imported to Cork – it was named for the London porters who drank it in large quantities – until the city began brewing for itself. It is now no longer made; only stout, the higher grade of the same species, is produced. Cork drinkers have their preferences, some always desiring Murphy's, some Beamish and Crawford's, and others the Dublin-brewed Guinness.

As with everything else, the production of stout and lager is now a highly mechanised, scientific and quality-controlled process. Hops come in pellet form, green hop extract. In the old days, little ships with names like *Betsey*

Margin notes:
Ballyvorisheen

Killavullen

Bandon

Malting barley
Brewing

Midleton
Beamish and Crawford
Murphy's
Cork city

Porter

and *Lavinia* came in with loads of English hops to the Cork quays. Malting is carried out at a new plant outside the city at Ballincollig, though Cork people still recall the smell and the rich dark smoke when malting was in progress in South Main Street.

Beamish and Crawford still have their complete series of old ledgers, in enormous volumes written in beautiful copper plate, recording, among other things, the small wages the men got – 6s (30p) to 15s (75p) per week – and the large profits which went to the owners.

Trees

Another feature of the changing face of Cork county has been the return of the trees. The destruction of the native forest cover has been described, and the planting by some of the big estate owners of ornamental woodlands. Extensive planting began in the early 19th century, following on legislation of the previous century which allowed the tenant a right to any trees planted provided they were registered with the County Clerk of the Peace. By 1850 Cork was the best planted county in Ireland and 52,000 acres, nine and a half million trees, were set between 1790 and 1860: six and a quarter million conifers and three and an eighth million hardwoods (ash, followed by beech and oak). In 1841 Cork had two and a quarter million hedgerow trees, too, but none of this planting was done in the mountainy west; it was all in the more fertile country around Cork city and along the Blackwater. Very few of these trees survive, as they were later to be felled and not replanted. Then came the official government plantings, with the foundation of the Irish Forestry Commission in 1908. Originally these plantings were thought of as purely commercial, more especially as a way to put rough mountain land to good use, but in the late 1960s the Forest and Wildlife Service changed its outlook completely, with the concept of the Open Forest. State forests were now to be not merely commercially profitable, they were to be a valuable amenity for the general public, who were encouraged to enjoy them. Picnic places, car-parks, forest walks and nature trails were laid out, and some species of trees were planted for their beauty rather than their commercial value.

Very large areas of County Cork are now under forest, and more and more hillsides are being planted. There are over 50 forests open to the public, and they come in all locations and in all sizes. At Glengarriff, the heart of the forest is the remnants of the old native woodland, and the visitor can drive or walk among the trees and enjoy views to the circling mountains. Gougane Barra is one of the most ambitious projects, with a motor road right round the great corrie at the head of the lake, and walks and nature trails leading from it. At Killeagh, Glenbower Wood is an old estate forest with an ornamental lake (drained recently) which served both to landscape the wooded valley floor and to work a mill at the village below. Farran, on the river Lee, is purely an amenity woodland, with a pond for the collection of wildfowl maintained there and a herd of red and fallow deer. Doneraile is restoring something of the glories of the old landscaped demense.

Gougane Barra

Glenbower Wood

Doneraile

Clashnacrona is in the gap of the glacial spillway through which the road from Dunmanway to Drimoleague runs, and a forest path ascends to its heights with enormous views. There are very splendid views of all West Cork and the coast from the forest trail at Lough Hyne, leading to the top of the adjacent hill. Near Fermoy the road and a good track takes you to the top of Corrin hill with its prehistoric cairn and hilltop fort. Currabinny, near Carrigaline, has a whole series of walks and wide views over Cork Harbour. Shippool and Inishannon give an opportunity to see the beauty of the lower tidal reaches of the Bandon River, with the glistening rush beds and the old wharfs, and rippling water latticed by a tracery of branches. Cullenagh (north of Dunmanway, and off the Coppeen-Cousane Gap road) has walks running down to a beautiful lake beyond which rise the rocky heights of Nowen Mountain. Rineen takes you around the head of the Castlehaven inlet with views across the water to the splendid plantations of rhododendrons on the opposite hillside. But the list of Cork's forests could go on, and on, and on.

Cork city itself is a curious mix. It has never considered itself an industrial town, yet it has always had numerous industries. They have ranged from elegant silversmith work to salt beef, and in the past have all been concentrated in or close to the city itself. Present day economic trends and Ireland's membership of the EC have changed the pattern; new industries, often multinational, are being established in industrial estates around the city, most particularly on Little Island, which now houses a variety of firms, and at Ringaskiddy, still in its initial stages of development. Two big employers in the heart of the city, both tied to the automotive industry, have lately closed, Dunlops in 1983 (modern tyres last too long and cars need fewer sets!) and Fords in 1984.

The Ford factory is of particular interest in that Henry Ford's grandfather came from County Cork, as already related. The Ballinascarthy Fords were not, though they left in the Famine years, the poorest of the poor. They already had relations in America, for John Ford's three brothers had left, looking for a better way of life, in the 1830s. Henry Ford (1863-1947) was

Clashnacrona

Lough Hyne

Currabinny

Shippool Inishannon

Cullenagh

Rineen

Cork city

Ford

The container port at Tivoli in Cork

the son of John's son William, who was 21 when the whole family emigrated, and who came to have his own farm in Dearborn. Farm work, a fall from a horse included, turned young Henry's thoughts to mechanisation. 'I have followed many a weary mile behind a plough and I know all the drudgery of it. What a waste it is for a human being to spend hours and days behind a slowly-moving team of horses when a tractor could do six times as much work! … I felt perfectly certain that horses, considering all the bother of attending them and the expense of feeding, did not earn their keep. … To lift farm drudgery off flesh and blood and lay it on steel and motors has been my most constant ambition.'

Henry saw, however, that the automobile needed to be made and accepted first. Once the car was on the farm, the tractor must follow. But the people thought a tractor needed to be very heavy in order to have a good grip. 'And this in spite of the fact that a cat has not much weight and is a pretty good climber. The only kind of tractor I thought worth working on was one that would be light, strong, so simple that anyone could run it and so cheap that anyone could buy it.' Just like his early Ford cars.

It was with tractors that Henry began in Cork, buying a large parcel of ground along the quays which had been the city park and racecourse. Work began in 1917 and the factory opened in 1919. It was not a purely sentimental choice, though Henry Ford said there was an element of that: 'My ancestors came from near Cork and that city, with its wonderful harbour, has an abundance of fine industrial sites. Cork has for many years been a city of casual labour and extreme poverty. There are breweries and distilleries, but no real industry. The best that a man could hope for was two or three days a week on the docks, for which he would receive sixty shillings (£3) or fifteen dollars, for the hardest kind of stevedoring.' What the Cork factory had to offer Henry was a good site, a plentiful supply of labour and an entry into the tractor market of Great Britain, which the First World War had drained of horses. (It is an ironical fact that the horse was the prime mover in the First World War, and that the internal combustion engine replaced it to some extent on the home front; while in the Second World War, petrol and oil were the great sources of energy, and the horse made a temporary comeback in a period of rigid petrol rationing.)

The Cork Ford plant, which paid £5 a week for an eight-hour day and five-day stint, had its problems, not least the severance of Ireland from Britain, which meant that the latter would tax imported parts from Cork. Fords founded their great factory at Dagenham in England and Cork went over to assembling cars, mainly for the Irish market, beginning with the famous Model T and ending with the Sierra.

Pfizer   Of the post World War II multinationals, Pfizer have a large plant at Ringaskiddy, which they began building in May 1969. Pfizer, like Fords, is another emigrants-made-good story, this time of two Germans, Charles Pfizer and his cousin Charles Erthart, who arrived in the USA in the mid-

1840s and started their little company in 1849. They had both been involved in the confectionery business, but decided to go in for high quality chemicals, starting off with 'Santonin', a vermifuge made from *Arte misia cina* with a sugar coating to disguise the bitter taste. The company and its range of products grew, especially the production of citric acid, used in so many ways, as in soft drinks and as a preservative of other foods. Their experience with deep tank fermentation producing citric acid led to work with the new wonder drug, penicillin, which originally was very difficult to produce even in small amounts. Pfizer claim to have had the first deep tank penicillin plant and went into mass production of the drug in 1943. Later, they were to discover and develop tetramycin.

In Cork, Pfizer have a large citric acid plant and an adjacent pharmaceutical one. In 1990 the citric acid section was taken over by the American company, Archer-Daniels-Midland (ADM). From its original planning the Pfizer plant was carefully landscaped and environmental hazards were taken into consideration. Molasses, the starting point for citric acid, and fuel oil, came in by the plant's own jetty and waste is taken out to be dumped at sea. The latter operation was both costly and not very environmentally desirable and from 1981 Pfizer set about finding ways of recycling the quantities of waste water which contained a sugar residue. In 1989 research gave the go-ahead for full-scale reclamation from the waste, which will produce methane which will be used in conjunction with Kinsale gas for the plant's energy needs. There is a large steam-producing plant which supplies steam for the whole works, and heat exchange units have been installed (by way of heating water) to utilise the surplus heat resulting from each process. This recycling of heat has been successful enough to be taken up, after the Pfizer experience, in the USA.

Penn Chemicals

Penn Chemicals, also in the Ringaskiddy area, have become increasingly aware of environmental problems and keep a constant patrol around their premises to check for any unwanted emissions. In fact, like Pfizer with its heat exchange, Penn is now 'exporting' its environmental know-how. Again, they go back to a small business started in America in the 1850s, and are named from Penn of Pennsylvania, who, of course, had a slight connection with Macroom through his father. The Cork factory, which went into production in 1975, has for its main product a new wonder drug for the treatment of stomach ulcers, cimetidine. It is very much a multinational process, as the first two stages of the drug's production are carried out in Switzerland and the rest in Cork. Another factory on Little Island makes the binding agent used when the cimetidine is eventually made up into tablets; the drug leaves the Ringaskiddy plant only in bulk.

Sandoz

Ringaskiddy is only slowly growing as an industrial, mainly chemical, estate. Sandoz began construction work on a huge plant in 1990, facing some considerable opposition on environmental grounds. There is a difficult balancing act between preserving the beauty and amenity of Cork

Elanco

Harbour and the development of factories where a single mistake could cause a major disastor

Elanco have a factory at Dunderrow, not very far from Kinsale, so carefully landscaped that you could drive past without seeing it. This Eli Lilly plant, mainly concerned with producing antibiotics, was constructed in the late 1970s and included the laying of a long pipe running right out to sea to carry waste products, hopefully out of harm's way.

Apple Computers

Faber-Castell

Apple Computers have a very large and growing plant in Cork at Hollyhill; Kilnamartyr produces kits to make your own toy soldiers. The list of modern County Cork industries is quite long and full of surprises. Faber-Castell came to Fermoy in 1955, the first German industry to come to Ireland after World War II, and before there was any official State aid for such ventures. Ireland was a good base from which to export and break out of the then high tariff walls surrounding Germany. Faber-Castell took over the old military barracks and installed sophisticated machinery to produce pencils and ball-point pens – a very far cry from their origins in 1761 when Kaspar Faber, a joiner, began to make his 'lead sticks' entirely by hand in Steinbei Nürnberg. However, the ever-increasing production of cheap ball-points made the Fermoy pencil factory less and less viable, and sadly it closed in 1990. Another Fermoy firm, this time of native origin and ownership, is O'Brien's Photo laboratories, using modern computerised machines for processing and printing colour films and with a reputation for high quality work.

Cork airport

Cork moved, formally as it were, into the air age with the official opening of its airport in 1961; the third of the Irish Republic's major airports, it had a 6,000-foot 17/35 main runway and a 4,000-foot 07/25 cross runway. The years 1989-91 saw an enormous expansion. The main runway was lengthened to 7,000 feet, new radar and navigational aids were installed and the terminal buildings were enlarged to handle the massive increase in line traffic. Iona National Airways of Dublin moved their flying school to Cork early in 1989; late that year the new European College of Aviation was founded,

Loading horses at Cork Airport after Millstreet International Horse Show

so that Cork is now Ireland's main centre for pilot training.

But Cork's aeronautical history goes back a lot longer than that, and the first person to see the enchanting view of Cork Harbour from above was a Mr Sadler in 1816. Balloons were around long before aircraft, and as far back as 1784 Cork had experimented with hydrogen-filled unmanned ones. Such a specimen was released from the Mardyke at 4 p.m. on 27 March and two hours later came to earth 18 miles away at Cooper's Hill. John Myneham, who lived there, had never seen such a thing before and the tube sticking out suggested to him the horns of the devil. However, he caught it and took it home to show to his neighbours. An accidental spark ignited the 'inflammable air' (hydrogen) which filled it, burning a man and a woman seriously. More of the crowd fainted or fled, 'fully convinced that Lucifer himself had got amongst them'. In that same year, on 14 April, a balloon that had been launched from Fleet Street in London, England, was found by Mr Finchett at Cork's Fair Hill – obviously they must have been having a period of persistent easterly winds.

*Mr Sadler
Balloons*

Then in June 1816, as Tuckey relates: 'Mr Sadler the aeronaut, arrived in this city. The car, suspended from his balloon, was of an oval shape and was elegantly finished. It was supported at each end by eagles, apparently rising from the shell of the nautilus, which was modelled in a most masterly style, it was lined with purple velvet finished with borders of shamrocks in gold; on the upper pannel [sic] was a mosaic railing, terminating with the Irish harp, so disposed as to form the elbows of the car, and on either side hung pendant the badge and star of the order of St Patrick, in gold embroidery encircled with wreaths of oak in relief. This splendid vehicle was attached by ropes of burnished gold, which appeared as pillars supporting the base of the canopy, round which were painted the twelve signs of the zodiac, relieved with clusters of silver stars. The canopy was formed of purple silk, studded with stars of gold, and intersected with spiral lines of oak, which were held by eagles, standing on the edge of the base, and between each of the eagles were the prince's plumes in gold, and drapery purple and yellow, richly embroidered, and trimmed with gold fringe and tassle; the whole surmounted with a rich coronet, and forming one of the most splendid and elegant vehicles fancy could picture.'

On 2 September 1816 a pilot balloon was let off from the yard of Cork's military barracks, presumably to judge conditions, and then a gun was fired to alert people to look skywards as Mr Sadler and his magnificent basket and balloon rose into the air. He was seen entering cloud, descending again, and then landing in the Ringabella district, on a Mr Hodder's farm. The latter was somewhat startled by, not to say afraid of, the extraordinary aerial visitation, but eventually plucked up enough courage to go forward and agreed to look after the balloon, while a Mr Foote first provided the aeronaut with a meal and then with a horse to ride back to Mr Hodder's, who by then had recovered enough to give him a bed for the night.

This first flight over Cork and Cork Harbour began at 4.40 p.m. and ended at 5.12 p.m. Sadler loosed a parachute for the people watching below to see, and waved a banner about when he thought he was too far off for them to see him waving his hat. Coming out of the cloud he described the view of 'the city and coast extending toward Bantry to the west, and Waterford to the east, I distinctly perceived, whilst the harbour of Cork, and the interior country, with its various mountains, formed a view sublime in the extreme'. Before landing, he carried out a pre-landing check, securing any loose articles that could be thrown about, and used a grappling iron to halt the craft as it touched down.

Blackwoods Magazine for August 1817 records 'Mr Sadler, junior' crossing the Irish Channel from Portobello barracks in Dublin to Holyhead, the first aerial crossing. 'On arrival, the 21-year-old Sadler junior was intrigued to see men working in a diving bell. '"I am just come from the clouds. I should now wish to visit the deep," and so persevering was he in his request, that the bell was prepared, and he went down to a depth of several fathoms, where he remained under water a considerable length of time.'

Lord Carbery

Lord Carbery of Castle Freke was one of the pioneers in powered flight and used to go looping his frail little craft at the local agricultural shows in Bandon and Clonakilty. In 1914 the *Skibbereen Eagle* remarked on his lordship's generosity in putting on his air show for £40, though judging by the value of money at that time, it does not appear particularly cheap.

William Sholto Douglas

In 1917, William Sholto Douglas of the Royal Flying Corps was sent to prospect for some eight sites for airfields in Ireland. In Cork, he chose

Fermoy

Fermoy, a small grass field which continued to be used for very many years afterwards, but is now no longer available. Meantime, the Americans had a

Aghada

wartime seaplane base at Aghada on the harbour.

Cork city

Cork city was long in getting its airport, and a long spell of wet weather delayed construction when it did begin. The site was the 500-foot hilltop just south of the city, close to a large field called Farmer's Cross, which had served as an airfield when necessary. A flying club had operated from there for a few years in the 1930s and, among others, trained Ruth Hallinan, who was the first woman in Munster to gain a pilot's licence, and who kept her own light aircraft at the Fermoy field in the years immediately preceeding World War II. At the present time there are several other airstrips in County Cork – a tarmac one of 455 metres at Bantry, and grass strips on Mallow racecourse and at Rathcoole between Mallow and Millstreet.

Bantry
Mallow
Rathcoole
Kilbrittain

As well as the long-closed Fermoy, two other Cork airstrips are now defunct: the 1,010 feet strip at Kilbrittain, which belonged to Winn Technology during its period of operation there in the 1970s, and Macroom, briefly

Macroom

in use in 1976/7. The latter was merely a grass strip in a field on a small hill about one and a half miles north of Macroom, but while it existed had the distinction of being Ireland's highest airfield, at 650 feet.

* * *

Cork then has experienced many changes and many developments over the centuries; Bronze Age copper mines on the slopes of Mount Gabriel, topped by the shining domes of an aircraft tracking station; air liners ousting the great ships that once steamed majestically in and out of Cork Harbour; new industries replacing the old; and even much of the very face of the country-side in a state of change and flux. Yet it remains a microcosm of Ireland, with something of everything; a county of many beauties and big enough to be full of surprises. It would need many volumes to tell the story of it all – this book has only set out to try to trace some of the themes that have made Cork, and Cork's people, what they are. It is the beginning rather than the end of a journey of discovering the county, a journey on which all can set out but which in the nature of things is not likely to have an end. Rather it can be a series of new discoveries about this great Irish county.

Appendix 1

The Great Little Roads of Cork

Many of the main roads and obvious routes around the county are very beautiful and command wide views, but the lesser roads are sometimes even more worthwhile and interesting to travel. This list is of some of the county's minor roads, which take one into its intimate recesses and into some of its loveliest scenery. Be warned that they are often narrow and twisting and demand care, especially when meeting other vehicles. They now all have tarred surfaces.

1. Roads, with access to forest parks, through the Nagles Mountains.
   Whitechurch - Daly's Cross - Killavullen.
   Carrignavar - Chimneyfield (very fine Mass Rock site in Forest Park close to road) **- Carrigacunna - Killavullen.**
   Glenville - Ballyhooly
2. Over the hills to **Ballyporeen**. From **Kilworth**, up the wooded **Araglin** valley, with its trees, fine old bridges and memories of iron smelting. From the head of the valley a mountainy road leads over the northern ridge and down to **Ballyporeen** in County Tipperary.
3. A complex of small roads twist in and out and over the Boggeragh Mountains, providing access to their many ancient monuments, to climbing on the hills with their far-ranging views.
   Coachford - Bealnamorive (waterfall hidden in Forest Park here) **- Carrigthomas - Millstreet** via pass between **Mushera More** and **Beg**. Branch routes allow one to drive right around **Mushera** and there are forest walks off it. The other small roads branching off this main route are all well worth following.
4. **Carriganimmy** to **Ballyvourney** by side road over shoulder of **Mullaghanish**, and through **Glendav Forest**. Wide views, forest walks; access to summit of **Mullaghanish** via RTE's road to their TV transmitter there.
5. **Kilmeedy Castle** (off **Carriganimmy - Millstreet** road at **Kilmeedy bridge**) and road over shoulder of **Claragh** mountains. Summit provides enormous panoramic views to Kerry, Limerick and Tipperary as well as Cork. Easy access to **Claragh** (east), hill-fort, hang-gliding launch spot, and to **Caherbarnagh** (west) with ancient hilltop cairn and beautiful corrie lakes below. Continue on road to valley below, to north and follow the side road, west into Kerry, passing a series of fine ring forts including **Caherbarnagh** itself, and some well-built old limekilns.

6. **Ballyvourney** to **Kerry** via **Coolea**, with a fine mountainy branch route from the thousand-foot crossing into the next county, which leads back under the cliffs of **Mweelin** to the **Reananeree - Ballingeary** main route. By leaving the main road again at **Carrig Lodge** one can follow a beautiful little back road with views to **Keimaneigh** and **Gougane**, which leads down into the latter place. From it, a branch route goes to the foot of the old **Lackabaun** pass over to **Kerry** – walkers only for the actual crossing.

   A minor road from **Ballymakeery** to **Reananeree** is also well worth exploring.

7. Roads around **Shehy Mountain**, with very fine views. The main line is **Coppeen - Shanlaragh - Cousane Gap - Kealkill** route. From the top of the **Cousane Gap**, by a standing stone, a very minor road runs north and west, and drops down onto the direct **Kealkill - Inchigeelagh** road (not the **Keimaneigh** pass) which goes between **Shehy** and **Douce**, with views back over Bantry Bay. From the **Inchigeelagh** end of this road another mountainy road goes over **Mount Prospect** back to **Togher**, on the east side of the **Cousane Gap.**

   Also from the **Togher** area, signposts lead to the Forest Park under **Nowen** at **Cullenagh**. Before this is reached, a very minor road climbs away through the rocky glacial spillway of **Bearboy**, just north of **Nowen** summit, and then runs down to **Bantry Bay**.

8. **Dunmanway - Bantry** via **Castle Donovan**. The more direct and more mountainy road, as against the present modern main road to its south.

9. The minor roads between **Ballynacarriga** and its castle, down to **Leap**, are an interesting complex taking one into the heart of typical inland West Cork. From **Leap** one can go on to **Glandore** and down the little roads to **Blind Harbour** and to **Myross** on the coast.

10. The routes around the **Mizen** peninsula and the **Sheep's Head**. These roads allow one to go down one side of each peninsula and return upon the other. The journey going west should be made in the morning, the returning, eastward one in the evening, so as always to have the light behind one. From **Kilcrohane** the **Goat's Path** takes one across the spine of the **Sheep's Head** peninsula and is particularly lovely in late summer when the dwarf furze and heather is in flower; a short and easy climb from the top gains the highest point of the Sheep's Head peninsula, **Seefin**, 1,136 feet.

11. **Eyeries** to **Allihies** via the **Cod's Head** with wide views, a rocky pass and walks down to the tip of the Head.

12. The southern main road crossings to Kerry are well known, the Healy Pass and the Tunnels road. But very beautiful is the minor road from the head of **Bantry Bay** up the **Coomhola valley** and over the county bounds to **Kilgarvan**, with particularly fine mountain and rock scenery on the Kerry side. From the summit, at about 1,000 feet, it is a short walk to visit

the rock-cut corrie lake of **Nambrackderg** (of the red trout) on the Cork side of the hills.

From the **Coomhola valley** a side road to the east climbs steeply up and then down again, through the **Bull's Pocket**, to **Carriganass Castle** near **Kealkill**. This is a very splendid little road both in its close-to, intimate prospects, which include a stone alignment, and in its wide outlooks beyond.

Appendix 2

High Cork

Cork is not generally thought of as a mountainous county but it includes many easy hills from which very wide views can be seen and some very pleasant rocky scrambles in the west. There are many very small hills, which would hardly be listed in a summary of Cork's mountains but which can be very well worth exploring. The main mountainy areas are the following:

1. **The Nagles**. Now extensively forested, and with forest walks. Access from the minor roads which traverse them. Highest point, **Knocknaskagh**, 1,406 feet. Prehistoric burial cairns on this, on the 1,340-foot summit to its north and on **Seefin**, 1,392.
2. **Mount Hilary**. Forests and access on the Banteer side. A long lump of a hill, 1,288 feet, with a cross and prehistoric cairn on its eastern end. Standing above and isolated in the Blackwater Valley, is a tremendous viewpoint on a clear day.
3. **Musheramore**. At 2,118 feet, the highest point of the **Boggeraghs**, with holy well close to summit. Easy access to it and other Boggeragh heights from the complex of minor roads there.
4. **Caherbarnagh**. At 2,239 feet, has burial cairn on lesser summit. Access from road over **Claragh** mountain.
5. **Mullaghanish**. At 2,133 feet, has extensive views into Kerry. RTE's private road to their summit TV mast makes access to this rather uninteresting height easy – but the views are very worthwhile.
6. **Shehy**, 1,796 feet and **Nowen**, 1,763 feet stand up dramatically and are features to be seen from far off all over the western half of the county. They command great views to the coast and its long sea inlets as well as far over Cork to Waterford.
7. The numerous small hills of the **Mizen** and **Sheep's Head** and around Lough Hyne are all of interest; the great lump of **Mount Gabriel**, the highest at 1,339 feet, being a considerable landmark.
8. **Knockboy**, on the county boundary at 2,321 feet, is Cork's highest mountain. Access from the summit of the Priest's Leap track. To its east, and readily reached from the Coomhola - Kilgarvan road, is **Akinkeen**, 2,280 feet. If transport can be arranged at either end, a ridge walk along the county bounds is possible from the summit of the Kilgarvan road via Akinkeen and Knockboy to the Priest's Leap track. Views are from Waterford in the east to the heights of Kerry in the west.
9. **Slieve Goill**, the **Sugar Loaf** above Glengarriff at 1,887 feet, looks like a baby Matterhorn from below in Glengarriff but is actually a long ridge

and easy to climb. To its north are two very fine corrie lakes, which can be reached either from the Sugar Loaf or from the head of the road up Coomarkane from Glengarriff Forest Park. Another road from the Park will bring you within walking distance of another corrie lake, the Barley Lake.

10. From the Healy Pass road there is very pleasant rocky exploring to be done along the main ridge to the north-east, to **Knockowen** (2,169 feet) and **Cushnaficulla**. Interesting views down into the deep valleys on the Kerry side, and high-level mountain lakes.

11. **Cnoc Daod/Hungry Hill**. At 2,251 feet, a most beautiful mountain with a rocky shelf, containing two lakes high on its face, from which a 700-foot-high cascade descends to Adrigole. The cascade was much visited by Victorian tourists but is only at its best after heavy rain. (Across the Healy Pass valley is Glen Lough and a deep corrie valley with many more cascades down its steep slopes). Hungry Hill can be climbed from Adrigole or from the Castletownbere side; it overlooks all Bantry Bay and across into Kerry. It backs onto more high summits which surround Glenbeg Lough, reached from Ardgroom by a minor road.

12. On the county border, part in Cork and part in Kerry, is a very fine horseshoe ridge walk, reached from Lauragh in Kerry and taking in **Tooth Mountain**, 1,969 feet, **Eskatarriff**, 1,875 feet, and **Lackabane**, 1,984 feet.

Appendix 3

Island Cork

Cork is one of the most highly 'islanded' counties of Ireland, and what follows is a list of the principal offshore ones, travelling from east to west.

1. **Capel Island.** Nature reserve. Lighthouse that was never lit.
2. **Ballycotton Island.** Lighthouse.
3. **Spike Island** in Cork Harbour. Military fortress built in 19th century, now used as a prison.
4. **Haulbowline Island** in Cork Harbour, now linked to mainland by bridge. Irish naval base and home of Irish Steel.
5. **Great Island** in Cork Harbour. Linked by bridges to mainland. Cobh is its principal town.
6. **Fota Island** in Cork Harbour. Linked by bridge to mainland. Fota House and wildlife park.
7. **Little Island** in Cork Harbour. Industrial estate. Now joined to mainland by reclamation works of long standing.
8. The rocky **Sovereign** islands off Oyster Haven.
9. **Inchidoney Island**, near Clonakilty. From the air still very obviously an island, though now joined to the mainland by reclamation and a causeway. Very fine strands.
10. **Adam** and **Eve Islands** in Glandore Harbour, two small rocky islets. The old sailing direction entering the Harbour is 'avoid *Adam* and hug *Eve*'!
11. **Rabbit Island/Oileán Bhríde**, between Adam and Myross. Rabbit seems to have been a surveyor's name, as the place had no rabbits! A long island, rocky stacks at the east end, grassy to the west. Inhabited until 1940 or thereabouts.
12. **High Island** and **Low Island**, off the coast in the same area, between Glandore and Castlehaven. High Island is high and cliff-bound; Low Island low and grassy and rapidly eroding. The two are very prominent landmarks off the West Cork coast.
13. **Myross.** Now joined to the mainland by a causeway and a shingle beach.
14. **The Stags**. A group of eroded fangs of rock off Toe Head, which from the mainland appear with surprising solidity, as if they were a craggy and solid island.
15. **Horse Island**, Castlehaven. Called, like many similarly named islands, from the belief that its grazing was particularly good for horses and would cure sick ones. Oileán Mo Lua in Irish, St Molua's island.
16. **The Kedge Islands**, between Toe Head and Baltimore. A small group of rocky islets, showing rapid erosion.

Principal Islands in Roaring Water Bay

17. **Sherkin Island**. Inhabited. A delightful mix of beach and rocky hill and tiny, flowery fields. Sherkin Island Marine Research Station.
18. **Cape Clear**. Inhabited; Irish-speaking. A high, rocky island of great interest and beauty. Bird observatory and Youth Hostel.
19. **Hare Island** or **Inishodriscol**. Inhabited. A flat-ish, fertile little island. Ferry from Cunamore Point on request.
20/21. **Ringarogy** and **Inishbeg**, in the lower reaches of the Ilen estuary and both linked to the mainland by bridges.
22. **The Skeames, East** and **West**, with remains of an early church. Rapidly eroding and probably one island when the church was built.
23. **The Calf Islands**. Three flat, grassy islands set in line in the middle of Roaring Water Bay. Inhabited within living memory.
24. **Horse Island**, with old copper mines.
25. **Castle Island**, with ruins of a small tower house. Meán Inis in Irish, Middle Island.
26. **Long Island**. Inhabited.
27. **Carthy's Islands**. A small group of islets between Castle Island and the Calves.
28. **Goat Islands.** A group of islets off the west end of Long Island.

29. **Fastnet**. Lighthouse on rock.
30. **Carbery Island, Furze Island, Cold Island, Lusk Island**. Small islets forming a group in Dunmanus Bay.
31. **Whiddy Island**. Sometime a deer park for Bantry House, and a fertile farming island; converted in part to a tank farm for Gulf Oil in the 1960s, for transhipment of oil from supertankers to smaller ones; on a care and maintenance basis since the *Betelgeuse* disaster of 1979. **Capel**

*From Cape Clear to Sherkin. On the right the old
signal-tower and lighthouse; in the middle distance
the new windmills generating electricity*

West Calf Island

Island and **Horse Island** are two small islets between Whiddy and the mainland.

32. **Garinish Island**. Off Glengarriff, has exotic gardens and Martello tower, in State care. Regular ferries.

33. **Garinish West**, further along the coast of Bantry Bay.

34. **Roancarrig Beg**. A small rocky islet with a lighthouse.

35. **Bere Island**. Inhabited. Hills rise to over 800 feet. Martello and signal tower, military forts still occasionally used. Glenans sailing school.

36. **Dursey**. Inhabited and linked to mainland by Ireland's only cable car. A long hilly island with the first signal-tower of the series that could pass a message quickly to Cork. Really just the tip of Beara cut off from the mainland by a very narrow channel through which there is a savage tide. In the 1950s the parish priest of Allihies, on a sick call to the island, drove to the pier, was taken over by boat and was then met by a saddle horse for the rest of the journey.

37. **The Bull, Cow, Calf** and **Heifer**. Rocky islets of varying size off Dursey. Remains of lighthouse on the Calf and existing lighthouse on the Bull.

Dursey Island

Capel Island

Appendix 4

An Eighteenth Century Industrial Estate

Arthur Young's account of Blarney

1776. September 15th, the Blarney Castle, S. J. Jefferys Esq., of whose great works in building a town at Blarney, I cannot give so particular an account as I wish to do; for I got there just as he and his family were setting out for France. I did not however let slip the time I had for making some enquiries and found that in 1765, when Mr Jefferys began to build this town, it consisted only of two or three mud cabbins; there are now 90 houses. He first established the linen manufactory, building a bleach-mill, and houses for weavers etc. and letting them to manufacturers from Cork, who have been so successful in their works, as to find it necessary to have larger and more numerous edifices, such as a large stamping mill for printing linens and cottons, to which is annexed another bleach-mill, and since there has been a third erected; the work carried on is that of buying yarn, and weaving it into linens, ten pence to thirty pence white; also diapers, sheeting, ticking, and linens and cottons of all sorts printed here, for common use and furniture. These several branches of the linen, employ 130 looms, and above 300 hands.

Another of Mr Jefferys' objects has been the stocking manufacture, which employs 20 frames, and 30 hands, in buildings erected by him; the manager employing by covenant, a certain number of apprentices, in order by their being instructed, to diffuse the manufactory. Likewise a woollen manufactory, a mill for milling, tucking etc broad cloths; a gigg mill for glossing, smoothing, and laying the grain; and a mill for knapping, which will dress above 500 pieces a year, but will be more, when some alterations now making are finished. A leather mill for dressing shamoy, buck or skins, fully employed. A large bolting mill, just finished, and let for £32 a year. A mill, annexed to the same, just finishing for plating, and a blade mill for grinding edge tools. A large paper mill, which will be finished this year. He has been able to erect this multiplicity of mills, thirteen in all, by an uncommon command of water.

The town is built in a square, composed of a large handsome inn, and manufacturers' houses, all built of excellent stone, lime and slate. A church, by the first fruits, and liberal addition of above £300 from Mr Jefferys. A market house in which are sold a hundred pounds worth of knit stockings per week. Four bridges, which he obtained from the county, and another (the flat arch) to which he contributed a considerable sum. Much has been done, yet is not the design near finished.

To show the magnitude of these works, and the degree of public good resulting from them, I shall mention the expense at which they have been executed. Respecting the principal bleach-mill, Messrs Forest and Donnoghue, under the Linen Act, took fifteen acres, at a guinea an acre, upon which they have expended £5,000 in erecting a linen-mill and a bleach green, twenty-five houses for twenty-five weavers' families, four looms in each house, a large dwelling house for themselves or their director; in each house, a man, his wife, three apprentices, two girls and two boys, besides young infants. In a short time the farm was increased, and land, which before had only brought half a guinea, then let for a guinea. The Linen Board advanced £500 to this work, and Mr Jefferys repaid them £1,400 of the £5,000. The old rent of the premises was £40 a year, the new rent £71. Another bleach mill, which cost Mr Jefferys £300 to which the Board added £300 and the person to whom it is let, £600 40 acres of land, formerly let at £10 a year, go with them. The whole rent now £80. To this mill is added since an oat mill, which cost £300, two tuck-mills, £200; a leather mill and kilns, £150; two dwelling houses, £300. A stamping mill, which cost Mr Jefferys £2,300 to which the Board added £300 promising £1,000 more when the works should be finished, which they have been these two years. Twelve printing tables are kept going, and sixty-five hands employed. Twelve printers. Twelve tire boys. Three print cutters. Eighteen bleach men. Six pencillers. Two tub-men. One clerk. One callender. One manager. Two draughtsmen. Four coppermen. Three carters. Beside the above sums, the manufacturer has laid out £500. The quantity of land occupied is 25 acres: old rent, £6 10s, new £113 15s.

A stocking factory, for which Mr Jefferys lent £200. The man laid out £300 himself; he occupies 50 acres before let at £20 a year; now at £76 11s. A gigg-mill, for which Mr Jefferys lent £300 till repaid by the Dublin Society, who granted £300 towards it, and the tenant laid out £200 the quantity of land he has is eleven acres, let at £5 10s, now at £36.

A manufactory of tape is established by which means six acres of land are advanced, from £2 8s to £9. They have three looms going, which make 102 pieces a day of 36 years each. The Dublin Society gave £20 to it. A paper mill which has cost Mr Jefferys £1,100 and is not yet let. A bolting mill, on which he has expended £1,100 the tenant £500 on adding an iron mill. Twenty acres of land, rent before £9 10s rent of the whole now £132 13s. The church has cost Mr Jefferys £500 and the first fruits £500 or more. The new inn, £250 and the tenant £300 more. Seventy acres of land before, at £20 a year, now at £83 9s. A dwelling house, £250, to which the tenant added £500. Ninety acres of land, before let at £54, the new rent is £74. Twelve cottages, and a lime kiln, which cost £280. Two dwelling houses and a forge, which cost him £150, and to which parliament granted £250 more. Upon the whole, therefore, Mr Jefferys has expended £7,630 in these establishments. Of public money there has been added £2,170, and the tenants themselves laid out £9,050 in all expended her £18,850 besides what Mr Jefferys laid out on bridges etc, in the whole, very near, if not full, £20,000 upon matters of a public nature. In all these establishments, he has avoided undertaking or carrying on any of the manufactures upon his own account, from a conviction that a gentleman can never do it without suffering very considerably. His object was to form a town, to give employment to the people, and to improve the value of his estate by so doing; in all which views it must be admitted, that the near neighbourhood of so considerable a place as Cork very much contributed: the same means which he has pursued would, in all situations, be probably the most advisable, though the returns might be much less advantageous. Too much can scarcely be said in praise of the spirit with which a private gentleman has executed these works, which would undoubtedly do honour to the greatest fortune.

Mr Jefferys, besides the above establishments, has very much improved Blarney Castle and its environs; he has formed an extensive ornamented ground, which is laid out with considerable taste; an extensive plantation surrounds a large piece of water, and walks lead through the whole; there are several very pretty sequestered spots where covered benches are placed.

Appendix 5

Mines in County Cork

Collieries of the North Cork coalfield
Garravesoge/Fairy Hill (2 miles S by W of Kanturk)
Coolclogh/Gurteen
Lisnacon/Killinane (1½ miles W Coolclogh)
Cloonbannin
Drominagh
Dromskehy North
Dysert (half mile S Mineville cottage)
Dromagh
Dernagree
Keale
Island
Cleanrath
Coal Pits
Duarrigle
Lisnashearshane
(List compiled from vol 1 *Memoir of the Coalfields of Ireland*, Dublin 1921)

Copper mines
Copper is very widely disseminated through the rocks of West Cork – grey copper ore in shales, weathering out on the surface as the green malacite and blue azurite, and in lodes as copper pyrites or 'purple ore', the variegated variety of pyrites. Accordingly, copper ores are reported from a great many localities, including the Anvil rock, one of the Stags. Profitable mining in the last century was, however, a different matter and geologist J.B. Jukes wrote (in the 1861 *Memoir of the Geological Survey of Ireland* for the district): 'The south-west part of the county of Cork is a district which perhaps more than any other, requires great caution as well as skill and prudence to mine with profit, and is a most delusive district to the speculator, for it contains so many of these specimens of "rich ore", many of which have not indicated the existence of much more ore than was actually seen in the specimen.'

The whole convoluted story of the copper mines of West Cork has recently been explored by D. Cowman and T. A. Reilly in *The Abandoned Mines of West Carbery. Promoters, Adventurers and Miners* (Geological Survey of Ireland, 1988).

Prehistoric copper mines may be difficult to distinguish from later trial pits. In local tradition small mines of unknown age were called 'Danes' or 'Old Men's Mines'. On Mount Gabriel and at Derrycarhoon the Bronze

Age workings were covered with peat and so lay untouched until the present day when it was cut away. J. Jackson (1980) lists the following as likely Bronze Age mines in County Cork:

on the Mizen peninsula:	Mount Gabriel
	Derrycarhoon
	Horse Island
	Castle Point
	Ballyrisode
	Callaros Oughter
	Scart
on the Beara peninsula:	Eyeries

The following seem to have been the principal 19th-century mines in Cork:

Copper:

Audley Mines:	Ballycummisk (also produced barytes)
	Cappaghglass
	Foilnamuck
	Horse Island (Roaring Water Bay)
	Rossbrin
Ballydehob Mines:	Ballydehob
	Boleagh
	Cooragurteen
	Kilcoe
	Skeaghanore
Deereennalomane	
Roaring Water Mines:	Kilkillen
	Laheratanvally (also produced lead)
	Leighcloon
Borlin Valley	
Berehaven Mines:	Allihies
	Cahermeeleloe
	Caminches
	Cloan
	Coom
	Kesloge
Balteen (nr Crookhaven)	

Carrigacat (near Crookhaven) – copper with auriferous gossan

Crookhaven Mines:	Boulysallagh – produced copper, silver, lead
	Callaros
	Cloghane, Mizen Head
	Crookhaven
	Killarry
	Mallavoge, Brow Head

Crookhaven Mines:	Spanish Cove, Kilmoe – copper, barytes, argentiferous lead

Sheep's Head Peninsula. Mines on tip of peninsula in Kilcrohane/Glanroon district, with auriferous gossan.

Skibbereen:	Bawnishall
Schull:	Castle Point
Coosheen Mines, Schull:	Castle Island
	Coosheen
	Gortnamona
	Long Island
	Schull

Manganese

Associated with copper and iron ore in the Glandore/Leap area. Occurs as pyrolusite and psilomelane.

Glandore Mines:	Aghatubrid (manganese, copper, iron)
	Derry – copper
	Drom – copper
	Keamore – copper
	Kilfinnan – copper
	Rouryglen – manganese and copper
	Gortagrenane – copper
	Little Island – copper

Lead

Occurs as galena. Mined near Bantry at Scart (Hollyhill mines) and at Ringabella (Ringabella and Minane) on the west side of Cork Harbour.

Barytes

Mined at Bantry and on Mount Corrin in the Mizen peninsula above Durrus, and at Lady's Well Mine near Clonakilty.

Slates

Worked at a great many sites, of which the largest were Drinagh and Benduff, both working into the middle of the present century. Slates were given female titles of honour according to size; in 1860, Benduff prices and sizes were:

Queens	28" x 36"	different widths	£1 10s per ton
1st Duchesses	24" x 12"		£5 per thousand
2nd Duchesses	22" x 11"		£3 15s per thousand
1st Countesses	20" x 10"		£2 15s per thousand
2nd Countesses	18" x 9"		£2 per thousand
1st Ladies	16" x 8"		£1 5s per thousand
2nd Ladies	14" x 7"		£1 per thousand

Appendix 6

Time Chart

BC

c. 7000   Arrival of first men in north of Ireland.

4000/3000 Neolithic farmers building court tombs in Northern Ireland.

Pre- 2000 The Bronze Age. Building wedge tombs and the Cork/Kerry stone circles. Hill top burial cairns.

1500-1000 Extensive growth of bog covering many early settlements.

AD

c. 400   Pre-Patrician saints including Ciaran of Cape Clear active in south of Ireland.

c. 450?   St Patrick's mission.

520?   Death of St Enda of Aran, traditional founder figure of Irish monasticism. St Finian founds Clonard.

524   Death of St Brigid. Monastic character of Irish Church becomes established.

c. 606   St Finbar makes monastic settlement in Cork.

c. 820   First Viking raids on Cork.

846   The Norse settle in Cork and build a town.

1014   Battle of Clontarf.

1170   Landing of Strongbow – Richard, earl of Pembroke.

1172   Diarmaid MacCarthaigh, king of Desmond, surrenders Cork to Henry II.

1177   Henry II grants kingdom of Cork to Robert Fitzstephen and Milo de Cogan, retaining control of the city of Cork and of the cantred of the Ostmen.

1297   Beginning of the Irish Parliament.

1348   The Black Death in Ireland.

1534   Act of Supremacy in England, marking start of the Reformation there.

1536/7   First Reformation Parliament in Dublin.

1586   Plantation of Munster.

1588   Spanish Armada.

1601   Battle of Kinsale.

1603   Accession of James VI of Scotland to crown of England.

1607   Flight of the Earls.

1641   Start of Irish Rising.

1642-49   Catholic Confederation of Kilkenny.

1645   Arrival of papal nuncio Rinuccini.

1646   The 'Ormond Peace'.

1649/50	Cromwell in Ireland.
1660	Restoration of Charles II.
1666	English act stopping export of live cattle from Ireland, thus giving the impetus to the development of the provision trade in meat in Cork.
1690	Battle of the Boyne. Cork city beseiged and captured by the Duke of Marlborough.
1692-1829	Exclusion of Roman Catholics from Parliament and all public offices.
1695	First penal laws against Roman Catholics.
1699	Legislation to halt export of Irish wool.
1707	'United Kingdom' established by formal union of Scotland with England.
1745	The great Jacobite rising in Scotland led by Prince Charles.
1771	The Bogland Act, marking the start of legislation to remove discrimination against Roman Catholics.
1796	French attempt invasion at Bantry Bay.
1797	Extensive but unsuccessful mutiny in British Navy in attempt to obtain some relief from the appalling conditions of service therein. French landing at Killala.
1798	Irish Rising.
1800	Act of Union. End of Irish Parliament in Dublin.
1815	Battle of Waterloo. Foundation of St George Steam Packet Company in Cork.
1829	Catholic Emancipation Act passed, removing remaining disabilities against Roman Catholics.
1838	Cork-owned *Sirius* makes the first scheduled steam passage to New York.
1845-47	The Great Famine
1867	The Fenian Rising.
1879	Land League founded.
1893	Gaelic League founded.
1914-18	World War I.
1916	The Easter Rising.
1918-21	The Anglo-Irish War.
1920	The first Republican mayor of Cork, Tomas MacCurtain, murdered by British forces, 20 March. Lord Mayor Terence MacSwiney died on hunger strike in London, 25 October. Cork city and City Hall burned by British forces.
1921	Anglo-Irish Treaty signed; followed by civil war in Ireland between those who accepted its terms and those who did not.
1939-45	World War II.
1941	Irish Shipping founded.
1961	Cork Airport operational.
1984	Ringaskiddy declared a Free Port.

Select Bibliography

(I list the major sources of information about the county, but not individual papers and articles)

Allen, D. H. *A History of Newmarket* (Cork Historical Guides) Cork 1973

An Foras Forbatha *Report on Areas of Historic and Artistic Interest in County Cork* Dublin (2nd reprint) 1975
> *Cobh. Architectural Heritage* Dublin 1979
> *Kinsale. Architectural Heritage* Dublin 1979

An Foras Talúntas *West Cork Resource Survey, 1960-63* Dublin 1969

Bandon Historical Journal (From 1984)

Barry, Michael *The Story of Cork Airport* Fermoy 1988

Barry, Tom *Guerilla Days in Ireland* Cork 1948

Bence-Jones, Mark *Burke's Guide to Country Houses* Vol 1. Ireland. London 1978

Bennett, George *The History of Bandon and the Principal Towns in the West Riding of County Cork* (2nd edition) Cork 1869

Bolster, Evelyn *A History of the Diocese of Cork* Vol 1, from the earliest times to the Reformation, Shannon 1972; Vol 2, from the Reformation to the Penal Era, Cork 1982
> *Mallow* (Cork Historical Guides) Mallow 1971

Brady, W. Maziere *Clerical and Parochial Records of Cork, Cloyne and Ross* 2 Vols Dublin 1863

Brunicardi, Niall *Haulbowline, Spike and Rocky Islands* (Cork Historical Guides) Cork 1968
> *Fermoy. 1891-1940* Fermoy 1979
> *John Anderson of Fermoy, the forgotten benefactor* Fermoy 1979
> *John Anderson, Entrepreneur* Fermoy 1987

Butler, Ewan *Barry's Flying Column* London 1971

Casserley, H. C. *Outline of Irish Railway History* Newton Abbot 1974

Cody, Bryan A. *The River Lee, Cork and the Corkonians* London 1859; reprint Cork 1974

Coleman, J. C. *Journeys into Muskerry* Dundalk n.d.

Coombes, James *A History of Timoleague and Barrymore* Timoleague 1969
> *Utopia in Glandore* Butlerstown 1970

Cork County Library and Cork City Library both hold extensive material relating to the county and original and microfilm runs of Cork newspapers from their earliest publication

Cork County Council 1899-1985 Compiled by Edward J. Marnane, County Secretary. Cork 1986

County Cork Sites and Monuments Record Office of Public Works, Dublin 1988 (A set of the six inch to the mile maps of the county on which are marked all the known archaeological sites together with a list of what they are. A four volume detailed description with illustrations is in preparation.)

Cowman, D. and Reilly, T. A. *The Abandoned Mines of West Carbery* Dublin 1988

Craig, Maurice *The Architecture of Ireland. From the earliest times to 1880* London 1982

Crowley, Flor. *In West Cork Long Ago* Cork 1979

Culloty, A.T. *Ballydesmond. A Rural Parish in its Historical Setting* Dublin 1986

Daly, Sean *Cork. A City in Crisis* Vol 1. Cork 1978

De Courcy Ireland, John *Ireland's Sea Fisheries* Dublin 1981

Disaster at Whiddy Island, Bantry, Co. Cork Report of the Tribunal of Inquiry. Dublin 1980

Donnelly, James S. *The Land and the People of 19th century Cork* London 1975

Donovan, Daniel *Sketches in Carbery* 1st edition 1876; reprint Cork 1979

Enoch, Victor J. *The Martello Towers of Ireland* Dublin n.d.

Foley, Con *A History of Douglas* Cork 1981

Forde, Frank *The Long Watch* Dublin 1981 (History of the Irish Mercantile Marine in World War II)

Gaughan, J. A. *Doneraile* Dublin 1968

Grove-White, James *Historical and Topographical Notes etc on Buttevant, Castletownroche, Doneraile, Mallow and places in their Vicinity* Cork 1905-1918

Guy's County and City of Cork Directory From 1875/76 onward

Gwynn, A. and Hadcock, R.N. *Medieval Religious Houses, Ireland* London 1970

Harbour Lights Journal of the Great Island Historical Society. From 1988

Harkness, David and O'Dowd, Mary (editors) *The Town in Ireland. Historical Studies* Belfast 1979

Hayward, Robert *Munster and the City of Cork* London 1964

Hodges, Richard J. *Cork and County Cork in the 20th Century*, together with contemporary biographies edited by W. T. Pike. Brighton 1911. Photographs and descriptions of the Big Houses and their owners prior to World War I.

Hogan, Sarsfield *A History of Irish Steel* Dublin 1980

Hollan, W. *History of West Cork and the Dioceses of Ross* Skibbereen 1949

Iris Muintir Mhathghamhna 'The O'Mahony Journal'. Organ of the O'Mahony Records Society. From 1971

Jennett, Sean *Cork and Kerry* London 1977

Journal of the Ballincollig Community School Local History Society From 1984

Journal of the Cork Historical and Archaeological Society From 1892. This is the principal journal in which historical and archaeological papers are published, relating to the county. Indexed.

Killawin, Lord and Duignan, M.V. *The Shell Guide to Ireland* London 1967

Kinsale Historical Journal Kinsale Heritage Society. From 1986

Leabhar Chluain Uamha (*The Book of Cloyne*) Cloyne Historical and Archaeological Society, 1977

Leask, H. G. *Irish Castles* Dundalk. Revised edition 1944
    Irish Churches and Monastic Buildings 3 Vols. Dundalk 1960

Lewis, Gifford *Somerville and Ross. The World of the Irish R.M.* Middlesex 1985

Lewis, Samuel *A Topographical Dictionary of Ireland* 2 vols. London 1837

McCarthy, Ivor A. J. *Geology of the Cork District* Cork 1988. Detailed geological map of the area based on the most recent research

McCracken, Eileen *Irish Woods since Tudor Times* Newton Abbot 1971

McCrath, Walter *Tram Tracks Through Cork* Cork 1981
    Some Industrial Railways of Ireland Cork 1959 (Includes the Allman Tramway, Bandon, Haulbowline Admiralty Railway, Cork Exhibition lines, Fords Railway in Cork, Cork Coal Gantry and Shannonvale horse Railway – horse-worked siding from the Shannonvale mills to the main railway line).

McNeill, D.B. *Irish Passenger Steamship Services* Vol 2, South of Ireland. Newton Abbot 1971

Mallow Field Club Journal Mallow from 1983

Malins, E. and Knight of Glin *Lost Demesnes: Irish Landscape Gardening 1660–1845* London 1976

Mersey, Richard *The Hills of Cork and Kerry* Dublin 1987

Milner, Liam *The River Lee and its Tributaries* Cork 1975
    From the Kingdom to the Sea: The River Blackwater in History and Legend Cork 1976

Mitchell, Frank *Reading the Irish Landscape* Dublin 1986

Mould, D.D.C. Pochin *The Irish Saints* Dublin 1964
    Captain Roberts of the Sirius, Cork 1988

Mulcahy, Michael *A Short History of Kinsale* Kinsale 1968

Milligan, Fergus *One Hundred and Fifty Years of Irish Railways* Belfast 1983

Murphy, Seamus *Stone Mad* London 1950

Newham, A. T. In the series *Locomotion Papers* Oakwood Press, Lingfield, Surrey.
    No. 24 *The Schull and Skibbereen Tramway*
    No. 39 *The Cork and Muskerry Light Railway*

Nock, O.S. *Irish Steam* Newton Abbot 1982

O'Brien, Daniel M. *Beara – A Journey Through History* Skibbereen 1991

Ó Conchúir, Breandán *Scríobhaithe Chorcaí: 1700-1850* Dublin 1982

O'Donoghue, Bruno *Parish Histories and Place Names of West Cork* 1986

O'Donoghue, Denis J. *History of Bandon* Cork Historical Guides. Cork 1970

O'Flanagan, J. R. *The River Blackwater of Munster* Cork 1844; reprint 1975

O'Flanagan, P. *Bandon* No. 3 in the Irish Historic Towns Atlas. Dublin 1988

O'Mahony, Colman *The Maritime Gateway to Cork* (Passage West) Cork 1986

O'Mahony, Jeremiah *West Cork and its Story* Bandon 1961; reprint Cork 1975

O'Murchadha, Diarmuid *Family Names of County Cork* Dublin 1985
    History of Crosshaven Cork Historical Guides. Cork 1967

Ó Ríordáin, Sean P. *Antiquities of the Irish Countryside* London 1942

Ó Síocháin, Conchúir *Seanchas Chléire* Dublin 1940. English version by R.P.
    Breathnach *The Man from Cape Clear* Cork 1975

O'Súilleabháin, Michael *Where Mountainy Men Have Sown: War and Peace in
    Rebel Cork in the Turbulent Years 1916-1921.* Tralee 1965

O'Sullivan, William *Economic History of Cork City to 1800* Cork 1937

Power, Patrick *Crichad an Chaoilli, being the topography of ancient Fermoy* Cork
    1932

Power, William ('Bill') *Mitchelstown through Seven Centuries* Mitchelstown 1987

Praegar, R. Lloyd *The Botanist in Ireland* Dublin 1934

Seanchas Chairbre Skibbereen. From 1982

Seanchas Duthalla Duhallow Magazine. From 1974

Sharrock, J. T. R. (Editor) *The Natural History of Cape Clear* Berkhamstead
    1973

Sherkin Island Marine Station, Sherkin Island, publishes technical and
    popular material relating to maritime research along the coasts of Cork:
    Journal from 1980, Proceedings, Sherkin Comment etc.

Sliabh Luachra Journal of Cumann Luachra. From 1982

Smith, Charles *The Ancient and Present State of the County and City of Cork* 1750;
    several recent reprints

Somerville Large, Peter *The Coast of West Cork* London 1974; reprint Belfast

Sullivan, T. D. *Bantry, Berehaven and the O'Sullivan Sept* 1908; reprint Cork
    1978

Taylor, George and Skinner, Andrew *Maps of the Roads of Ireland* 1778; fac-
    simile reprint, Shannon 1969

Townsend, Horatio *Statistical Survey of the County of Cork* Dublin 1810

Wain, H. *History of Youghal* Cork 1965

Webster, Charles A. *The Diocese of Cork* Cork 1920

Weir, Anthony *Early Ireland, a Field Guide* Belfast 1980

Williams, R. O. *The Berehaven Copper Mines* Sheffield 1991

INDEX

304

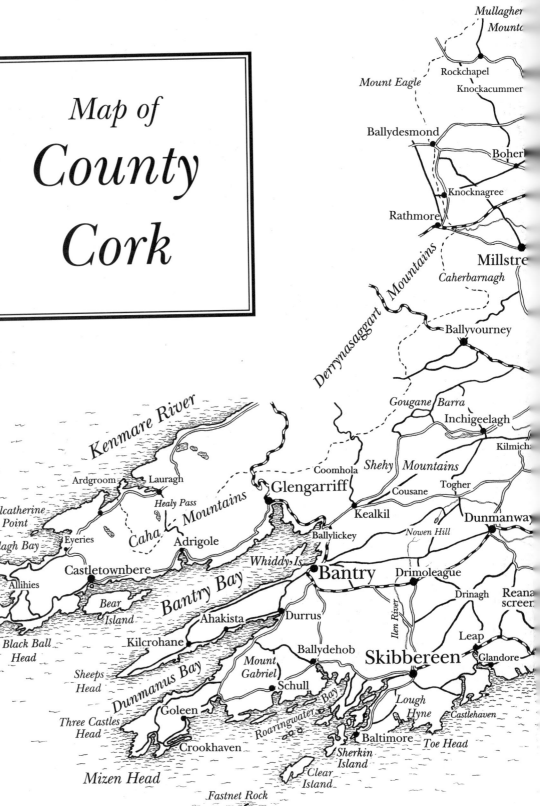

Map of County Cork

Mullagher
Mount

Rockchapel

Mount Eagle

Knockacummer

Ballydesmond

Boher

Knocknagree

Rathmore

Millstre

Caherbarnagh

Derrynasaggart Mountains

Ballyvourney

Kenmare River

Gougane Barra

Inchigeelagh

Kilmich

Coomhola

Shehy Mountains

Ardgroom
Lauragh

Glengarriff

Cousane

Togher

Dunmanway

Healy Pass

Kilcatherine
Point

Caha Mountains

Kealkil

Nowen Hill

Coulagh Bay

Eyeries

Adrigole

Ballylickey

Cods
Head

Whiddy Is.

Bantry

Drimoleague

Reana
screen

Allihies

Castletownbere

Bantry Bay

Drinagh

Dursey
Island

Bear
Island

Ahakista

Durrus

Ilen River

Leap

Black Ball
Head

Kilcrohane

Ballydehob

Skibbereen

Glandore

Dursey Head

Mount
Gabriel

Lough
Hyne

Castlehaven

Sheeps
Head

Dunmanus Bay

Schull

Roaringwater Bay

Three Castles
Head

Goleen

Baltimore

Toe Head

Crookhaven

Sherkin
Island

Mizen Head

Clear
Island

Fastnet Rock